NORTHWOODS WILDLIFE
WILDLIFE
A WATCHER'S GUIDE TO HABITATS

NORTHWOODS WILDLIFE

A WATCHER'S GUIDE TO HABITATS

JANINE M. BENYUS

Produced By
North Central Forest Experiment Station
USDA Forest Service
St. Paul, Minnesota

FROM THE NORTHWORD
NATURE GUIDE COLLECTION

Copyright © 1989
Lake States Interpretative Association

Designed by Moonlit Ink, Madison, Wisconsin

Cover illustration by Vera Ming Wong

Published By

NorthWord Press, Inc.
Box 1360
Minocqua, WI 54548

For a Free Catalog describing NorthWord's line of
nature books and gifts, call 1-800-336-5666

ISBN-1-55971-003-9

The area covered by the "Northwoods Wildlife Guide"

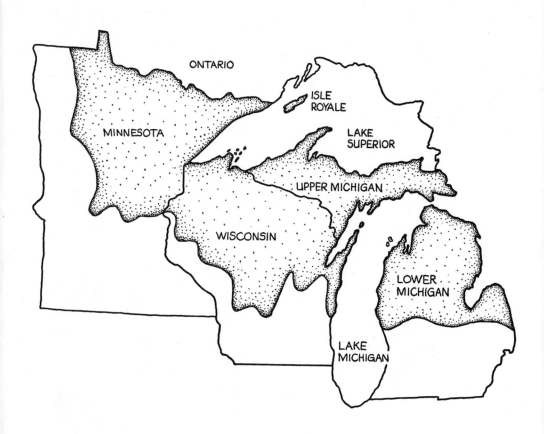

HABITAT KEY

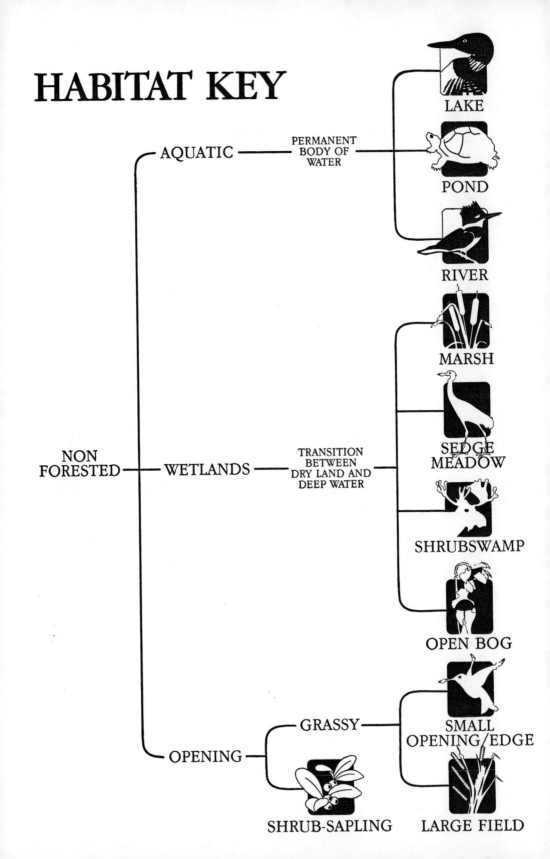

AQUATIC — PERMANENT BODY OF WATER

LAKE

POND

RIVER

NON FORESTED — WETLANDS — TRANSITION BETWEEN DRY LAND AND DEEP WATER

MARSH

SEDGE MEADOW

SHRUBSWAMP

OPEN BOG

OPENING — GRASSY

SMALL OPENING/EDGE

SHRUB-SAPLING

LARGE FIELD

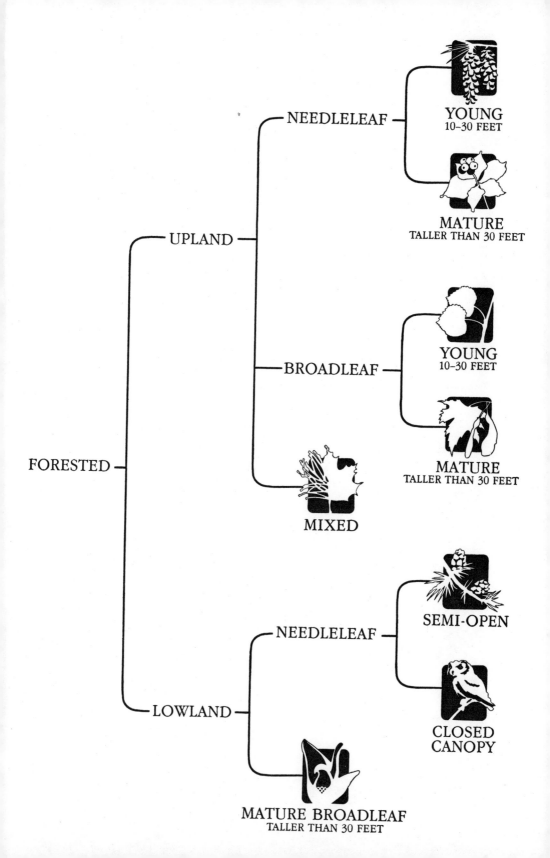

FORESTED

UPLAND

NEEDLELEAF

YOUNG
10–30 FEET

MATURE
TALLER THAN 30 FEET

BROADLEAF

YOUNG
10–30 FEET

MATURE
TALLER THAN 30 FEET

MIXED

LOWLAND

NEEDLELEAF

SEMI-OPEN

CLOSED
CANOPY

MATURE BROADLEAF
TALLER THAN 30 FEET

Acknowledgments

Writing this book was like sweeping a net through a teeming ocean of information about northwoods ecology. To the hundreds of researchers whose work was part of this "catch," I offer my sincere thanks. Of particular help were the USDA Forest Service scientists at the North Central Forest Experiment Station and the wildlife biologists on the seven National Forests in Minnesota, Wisconsin, and Michigan.

I owe a special debt of gratitude to Richard Buech, Research Wildlife Biologist at the North Central Station. Dick saw a need for a book like this, and his imagination and support helped bring it to life. Thomas Nicholls, Project Leader of the Wildlife Habitats Research Project in St. Paul, was another enthusiastic supporter.

I was fortunate to work with exceptional research assistants. Velma Webb spent a summer computerizing the National Forest inventories used to create a wildlife-habitat chart. Mark Nelson had the yeoman's task of managing that database as it grew and grew. He also scanned the habitat preferences literature and assembled the "Volunteer and Educational Opportunities" section. Christian Martin laid the foundations for the habitat profiles, drew up flora lists, and created the "Hotspots" section. Bruce Edinger's portrait of a year in the northwoods became the "Monthly Almanac" section. From start to finish, Julia Byrd, Mary Peterson, Marnie Schmidt, Diane Veilleux, and Barb Winters provided professional publication support.

When we sent the outline of this book out for review, we did what ecosystems do: we reached across the boundaries of discipline, geography, and bureaucracy. Staffs of the following groups provided helpful insight. The National Audubon Society (and local chapters), National Wildlife Federation, The Nature Conservancy (Minnesota field office), Wildlife Management Institute, Sigurd Olson Institute (Ashland, WI), Environmental Learning Center (Isabella, MN), Northwoods Audubon Center (Sandstone, MN), Woodlake Nature Center (Bloomington, MN), The Association of Interpretive Naturalists, Michigan United Conservation Clubs, the state ornithological unions, the Bell Museum of Natural History (Minneapolis, MN), the state universities, the state departments of natural resources, USDI Fish and Wildlife Service, USDA Forest Service, USDI National Park Service, USDA Soil Conservation Service, and the USDA Agricultural Extension Service.

For their careful review of part of all of the manuscript, I am indebted to: Kim Chapman (The Nature Conservancy); Paul Benson-Lender, Francie Cuthbert, John Moriarty, Gerda Nordquist, and Sara Webb (University of Minnesota); Michael Penskar (University of Michigan); Joan Galli, Pam Perry, Lee

Pfannmuller, and Steve Wilson (Minnesota Department of Natural Re-
sources); Dorothy Anderson (US Agency for International Development); L.
David Mech (USDI Fish and Wildlife Service); Richard Buech, Tom Crow,
Jay Hutchinson, Mark Nelson, Dale Nichols, Thomas Nicholls, Lew Ohman,
John Probst, Lynn Rogers, Sandy Verry, and Robert Wray (North Central Forest
Experiment Station). For showing me their favorite places on the Forest and
teaching me about habitats in the process, thanks to Jane Cliff (Chippewa
National Forest), Pete Griffin (Huron-Manistee National Forest), and Wayne
Russ (Superior National Forest).

Table of Contents

About This Book. 1

What's So Special About The Northwoods? 5

What Is A Habitat? 17

Observation Tips. 33

Habitat Guide 51

   Habitat Key 52
   Lake 55
   Woodland Pond. 73
   River and Stream 89
   Marsh 111
   Sedge Meadow. 127
   Shrub Swamp. 143
   Open Bog. 159
   Small Woodland Opening/Edge 171
   Large Field. 185
   Shrub-Sapling Opening 201
   Young Upland Broadleaf Forest. 221
   Mature Upland Broadleaf Forest 233
   Young Upland Needleleaf Forest. 251
   Mature Upland Needleleaf Forest 259
   Mature Upland Mixed Forest 275
   Mature Lowland Broadleaf Forest 291
   Semi-Open Lowland Needleleaf Forest. 303
   Closed-Canopy Lowland Needleleaf Forest 317
   Wide-Ranging Wildlife 335

Wildlife Watching Hotspots 347

Wildlife Events Calendar 373

How To Go Beyond This Book. 413

Common and Scientific Names 427

Index 435

ABOUT THIS BOOK

Who's It For?

This is a book for people who get goosebumps when they hear a yodeling loon, a bellowing moose, or the snort of a vanishing doe. It's for people who are curious about what they see, smell, hear, and touch in the outdoors. It's for explorers of new places, as well as those who are still amazed by the places they know best. If you love the northwoods, and you'd like to know it even better, this is your book.

What's It About?

This is an insider's guide to the northwoods. With it, you can visit any woodland or waterway, and easily know what habitat you're in and what kind of wildlife you may see there.

The guide is divided into 18 different types of wetlands, forests, and fields that are found in the northwoods. Each has a unique character—a constellation of plants and animals that live there because of what the habitat has to offer them. A needleleaf forest has a different community makeup, and different sources of food, cover, space, and water than a broadleaf forest. This book will help you to recognize those differences.

It will tell you how each habitat originated, how it changes over time, and why it attracts a certain community of birds, mammals, reptiles, and amphibians.

Once you know where you are, the Northwoods Wildlife Guide can tell you what types of wildlife to look for. You'll learn where in the habitat they are likely to be, as well as what they are doing there and why. While there is no way to guarantee that you'll always see wildlife, this insider's knowledge may help you to spot creatures that you would ordinarily miss.

You don't have to have a technical background to

Marten.

use this book. Although we looked to researchers for much of the information, we've tried to weed out the scientific jargon and spotlight the stories that we thought might interest you.

Most of the stories are about survival—about the various ways plants and animals adapt to their environments. Each species adapts to take advantage of what its habitat has to offer. The adaptors survive, and their ingenious strategies are passed on to future generations. These survivors are connected, either as predator and prey, parasite and host, partners in a mutually beneficial relationship, or as competitors for sunlight, food, water, and space.

We too are connected to the organisms that live in the northwoods. Our actions affect their well-being, sometimes positively and sometimes negatively. This book is about all these links: the survival link between an organism and its habitat, the links between organisms in a community, and our link to those organisms.

Once aware of these connections, our hope is that you will be personally committed to making sure there is enough quality habitat for all wildlife in the northwoods. As land-use pressures increase, your say in how we use public land is going to be more important than ever. We need "informed, disquieted, articulate, land-loving citizens" to become involved in the fight for habitat diversity and maintenance. We hope this book will be a step in informing and involving all those who read it.

What's Inside?

What's So Special About the Northwoods? starts on page 5. Here's a primer for the northwoods, a land that is uniquely situated between ecologically opposite worlds to the north and south. Shaped by glaciers, renewed by fire, redesigned by logging, and annually innundated with snow, the northwoods is both a challenge and a bounty to wildlife. This section looks at the elements that make the northwoods a world apart.

What Is a Habitat? starts on page 17. This section

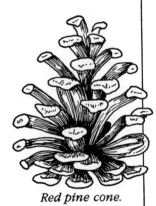

Red pine cone.

2

will help you to really "see" what you are looking at in the northwoods. It talks about how animals relate to their surroundings. You'll learn why animals prefer certain habitats, why we need to manage habitats, and how we can provide for wildlife along with an array of other uses. Finally, you'll learn what we don't yet know about wildlife habitats and how research might illuminate those dark areas.

Observation Tips starts on page 33. Expert wildlife watchers (e.g., photographers, researchers, trackers, birders) know how and when to stalk wild creatures or lure them into view. Their secrets will help you better your odds of seeing wildlife and interpreting their signs.

Habitat Guide starts on page 51. Eighteen different plant and wetland communities are described here. You'll learn about their origins, their special adaptations to soil and climate, and the unique value they hold for wildlife. By understanding how they differ, you'll see why a distinct community of wildlife is drawn to each one. Once you learn to recognize the habitat you're in, you can become familiar with what lives there and why.

Wildlife Descriptions follow each habitat. People who spend a lot of time in the woods have a "search image" for each habitat they visit. That is, they know which birds and animals they can expect to see there, and therefore, they know exactly what to look for. This section will give you a search image for each of the 18 habitats. The write-up for each species will tell you where in the habitat to look (e.g., on the ground, in the canopy, on the trunk) and a bit about how that animal uses the habitat to supply its needs. Knowing these patterns will help you to focus in on parts of the habitat where you'd be most likely to see the resident species.

Wide-Ranging Species starts on page 335. Some of our more interesting species, such as the great horned owl and the black bear, spend their time in a variety of habitats. We've given them their own chapter because they are so adaptable and are therefore diffi-cult to "pigeon-hole" into one habitat. Other species in this chapter need not only variety but also large, uninterrupted spaces to roam in.

Wildlife Watching Hotspots starts on page 347. Some areas in the northwoods are known for their spectacular congregations of wildlife, especially dur-ing certain times of year such as breeding or migra-tion. These hotspots are often on public land such as refuges, and are managed to provide for wildlife needs. Other places, such as Hawk Ridge in Duluth, are geographically strategic and serve as funnels or magnets for migrating bird species. A map of each state is provided, keyed to hotspots where viewing opportunities are excellent.

Wildlife Events Calendar starts on page 373. This calendar will give you a month-by-month rundown of important wildlife activities such as hibernating, incubating, nest building, migrating, molting, and mating. Use it to plan your outings so that they co-incide with wildlife's most active periods. Good tim-ing increases your chances of seeing wildlife.

How to Go Beyond This Book starts on page 413. No one book can be a complete treatise on wildlife, so we offer a list of readings and courses to help round out your knowledge. Of course, there's no sub-stitute for what you can learn from actually watching wildlife in the act. After reading this book and trying it out in the field, we hope you'll be charged with enthusiasm for wildlife watching. There are several volunteer organizations that could benefit from your enthusiasm, and we've listed them in this section.

WHAT'S SO SPECIAL ABOUT THE NORTHWOODS?

A Transition Forest

We in the northwoods live at the seam of two worlds. To the north, the vast needleleaf, boreal forest of Canada stretches to the tundra. To the south, broadleaf trees spread their branches to the tropical tip of the continent. Here, in the zone of in-between, the inhabitants of both forests flourish, mingling to create a forest community unlike any in North America.

Bald eagle.

In the top half of our region, the influence of the northern forests is strongest. From here, fingers of white spruce, balsam fir, tamarack, and quaking aspen reach southward to meet the rising influx of sugar maple, American beech, and American basswood. Also, sprinkled throughout the region are residents such as red pine, eastern hemlock, yellow birch, and eastern white pine, all of which have ranges centered in the eastern transition forest.

This blending of resident, northern, and southern species sets up unique types of competition and food chains that include plants, animals, insects, and even microscopic life from each community. Only in a transition forest, for instance, could snowshoe hares (from the north) run next to cottontail rabbits (from the south), while great gray owls dine on southern flying squirrels.

This mingling of worlds is a recent phenomenon and thus is still in a highly unsettled state. Not long ago (geologically speaking), this region was completely devoid of forests—a rocky wasteland dripping with the remains of a retreating glacier.

The Big Chill—
A Glacial History

The northwoods is one of the most recently uncovered places in the world. Less than 10,000 years ago, while civilization was well underway in the Middle East, parts of the northwoods were still under an ice cap that stood 2 miles high in places. The enormous weight of the ice caused the lower layer to bulge outward in all directions, bulldozing mountains and gouging the earth as it moved. Frigid air swooped down from the front of the glacier, creating a wide fringe of tundra wherever it went.

When the glacier finally stopped and began to melt backwards, great muddy torrents roared over its cliffs and rushed out through tunnels in its face. Their payload of crushed rock, gravel, sand, and ice settled over hundreds of miles to form the lake-splattered landscape that we know today.

Glacial Souvenirs

Mementos of the glacier's passing are with us everywhere. On some rock ledges, for instance, you can still find deep parallel grooves that were gouged by rocky "teeth" embedded in the moving ice. Eventually these boulders were dropped here and there by the melting glacier to become today's randomly strewn "erratics." Sometimes a glacier would pause; that is, it would melt backward as fast as it inched forward, so that its edge would stay in one place. As it melted, it would deposit rock debris in a ridge along its edge. The longer it paused, the higher these "moraines" would pile, forming some of the hills you see in the northwoods today.

In this way, the glacier imported new types of rock into some parts of the northwoods, and uncovered original bedrock in others. These crushed rocks became the parent material for our soil, another of the glacier's legacies. In the eastern part of our region, where the bedrock was soft and easily eroded, the glacier picked up and deposited a blanket of pulverized rock hundreds of feet thick. The soil from these remains is deep and rich. In the west, the older bedrock was so hard that even the glacier could not erode it. Here, the soil is still thin and studded with bedrock outcroppings.

The greatest monuments to glacial action, however, are the thousands of lakes, bogs, marshes, and other wetlands that puddle our region. These wetlands were created in a variety of ways.

Some filled up the large shallow dents where the sheer weight of the glacier had bent the land beneath it. Others were formed when huge blocks of ice broke off from the face of the glacier and became buried in tons of silt and rubble. When these blocks finally melted, the debris on top slumped to form a basin, or a "kettle hole," which often filled with water. Some lakes backed up behind natural dams made of glacial debris. In other places, peatlands built up slowly on the flat sand plains laid down by icy meltwaters.

This vast collection of waterways is a feature of a young and undrained landscape. Eventually, over thousands of years, the northwoods will erode to form a deeper drainage system characteristic of older landscapes.

Life On the Heels of the Glacier

The living landscape was also shaped by the ebb and flow of the glacier. As the last ice mass retreated to the north, plants and animals from unglaciated areas were free to migrate into the newly exposed areas. Lichens, mosses, and other tundra plants led the parade, moving an average of 50 miles a century. Through chemical and physical means, they helped to transform the rock surface into soil, giving grasses, shrubs, and tree seedlings a place to sink their roots.

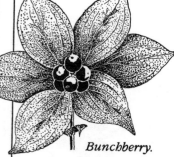

Bunchberry.

The first trees to arrive were the arctic conifers such as black spruce, tamarack, and balsam fir, mingled with the hardy leaf-dropping pioneers—paper birch and quaking and bigtooth aspen. Next came a sudden warming trend that accelerated the thawing and shrinking of the glacier. Summers probably became too hot at this time for spruce to regenerate, and it followed the retreating glacier back up north. Jack and red pine and American green alder filled in behind spruce, followed by eastern white pine and oaks.

The prairie made inroads into the east during this warm period as well.

Gradually, over the last 7,000 years, the climate has begun to cool off and become moister, sending the prairie back to the west, and allowing the pines and the oaks to expand farther south. Newcomers into this cooler environment included sugar maple, eastern hemlock, and American beech (which is so new it hasn't made it to Minnesota yet). Some experts expect this cooling trend to continue and insist that we are now simply between ice ages!

In the short time since the last ice age, we humans have managed to rival the glaciers in our ability to temper the character of the land. Today's wetlands and forests (those that remain undrained or unpaved) bear the marks of many centuries of human inhabitance.

Axes and Asphalt— A Human History

Indians moved into the northwoods practically on the heels of the retreating glacier. They made their living from the land—hunting, fishing, farming, and collecting wild foods—in what was essentially a subsistence economy. In the 17th century, the French arrived and set up a lucrative fur trade, exporting skins to markets throughout the world. In a short time, the trappers came close to eliminating some animals, especially beaver, from the region. Even this disruption was minor, however, compared to what was in store for the northwoods when the loggers arrived.

The Logging Era

Beginning in 1830, it took loggers only a century to harvest most of the towering red and eastern white pines that the region was famous for. Devastating fires spread in the discarded tops and branches, opening the landscape to the drying and heating effects of the sun. A few areas were burned so frequently and intensely that they became sterile. In soils that could have nurtured pines, there were usually too few mature trees (seed sources) left standing. In some places

Lofty white pines once covered the northwoods.

8

where white pine was able to come back, it was later wiped out by blister rust, a disease accidently introduced from Europe. Ultimately, the magnificent pines were replaced by a generation of aspens, paper birch, and jack pine.

Unlike the clearcut pines, broadleaf forests were "selectively" cut. That is, one kind of tree was harvested at a time, leaving the forest canopy and floor nearly intact. Trees that could grow in the shade of the partial canopy did well and eventually overshadowed the original sun-loving trees. Sugar maple is an example of a shade-tolerant tree that has come to dominate many of the broadleaf forests in the northwoods.

A New Responsibility

Some of these changes, such as the conversion of pines to aspens, could have happened naturally as a result of fire, windthrow, insects, or disease. But under natural conditions, without our axes, oxen, or logging barons, these changes would have taken hundreds or even thousands of years. By accelerating this timetable, we have placed an indelible mark on northwoods forests, and taken our place as major players in the ecosystem.

Today, nearly 50 million people live in the drainage of the Great Lakes, and a third of the population of Canada and the U.S. live within a day's drive of the Lakes. In our quest for space and resources, we have drained many of the wetlands and fragmented much of the forest cover. The waste products of our industries, automobiles, and agriculture have accumulated in the water, air, and soil.

As we have become more aware of our power to rival glaciers, we have also begun to accept our responsibility to the land. Sound resource management and sensitive land-use planning are two ways we now try to lessen the stress we put on our environment. One of the modern tools we use to manage forests is actually one of the age-old elements that helped shape the northwoods—fire.

Fire—The Great Starting Whistle

Fires were a fact of life in northern forests long before loggers set the land ablaze. Native Americans used fires to drive game and manage vegetation, and lightning lit up the land when it was dry. As a result, our native vegetation is adapted not only to survive a fire, but to thrive in its passing.

A wildfire usually begins with the touchdown of lightning, and can be whipped by winds into a roaring storm of flame, heat, and sparks. In its wake, it can leave blackened scars in a once lush expanse of green.

Within a few years after a fire, however, a northwoods firescar is usually pulsing with life again. For all its seeming destruction, fire plays a key role by opening the tree canopy and enriching the soil with nutrients.

Before a fire, nutrients such as phosphorous, magnesium, and calcium are locked up in living vegetation and in fallen needles and leaves on the forest floor. A fire can release these nutrients quickly, accomplishing in a few minutes what decay organisms take several years to do. When this stifling layer of needles and leaves has been burned off, rootlets can easily penetrate the mineral (inorganic) soil to reach water and newly released nutrients. Intense fires also remove the overstory trees, exposing the forest floor to full sunlight. This rich infusion of sun and nutrients is a great boon to the plant "phoenixes" that rise from the ashes.

Nature's Fire Chasers

Individual eastern white and red pines, with their thick outer bark and lofty canopies, often survive an intense fire, showering the ground with cones and seed. The young pines will do well in the full sun, provided they do not have to compete with the opportunistic pioneers—aspen and birch.

After flames consume the parts we see, the underground aspen goes to work, sending root suckers skyward to become the stems of new trees. Seeds from unburnt aspen stands blow in to complete the inva-

10

sion. Paper birches also rebound quickly, sprouting in clumps from the base of dead parent trees. In a race for the sun, birches and aspens usually outpace other contenders, spreading leafy canopies that eventually shade out the competition.

Jack pine, like aspen and birch, does best in full sun, and is even better adapted to fire. A portion of its seed crop is housed in resin-sealed cones that open only when heated to a high temperature. This insures that the seeds will reach the ground at the opportune time—when a fire has removed competitors, released nutrients from burned vegetation, and exposed the mineral soil that jack pine requires. The fact that jack pine is the second most abundant tree after aspen in the Lake States is a testimony to its hardy comeback qualities.

Just as fire selects for its own type of forest (that of sun-loving pioneers), the absence of fire creates its own type of forest too. Shade-loving species such as white spruce, balsam fir, and sugar maple grow beneath the pioneers, slowly biding their time. When the "umbrellas" above them topple with old age, the understory trees shoot up and become dominant. Because they can tolerate shade, these new dominants will nurture seedlings of their own that will eventually replace them. A forest like this can perpetuate itself for generations in the absence of fire.

Eastern white pine cone.

Jack pine cone.

Setting Fires for Wildlife

The age of modern firefighting tends to encourage this sort of self-perpetuating forest by protecting it against fires. To promote fire-adapted species such as pines, land managers sometimes set fires or let natural ones burn under their supervision. Controlled burns are set in Michigan, for instance, to encourage the growth of young jack pine forests, where the endangered Kirtland's warbler nests. The need to set fires, in a region that was once torched by frequent conflagrations, is one more example of human influence on the northwoods ecosystem.

Winter—The Ultimate Test

No survey of the northwoods would be complete without a look at winter: the long, deep, and silent challenge. In the coldest parts of the northwoods, temperatures may dip below zero for days or weeks at a time. The lakes freeze hard and deep, sandwiching fish and water mammals between the lake bottom and a lowering ceiling of ice. In the snowiest sections, where a total of 25 feet of snow falls, an average snowbank could bury a standing person. Animals that stay in this sort of climate for the winter lead a double life, blessed by the plenty of summer and tested by the rigors of winter.

The White Habitat

One of wildlife's greatest tests begins with the first papery snowfall of the year. To us it is a peaceful, welcome sign of the new season. The ground becomes a canvas on which we can follow wild dramas of pursuit, near-escape, and capture. But for the birds and mammals that leave these tracks, snow is far more than a canvas. It is a powerful force that each must contend with or succumb to.

Snow can be a feeding platform for a hare . . .

Snow transforms the contours of the habitat, and creates at least two new dimensions: above the snow and beneath the snow. For some animals, snow covers up food sources, and for others, it provides access to new food. For example, snow on trees, called "qali," covers the cones that crossbills, chickadees, and red squirrels depend on. They must either move to areas where winds have been strong enough to blow away the qali, or resort to caches stored under the ground. For snowshoe hares, however, qali is a blessing because it bends the supple branches of birches and alders, bringing the tender growing tips within the hares' reach.

Snow on the ground, called "api," can also be a help or a hindrance. When the snow is solid enough, it gives the snowshoe hare a platform to reach even higher up on trees than it normally could have. Hares "reciprocate" by leaving pellets of manure that help to fertilize the saplings in the spring.

After it falls, snow goes through a series of changes that create an undercover haven for small mammals. The layer closest to the ground begins to melt because of the heat flowing from the earth, and the six-sided flakes lose their water to the colder crystals above. Gradually, the bottom layer opens into a low-ceilinged room, laced from top to bottom with delicate, hollow pyramids of ice. The air inside is warm and moist, illuminated by a pale blue light filtering through the snow. Even in temperatures that would freeze a small shrew solid, these underworld corridors rarely go below 20 degrees F. Small mammals go about their business with plenty of headroom, no chilling winds, a supply of food on the forest floor, and few predators (except for the extremely narrow weasel that can negotiate the tunnels, and the great grey owl which can hear prey through 2–3 feet of snow).

Occasionally, small mammals will build shafts up to the surface which allow them to expand their foraging range. It's during these excursions that owls and other aboveground predators finally have a chance to pick off these well-protected rodents.

Sometimes after a thaw, the surface of the snow will refreeze and crust over. If it's not hard enough to stand on, crusted api can be a hazard for long-legged deer and moose. They occasionally fall through the crust, burning energy in their struggle, and tearing their legs on the jagged ice. The avalanche of snow knocked loose by their hooves temporarily blocks the under-snow corridors for smaller mammals as well.

Because traveling is so difficult and energy-consuming in deep snow, deer and moose tend to yard up for the winter in areas where they can maintain trodden trails through a protected stand of woody food. Dense needleleaf forests are ideal because snows are not as deep, winds are not as driving, and the canopy traps some of the heat that would normally escape to the open sky.

. . . or a snug tunnel for a mouse.

13

Closed for the season.

To Be a Tree in Winter

Just as wildlife must prepare for and react to the northwoods seasons, vegetation must also adapt or perish. Trees and woody shrubs must be able to survive a season without water (it may be frozen in the ground), and accomplish most of their growing during the short season of warmth.

Needleleaf trees, denizens of the truly frozen boreal zones, are well-adapted to snow and cold. Their tiny "leaves" expose a minimal surface area and are coated with wax to cut down on the amount of moisture lost to the drying winds of winter. Their umbrella-like branches hold a "mantle" of snow that actually covers, and, in effect, insulates many of the needles. These branches are designed to flex downward with snow, recovering when it melts or blows away.

Moisture within the needles is stored between cells rather than within cells to reduce the rupturing that can occur when the water freezes and expands. In this state of cold storage, the tree's sap is immobilized and concentrated with sugars. This thickened sap is a natural antifreeze that keeps ice crystals from forming even at cold temperatures.

Evergreens are adapted to make the most of a short growing season as well as a hard winter. They drop their needles gradually, throughout the year, so that at any one time, there is an overall green canopy. Thus, evergreens can work overtime to make food, taking advantage of the warm sun in early spring and late into the fall. They are also able to hold onto nutrients for a little longer by retaining their leaves for 3 or 4 years.

Broadleaf trees use a different strategy to get through a winter without water. Before the snow flies, the trees reabsorb most of the nutrients from their leaves, and store them in sap and in horizontal "rays" in the trunk. Miniature versions of next year's leaves are folded inside buds that are wax-coated to resist drying.

As the days grow shorter and colder, the trees drop their leaves entirely to eliminate the "leak" of water

14

vapor through the pores. With the food-producing factories shut down, the sap thickens and no longer flows through the tree. Its sugary antifreeze keeps it from crystalizing despite freezing temperatures. Come spring, these sugars will give opening buds a "jump-start," even before nourishment is available from the soil. When soil water begins to flow, broadleaf trees will reap their final reward—fallen leaves from years past, now decayed, create a warm, moisture-holding mulch.

Leaf-dropping trees also avoid damage by presenting less of an obstacle to limb-breaking winds. Some broadleaf species, such as alder and aspen, further resist breakage by having supple branches that bend rather than break under the crushing weight of an ice storm or a normal season's snowfall.

Sometimes, however, the burden of ice or snow is too heavy for any tree to handle. When a branch or a trunk breaks, an opening to the sun is created. This opening tends to "grow" over the years. In summer, the branches on the opening side of the tree grow profusely in the sun, causing the tree to become lopsided. When winter storms weigh down these branches, they can easily take the tree down with them. One by one, the trees fall into the opening and enlarge it. Eventually, a healing point is reached when the opening becomes large enough to let wind blow the snow (and the pressure) off the branches.

Northwoods organisms are routinely tested by snow, by fire, and by human intervention. The winners in these contests are those organisms that have adapted ways to squeak through the worst and spring back when conditions are good. In the heart of this book, you'll read about some of the plants and animals that have passed the test and proved that they have what it takes to survive here in the changeable, rigorous, and bountiful northwoods.

WHAT IS A HABITAT?

A Home Base

A habitat is an organism's home base, the place where it finds the combination of water, food, cover, and space that it needs to survive. A good habitat provides a hospitable climate, a reliable source of food and water, and ample places for resting, hunting, playing, hiding, and raising young. The sum total of an animal's needs is expressed in its habitat.

In this book, we use the word habitat to describe various aquatic and plant communities in different stages of development. Each community, from deep lake to dark forest, offers a different menu of the essential ingredients for life, and thus attracts a different wildlife clientele. To help you recognize their differences, we have drawn an idealized version of each habitat.

In real life, you may not run across the "pure" needleleaf or "pure" broadleaf forests that are pictured here. You are more likely to see a mixture of habitat types, one blending and shading into the other. When identifying them, go with the feature that is **most** obvious. For instance, are **most** of the trees large (mature) or small (young)? Are they broadleaf or needleleaf? Look at the lay of the land: are you in the uplands or lowlands? By asking these three questions, you'll soon be able to tell whether you're in a "young upland needleleaf" forest or a "mature lowland broadleaf" one. The eight aquatic habitats and the three opening (field) habitats are even simpler to identify. You can use the habitat illustrations at the beginning of each section to verify your guesses.

As you get more involved in habitat study, you'll begin to notice even finer distinctions than those we have drawn here. The kinds of plants that grow on a site "say something" about that site—about its soil,

Pileated woodpecker.

moisture, microclimate, topography, past use, resident organisms, etc. In turn, an animal's presence on the site indicates that the site has certain features it needs to survive. The best way to predict what animals and plants you'll see on the site is to analyse these factors—a job for a powerful computer too heavy to carry in the field. For our purposes, plant communities do a good job of symbolizing the arrangement of food, water, space, and cover called "habitat."

How We Matched Wildlife with Their Habitats

Animal communities, like the plants around them, are not "fenced in" by human-conceived habitat boundaries. In fact, most wildlife species cross from one community type to another to satisfy all their needs. Many amphibians, for example, spend the early part of their lives in water, moving to land as they mature. Some birds of prey nest in dense forests but skim over grasslands in search of prey. Moose and deer find their summer range in one habitat and their winter range in another.

How, then, did we pick out one habitat for each of the wildlife species in this book? First, we acknowledged the fact that species may use more than one habitat. Then, we chose what's called the "preferred habitat" for each species, that is, the place where they spend **most** of their time. Often, this is where they breed and raise their young. We concentrated on the times when you'd be most apt to be out wildlife watching—spring, summer, and fall.

The strong connection between animals and their preferred habitats is no coincidence. As you will see in the next section, those with the strongest connections have special adaptations that help them excel in their habitats.

Eastern garter snake.

18

Why Do Some Species Have Preferred Habitats?

Over the long span of evolutionary time, animals have developed more efficient ways to use the resources offered by their habitat. Special behaviors and physical traits give them an edge over other organisms competing for the same resources. It's to their advantage, then, to spend most of their time in the habitat that they specialize in, the one where they have the best chance of surviving and reproducing.

You can almost predict where an animal will make its home by noticing some of its adaptive characteristics such as body size and shape, bill or paw design, coloration, or special mating practices. Trunk "hitchers" such as woodpeckers and squirrels have sharp claws and opposing toes to get a grappling-hook grip on bark. Flying squirrels come equipped with skin parachutes to transport them from tree to tree. Birds that raise their young on the forest floor are usually camouflaged in feathers that resemble fallen leaves. Red and white-winged crossbills have beaks that "scissor" together to help them pry seeds out of needleleaf cones.

What is not so important to survival is usually not as well-developed. Animals that dwell in forests, for instance, where visibility is often obstructed, are not known for their keen vision. They make up for this by having a well-developed sense of smell, sharp hearing and, in many birds, well-developed voices. Likewise, lake-dwelling common loons have powerful legs placed far back on their bodies—in a perfect position for diving, but very clumsy for walking on land.

Populations develop these specialized adaptations through a process called natural selection. Natural selection, or "survival of the fittest," favors the better adapted individuals in a population. These individuals tend to live longer and produce more offspring than poorly adapted individuals. As their adaptive genes are passed on again and again, the population as a whole begins to reflect an affinity for the habitat.

Of course, the degree to which species "prefer" one habitat over another varies. Some species, such as the adaptable and ubiquitous American robin, have found that flexibility is the best way to survive in many different habitats. They are called generalists (see Wide-Ranging Wildlife, page 335).

Other species have a narrow range of tolerances under which they can survive. They are specially equipped to compete well in a certain environment, and outside of it, their survival chances drop. The Kirtland's warbler, for example, will only nest in jack pine and red pine stands of a certain age and density. Many of our narrowly adapted species, like the Kirtland's, are rare or in danger of becoming extinct.

What Makes a Good Habitat?

How do species "know" which habitats they would do best in? For some, it is a matter of simply returning to where they were born. For those that must choose new habitats, there are certain signs and stimuli that seem to attract them. Researchers are not yet sure of all the factors that spell success to an organism looking for a home, but a few of them are discussed below.

Structure: The general look or the "gestalt" of the environment—its structure—is what most birds seem to key in on. A habitat's structure includes the shape, height, density, and diversity of the vegetation as well as other general features of the terrain.

Some of these visual clues may have little to do with survival per se, but are, rather, indicators that this would be a good place to raise a family or look for food. For example, some grassland birds will bypass a meadow that is green in the spring. A brown meadow will be chosen instead, not because brown is better for survival, but because this indicates that it will green up later, and be at the perfect height when nesting season dawns.

For many species, the life form of the vegetation, that is, whether it's a grass, shrub, or a mature tree, seems to be more important than whether it is a bluestem, hazel, or spruce. A variety of life forms makes up the architecture of the community, and

Silver maple.

determines how species will be distributed in the habitat.

Vertical Layers: Every habitat in this book can be looked at in terms of its different vertical layers. A lake has a top layer; a darker, colder lower layer; and a bottom. A forest may have a tree canopy, a shrub layer, and a covering of herbaceous plants on the forest floor. Even a grassy opening has layers: a grass layer, surface level, and underneath, a root zone. Each zone, in turn, has its own inhabitants, adapted to take advantage of "niches" (ecological roles) in that zone.

In the basement of the forest, for instance, moles and woodchucks burrow underground, looking for food and churning up soil nutrients in the process. Around them, the wrecking crews of fungi, bacteria, insects, and other organisms are breaking down the deluge of fallen leaves, twigs, buds, petals, pollen, flesh, feathers, and waste. All life that sways or walks on top of the forest floor winds up beneath it, to be broken down and taken up again by plant roots.

On top of the forest floor, amid a carpet of green plants, flickers turn over leaves to find insects, and many species of shrews, mice, salamanders, and reptiles patrol leafy runways for food. Grouse and other ground nesters lay low and wary, using the intricate patterns of their plumage to secrete them.

The next layer of shrubs provides berries and succulent leaves for moose, deer, bear, and other wildlife. This layer is especially important in the ravenous feeding binges of spring and fall.

On the top story of the forest, the limbs of the trees lift their leaves to the sun, fueling the photosynthetic (food-making) engine that runs the community. Here, woodpeckers and nuthatches probe for insects, and pine martens chase down red squirrels. Even the canopy itself is subdivided, however, with certain birds frequenting the lower branches, some perching on the very edges, and others patrolling the sunlit tops of trees.

Horizontal Zones: Horizontal zoning is also important in a habitat. For instance, the character of a stream changes as you move along it; its riffles, deep pools, and shallow backwaters create different conditions. As you move across the forest floor, there is a mosaic of shade broken by patches of sunlight. In the same way, the interior of a forest or a marsh differs greatly from its perimeter. Notice, for example, that yellow-headed blackbirds tend to claim the center of a marsh, while redwings take the fringes.

The layers in a forest are zones of opportunity for wildlife. The more layers there are for nesting, feeding, and hiding, the more different kinds of wildlife you are likely to see.

Each distinct area in the habitat offers wildlife a slightly different combination of food, water, space, and cover. Zoning allows many species to occupy the same habitat without competing for the same resources. Like a smoothly functioning crew of newspaper reporters, each animal has its "beat," and among them, all the resources in the forest are scouted out.

Complexity: As a forest ages, its structure changes. It becomes more complex as it adds new layers, and the complement of resident wildlife also changes. When shrubs and thickets are added to an area of grasses, there is a new opportunity for secretive birds and berry-feeders to make a living. By adding a layer of trees, a whole new set of possible nest and foraging sites opens up. The elaborate architecture of the canopy affords different places with different temperatures and humidities for insect prey to breed. As the canopy grows higher, open space is created between the lower branches and the ground, allowing birds like eastern wood-pewees and American redstarts to fly from perches and catch insects on the wing.

Studies have demonstrated that the variety of species increases in a series of habitats from grassland through shrubland through mature forest. This occurs in part because there are more vertical and horizontal zones in later stages, and thus, more opportunities for a diverse mix of wildlife.

Patchiness: Within a habitat, disturbances, such as windstorms, insect and disease outbreaks, floods, rockslides, logging, or fires can disrupt one type of habitat and add patches of an earlier stage of forest development. This patchiness adds diversity to an area, and allows it to accommodate species that need both young and mature vegetation.

Edge: An altogether unique habitat called an "edge" is formed where two types of communities or vegetative stages meet. Examples of edges are where a marsh turns into a shrub swamp or a field blends into a forest. It's a corridor of contrasts, with plenty of vertical and horizontal variety. Species from the separate communities meet at the junction, joined by edge species that are specially adapted to live in this transition zone. The result is a community more diverse than either of the adjacent ones.

Size: Size is another factor that determines whether a habitat is suitable for an organism's needs. Some species require elements that can only be provided by large, undisturbed blocks of habitat. Long-distance migrants such as ovenbirds tend to nest only in the interior of extensive forests. They usually produce only one brood a year in open ground nests that require dense cover from overhead. In areas that are too small or patchy, these nests can be easily parasitized or discovered by predators, and the long-distance migrants will be hard pressed to reproduce. These species that need large, undisturbed habitats are called "area-sensitive."

With axe and plow and bulldozer, humans tend to subdivide these large expanses, leaving "islands" of good habitat within a surrounding sea of roadways, farms, or suburban lawns. Researchers have found that the smaller these islands are, the fewer species they can support. These individuals are more vulnerable to predators and competitors from the habitats that surround the island. If one population on the island gets in trouble, there may be no similar habitat close enough to provide replacements to help rebuild it. All of these factors may work together to shrink and simplify the roster of wildlife in fragmented forests.

Special Features: Besides variety and adequate size, there are other essential requirements that must be met if a habitat is to support certain species. The presence or absence of snags (standing dead trees), food plants, singing posts, or water can make or break a site. The habitat can be ideal in every way, but if it doesn't supply one ingredient essential to an animal's survival or reproduction, the species will not be found there for long.

Other Organisms: Another factor that contributes to an animal's success in a particular habitat is the interaction it has with members of the surrounding community, such as competing species, predators, parasites, and disease organisms. No plant or animal

lives in isolation; it lives in an environment that has
been changed, or, in part, created by other plants and
animals that live there.

Sugar maples, for instance, enrich the soil under
them by dropping leaves that are rich in nutrients.
Ground plants flourish in this rich fertilizer. Eastern
hemlocks, on the other hand, shed acidic leaves that
resist decay and "lock up" vital nutrients, discouraging most ground plants. A large population of
meadow voles in a field may create prime habitat for
a short-eared owl, but competition from other hawks
or owls may force it to hunt over habitats that are less
than ideal. These relations are a dynamic feature of
the habitat and determine whether a species will
thrive or falter.

As you can see, wildlife key in on a variety of features when selecting a place to live. Ultimately, however, the test of a good habitat is this: 1) can a species
keep itself alive there, and 2) can it successfully reproduce there? In the modern northwoods, where
human habitats often overlap with natural ones, the
challenge to maintain enough prime habitat requires
conscientious management.

Osprey.

Why Manage Habitats?

Even the best habitat can support only so many individuals of a given species without damaging the
system. This limit is called the "carrying capacity" of
the habitat. Changing the habitat so that it is more
or less usable by different species can boost or reduce
this carrying capacity.

Change Is Inevitable

Natural forces such as storms change habitats frequently. With each change or transformation, some
species benefit and others suffer. For instance, if a
severe windstorm were to topple many large trees,
the wood thrush may lose its shaded home, but the
rufous-sided towhee and white-throated sparrow may
find the new, tangled jumble to their liking.

In the same way, humans can alter habitat, creating
ideal conditions for some species while making it

untenable for others. Physically, habitats can be created, destroyed, enlarged, reduced, or fragmented into "islands." Biologically, they can be altered by competition, the introduction of non-native species, air and water pollution (including channelization and drainage), and toxicants (such as insecticides, herbicides, and heavy metals). For wildlife, these changes may imply a loss of food, restricted movement, or stress. With each new housing development or industrial park we build, we reduce the habitat supply upon which wildlife populations depend.

But why can't species simply move into adjoining habitats that haven't been disturbed? They can of course, provided the new habitat isn't already occupied, and that it is able to meet all the species' requirements. Displacing wildlife into less-than-ideal habitats will eventually diminish their population. In some cases, highly sensitive species have nowhere to turn. They simply fade away and become locally extinct. Their absence will change the makeup of the wildlife community, and their loss will be felt.

The Danger of Extinction

When a species disappears from an ecosystem, the role or function that it played also disappears. Perhaps it was an important prey species. Or maybe, as in the case of insect-eating birds, it was helping to keep pest numbers at a manageable level. It may have been building cavities or underground burrows that other species used regularly. Perhaps it was inadvertently "planting" oaks by burying acorns throughout the forest. These functions are now missing, and the entire ecosystem suffers.

When extinction occurs worldwide, the loss is even more profound. To lose even one species punctures a hole in the larger biological system that nourishes and replenishes all life, including human life. And because each species is genetically unique, it cannot be "reinvented"—the puncture cannot be mended.

From a practical standpoint, we humans lose in the short as well as the long run. We forfeit the opportunities that the organism may have presented for breakthroughs in medicine, agriculture, pest control,

Lynx.

and environmental monitoring. Consider, for instance, that half of all medical prescriptions are derived from plants and animals, but that only 2 percent of all species have been investigated for their commercial value. If the rate of extinction continues to rise as it has, we could lose up to one-fifth of all the earth's living species by the year 2000.

It's important to remember that extinction itself is a natural process that has occurred throughout the ages. There is, however, a key difference between natural and human-caused extinction. In the past, as species became extinct, they were replaced by new ones that had become better adapted to the slowly changing environment. Ecologists Paul and Anne Ehrlich compare this process to a faucet running new species into a sink, while extinction drains them away. Throughout most of the earth's history, the faucet ran in more species than the drain let out, so the number of species increased over the ages. That is no longer the case; today, species disappear much more rapidly than they appear. We've managed to widen the drain by overexploiting organisms and altering habitats everywhere. These same actions interrupt the flow from the faucet, thus weakening the ecosystem's ability to replace species and heal its wounds.

When considering the entire range of endangered life, from lichens to snow leopards, some conservationists estimate that we are now losing one species a day. By the end of this century, that could move to one an hour. At that rate, fewer new and better-adapted species—the rightful heirs—will have a chance to evolve.

By shattering the integrity of ecosystems, we go against what Aldo Leopold called the first rule of intelligent tinkering, that is, to save all the pieces. We don't yet know how important each species is, and by reducing diversity today, we reduce the information and choices available to those who come after us. Lee M. Talbot, of the President's Council on Environmental Quality, equates this to passengers in a spaceship who, in an effort to give themselves more room, throw out part of their life-support system because they don't yet know what the equipment is for.

The unpredictable benefits of a species are reason enough to work for its protection. After all, a species is truly useless only when it is extinct.

Tough Choices for Land Managers

The Spirit of the Law

Thankfully, the desire to keep our ecosystems intact has become part of our national consciousness. In legislation that tells federal resource agencies how to manage public land, the American people have issued a two-pronged challenge:

1. To maintain self-sustaining populations of all native species and desired non-native species.

2. To provide for specific numbers of certain species in certain areas (game, sensitive, endangered, or aesthetically unique species).

Maintaining these species begins with maintaining enough of the right kinds of habitat. Unfortunately, this is not a simple matter of leaving ecosystems alone or preserving small tracts. Humans have been a major player in forest succession in the Lake States for a century and a half, and we are still competing with wildlife for space and resources. Because of the hand we've had in shaping the forest, we now have a responsibility to that forest. Providing for all species that are native to this area is just one part of "our end of the bargain."

Providing for all native species is perhaps best accomplished by "keeping all the parts," and providing for the full spectrum of habitat types. Mixing many habitats creates an assortment of niches that support, in turn, a greater variety of wildlife.

Some researchers believe that a diverse community may be more stable than a simple one because of its complex web of interconnections. When one part of the system breaks down or is disturbed, a diverse community has more mechanisms for recovery, and thus, a cushion against catastrophe.

Managers must be careful not to carry diversity too far however. Breaking up habitats into smaller and

Red pine seedling.

smaller patches of different ages or types tends to
select for generalists or species that are adapted to
transitions and disturbance. Specialized species, such
as those that need mature, extensive forests, will suffer in a too highly diversified landscape. A balanced
mosaic of large and small blocks with corridors of
"edge" between them is often the ticket.

How is this mix of habitats created and maintained?
Some of the tools used to carve out new habitats or
to diversify existing ones are controlled burning,
thinning, water impounding, seeding, and mowing
fields. Activities such as these are rarely taken solely
for the benefit of wildlife, however, because wildlife
is but one of many resources in a forest.

Wildlife, Yes, But Other Uses Too

Land managers are asked to provide for a mix of other
resources including recreation, water, forage, and
timber. Actions that enhance one resource ultimately
affect all others, including wildlife.

Clearcutting a mature forest, for instance, affects
some species positively and others negatively. Ini-
tially, it makes room for a whole community of field
and shrubland organisms that couldn't have survived
under the canopy. On the other hand, the cavity nests
of woodpeckers and nuthatches are gone, and these
species have had to move on. So, in effect, *responsible*
management actions do not destroy a habitat; they
simply transform it into something else, changing the
species composition in the process.

The largest and most well-funded opportunities for
transforming habitat come in the form of timber sales.
These affect large acreages in a dramatic way. Removing timber can create conditions similar to various successional changes. It can also create horizontal and vertical diversity within an area. This is
not to say, however, that good timber management
is always good wildlife management. Making timber
sales work for wildlife requires careful planning.

There are many ways timber sales can be modified
to enhance wildlife habitat, such as leaving snags or
uncut clumps of vegetation, cutting a mosaic of irregularly shaped clearcuts, or creating stairstepped

edges around clearcuts. These enhancements are not accidents, however—they require good communication between the wildlife biologist and the forester who lays out and executes the sale.

Laws have been passed to formalize this integration among timber, wildlife, and the rest of the resources on our forests. Every National Forest must publicize its plans for managing this mix of resources. Through the public involvement portion of that process, you now have a say in how resources are allocated and what has priority where. To help all of us make better decisions about public lands, we need to know more about the needs of wildlife communities and how our activities impact them.

Where Do We Learn About Wildlife Needs?

There are nearly 400 vertebrates (organisms with backbones) in the northwoods. Each has a unique set of habitat requirements that change with season and stage of life. In contrast, there are only about 40 commercial tree species in the Lake States, and most of them have been researched thoroughly. Wildlife researchers cannot yet echo this claim. They face the monumental task of answering the following questions for all 400 species: Where can we expect to find them? Which are their preferred habitats, and which are their second choices? Most importantly, why are they there? What factors determine whether a habitat is suitable for a particular wildlife community? What size habitat do they need? How adaptable are they? Can they survive a wholesale alteration of their habitats? Can they survive elsewhere?

Understanding wildlife needs can help managers tailor their activities to preserve or create suitable habitats. If they know what limits wildlife populations, they can work to remove these barriers. In turn, healthy wildlife communities can provide feedback to us about the stability and integrity of our own environment.

When animals disappear despite legal protection, it's an indication that something is awry with the environment. And because that environment is our habitat, our life support, the problems facing wildlife face us as well. The humility that comes with this realization may be, after all, the key to our own survival.

Wild turkey.

OBSERVATION TIPS

Now that you have a guide to habitats, you have a better idea of where to look for wildlife. Looking at the right time of day or season is as important as looking in the right place. To help improve your timing, we've noted peak activity periods for individual wildlife species in the "look for" portion of each animal's description.

After you master the where's and when's, the next step is to learn how to get close to wildlife, a skill that birders, photographers, and other wildlife enthusiasts are always perfecting. The following section offers some tricks of the trade, including how to lure and stalk wildlife, how to really look, how to read wildlife signs, how to avoid disturbing wildlife, and most importantly, how to think like an animal.

Think Like an Animal

By their very nature, wild creatures are in the business of being elusive. For those that hunt as well as those that are hunted, survival depends on not being seen. To this end, animals employ an astonishing variety of guises and strategies that render them nearly invisible to each other and to us.

Seeing "invisible" wildlife is easier if you know something about how they "think." If you were a white-tailed deer, for instance, and became suspicious that a human being was in your home range, what would you do? Deer, like many keen-nosed animals, often circle an area to get a whiff of an intruder before they will approach. Knowing this, you'd be wise to keep glancing backward as you walk, looking for a deer that may be circling behind you to catch your drift.

But where do you learn to think like an animal? One way is to read life history accounts like those in this field guide and others like it. Here you'll learn about the habits and motivations of mammals, birds,

Marsh wren.

Deer-bitten twig.

White-tailed deer antler.

reptiles, and amphibians. Another excellent source of wildlife knowledge resides not in books, but in the woods themselves.

Forests, fields, and wetlands are literally filled with the signs and signatures of wildlife. A shed antler, a chewed twig, or a drop of blood in the snow are all clues to a rich drama of natural history. Learning to read these signs can help you imagine what it is like to be an animal: to stalk prey, find a place to sleep, elude your enemies, and build a safe place for your young. Putting yourself in an animal's skin actually increases your chances of seeing the animal you're imagining. To further increase your odds, station yourself in the right habitat, at the right time of day, during the right season of the year.

Look in the Right Places

Preferred Habitats

If you are looking for a particular bird, mammal, reptile, or amphibian, think about what they need every day to survive. Given their size, coloration, and method of nesting, what kind of cover would hide them well? What kind of food do they need at various times of the year? Do they need to be near water during part of their lives? Where would they best be able to provide for these needs? Species tend to prefer areas where all their needs can be conveniently met, and these preferred habitats are the best places to look for them.

The Right Part of the Habitat

Now, if you were a bird or a snake in its preferred habitat, where would you most likely forage for food, build a nest, or sleep? In a wildlife community, different species use different parts of the habitat to meet their needs. Wood warblers use separate "layers" of the same tree. On a single spruce, for instance, a magnolia warbler may be in the lower branches, a bay-breasted warbler in the midsection, and a blackburnian warbler may be prowling the treetop. Along the trunk, a woodpecker uses its special bill to poke into crevices, and at the base, a shovel-footed rodent

34

engineers a subterranean tunnel. A red crossbill in the cone-laden branches of needleleafs has a scissored bill designed to persuade seeds out of cones. In the nearby lake, a great blue heron walks on stilts in the shallows, while a streamlined common loon dives deep into the center. Knowing which "piece of the pie" each species uses can help you catch them in action.

Look at the Right Time of Year

Spring

In some ways, spring is the best time for wildlife watching. Animals, especially birds, are often less elusive in mating season, simply because many of them are actively trying to be noticed by potential mates. Before the leaves pop out, the view can be excellent.

Spring is a good time to listen for chorusing frogs.

Birds: Spring is a good time to watch migrating birds, especially where they may be concentrated along narrow migration routes (see Wildlife Watcher's Atlas). As each week passes, a new species will be winging its way north. The warbler wave may paint splashes of color on every branch and give you a chance to see species that you may not see the rest of the year. Besides being decked out in colorful breeding plumage, many birds perform conspicuous courtship displays in spring.

Mammals: Hungry mammals recovering from the rigors of winter or just emerging from hibernation are busy regaining weight and breeding. White-tailed deer, snowshoe hare, and moose search for succulent buds and shoots, especially along roadsides and in openings where such food appears first. Young beavers and male black bears may be shoving off to find territories of their own.

Amphibians: Ponds are a good place to see noisy, springtime congregations of various kinds of frogs. They are most conspicuous when breeding because they are trying to attract one another—with sounds you can hear. Salamanders are laying eggs in jelly-like masses under logs, in moist leaf litter, or in the water. Many are migrating from their hibernating places to ponds for breeding.

Reptiles: Emerging from hibernation, snakes may be on the move to their summer grounds, or basking in the first warm sun of the year. Look in places that the sun warms during the day—rocks, logs, or the dust of unused forest roads. Look for pond turtles lined up on partially submerged logs.

Summer

Food is plentiful and the weather is forgiving. Most of the breeding residents are now on board, but tougher to see because of heavy foliage.

Birds: Late-arriving birds nest now. Waterfowl may move to dense marshes in flocks to shed their flight feathers. In late summer, the early migrators flock together before going south.

Mammals: Young mammals are being raised and taught to fend for themselves. Now is a good time to see family groups traveling together.

Amphibians: Many leave the ponds now and can be found hopping or creeping about in dryer habitats. Some salamanders cross highways during warm summer rains.

Reptiles: Summer is a time for eating, shedding skin, basking, and avoiding predators.

Fall

As trees and bushes produce their crop of berries and nuts, wildlife is either gorging or storing these foods for the coming winter.

Birds: Waterfowl, raptors, and songbirds migrate to southern wintering grounds, sometimes in spectacular flocks. Before leaving, some species fatten themselves on wild berries and grains, often feeding in flocks.

Mammals: Male deer and moose are in rut, stomping through the woods after does with their necks engorged and their antlers itchy with shedding velvet. Black bears frequent oak stands. Mammals that

Berries are a favorite fall food.

36

will remain active all winter are stashing large caches of food. Hibernators are adding a layer of insulating fat, and beginning to slow down (temperature and heart rate) as they ease into a long winter's confinement.

Amphibians: Frogs and salamanders are moving to underwater and underground wintering spots (hibernaculas).

Reptiles: Snakes and turtles are also moving to hibernaculas.

Winter

Movement is less obscured by vegetation, and the tracks of shy gray wolves, lynx, martens, minks, and river otters can be found in the snow. Many dramatic chase-and-capture scenes are enacted on this canvas and left as hieroglyphics for us to decipher.

Birds: Those that stay the winter must feed frequently and roost in sheltered places to conserve energy. Late in the winter, some birds begin to pair off and breed.

Mammals: Many are hibernating, or sleeping away the coldest days. Deer congregate in northern white-cedar swamps where they create communal trails in the deep snow. Wolves travel windswept lakes and ridges where snow may be packed down. Mice, voles, and shrews travel in roomy corridors under the snow, feeding on food on the forest floor. Beavers and muskrats are warm and dry inside their raised lodges; you can sometimes see plumes of water vapor rising from the chimneys of their houses. In late winter, squirrels begin to chase each other and mate. Tracks are everywhere.

Amphibians: Frogs are buried alive in mud at the bottom or banks of lakes and ponds. They breathe a sort of muddy oxygen. Salamanders are tucked underground or under a leafy blanket.

Spotted salamander.

Reptiles: Snakes are hibernating in groups, often with other kinds of snakes. Turtles under the ice breathe through an all-purpose opening called the cloaca, where sensitive tissues act like gills to filter oxygen out of the mud and into the blood.

Look at the Right Time of Day

Twilight

Activity usually peaks around sunrise and sunset. Animals that work best at twilight are afoot, as are creatures that are just setting out for or getting back from a night's hunt.

Daytime

Woodpeckers, red squirrels, hawks, and a variety of other creatures are active during the day. High noon is usually too hot for much activity, and many animals are in day beds at this time.

Nighttime

A whole world comes alive behind the mask of night. Owls and flying squirrels with huge, light-gathering eyes are stalking and dodging one another. Four-footed carnivores are zigzagging back and forth, tracking their prey by scent. Let the full moon be your searchlight, or use it as a backdrop to help you count highflying flocks of migrants that pass across its face.

When It Rains

Many wildlife species are afoot during light, warm showers. Frogs, toads, and salamanders do much of their traveling during rains because the humidity helps keep their skin moist. Birds can be seen bathing in the newly formed puddles or drenched grasses left by a rain. If rains are heavy enough to flood low-lying areas, swallows and martins will skim the gras-stops searching for washed-out insects that have climbed up to avoid drowning. Likewise, hawks will perch to feast on the procession of escaping rodents, reptiles, and amphibians.

How to Look—
New Ways of Seeing

Use Peripheral Vision

Practice seeing things and distinguishing shapes and colors out of the corner of your eye. You'll find you notice more because you're using the full range of possible sight. This will come in handy when an animal approaches you from either side and you don't want to frighten it by turning your head. Animals will sometimes allow you to approach closer if you don't confront them with a head-on stare, a gesture that signals aggression in most wild codes.

Extend Your Senses

Technology enables us to see like the hawks and owls see, and to bring home the sights and sounds of our visits on film and tape. Here are some ideas:

Many birders use 7×35 or 8×40 power binoculars.

1. Binoculars, tripod-mounted spotting scopes, and zoom lenses on cameras bring the world closer and in sharper focus. The trick to locating birds or animals with binoculars is to first find them with the unaided eye, and then, while still watching, bring the binoculars to your eyes.

2. For observing night life, cover the lens of your flashlight with a red filter, such as the gels used for theatrical lighting. Many animals see red as black, and will not notice your light.

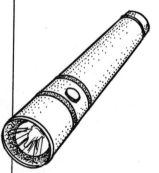

Discover the nightlife with a red-filtered flashlight.

3. Try sprinkling fluorescent powders on the ground in areas where mammals are likely to walk. The trails they leave with every footfall can then be followed with the help of a black light.

4. Use a tilting mirror mounted on a telescoping pole to see inside a nest that is above you (use caution so as not to disturb the nestlings!).

5. Trained spotting dogs can be used to follow scent trails and point out wildlife.

6. Parabolic reflectors can gather faint sounds, and tape recorders can capture them.

7. Snorkeling or SCUBA gear can bring you face to face with aquatic wildlife.

Stalking

Follow Tracks and Trails: Look for paths of all sizes, from tiny runways chewed in the grass to well-rutted deer paths. These "highways" see a lot of wildlife traffic throughout the day and night.

Keep the Wind in Your Face: Travel upwind so that smells in the air ahead of you are traveling from the animal to you and not the other way around. Most animals associate the smell of humans with danger.

Keep the Sun at Your Back: This is especially true if you hope to photograph your subject. Colors and shapes are easier to pick out if the sun is not in your eyes.

Advance When Wildlife Is Occupied: Wait to move until the animal is busily engaged in eating, grooming, etc. At the slightest sign that it is listening—

There's an art to getting close to wildlife without spooking them. With practice and patience, you can learn to see wildlife wherever you go.

tensing, ear twitching, raising its head—you should freeze. Move only when it's relaxed and occupied. You can get within a few feet of a drumming ruffed grouse this way.

Keep Cover Between You and the Animal: Move behind vegetation to keep the animal from seeing your silhouette. When you want a look, peek around (not over) the bush or boulder. Keep close to the ground when on hilltops.

Stalk From the Water: Land animals usually don't expect danger from the water, so you may be able to sneak up in a canoe, waders, or in a portable, camouflaged blind.

Hiding

Locate High Visitation Sites: Some parts of the habitat are more heavily used than others, such as water borders, trail intersections, natural springs, scent stations, den sites, or knolls with a good view of the surroundings. These are good places to hide and wait. Another good place is anywhere near the carcass of a large animal. Sit where you have a view of an area you haven't walked through; here, wildlife may not yet be aware of your presence. Remember that most wildlife won't cross open fields to get to you; make sure you sit in areas where they will have cover for safe travel. Try to sit with the sun at your back so wildlife will have to squint to see you.

Camouflage Yourself: Remember that resident animals are intimately familiar with every stick and stone in their environment. You are something new in the picture. To minimize your strangeness, dress in natural colors, cover your face and hands (camouflage netting, gloves, or face paint), and move with slow, measured movements. Mask your scent by storing your clothes with a sachet of pine and bayberry. Make sure you use only unscented soap and shampoo. If you sit out in the open to wait, sit against a tree or rock so your outline is not so obvious. If you stand, make sure a long shadow or your reflection in the water doesn't betray your presence.

"Take only pictures, leave only footprints."

Conceal Yourself: Natural blinds include up-turned roots, downed logs, cattail clumps, and boulders—anything large enough for you to hide behind comfortably. You can also rig an artificial blind, but it may take wildlife in the area a week to 10 days to get used to this foreign object in their territory. Set the blind out well before you want to use it. Even cars have been used as blinds; for instance, biologist Hope Ryan's observations of coyote dens were made from a parked van. Stands placed high up in trees may give you a chance to observe larger animals that rarely look up for danger.

Animals Can't Count: Wildlife may get used to the blind, but they will still be alarmed when you arrive. Ask a friend to walk with you to the blind. When you go in, have your friend keep on walking. Wildlife in the area may perceive that the human danger has passed and may go about their business sooner.

Go Out on a Limb: Some bird species, especially warblers, vireos, and kinglets, will come up to investigate if you approach them at their level. Climb a tree and try it. Or better yet, begin a second childhood—build a treehouse!

Act Nonchalant: The "behavioral blind" technique has been used to study and photograph larger animals. The idea is to let yourself be seen while engaging in passive, natural activities like digging or "preening." Animals can sense tension, and usually shy away from it. If you keep your eyes averted and your body relaxed, chances are they will be more comfortable around you, and you will be able to watch them out of the corner of your eye.

Luring Wildlife

Pishing: With your teeth together, exhale the word "pish" a few times. This sounds like the alarm call of many birds, and will draw others that want to investigate. Pishing is especially effective during the breeding season when birds are highly protective of their territories. It works best when birds in the area are already giving chip calls, signalling concern over your presence.

Squeaking: By either kissing the back of your hand or using a handheld caller, you can produce squeaks and squeals that sound like a rabbit or a mouse in its death throes. To predators such as foxes, coyotes, bobcats, owls, and hawks, this is the sound of an easy meal, and will often bring them running. This, in turn, may prompt flocks of birds to begin "mobbing," i.e., swooping and dashing at the predator to get it to leave the territory. You can also buy calling devices that imitate the sound of a bird in distress, which will attract raccoons and other predators. These calls are most effective in April, May, and August during the 3 hours before dark.

Handheld caller.

Imitating Calls: One of the reasons male birds sing is to warn other birds that this is their territory—no trespassing. By imitating a bird's call or playing a tape of it, you may convince the resident male that an intruder is on hand. Within a few minutes he should be close by, singing his heart out. You can also induce a group of frogs to start chorusing by playing a tape of a frog's call. (See warnings about wise use of recordings below.)

Rattling Antlers: Rattle the tines of deer antlers together, scrape gravel, and beat the bushes with the antlers to imitate the sounds made by two bucks fighting for a doe. This may bring other bucks to investigate during rutting season (fall).

Waving Bright Objects: Some animals, such as deer, bobcats, and ground squirrels are full of curiosity. If you are well-hidden, you may be able to lure one of these animals out by waving a bit of colored cloth or a piece of aluminum.

Reading Telltale Signs

Some days are bound to pass when no amount of stalking or hiding or luring will bring a wild creature into view. On these days, you can be just as richly rewarded by finding the **signs** of animal activity, the clues that hint at the sequestered community around you.

Speaking of signs, Tom Brown, expert trapper and author, says, "I learned to track not animals but disturbances, things knocked out of place, minute and indistinct traces, the ghost of a print, a stone turned wrong-side up, a fragment of hair on a branch." These indistinct traces are like ruins that you can reconstruct with your imagination to flesh out the whole story of an animal's comings and goings. This story, told through signs, can be as vivid as one that unfolds before your very eyes. Use the following checklist of clues next time you go looking for wildlife.

Signs of Feeding

- ☐ Holes in trees
- ☐ Sap
- ☐ Drilling dust
- ☐ Divots
- ☐ Holes in mud
- ☐ Nipped twigs
- ☐ Stripped logs
- ☐ A hidden store of nuts, seeds, mushrooms, cones
- ☐ Pine cone scales
- ☐ Opened nuts
- ☐ Rodent skins
- ☐ Carcasses
- ☐ Plucked feathers
- ☐ Hair and bones

Nests, Dens, and Shelters

- ☐ Holes in trees
- ☐ Burrows in ground
- ☐ Matted-down areas in vegetation
- ☐ Nests
- ☐ Holes in banks
- ☐ Lodges
- ☐ Downy feathers on rim of nest

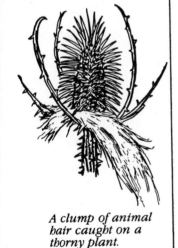

A clump of animal hair caught on a thorny plant.

☐ Fresh green sprig in nest
☐ Feeding platforms

Beaver Dams and Canals

Tracks and Trails

☐ Dry trails in dewy grass
☐ Runways
☐ Otter slides
☐ Tunnels in snow
☐ Underground burrows
☐ Dust baths

Body Waste and Castoffs

☐ Whitewash
☐ Soft droppings ("cowpies")
☐ Hard droppings
☐ Pellets of undigested bone and hair
☐ Snake skins
☐ Molted feathers
☐ Shreds of antler velvet
☐ Clumps of shed fur
☐ Skulls and bones

Markings

☐ Claw marks on trees
☐ Wallows and scrapes
☐ Urine and scent stations
☐ Scat piles
☐ Antler rubs

Sounds

☐ Breeding calls
☐ Territorial calls
☐ Aggression calls
☐ Alarm calls
☐ Family communication

A molted feather.

Caught in the Act— Behavior Watching

Behavior watching can be the most addictive of wild-life watching activities, but it is a decidedly construc-tive addiction. There is much to be learned about the behaviors of even the common species, and much of this work is being done by amateurs. By taking notes

45

on what you see, you can begin to build your own understanding of wildlife behavior, while possibly adding new discoveries to our knowledge of these species. For more information on taking notes, see the Wildlife Events Calendar on page 373. For information on amateur wildlife watching groups, see the How to Go Beyond This Book section on page 413.

Etiquette for Wildlife Watchers

Don't Bankrupt an Animal's Energy: If you are reading this book, you are probably a dyed-in-the-wool wildlife lover, and would do whatever you could to see wildlife prosper in the Lake States. You may be surprised, then, to learn that some of your actions, though well-intended, may be harmful to the species you are admiring. Here's why.

Each habitat provides animals with a certain energy budget they can expend. Part of this budget is spent in reproduction, part in their own maintenance, and part in protecting themselves from predators. It takes energy to be on the alert for danger, and to freeze or flee at an intruder's approach. The heart beats faster and breathing gets more intense, robbing the animal of energy needed for other survival tactics.

Most animals perceive you as a possible threat. They will let you get just so close before they instinctively freeze, flee, or actively defend their territory. One disturbance won't harm them, but repeated or prolonged disturbances may bankrupt their energy. You can help by limiting the time of your visits, and observing animals from a distance that they consider safe.

Keep Your Distance: How do you know when you are too close to an animal? If the animal shows the following signs, you are in the "disturbance range" and you should sit quietly or move slowly away. Remember that binoculars and spotting scopes can bring you close to the animal without endangering it.

MAMMALS

- Head raised high and ears pointed toward you.
- Skittish: jumps at sounds and movements.

46

- Moves away or lowers its head with its ears back in preparation for a charge. Hairs on neck and shoulders may stand up.
- Aggressive or nervous behavior.

BIRDS

- Head raised, looking at you.
- Skittishness.
- Excessive preening, bill wiping, or pecking at dirt or food.
- Alarm calls, repeated chirping and chipping.
- Distraction display, i.e., broken wing or tail spread.

REPTILES

- Rattling or hissing.
- Playing dead.
- Snakes raise their upper body, open their mouths.
- Striking.

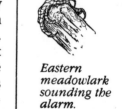

Eastern meadowlark sounding the alarm.

Be Especially Considerate of Nesting Animals:
Birds and animals that are raising young are especially sensitive to disturbance. Your presence may keep parents away from nests or dens at a time when eggs need to be kept warm or young need to be fed. If disturbed often enough, parent birds may desert young, or their nearly fledged young may leave before they are ready to fend for themselves. Also, predators may follow your scent trail to a nest they might otherwise have missed.

Before approaching a nest, always scan the area with your binoculars to see if the female is on the nest or nearby. Use the stalking techniques above to keep her from being alarmed. If you are taking pictures, you may be tempted to cut or move vegetation to get a better shot. Remember that this vegetation may provide needed shade or cover from winged predators. Better to leave the vegetation in place and limit your stay to 15 minutes or less.

Use Tape Recordings Sparingly: Tape recordings of bird calls can be used to lure a resident bird into view. The bird interprets the call as a challenge from an intruding male, and will usually respond with its own call or with a personal visit. If you are in a heavily used recreation area where other wildlife watchers may be playing calls, use caution not to overtax the defending bird. If harassed too often, some wild creatures will desert a habitat, even if it provides the ideal combination of survival needs. They may be forced to move to an inferior habitat, and then work harder to find what they need.

Never use recordings to lure rare or endangered species or species that may be nesting out of their range. These animals are under enough stress already.

Replace Rocks and Logs You Overturn Looking for Reptiles and Amphibians: For many creatures, rocks, logs, and piles of debris are homes, feeding sites, and places of refuge. If you lift these shelters to look, make sure to restore them exactly as they were.

Never Allow Pets to Dig Up, Chase, or Harass Wildlife.

Cut Motorboat Speed Near Shore: Besides frightening wildlife on the banks, a boat wake can cause serious erosion on the shore. This may interfere with breeding reptiles and amphibians, emerging hibernators, nesting loons, and feeding shorebirds.

Familiarize Yourself With Bear Safety: Don't tempt bears by leaving food out at a campsite, or even worse, bringing it into the tent with you. Black bears are rarely interested in fighting with you, but they are interested in your food. Methods of hanging food out of bears' reach and other bear-proof strategies can be gleaned from pamphlets available at National Forest visitor centers.

Don't Get Between Large Animals and Their Young: Moose are notoriously loyal mothers. If a cow senses that you are endangering her calf, she may charge, and she and her flying hooves mean business.

Back Up Slowly: When you and an animal come face to face, avoid direct eye contact; it may be interpreted as a threat gesture. Try to suppress your urge to run. Backing up slowly is a submissive act, and most animals will be satisfied that you are "crying uncle."

Respect the Rights of Your Own Species: Give other wildlife watchers a good name by always asking landowners' permission before using their land. Always walk the edges of plowed fields, rather than through the crops. Leave the land as you found it. And if you run across other rapt observers in the woods, remain quiet so you don't frighten the animals they are watching.

White-tailed deer.

HABITAT GUIDE

How to Use This Guide

1. Turn to the key on page 52, and use it to help you identify the type of habitat you are looking at. You'll need to determine whether it's:

NON-FORESTED

Aquatic (permanent body of water)
Wetland (transition between dry land and deep water)
Opening (field of grasses, forbs, shrubs, or saplings)
Or

FORESTED

Upland (broadleaf, needleleaf, or mixed forest)
Lowland (broadleaf or needleleaf forest)

Read the short description under each heading to help you decide. Turn to the page shown to find a more complete description and illustration of each habitat.

2. Study the habitat illustration. Look for characteristic plants that are pictured, and try to learn some of their names. Read about how the habitat began, what it may eventually become, and how plants and animals have adapted to survive there.

3. The Wildlife Action section will tell you where in the habitat to look for wildlife, e.g., tree trunk, forest floor, edge of water, and so on.

4. Read about the wildlife species you are likely to see. Follow the "Look For" and "Listen For" instructions to find signs and sounds of the species.

5. You now have a "search image" for each habitat—you know what animals you might see and where you might see them. Keep this image in mind next time you visit the habitat.

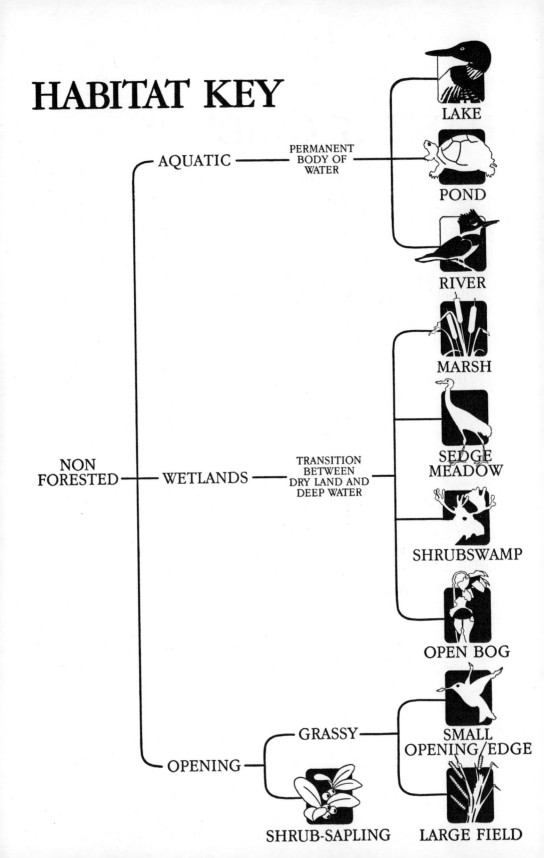

HABITAT KEY

AQUATIC — PERMANENT BODY OF WATER

LAKE

POND

RIVER

MARSH

SEDGE MEADOW

NON FORESTED — WETLANDS — TRANSITION BETWEEN DRY LAND AND DEEP WATER

SHRUBSWAMP

OPEN BOG

OPENING — GRASSY — SMALL OPENING/EDGE

SHRUB-SAPLING

LARGE FIELD

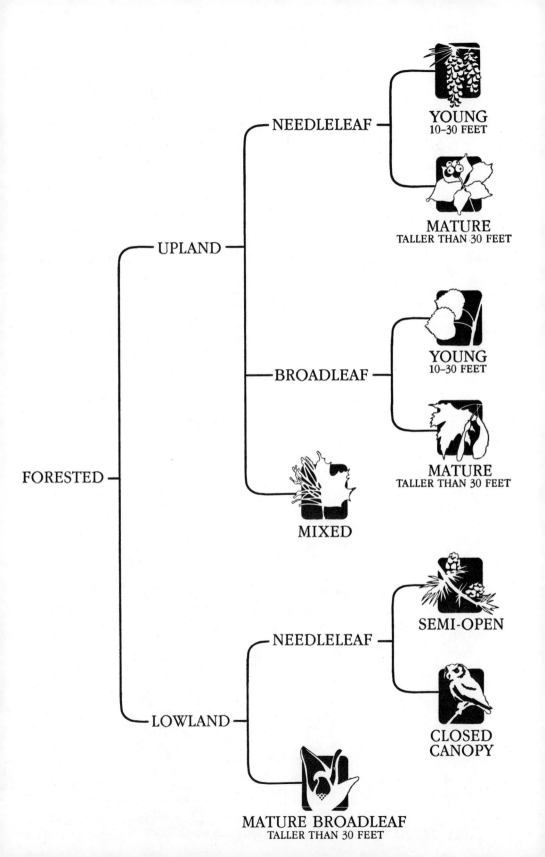

FORESTED

UPLAND

NEEDLELEAF

YOUNG
10–30 FEET

MATURE
TALLER THAN 30 FEET

BROADLEAF

YOUNG
10–30 FEET

MATURE
TALLER THAN 30 FEET

MIXED

LOWLAND

NEEDLELEAF

SEMI-OPEN

CLOSED
CANOPY

MATURE BROADLEAF
TALLER THAN 30 FEET

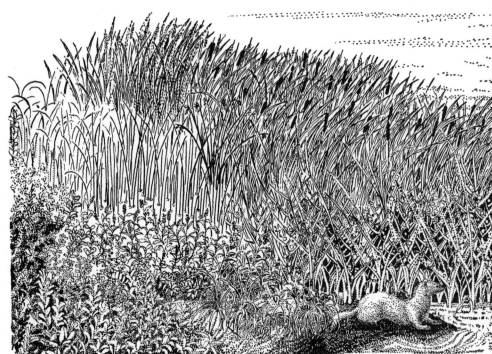

LAKE

©1988 Vera Ming Wong

A white-tailed deer, sweltering in the sun and pestered by flies, wades into a protected part of the lake. Nearby a great blue heron stands with stately patience, waiting for the shallows to yield a passing meal. A mudpuppy waves its gills as it prowls the murky bottom, and the shell-home of a snapping turtle parts the stalks of green like an invisible hand.

Overhead in the squint of the sun, an osprey tucks its wings and rockets toward the lake. In the moment before it meets its shadow, it snaps open its wings and drives down its muscled legs. A shimmering perch rolling to the surface hesitates too long, and is plucked up and borne away by four needle-tipped talons.

What Is a Lake?

Lakes are bodies of permanent, open water greater than 10 acres, and usually deeper than 6 feet. In winter and summer, the temperature of the top layer of water in a deep lake differs from that of the bottom (think of the cold spots you can feel under you when swimming in a lake). The exposed shoreline may be windscoured and wavebeaten, with rocks and cobble at its edge, whereas more protected parts of the lakeshore will be mucky or silty, and will support a marsh-like mix of emergent plants (growing partly above and below the water surface). Submerged aquatic vegetation may be found in the open water, but in

1. *Great Blue Heron*
2. *Common Loon*
3. *Bald Eagle (& nest)*
4. *Osprey*
5. *Snapping Turtle*
6. *Mink*
7. *Leatherleaf*
8. *Water Smartweed*
9. *Sedges*
10. *Bulrushes*
11. *Cattails*
12. *Bur-reeds*
13. *Pondweed*
14. *Pipewort*
15. *Three-way sedge*
16. *Spike rushes*
17. *Silverweed*
18. *Sweet Gale*
19. *Aspen & Birch Trees*
20. *Horsetails*
21. *Speckled Alder*

the deepest portions, a lack of sunlight will prohibit plant growth.

Origins

Most lakes in this part of the world were glacier-made, settling into kettle-shaped depressions left by melting ice chunks, or washing into basins gouged out by the glacier's blade. Other lakes backed up behind dams of gravel dumped by the melting glacier. Born on these newly scoured rockbeds, the lakes were pure and rather sterile at first. Then microorganisms began to appear, and inflowing streams carried in organic material and great loads of eroded sediment that settled in the lake to create a rich, muddy bottom. Plants and animals soon invaded these holding tanks.

The process that began with the glaciers is still occurring; lakes are slowly aging and changing all across the northwoods. As their beds fill with silt and organic muck, the lakes gradually become shallower. Sun can reach more of the lake's bottom, and plants along its edges creep toward the center. Over time, the river that flows out of the lake may erode the notch, or lip, over which it spills. If this notch erodes through, much of the water in the lake may suddenly drain out. As the basin fills with plant and animal remains and dries, it may pass from pond to marsh to wet meadow to swamp, until eventually, a forest may stand where waves once rolled. A disturbance at one of these later stages can set back the clock, however, delaying the succession for generations.

Fall and Spring Overturn

One characteristic of large, deep lakes is the layering in the water. Whereas a pond tends to be shallow, with a relatively uniform temperature between the top and bottom, a deep lake has an upper layer of sunwarmed water (in the summer) and a colder layer below. The warmer water is lighter; it floats on top of the cold layer, but doesn't mix with it. Wind along the surface of the lake circulates the warm layer of water with itself, but does not stir it down to the bottom.

In the fall, the tables turn. The top layer begins to cool until all the water, top to bottom, reaches the same temperature, disrupting the layering that stabilized the lake during the summer. Gusty fall winds are now free to mix the unstable water all the way down to the bottom, circulating nutrients in what is called the fall overturn.

In the winter, the layers become distinct again. Dropping temperatures freeze the surface and cool the top layer of water to near 32 degrees, making it colder than the lower layers. When the spring sun thaws the ice, it warms the top water until the lake once again reaches an even temperature. The kite-flying winds of spring cause the lake to turn another somersault.

Layers of Life

The open water of a lake has several distinct layers of life:

The Surface (On Top): The very top layer is the ceiling or the surface of the water. Because water molecules cling to each other more strongly than they do to air, they form an elastic "skin" that is firm enough for some life to skate on, run on, land on, and float on. Whirlygig beetles gyrate to create ripples in this skin. They "read" the returning ripples to learn about obstacles (possible prey) also sitting on the surface.

The Surface (Underneath): A whole world of insects, snails, and microscopic organisms hang upside down from the underside of the water surface.

Upper Layer: Just below the surface is a layer of water warmed by the sun and populated by free-floating algae, diatoms, and tiny animals with nearly transparent bodies, such as rotifers, water fleas, and copepods. When these plants and animals die, their bodies settle down to the lower, colder layer of the lake, and build up a rich blanket of organic debris on the muddy bottom.

Lower Layer: A complex community of plant and animal decomposers survives in the depths by breaking down the food that filters from above. Insect larvae, clams, snails, tubeworms, etc. live in the muck of the lake bottom.

Other zones of life occur closer to shore, where the bottom slopes up and the water is shallower.

Quiet Coves: These plant-filled edges can resemble marshes, ponds, or even bogs. In the shallows, plants are able to sink their roots in mud while reaching up for sun. A wide variety of animals and fish use these plants for food, nesting, concealment, and structural support (a place to cling to). The shoreline is muck, peat, or sand.

Exposed Beaches: Shorelines can also be sculpted by the actions of waves and wind. These beaches have fewer plants, and tend to be lined with gravel, cobbles, or rocks.

Value to Wildlife

Lakes have size and depth. They're deep enough for divers such as loons and mergansers, as well as bottom feeders such as mudpuppies. They can also accommodate predators like the osprey that require a large supply of fish.

In addition, a lake has habitats at its edges: bays, inlets, and coves—quiet places where pond, marsh, or bog-like conditions may occur. Turtles, frogs, and molting waterfowl, for instance, often find refuge in a cove of bulrushes or water lilies that is protected from winds and waves. Wading birds haunt the shallow water and tall grasses that often rim the lake. In places where a shield of land vegetation grows right to the edge, mammals are afforded safe access to water and food. On the less protected shores, winds and waves can create a shoreline that is rocky and exposed, attractive to gulls, terns, and cormorants. Finally, islands in lakes provide relatively secure nesting opportunities for loons, herons, cormorants, and egrets.

BLUE ACRES
There are 17,000 natural lakes in Minnesota, 11,000 in Michigan, and 8,700 in Wisconsin. Ninety-five percent of the people in Minnesota live within 5 miles of recreational water. It's no wonder this state has the highest number of boats per capita in the country!

Acid precipitation threatens to quiet some north-woods lakes. Fish cannot reproduce in highly acidic waters, and other forms of aquatic life succumb to early death as well. Many lakes are currently protected by the buffering action of nearby soils; if these soils become too acidic, however, they may lose their buffering ability, and allow metals such as aluminum, manganese, mercury, lead, copper, and zinc to leach into the water. Lakes that are in bedrock regions and sand plains are in the greatest danger because of the already low buffering capacity of their surrounding material.

Wildlife Action

Dawn and dusk are the best times to observe lake life. Look high above for circling ospreys and eagles. Follow them with your binoculars after a catch and you may be rewarded by spotting a huge nest, complete with hungry, bawling nestlings, atop a towering shoreside pine. Listen for screaming black terns, wheeling over the water in search of darting fish. Along the surface of the lake, watch for loons and mergansers, and try to follow them with your eyes as they dive and reappear somewhere else on the lake. Watch the shoreline for skittering sandpipers. During migration, watch for rafts of grebes, common golden-eyes, redheads, and buffleheads. If the lake has a fringe of pond or marsh plants, it will be host to frogs, snakes, turtles, mammals, and birds common to both the pond and the marsh. Look at the muddy edge of the lake for the signatures of night visitors such as raccoon, mink, red fox, and white-tailed deer.

GREAT BLUE HERON

A school of perch drifts lazily into the cool shadow of a heron standing in the shallows. They veer instinctively, but not all escape. With lightning speed, a daggerlike bill splits the water, clipping shut on the last of the school. With its long, sinuous neck, the heron lifts its bill, flips the fish skyward, and ducks to swallow it whole. After a well-deserved stretch, the hunter resumes its statue-like freeze, eyes scanning the shallows with telescopic accuracy.

Great blues are among our most elegant and stately birds. They stand 4 feet tall on long, stiltlike legs, and their wings span an amazing 6 feet. Even the slightest breeze will carry them aloft with steady, measured wingbeats.

These towering waterbirds also choose towering nests, as high as 130 feet up in a tree. They tend to nest in crowded colonies ranging from a few nests to a thousand, with 50 being the average. If you happen across a heron rookery in springtime, there'll be no mistaking it. You'll hear it long before you see it— a raucous party of eerie screams and squawks. As you move closer, you'll whiff the stench of decaying fish and excrement that the young eject over the sides of the nest. If agitated enough by your presence, nesting herons will whitewash you, or even regurgitate their last meal on your head (shades of boiling oil over medieval city gates!). Although this defense mechanism helps repel some intruders, the constant rain of harsh excrement over many years often poisons and kills the trees, which in turn threatens the rookery.

Despite their unique defenses, many fledglings are lost to vultures, owls, and tree-climbing mammals. Others are jostled out of the nest by aggressive siblings, or lose their balance during their flying-in-place exercises. It's a long way down, and even if the young birds survive the fall, they are likely to starve or become a meal for another hungry creature. Of the 4 or 5 nestlings that hatch, only 2 or 3 will survive. They will eventually learn the wade-and-wait method of fishing, turning to insects, frogs, snakes, and even birds and mammals when the fishing is poor.

Look for great blue herons: standing in the shallows along lakes, ponds, or river shores, especially at dusk and dawn. As you come close, watch the heron extend its neck, watching you while preparing for flight. If you get too close it will push off with its long, springy legs and lift itself to another fishing spot. Eventually it may circle back to where it was when you disturbed it.

Great blue heron.

Look for nests: large stick structures, alone or by the dozens, high in tall trees, often on islands. Air traffic patterns around a rookery may lead you to one. At dusk, when parents are bringing food for their young, many herons in an area will be homing in on the rookery, much like planes queuing in the sky at a busy airport. Look for the smaller, completely white great egret that also builds its nest here. You should watch from a distance, however, because even minor human disturbance can force wary parents to abandon the rookery, or cause young to leave the nest before they can fly or survive on their own.

Listen for: honks, squawks, and croaks especially in the vicinity of nests.

COMMON LOON

If you think the echoing laugh of a midnight loon sounds primeval, you're absolutely right. Loons are among our oldest birds, with an ancestry going back 45 million years.

The haunting music of today's loon has been compared to the bugling of a bull elk or the singing of a humpback whale—all guaranteed to send shivers down your spine. Loons have at least four different types of calls (tremolo, yodel, wail, and hoot) that they use at various times to greet one another, express alarm or worry, defend their turf, or simply identify each other in the dark. An aggressive tone seems to characterize the penguin dance, in which a male stands upright on the water by wildly beating his feet. Night chorusing, performed by many birds especially in spring, can be heard for up to a mile. The yodel, which rival males hurl back and forth across their invisible "fences," is unique to each loon that utters it and can be used to identify individuals. Loons are perhaps best known for the tremolo, which writer John McPhee calls "the laugh of the deeply insane."

Although loons have been clocked at flight speeds of over 100 mph, flying is not their forte. In fact, their skeletons and bloodstreams have evolved to favor diving rather than flying, giving them several solid bones that make diving easier but make take-off a bit of a chore. Before they dive, loons expel air from their lungs and flatten their plumage to squeeze air out of their feathers. They sink quickly and then "fly" through the water, propelled at high speed by their enormous webbed feet. Each webbed foot is 4 by 5 inches; a comparable human foot would wear a 45 triple R shoe!

As they travel, their circulatory system reduces their heart rate and rations out oxygen so that their most vulnerable tissues are assured enough oxygen, even for 100-foot or deeper dives. Loon watchers often fear that they have lost their loons when they don't see them resurface after 10 minutes or so. Chances are the loon has resurfaced several times, sneaking a breath and then departing for the depths again, barely rippling the water with its movements.

Look for common loons: swimming and diving, ducking under the water to pursue their favorite meal—fish. Biologists estimate that a pair of loons with 2 chicks will eat a half ton of fish in the 15 weeks it takes to raise their family. They prefer clear lakes with good fishing visibility, enough depth to dive away from enemies, and enough room to allow them to take off (they use up to a ¼-mile "runway") and clear the surrounding trees. An ideal loon territory has at least 2 nest sites, a protected "nursery" for teaching and feeding the young, and an abundance of food. Territories average between 50 and 200 acres, depending on whether the pair holds the whole lake or a bay on a lake.

Common loon.

Don't disturb nests: which may be found at the edge or within 16 feet of water, frequently on the leeward (out of the wind) shore of islands. Loons' feet are so far back on their bodies that walking upright is difficult, so they try to spend as little time as possible on shore, always within close range of water. Nests are hastily assembled piles of vegetation, and shortly after hatching, loon chicks hit the water and never look back.

Look for chicks: riding on their parents' backs. This is more than just a joy ride. Young loons, because of their downy feathers, are easily soaked, and could die from exposure if wet.

Look for flocks: of 15–20 loons gathering on lakes in the fall before migrating to the Atlantic coast, where they spend the winter. Some remain alone or in groups of 2 or 3.

Listen for: tremolos, wails, yodels, and hoots. The tremolo signals alarm, annoyance, or worry. Wailing carries messages and opens and closes night choruses. The yodel, a weird and almost bloodcurdling cry, is used in squabbles over boundaries. The hoot is a soft call between family members.

BALD EAGLE

Bald eagle.

Ben Franklin tried to warn Americans about their popular favorite in the contest for a national emblem. Delving into the eagle's "checkered" past, Franklin found some objectionable behaviors, including scavenging and even thievery. The wild turkey, he argued, would make a more deserving mascot, despite its less noble appearance (at least by human standards).

In one sense, Franklin's allegations were true. Eagles are feeding opportunists, and will scavenge for dead fish if they are available. (They also, of course, scoop their own live prey from the water, and will eat birds and mammals as well as fish.) And yes, they do sometimes force ospreys to drop their freshly caught fish, then dive with blinding speed to retrieve the catch. We now see that these feeding strategies are not character flaws, but rather, signs of the eagle's superior ability to adapt to its habitat.

Although Franklin had good reason to be partial to the intelligent wild turkey, the eagle was also a good choice for a national emblem. Its noble bearing aside, the eagle is a master aerialist, a great nest architect, and above all, a tenacious survivor. If you are lucky enough to see one sailing above the lake, slowly spiralling into the blue, and then diving at breathtaking speeds towards the water, you'll know why the eagle was chosen to represent us over 200 years ago.

Pesticides in the environment have led to the thinning of eagle eggshells. As regulations diminish the use of DDT, the populations seem to be increasing again. The Chippewa National Forest in Minnesota has the highest breeding density of bald eagles in the lower 48 states.

Look for bald eagles: perched motionless in tall trees overlooking a lake, or soaring in the open. On a lake with a good store of fish, eagles will spend 3 to 4 hours a day hunting. Food is brought to the nest most frequently before 9 a.m. and after 3 p.m., with a regular feeding at 4 p.m. Rather than flying directly to the nest, eagles will first land in nearby "pilot" trees to look for possible danger before giving away the nest's location. In the spring you may be lucky enough to see a courtship flight, where a pair flies together at great heights, locking talons and falling several hundred feet in a series of somersaults. In the fall, look for eagles at hotspots such as Hawk Ridge in Duluth, Minnesota.

Look for nests: huge platforms of sticks and debris placed 5–30 feet below the top of a tall, living tree (preferably eastern white pine) with a clear view of the surroundings. Nests are added to year after year, and sometimes reach heights of 12 feet and diameters of 8½ feet. They are the largest nests built by a single pair of birds. One nest in Iowa, which eventually crashed to the ground after 40 years of use, weighed an astonishing 4,000 pounds.

Listen for: a squeaky, cackling, almost gull-like "kar kar kar." Head is often lowered and the wings are depressed and quivering as the call is given.

OSPREY

This extraordinary angler is well-equipped for its livelihood. It has legendary eyesight, a torpedo-like body for swift dives, and feet that are studded with spines for holding slippery prey. After nearly 8 dives out of 10, the fish hawk emerges from a roostertail of spray with a finny meal between its talons. One of its toes is reversible to help it carry up to 4 pounds

Osprey.

of fish. It carries its catch to a nearby perch, keeping one cleated foot near the fish's head and one pinned farther back to keep it from struggling.

Occasionally, ospreys are intercepted after their flashy catches by opportunistic eagles. After a few threatening swoops from the larger eagle, most ospreys fumble their fish, and the eagles dart down to snatch the falling prize. In most areas, eagles are not numerous enough to pose much of a threat, however.

A greater threat is the disappearance of prime fishing habitat, illegal shooting, and egg collecting. On the positive side, humans have provided for future osprey generations by erecting thousands of artificial nest platforms and by banning DDT, a pesticide that accumulates in fish bodies and leads to thinning of eggshells.

Look for ospreys: perched on lakeshore trees, flying reconnaissance, or hovering 30 to 100 feet over the water. They prefer feeding in shallow areas where fish such as pike are near the surface. Typically, males do all of the hunting for the growing brood, from early morning through evening. In spring, look for soaring, aerobatic flights where a courting pair dive, circle, and chase one another, screaming aloud.

Look for nests: alone or in colonies. Built of large sticks and debris, 3 feet across, 1–2 feet deep, in the top of a dead tree up to 130 feet high, and visible for miles. The pair return to the nest, adding new nest material each year. Record nests have been as much as 10 feet high and weighed half a ton at the end of several generations. Ospreys will also accept artificial nesting platforms.

Listen for: short, melodious whistle: "chewk chewk chewk." Its voice is feeble for a bird this size except in display when the screaming can be heard from a distance.

SNAPPING TURTLE

The snapping turtle is a reptilian Jekyll and Hyde. In water, these turtles are docile and uninterested in anything but getting away quickly. But let the same animal venture onto land, to lay eggs for instance, and you've got a turtle of a different stripe. On the defensive, a snapper will lunge, snapping its knife-sharp jaws with great speed and accuracy. Once the turtle grips its attacker, it holds on with bulldog stubbornness; in fact, the jaw muscles often have to be cut before they'll loosen their hold. Drop the same turtle into the water, and it will immediately mellow, crawl to the bottom, and slowly creep away.

In their underwater domain, snapping turtles play an important role, both as consumers of large quantities of fish, plants, and carrion, and as food sources themselves. A female snapper will produce 500–1000 eggs in her lifetime (from 10 to 96 per clutch), 80 percent of which will be eaten by predators such as foxes and raccoons. Hatchlings and young turtles are also on the menus of a number of large birds and fish. Those turtles that do survive their first few months become successful predators themselves.

They do most of their stalking underwater at night, sneaking up on slow-moving fish and crayfish, much like cats sneaking up on mice. As they approach, they lift themselves up on their hind legs and lower their front legs, building the leverage they'll need for a powerful lunge. They wait patiently until their target is within reach, and then, in one swift movement, they thrust their head and neck forward while opening their jaws. This open-mouthed lunge creates a vacuum with which they suck in the fish along with lots of water and vegetation. Smaller prey are seized and swallowed intact, but larger prey are held in the mouth and torn to pieces with the long foreclaws. An occasional duckling or mammal will be dragged underwater and held there until it drowns.

The best defense against an attacking, landlocked snapper is to step aside. Because of the way they are designed, a snapper can't change direction once they begin lunging forward. This poses no problem to the snapper that's hunting crayfish, however, because crayfish instinctively back up when attacked. But fish, which dart to the side, tend to escape the snapper's jaws more often.

Look for snapping turtles: in shallow, weed-choked back bays of lakes or other shallow water with a mud bottom and abundant vegetation. Rather sluggish during the day, they crawl slowly along the bottom with just their eyes and nostrils above the water. Sometimes you'll see their ridged upper shell, often covered with algae and perfectly simulating a slime-covered rock. In June, you may find females on land laying eggs, especially between 5 and 9 a.m. and 5 and 9 p.m. It's best to observe from afar.

Don't disturb nests: in riverbanks, sides of hills, road shoulders, muskrat houses, fields—usually in the open where sun can reach and warm the eggs. Females dig a 4–7-inch-deep, flask-shaped chamber with their hind legs, deposit anywhere from 10 to 96 (usually 25) eggs the size of ping-pong balls, then cover them with dirt. They will travel miles to return to this site each year. Young bottle-cap sized turtles emerge in the fall (some overwinter in nest) and crawl toward bodies of water. Researchers have suggested that perhaps the turtles "see" distant water reflected in the form of polarized light in the sky.

In the winter: snappers hibernate in large groups in muddy lake bottoms, beneath logs or plant debris, or in abandoned muskrat burrows or lodges. They breathe oxygen through blood-rich tissues just beneath the skin at the base of their tail.

Listen for: loud hissing of snappers disturbed on land.

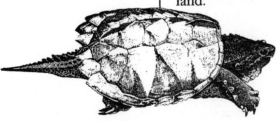

Snapping turtle.

MUDPUPPY

Every few years, the papers carry a story of an angler who's discovered a strange and ominous creature nearly a foot long, with red, feathery gills around its head, the body of a fish, and the legs of a lizard. A creature new to science? More likely, it's the mudpuppy, one of the family of giant salamanders that have been said to "look more like bad dreams than live animals." Many mudpuppies meet their demise at the knives of superstitious and uninformed anglers or scuba divers. The name itself comes from an erroneous belief that these "water dogs" bark.

Actually, mudpuppies are non-poisonous and beneficial, strange only in that not many people know about them. Their delicate gills, waving like crimson feather dusters in the current, filter oxygen from the water and allow them to live their lives at the bottom of lakes. The condition of their gills tells much about the water quality. In warm, foul water, these aquatic "lungs" are large, bushy, and constantly moving to get oxygen. In cool water with plenty of dissolved oxygen, the gills are small and contracted.

In the fall, mudpuppies congregate in large numbers in the shallow, moving water to breed. As part of the nuptial dance, males have been seen swimming and crawling over the female, passing over her tail and between her legs as she stands upright on hind legs and tail. Males deposit small stump-shaped structures of jelly called spermatophores in front of her. Each is topped with a cap of sperm that the female nips off with the lips of her cloaca (an all-purpose opening on the underside of the body).

The female builds a nest cavity under rock slabs in at least 3 feet of water, with plenty of weeds and rocks to provide cover. She lays up to 180 pea-sized eggs, each attached by a stalk to the underside of the nest's rocky roof. She guards and aerates the eggs for 2 months, blocking the entrance with her own body.

Look for mudpuppies: at the bottom of lakes and rivers, and among rocks and logs piled below dams and bridges. Fishing parties often see them swimming along the surface, attracted to night lanterns. They are active throughout the year, in the daytime in murky water, and at night in clearer waters. They feed on crustaceans, insect young, fish, earthworms, snails, and amphibians they capture along the bottom, mostly at night.

Look for nests: under rocks in at least 3 feet of water. The female can be seen lurking in the downstream-facing entrance.

In the winter: mudpuppies move to deeper water where they are active during the day. They have been found at a depth of 90 feet in Lake Michigan.

Mudpuppy.

Common loon.

©1989 Vera Ming Wong

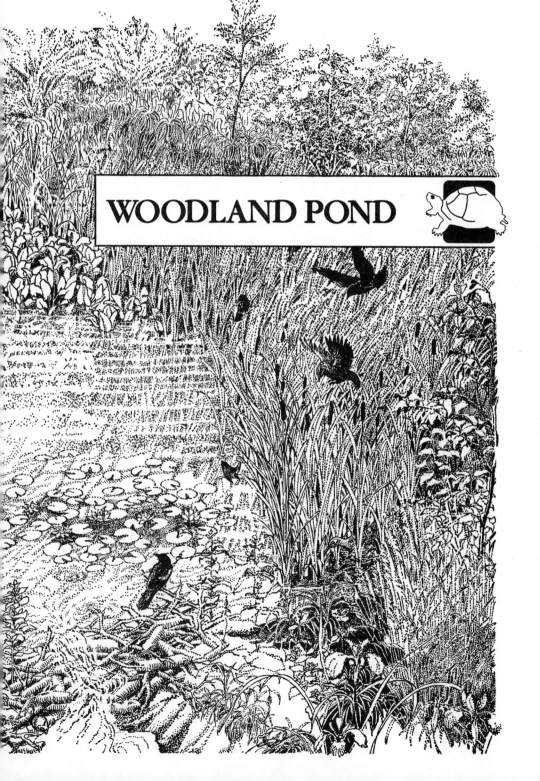

WOODLAND POND

A mirror of still water reflects the upside-down trees of the surrounding forest. The reflection ripples occasionally with the jerky waltz of a waterbug, or the slap of a feeding fish. Mergansers patrol low on the surface, diving occasionally to "fly" underwater. Closer to shore, lily pads offer islands of dry land for dragonflies and spiders. Frogs dangle their legs among the pads, kicking sporadically as they struggle to eat or avoid being eaten. Mallards and coots paddle with the frogs, feasting on the bloom of tiny duckweed floating there. A water snake plows its slender head through the water lilies and into the thicker tangle of arrowhead and bulrushes closer to shore. In the mud of the pond's edge, water seeps into the recent tracks of a raccoon.

What Is a Pond?

A pond is a body of permanent water less than 10 acres in size, and usually less than 6 feet deep. Unlike deeper lakes, which have separate warm and cool layers, pond water has a relatively uniform temperature from top to bottom. Ponds are shallow enough to allow sunlight to penetrate to the lower layers, so that rooted plants can grow from shore to shore. A fringe of marsh or bog plants often rings the pond, providing abundant food and shelter for pond dwellers.

1. Beaver
2. Wood Duck (male)
3. Mallards (male and female)
4. Red-winged Blackbird
5. Virginia Rail
6. Marsh Wren
7. Aspen
8. Speckled Alder and Pussy Willows
9. Cattails
10. Arrowheads
11. Pickerelweed
12. Pond Lilies
13. Swamp Loosestrife
14. Blue Flag (Iris)
15. Northern Spring Peeper
16. Water Milfoils
17. Drowned Trees
18. Bluejoint Reedgrass

Origins

Many woodland ponds are the legacies of glaciers; they sit in the small, shallow "thumbprints" left by the retreating ice. Other ponds are simply the older versions of lakes, which shrink and become shallower each year as dead plants, animal remains, and silt accumulate on the bottom. New ponds may be formed when beavers dam up streams or when meandering rivers twist back on themselves to form separate "U"-shaped ponds.

However it arises, the pond is a short-lived phenomenon. The plants around its edges are constantly expanding their empires, arching a tangle of stems farther and farther into the center of the pond. Swamp loosestrife (water-willow) "walks" toward the center at a rate of a yard per year. Plants sprout from these stems, and sediment and debris catch on the tangle, building a layer of soil on which other plants can take root.

In as little as a century's time, a pond can be born, colonized by plants, filled in, and rippling with wet meadow grasses. As these grasses release the remaining water to the air, the soil slowly becomes dry enough for tree seedlings to grow, and what was once a pond becomes a forest. (Of course, as with all of nature, this "schedule" is highly variable, and can be interrupted, delayed, or accelerated by other environmental factors.)

Roots Under Water

On land, plants are surrounded by a generous envelope of air that percolates through the soil and supplies the roots with oxygen. For them, the biggest challenge is to find and compete for water. For pond plants, the challenge is reversed. They are surrounded by water, which they "drink" through their submerged leaves and stems; but, because their roots are water-logged in mud, they don't get enough oxygen. To compensate, some pond plants develop special root tissues that reach up to the surface to "breathe." Most simply acquire oxygen through photosynthesis (using the sun's energy to make food from water and carbon dioxide). They are equipped with special air reserve tanks in their stems to store this oxygen for nighttime or cloudy days. These loose, open cells also provide the buoyancy needed to help the plant float. One mosquito larvae pierces these cells to get air.

Because many pond plants extend above as well as below the water, two kinds of leaves—one adapted to water, the other to land—may be present on the same plant. This split personality even occurs on the same leaf in the case of floating water lily pads. The top surface has a waxy cuticle to protect it from drying winds, as well as special pores that allow it to breathe the way land plants do. The undersurface has no need for a waxy cuticle or air-breathing pores, and it is attracted to rather than repelled by water. If a strong wind flips the leaf, the waxy top will not "stick" to the water surface. Usually, the next gust will right the leaf again, putting the pores up in the air, where they belong.

Floating to Survive

Besides holding pond plants up, the buoyant properties of water also help them reproduce, move to new places, and survive the winter. Wild celery, for instance, sends its flowers to the surface to open. Male plants release pollen grains that float or blow along the surface to female flowers. Hornwort, a submerged plant, actually flowers and is pollinated underwater, making it the botanical equivalent of the whale (a mammal that has severed all ties with the land). Dispersal of pond plants is also helped by water. Many fruits are shaped like tiny boats, and are swept over the surface by wind or current. When ripe, they break open to release seeds that eventually drop to the bottom, sometimes far away from the parent plant.

Pond plants survive winter in equally ingenious ways. Duckweed, for instance, a floating plant with a single leaf the size of a match-head, begins to store starch as the summer progresses. By fall, it is so heavy that it sinks to the bottom to wait out winter. Here, it uses up its stored starch, and by springtime, it is

76

light enough to bob back up to the surface. Other plants die back to their roots, but subsist on the starch in their tubers. Arrowhead tubers are so heavily used by rooting ducks that they're known as "duck potatoes."

Value to Wildlife

Woodland ponds are generally more secluded and protected than lakes are. Birds and animals approaching the pond usually have a fringe of heavy vegetation they can hide in, and in some cases, they can raise their young and hunt for food here as well. Once they reach the shoreline, they find a smorgasbord of water-based foods, including plants, fish, crustaceans, insects, amphibians, and reptiles. From water lily to duckweed, the plants in a pond provide food, both in themselves and in the animal life they harbor.

In the summer, pond water tends to be warm and shallow throughout, providing good fishing for wading shorebirds, and good foraging for dabbling ducks. Frogs and salamanders descend in droves in the spring to breed in the quiet, weed-choked water at the pond's edge. The relatively small acreage and large plant community in the pond cuts down on waves and provides a stable place for these amphibians to lay their eggs.

Wildlife Action

Three important pond zones to watch are the shoreline, the fringe of plant life at the shallow water margin, and the zone of open water in the center. At the shore, watch for fresh tracks of minks, otters, beavers, moose, fox, deer, skunks, raccoons, herons, sandpipers, and wood ducks. Here, turtles lay their eggs in sandy areas (where they won't get water-logged), and hibernating water snakes and salamanders may burrow under mud, rocks, or logs. Watch for songbirds hunting insects that are attracted to the flowers that grow along the shore. Watch for flotsam—water lily tubers, debarked sticks, and other "table scraps" left by feeding beavers and muskrats.

WHAT'S THAT SMELL?
An explosion of microscopic algae can paint the pond green. As the algae die, their remains filter to the bottom and decompose, creating the well-known smell of a summer pond. The organisms that break down their remains use up so much oxygen that fish may begin to die, adding to the pungent odor of the algal bloom.

In the shallows, dabbling ducks such as mallards and black ducks will be up-ending in the tangle of rooted and floating plants. Watch for "trains" of ducklings following the females in spring. Star-nosed moles will dive and swim in their silver coating of air bubbles. Watch as shadowy tadpoles scrape the algal coatings off plant stems, stones, and the bottom with their horny, rasping mouths. Herons, egrets, and bitterns wade and wait for fish in the shallows.

Farther out, geese and swans use their long necks to reach plants in deeper water. The up-periscope nostrils of frogs and turtles dot the open water between the plants. Water snakes sneak up on frogs, toads, and salamanders, unhinging their jaws to swallow them whole. Diving ducks, grebes, and terns fish still farther out on the open water.

By all means, stay until sundown. At dusk, bats fly erratically over the pond, sending out and receiving the echoes of their own signal as a way of navigating by sound. Swallows furrow the surface of the water as they scoop up a drink on the fly. Breeding frogs begin their raucous chorus of calls, and a family of beavers repairs a dam that, in some cases, creates and keeps the pond a pond.

WOOD DUCK

The first time you see a "woodie," you may rub your eyes in disbelief, especially if it's perching in a tree at the time. Here is a duck that looks like an exotic oriental mandarin, gleaming with iridescent color, and walking—with webbed, waterpaddling feet—along a branch! This duck in a tree is *Aix sponsa* (from the Latin and Greek words for "bride of the water"), a duck that nests in trees and sometimes waddles deep into the woods for acorns, beechnuts, and berries.

More than any other northwoods duck, woodies are adapted to life on land. Their legs are farther forward than puddle ducks to enable them to walk and run with ease. Their feet, with sharp claws and strong hind toes, are built for perching on tree limbs. Their bill is narrower than that of dabblers, to help them pick up seeds and nuts. And, when flying in and

78

around branches and trunks, their broad wings give them an advantage.

Wood ducks begin their lives in the dark recesses of a tree cavity. After only a day of brooding the new hatchlings, mother wood ducks fly to the base of the tree or to a nearby limb and begin calling their young. In response, the 8 to 10 downy chicks begin to jump towards the cavity opening in chaotic, cornpopping excitement. The opening may be several feet above the floor of the cavity, a distance the young woodies have to overcome if they are to see the light of day. If they can't reach the opening in one leap, they jump as high as they can and anchor their claws in the woody lining of the cavity. From here, they hop again, hitch, and hop again, until they reach the rim of the entrance to the outside world. Without a moment's hesitation, they leap into open space, falling sometimes as much as 60 feet to the forest floor below. Weighing less than an ounce, however, these puffballs are rarely injured by their fall.

One by one, they leave the nest and form a long parade behind their mother. Cautiously wending its way through the underbrush, it may take as long as a day for the entourage to reach the water. Here they learn to swim, fly expertly through heavy woods, and freeze when the hen signals danger. Studies have demonstrated that females will migrate back to the exact area where they were raised to raise their own young.

Wood duck.

Look for wood ducks: perching on the limbs of trees near or in ponds, preening on a fallen mossy log, dipping for water plants in shallow water, flying through the treetops, or sleeping at night on the water under dense woody cover. They feed on the land more than other ducks, relishing acorns, insects, seeds, nuts, berries, and wild fruits. They have flexible home ranges, perhaps because of the up-and-down water levels of some woodland ponds. When the water level changes, woodies move to other ponds that meet their need for shallow water (less than 18 inches deep) with a brushy overstory, stumps for perching, cavities for nesting, and food sources.

Look for cavity openings: 5–50 feet up (preferably over 30 feet) in trees at least 16 inches in diameter. Openings are at least 4 inches wide, created by woodpeckers or other natural causes. Don't hold your breath waiting for a woodie to fly at top speed into the nest hole—that's an old wives' (or husbands') tale. The use of artificial nest boxes has been a real boon to this duck, given the intense competition among many birds and mammals for cavity nests.

Look for flocks: of hundreds of woodies roosting in the evenings on certain waterways in fall and early winter.

Listen for: a loud, squealing "weeeek weeeek" as the hen lands on the pond. She may be taking a break from incubating the eggs in the woods, and is alerting the male of her arrival. She needs to be loud because of the muffling effect of the woody obstructions surrounding the pond.

MALLARD

Mallard.

The mallard is the most abundant duck in the Northern Hemisphere, the most widely distributed duck in the world, and most likely, the ancestor of our domestic ducks. In the three Lake States alone, an estimated 300,000 mallards arrive each spring to breed. The Mississippi Flyway has been called the mallard flyway, with more than 3 million birds overwintering there, more than along any other flyway. These high numbers are surprising if you consider that mallards lose half of their population each year to natural causes and hunting.

The "ice breaker" is one of the last ducks to leave in the fall, and among the first to arrive in the spring. They arrive in "U" or "V" flocks of 40 to 60, joining other flocks in large water areas. Soon after they arrive, they break up into pairs and disperse to smaller ponds, preferring waters less than 16 inches deep. Shallow water is ideal because mallards are dabblers, that is, they "tip up" when they feed, nibbling aquatic plants along the bottom of ponds with their bills, while their tails remain visible above the water. They also favor the seeds of sedges, smartweeds, meadow grasses, grain from fields, mosquito larvae, and acorns.

In mid-May, male mallards, or drakes, gather in large marshes by the hundreds. Here they molt into a flightless "eclipse plumage" that will last a month. Grounded for a while, males must depend on "safety in numbers" to escape predation. Females join them later when the broods are fully grown and no longer under their tutelage.

Look for mallards: during the day, dabbling in ponds with shallow feeding areas and suitable upland nesting sites nearby. Watch when they fly away; like most pond ducks, they use the small space well, flying straight up from the water rather than taking a running start. They may also be found feeding in grain-fields late in the afternoon and at night. In fall and spring, flocks are in larger, marshy areas.

Look for nests: mostly within 100 yards of water on dry upland sites with plenty of tall, weedy, or grassy cover.

Listen for: female's series of loud quacks gradually getting softer. Males utter soft reedy notes.

BEAVER

Humans and beavers share a unique trait among mammals: we are both able to change our surroundings to suit our needs. Beavers do it without engineering degrees, but their dams and canal networks often surpass ours in terms of their ability to control floods, conserve water, create wildlife habitat, and leave rich-soiled, farmable land.

When beavers build dams, they are solving a basic problem: the existing stream or lake is too shallow to travel safely, overwinter, or raise young in. By raising the water level, beavers will have a safe place to build a lodge and cache their food, a waterway on which to transport building and food branches, and a protected means of getting to the newly-flooded shore where delectable aspen, birches, and willows grow. Beavers eat the bark, twigs, and leaves of these

DIM LIGHTS AND LONG NIGHTS
In the winter, the light under the ice is so dim that circadian rhythms tend to break down. Instead of the normal daily cycle, beavers experience a 26–30-hour day, with longer periods of inactivity. This schedule helps them to conserve energy.

AT HOME UNDERWATER

Beavers are living showcases of adaptation. Their fur is waterproofed with anal gland secretions and insulated with a layer of warm, trapped air. Their webbed feet, which propel them like torpedoes through the water, also carry special split claws for combing their fur. Their huge lung capacity, flap-shut nostrils and ears, and transparent eye "goggles" allow them to dive and stay underwater for up to 15 minutes. To help them breathe while they are toting branches underwater, their lips close behind their teeth, and their air passage is separated from their larynx. Their broad, flat tail is handy not only for sounding alarms, but also for dissipating heat like a radiator.

trees, not by climbing and browsing, but by cutting them down and carrying them into the water to eat.

It takes a beaver less than 10 minutes to fell a 3-inch diameter tree, but they've been known to labor for hours over record 60-inchers. Contrary to popular belief, however, beavers don't have much control over which direction the trees fall. Most topple toward the stream simply because sunlight has added more branches, and thus weight, to that side of the tree. After felling a tree, they shear off the branches and buck them into segments that they can drag toward the water. To gain safe access to more food, beavers may build canals through pond vegetation to reach the forest edge.

It takes 1,000 woody saplings and shrubs a year to feed and house 9 beavers (a family), nearly a ton of bark to survive the winter alone. Thus, prime beaver habitat includes early dense forests where aspen and birch saplings are abundant. Cutting these trees opens the area to more shrub and sapling development, or, in some cases, it gives understory trees room to grow. Trees in the understory are frequently members of the next successional stage. By making way for them, beavers accelerate the "aging" process of a forest along the edges of their ponds.

Beaver ponds that have been abandoned (when food supplies run out) may eventually support brand new forests. After the repair team is gone, the dam may weaken, allowing the pond to drain. Nutrient-rich silt accumulated on the bottom now forms a rich bed for grasses and meadow vegetation. Trees may eventually colonize the sundrenched area, creating a forest where beavers once paddled.

Look for beavers: where streams have been backed up into quiet ponds. They are much larger than muskrats (45–60 pounds vs. 2–4 pounds for muskrats), and their tails don't show when swimming. They are quite punctual, leaving the lodge every day at dusk to feed. Most of their work is done at night, except in the fall, when they may be seen during the day caching their winter store of tree limbs by the lodge.

Look for lodges: along the bank or in the middle of the pond, built of logs and sticks and plastered with mud, 5–6 feet above water level and 12–14 feet wide. Beavers create a lodge by first piling sticks on the lodge site. They then dig up to the center of the pile to create a dry chamber above the water level. Then they begin to add mud and other debris to the outside, mostly along the sides. Because relatively little mud is added to the top, air passages remain at the apex of the lodge, and function much like a chimney. In cold weather, warm humid air rises like smoke from the peak of the lodge. The outside of the lodge freezes solid, preventing predators from scratching their way in. Birds often roost atop the lodges, and northern harriers and Canada geese may even nest on them.

Look for dams: 2–10 feet high and as long as 2,000 feet across the stream channel. The butt end of the trees faces upstream, and the branches spread downstream where they become anchored in the streambed. The loose framework of branches is porous at first so it isn't washed away by water. Later, after a mesh of branches forms, beavers begin to plaster them with mud, creating an effective barrier. During floods, spillways open naturally in the dams and release pressure. Beavers repair them after the water level subsides. If you can get close enough, look for the scats and tracks of other animals that use the dam as a bridge across wet areas.

Beaver.

Look for stumps and gnaw marks: on trees around the pond. The gnaw marks may be up higher if the beaver was standing on snow. Look also for broad tooth marks on bright white peeled sticks, signs of beavers snacking on the bark of their building materials. In the summer, however, they also eat succulent aquatic plants, such as water lily shoots, and the leaves of trees, shrubs, and ground vegetation.

Look for channels: extending to the forest edge, large enough for a beaver to float a limb or trunk on.

Look for "mud pies": mounds of mud on the shore that beavers mark with urine containing a sweet-smelling oil from their castor glands. Presumably, beavers use these scent mounds, especially in the spring, to advertise their territory. Humans communicate with this oil as well, using it in the making of perfume! (Medicinal castor oil is from the castor-oil plant, not from beavers.) There may be anywhere from 40 to 120 of these mounds within the home range of a beaver family.

Listen for: the sharp crack of a beaver's flat tail slapping the water. This telegraphs the message "Danger!" to the rest of the beaver family. By protecting its relatives, the tail-slapper also protects some of its own genes, even though it risks giving away its own location to a predator. If close enough, you can easily hear the whining and whimpering of beaver kits through the walls of the lodge. In late summer, listen for the whining of the young as they beg food from older family members. Angry beavers produce a nasal blowing sound.

CENTRAL NEWT

Witches may have been on to something when they called for "eye of newt" in their potions. Newts have an almost magical capacity to change forms depending on their surroundings.

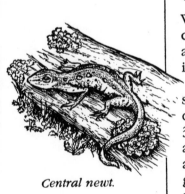

Central newt.

They begin life in the water, hatching from eggs, sprouting gills, and looking very much like tiny mosquito "wrigglers." Gradually, they grow to be 1¼ to 3½ inches long. In early fall, some larval newts begin a transformation that allows them to leave the water and survive as land animals. They lose their gills, grow lungs, trade in their smooth skin for sandpaper-rough skin, sprout hair-like filaments inside their mouth, and change their coloring from green to rusty brown. In this "eft" stage, they live in the forest among damp leaves and rotting logs, managing to avoid most predators because of highly poisonous skin glands in their back (their bright coloring warns predators about their foul taste).

After 2 or 3 years, they return to the water to breed, changing once again into smooth-skinned swimmers.

Their tubular tail becomes vertically flattened, forming high fins on top and bottom. Their toes flatten to perhaps aid in swimming. For the rest of their adult lives, they live in water.

Unless of course, their environment changes. If their pond dries up, the amazing newt transforms again into a rusty red landlubber, and survives quite well on land until the pond refills, enticing the newt to once again switch identities. They seem to be able to vacillate endlessly if need be.

Also remarkable are the newt's regenerative powers. If they lose a limb or tail in a close encounter with a predator, they will readily grow another in its place. So that nothing goes to waste, the highly adaptive newt eats its own molting skin. In July and August, even their own young become an important part of their diet, in addition to insects, tadpoles, frog and salamander eggs, snails, leeches, mollusks, spiders, and mites.

Look for adult central newts: swimming along the bottom of ponds, especially where there are lots of underwater plants for them to climb on and hide in. They are active during the day in spring and summer, as well as under the ice in winter.

Look for the eft stage: by turning over damp leaves, logs, bark, and rocks in dense, moist forests (remember to replace what you displace). Look for them moving about on warm rainy days, migrating from water to land, or feeding. They curl their tail over their back when threatened.

Look for eggs: 200 to 375 of them, laid in April, singly or in groups of 12 to 140. A thick, jelly-like coating around each egg allows it to rotate freely in the cluster.

In the winter: efts hibernate under logs and debris.

NORTHERN SPRING PEEPER

You may have to crunch through a fading crust of snow to get to the edge of the pond when peepers are calling. They are among the first frogs to herald springtime in the north. To find them, follow the chorus that has been said to sound like sleigh bells.

The frogs responsible for this cacophony are surprisingly small, only slightly more than an inch long. When they sing, their throat sac balloons with air and seems almost larger than their bodies. The males are calling to lay claim to their territory. When a neighboring male gets too close, the flute-like peep will change to a trill. If the newcomer doesn't get the message, a fight may ensue, with one frog finally being ousted.

Tadpoles hatch from as many as 1,000 eggs laid by each female, and transform into frogs in July. They climb onto land and may move long distances from their breeding areas in summer and fall. At this time, you may be fooled by the spring peeper, because its calls may come not from the pond edge, but from the branches of a tree in the forest. Like other members of the treefrog family, the peeper has special disks on its toe tips that enable it to climb trees. After hibernating under the moss and leaves of the woodlands, the peeper will make its way back to a pond, where its familiar chorus is best known.

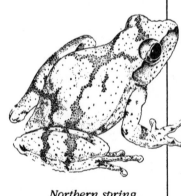

Northern spring peeper.

Look for spring peepers: in and around ponds in the spring, calling from the surface of the water or an elevated perch such as a blade of sedge or a log. In the summer or fall, look in shrubby openings, sphagnum swamps, and moist thickets where peepers will be hunting insects or calling from the branches of trees and bushes. During the heat of midday, they seek shelter under rotten logs, leaves, and rocks. They are especially active in rainy weather. In winter, they hibernate in the woods under moss and leaves, and may be seen migrating toward ponds during the first spring rains.

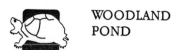

Look for white eggs: 800–1,000 of them, laid singly or in small clusters, attached to underwater plants near the bottom of shallow, weedy ponds.

Listen for: a long series of piercing, high-pitched, flute-like peeps given with regular pauses of about a second between each peep. They might be mistaken for bird calls, or, at a distance, for sleigh bells. In summer and fall, when peepers move long distances from breeding ponds, listen for single calls from woods and shrubby openings.

Wood ducks.

©Vera Ming Wong 1969

RIVER AND STREAM

Cradled where the land folds, a ribbon of water flows without stopping—24 hours a day, 12 months a year. Along its many miles of shoreline, kingfishers rattle, wood turtles splash, and beavers slap their tails. In the wilder places, otters porpoise in the rapids and bellyslide down the muddy banks. Trout swirl in the eddies, and above them, water shrews run on a tight drum of water, then dive, wrapped in silvery suits of air. Wriggling mayfly larvae along the stream bottom rise and hatch, breaking the surface with their new, translucent wings. As the sun sets behind the trees, swallows and bats dimple the water, gathering a portion of the hatch for their young.

What Is a River or Stream?

Streams and rivers are bodies of water in motion; smaller bodies are usually called streams, while the larger ones are called rivers. The stream or river habitat includes the water itself, the bed, the banks, and the vegetated areas along the banks. It is difficult to characterize a river or stream along its entirety because it is constantly changing. The same stream may have fast, rocky stretches near its source, and slower, muddier stretches near its outlet. With practice, you can learn to recognize the distinct plant and animal communities that are adapted to these varied conditions.

1. *Water Shrew*
2. *Northern Water Snake*
3. *Northern Waterthrush*
4. *Wood Turtle*
5. *Eastern Phoebe*
6. *Silver-haired Bat*
7. *Bank Swallow (colony)*
8. *River Otter*
9. *Raccoon*
10. *Belted Kingfisher*
11. *Pondweed*
12. *Water Shield*
13. *Arrowhead*
14. *Cattail*
15. *Wild Rice*
16. *Speckled Alder*
17. *Sandbar Willow*

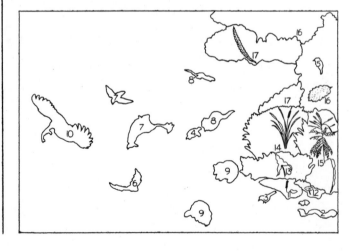

90

Origins

Rivers and streams flow from upper lands to lower lands, directed by gravity. They often begin when water from precipitation, seepage, or a spring collects in a basin and overflows its banks. The outflowing water eventually erodes a notch in the lowest part of the bank. When this notch becomes deep enough, a steady flow of water drains from the basin, creating a stream. As it flows through the landscape, it grows in size. Water drains into it from the surrounding land, washing in silt, nutrients, and fragments of plants and animals from the banks. Other streams and their tributaries join and expand it until it becomes a wider, slower, and cloudier river.

Changeable and Challenging

As a Greek philosopher once observed, you can never put your foot in the same river twice. Yard by yard, the river changes, offering a variety of habitat conditions for a diverse gallery of organisms. Life takes its place along the river according to where it is best adapted. Some organisms prefer the slow backwaters at the downstream end, while others brave the demanding currents near the headwaters. Depending on the force of these currents, the stream bottom may be muddy or rocky, sandy or gravelly, each attracting an entirely different bottom-dwelling community.

The river changes with the seasons as well. In the spring, when the snowpack of the northwoods is melting, small streams can turn into raging torrents, ripping away bankside plants and dislodging rocks and logs. Later in the summer the headwaters of a small stream can begin to dry up, stranding less adaptable plants and animals that have settled there.

The river's character can also change depending on what flows or seeps into it. Bank erosion can cause large plumes of silt to block the sun from free-floating and rooted plants. Pollutants in the form of agricultural runoff, sewage, or heat discharge can also disturb the stream habitat. In areas where acid precipitation is prevalent, streams become a unique target, receiving a heavy dose of runoff from melting snow and heavy spring rains. Acids have been accumulating in the snowpack all winter, and the spring thaw releases them at a time when fish and other aquatic stream life are at a sensitive stage of development.

Life in the Fast Lane

Current—the overwhelming force of moving water—distinguishes rivers from other aquatic habitats. To live in a world that is in constant motion, stream organisms must either overcome the current, flow with it, or avoid it entirely. In the fastest part of the stream, those that are not swimming, anchored, or sheltered will be swept away.

On the positive side, current is also the conveyor belt that carries food to downstream organisms. This floating food—plants torn free of roots, bits of decaying plants and animals, small animals ripped free of holds, free-floating microscopic life—flows by quickly and never remains in the same place for long. Many successful organisms have learned to use this current to help them "snag" their meals.

As an example of the various methods of adapting to a fast-paced world, consider the community of organisms on the many sides of a midstream boulder.

On **top of the rock**, animal and plant life must cope with the force of water washing over the rock. In an ultrathin layer along the top of the rock, the friction between the rock and the rushing water slows down the current. The insect inhabitants of this "boundary layer" (e.g., the immature stage of black flies) are equipped with flattened bodies, clinging hooks, sticky saliva, suction devices—anything that will root them to the spot. Single-celled plants called algae cling to the rocktop by the thousands, forming the slippery coating that makes river rock walking so treacherous.

The **upstream-facing side of the rock** presents a wall to the speeding current, and the insect young that live here are actually pressed against their home base by the current. Some are equipped with filters to strain the water for nutrients. Caddisfly larvae string a silken net out from the rock to catch food as it flows by.

On the **downstream side of the rock** is a protected
eddy where snails can graze on algae without clinging for dear life. In the shadows **beneath the rock** is
an even more protected habitat where burrowers and
flattened stoneflies and mayflies live. These organisms have adapted to moving water by simply avoiding the current.

Other important habitats occur **in-between rocks,**
or in crevices where leaves or rotting sticks are caught.
In the **water around the rocks,** swimming organisms
must maintain their position despite the current, and
here, adaptations include special upstream and
downstream orientation mechanisms.

The plants in this flowing world are sleek, flexible,
and able to regenerate themselves from broken fragments—traits that come in handy given the tearing
force of their environment. To help replace those
plants that are swept downstream, algae in swift
streams produce new generations faster than other
types of algae. Larger plants of the streambed, such
as fountain moss, water hypnum, liverworts, and true
watercress, have short stems and small leaves that
produce less drag in the current. Cushion mosses are
clumped and rounded, allowing water to flow over
and around the plant without dislodging it.

*WALKING
WATERFALLS
Waterfalls "walk"
upstream by under-
cutting the lip of
resistant rock that
they cascade over.
Once the overhang
is severe enough,
the lip falls in on
itself, and the water-
fall moves back.
St. Anthony Falls on
the Mississippi River
has moved 10 miles
upriver this way.*

At a Slower Pace

Downstream, where the current subsides, and the
suspended matter has a chance to settle out, the river
shows a different face. The bottom is more likely to
be covered with a fine silt or mud, making conditions
ideal for burrowing worms and mussels. These bottom dwellers would be ground to bits farther upstream, where forceful water scours the streambed,
tumbling rocks and gravel in its passing.

Plants growing in these slow-moving waters are
more likely to be those adapted to pond life. These
plants offer many surfaces for algae to grow on, thus
providing a food source for animals such as tadpoles,
which scrape the algae with their rasping mouths.
Plants also provide hiding places for water birds and
safe spots for frogs to lay eggs.

While life is easier in some ways in the backwaters, it is more difficult in another sense. Unlike the tumultuous beginnings of the river, where wave crests mix air and water, the slower backwaters may have limited supplies of dissolved oxygen. With life-giving oxygen at a premium, only those plants and animals that can tolerate low concentrations can survive. Carp and catfish, for instance, can live where trout and whitefish would never survive.

Value to Wildlife

Rivers, like other aquatic habitats, provide a unique menu of food items to visiting wildlife—fish, crustaceans, aquatic insects, plants, and an assortment of amphibians and reptiles. Rivers are unique among these habitats, however, in that they offer a lot of shoreline per acre of water. These banks provide easy access to drinking water, protected sites for dens and nests, and a sunny spot for berries and other fruit-producing shrubs to grow. This vegetation along the banks provides cover for animals that breed, feed, or hunt along the shores. Where humans share the habitat with wildlife, bridges are a common feature of rivers. The eastern phoebe is one species that has adapted to take special advantage of the protection that bridge beams offer.

Wildlife Action

The streambank and the airspace above the stream are the best places to look for wildlife. Scout along the shore for the pawprints of otters, minks, and raccoons hunting here for crayfish and turtle eggs. White-tailed deer, black bear, and moose will also come to the stream to drink and dine on aquatic plants. Great blue herons will wade along the shore while spotted sandpipers delicately pick their way in the mud. River otters slide into the water from the bank while turtles plop from logs. Beavers seeking to dam the stream may be cutting aspen along the bank. Above the water, look for the acrobatic dusk flight of belted kingfishers, bank swallows, and silver-haired bats. In the water itself look for salamanders in their aquatic stage, mudpuppies, painted turtles, water shrews, and tadpoles.

BELTED KINGFISHER

At first, the tasseled head and spear-shaped bill look too large to belong to a pigeon-sized bird. But when you see the kingfisher in action, plummeting from high above the water to snag a fish, you appreciate the impact that the powerful head and neck are designed to absorb. Back on its feeding perch, the kingfisher will flip a small fish into the air, and throw back its head to catch it. Larger fish will be swallowed whole also, but may be left sticking out of the kingfisher's bill until the digestive juices at the other end reduce the prey to size.

Kingfishers also use their bills for digging 3–7-foot tunnels in cutaway, exposed banks. As they work, they kick a fountain of flying sand out of the tunnel with their feet. At the end of this upward sloping tunnel, they dig a flattened sphere for a nest. Although their favorite nest sites are in riverbanks, they may also nest inland, but usually no more than a mile from their fishing grounds.

Belted kingfisher.

Parent kingfishers teach their young to fish by denying them "handouts" for a while and then dropping stunned fish onto the water's surface. Driven by hunger, the nestlings soon get the idea and dive down for their own dinners. When they are first hatched, kingfishers have no feathers. Within a week, pin feathers grow in, encased in sheaths, making each nestling look like a miniature porcupine. A couple of weeks later, all of the feathers burst from their sheaths in less than 24 hours.

Part of the kingfisher's scientific name is *alcyon*, which harks back to classical mythology. According to the legend, Alcyone, daughter of Aeolus, was so distraught when her husband died in a shipwreck that she threw herself into the sea. The gods took pity and transformed the couple into kingfishers that would roam the waters together. Supposedly, kingfisher nesting days were times of exceptional calm at sea, still referred to as "halcyon days."

Look for belted kingfishers: flying low over rivers, especially along shallow borders where water is clear enough to see fish. As you canoe, a kingfisher may give a startled call and fly ahead of you. When it reaches the end of its feeding territory (typically 500 yards long), it will circle back for another pass. During nesting season, a pair may command a strip of shoreline from 250 to 5,000 yards long. Spring is a good time to look for kingfishers collecting food for their young from 4 a.m. to 11 p.m., at a rate of one fishing trip every 20 minutes.

Look for openings: 3–4 inches wide, about a foot from the top of a cutaway exposed bank, where the topsoil shades into sand. The opening may have two grooves at the base where the birds' feet have worn it away when leaving and entering. Behind this entrance is a tunnel that leads to a dry nest cavity. Nestlings instinctively keep this cavity clean by loosening dirt from the walls, and thus burying their droppings. Look for other "probe holes" around tunnel entrances where birds have started, then abandoned digging.

Look for perches: usually on a dead branch of a tree with a good view of the water, no more than 100 feet from the nesting tunnel. This is where the kingfisher will carry back its prey to pound against a limb and then eat. Below the perch tree you may find clumps of tunnel soil from the kingfisher's feet. Locate the several exposed perches that the kingfisher repeatedly visits along its river "beat."

Listen for: a penetrating "k-k-k-k-k-k" rattle given on the wing or when perched to ward off intruders. It sounds like the amplified clicking of a fishing reel.

BANK SWALLOW

Down by the water some autumn evening you may notice a sudden cloud passing over the last of the sun's rays, a dark cloud that twists, turns, billows, and cartwheels, chirring like the heart of a giant machine. If you are lucky, you'll see it pour as if from a funnel into the branches around you. As many as 250,000 swallows at a time (a Toledo, Ohio flock) migrate south in a single motion to escape the harsh northern winters.

Bank swallows are gregarious throughout the year as well. When it comes time to nest, a colony of swallows will perforate a sandy, exposed bank with hundreds of nesting holes. After several years, the carved bank looks like a miniature version of the ancient Mayan villages that were honeycombed into cliffs. When the young birds hatch, they wait at the openings, clamoring for their parents' attention. You may see the hind ends of the young birds as well, because these fastidious housekeepers dispose of their wastes outside the tunnel entrance.

Why do bank swallows feed in groups and nest in colonies? Some researchers suggest that because large numbers of birds can search a big area, individuals that are part of a group may have a better chance of finding or learning about random swarms of insects than a lone bird would. And, although flocks are obviously more conspicuous to predators, individuals can rely on the other group members to alert them to danger. Despite this security system, some land predators such as skunks and minks do make off with young swallows. Another threat to swallows is the automobile, especially if the nesting colony is next to a road.

Bank swallow.

Look for bank swallows: skimming just above rivers to catch insects emerging from their aquatic stage. You may see great numbers in premigration flocks, hunting over fields and ponds, or spaced on a power line as evenly as beads on a bracelet.

Look for openings: cut into the vertical face of a sandy riverbank, roadcut, gravel pile, or clay bank.

Holes number anywhere from one to several hundred, concentrated just below the grassy top of the bank, or in the seam between two layers of firm soil. Nests of loosely woven grass and feathers are placed at the end of these tunnels.

Look for sand ridges: deposited on the ground beneath honeycombed nesting banks.

Listen for: a harsh, gritty twitter, multiplying to a cacophony when flocking.

EASTERN PHOEBE

Before people arrived in the northwoods, phoebes built their nests in the crevices of rocky cliffs, under the roots of fallen trees, or on stone ledges in deep ravines. Here the pair would raise their one or two broods a year, flying busily back and forth, making as many as 845 trips a day to feed the hungry nestlings.

When people began to "tame" the wilderness, build roads, and span streams with bridges, some phoebes still relied on their rocky retreats. But many of the birds took advantage of the new arrivals, attaching their mud and grass nests to the girders of bridges, eaves of houses, and beams of barns. These structures often proved to be perfect perch sites overlooking fields or water, just what phoebes look for in the wild. Due to their tremendous adaptability, phoebes have thrived since the arrival of settlers, and are now a commonplace bird at bridge-side picnics and barnyards.

Look for eastern phoebes: darting over the water in search of flying insects, especially near bridges. Watch for them lazily wagging their tails (a characteristic feature) on a perch overlooking a streamside clearing. You can often find them near human settlements.

Look for nests: on a sheltered ledge, typically less than 15 feet off the ground. The ledge may be natural (e.g., rock crevices in cliff walls) or man-made (e.g., bridge girders, eaves of houses, doorsills, porch rafters, tops of shutters). To find the nest, first locate the male phoebe, which will arrive early in the spring

Eastern phoebe.

and perform fluttering display flights to "show" the
female potential nest sites. Later, you can follow the
female to the site she chooses. The nest is a cup of
mud and moss, lined with grasses, feathers, and hair.
A new nest may be built atop an old one for 4 or 5
years running.

Listen for: "fee-bee, fee-bee" with the accent on
the first syllable, repeated many times. Other calls
include a chirp, chatter, and "t'keet."

RACCOON

Anyone who's tried to raccoon-proof a garbage can
can attest to the puzzle-solving abilities of the adaptable, indomitable raccoon. One homeowner who had
raccoons denning in her chimney was advised to start
a fire and smoke them out. "We tried that," she said.
"But they came down, shut the flue, and smoked us
out!"

Raccoon.

From the tip of their nose to their foot-long tail,
raccoons are built to take advantage of their habitat,
avoid predators, and reproduce successfully. Their
two coats of fur, a bristly outer one and a dense un-
dercoat, thicken up in the northern reaches of their
range to help them make it through winter. The coat
itself is two-toned—dark above and light below, a pattern that many animals have evolved to counteract
the effects of light and shadow. The light underbelly
tends to soften the shadow beneath their bodies, so
predators have a harder time recognizing the prey
animal as a three-dimensional object. By "flattening
out" against the background, raccoons can often escape detection.

The most unique adaptation that raccoons have is
their highly developed sense of touch. Using only
touch, they are able to distinguish between two objects as well as humans can. In fact, raccoons let their
long, facile fingers do the hunting in streams with an
action called "dabbling." With eyes diverted elsewhere, raccoons will poke their fingers into crevices
and run their paws over the surface of a streambed
as if braille reading or touch typing. When they "spot"
a crayfish in its burrow they lunge forward and pull

up their catch. On a good day, a raccoon can snag a crayfish every 3–4 minutes. They also eat frogs, fish, mollusks, insects, birds and eggs found near streams, as well as fruit, berries, nuts, and small rodents from upland forays.

Raccoons, by the way, don't actually "wash" their food. They do manipulate it with their dexterous front paws and dunk it, but observations have shown that a raccoon will then eat the prey, whether it is dirty or not. Researchers are still pondering the reasons for this behavior.

As winter approaches, raccoons begin storing fat in amounts that can double the weight of a cub and account for 9 pounds on a 30-pound adult. Though they are not true hibernators, they are dormant for days or even weeks during bad weather, living off this extra fat. The family will den up together, venturing forth occasionally when the temperature is milder. Although very few things will eat an adult raccoon (they are fierce fighters), cubs may be eaten by bobcats, lynxes, fishers, wolves, eagles, and owls.

Look for raccoons: dabbling at the streamside, shuffling along the ground, or climbing on the branches of a large, mature tree at night. Daytime resting sites include: tree crotches, shelflike cavities in rocks or beneath the roots of a wind-toppled tree, a squirrel's leaf nest, a ground bed, or even the top of an abandoned muskrat house. When it's sunny, they love to drape themselves over limbs or rocks to bask.

Look for dens: in tree cavities, hollow limbs, ground dens beneath rocky ledges, or in abandoned woodchuck, skunk, or Virginia opossum burrows. A typical cavity den is 26 feet up a tree and has a horizontal, elliptical opening that measures 6 inches by 4 inches and faces south. Look for raccoon hair on the trunk.

Look for tracks: handlike with 5 toes, 2½–4½ inches long, along muddy shores. Tracks disappear where the raccoon has entered the water, and reappear when it climbs back on the bank.

Look for "scat stations": piles of crumbly, 2-inch-long droppings atop a limb, rock, or tangle of woody debris. Family groups traveling together in late summer through winter will use the same scat station, choosing a place along the bank that other raccoons will easily see.

Look for "eyeshine": an orange-red reflection when a headlight catches a raccoon's eyes.

Try calling: raccoons with a device that imitates the sound of a bird in trouble, or a "coon talker" that emits a low-pitched growl.

Look for claw marks on trees: with smooth bark. A 5-claw pattern about 2½ inches wide is left when a climbing raccoon slips.

Look for dug-up turtle eggs: or the remains of a bird's nest full of eggs. Turtles lay eggs in a covered hole in sandy soil, and raccoons dig them up for dinner.

Listen for: churring, twittering, and growling of young, and piercing alarm screams from fighting adults.

SILVER-HAIRED BAT

The Latin name for this bat means "shaggy bat that wanders at night." But while the zig-zag flight of this bat may seem like wandering, it is actually the bat's highly precise method of tracking down flying insect prey. The method is called echolocation, or "locating objects by the echoes of their calls." It works like this: as the bat flies back and forth across the stream, it sends out 10 to 20 high-pitched calls a second, listening for sounds that bounce off any object in the way, such as an insect. When it "hears" something, it speeds transmission to 250 calls per second, and receives, in the feedback, a detailed sonar picture of where the insect is, and how fast and in what direction it is traveling.

A bat may eat half its weight in one night, catching up to 150 insect meals an hour. Among the bat's favorite foods are the winged insects emerging from

Silver-haired bat.

101

A BAT REPUTATION

Americans are among the only people who seem to fear bats. Other cultures use bats to symbolize good fortune, happiness, or hospitality. Europeans put bat boxes in their backyards to encourage bats to nest. When you consider that bats devour 500 mosquitoes an hour, you too might want to invite one to your next barbeque. But will bats give you rabies? Only 1/2 of 1% of all bats in America have rabies. Only 1 case of bat-transmitted rabies is reported every 3 years. On the contrary, these fascinating creatures are anything but harmful. If they fly close to you, it is not to get in your hair or to bite you, but rather to prey on mosquitoes that are moving towards you. How's that for hospitality?

their wormlike underwater stages—the same type of insects that trout rise to. Anglers who try to imitate the hatch on a trout stream may also fool the silver-haired bat. There are reports of this bat diving for dry flies that resemble the real insects they thrive on. Sometimes they find themselves in the water, and are surprisingly swift, powerful swimmers, even when "flying" against the current.

At migration time, bats may climb to a cruising altitude of more than 10,000 feet. The homing ability of the "wanderer" is said to be so keen that bats moved as far away as 94 miles have found their way back easily.

Look for silver-haired bats: dipping down along the surface of a river at twilight or hanging in the trees along the banks. Their flight is fluttery and meandering, moving from the trees to the river and back again. Look for the distinctive silver tips on the ends of their fur. Although silverhairs may sometimes be seen feeding and drinking with other types of bats, they are not communal roosters or colonizers like many bats.

Listen for: a highpitched squeak and chatter as a bat flies by. The silverhair's radar signals are lower in frequency than most bats, and some humans may hear them.

RIVER OTTER

An early morning mist crouches over the river and tangles in the weeds along the banks. Just barely, you see a slippery brown curve break the surface and disappear. Behind it another curve appears, and then another, until you can't deny what you are seeing. It must be the outline of a sea serpent, a good 30–40 feet in length!

What startles many a sleepy eye on our rivers is actually the frolicking of an otter family, 6 or 7 strong, playing "follow the leader." Otters are extremely social animals, and this sort of interaction, which to us looks like play, is an important part of the bonding between family members. Other "sports" such as somersaults, balancing sticks on their nose, chasing their tail, and juggling pebbles may help to sharpen their swimming or hunting skills.

One of their favorite sports is downhill belly-sliding, whether on wet grass, mud, or snow. A traveling otter thinks nothing of going out of its way to test drive a promising hill. They also use sliding as a shortcut in the snow, and can reach speeds of 15–18 mph by galloping, hopping, and sliding across the snow.

River otter.

In the water, they are our premier swimmers, equipped with a streamlined body and webbed feet for thrust. They can shut their nose and eyes watertight for diving, and their lungs can hold out for as much as a ¼ mile of underwater swimming. Their broad head has eyes set high so they can peer above the water when swimming, easily scouting even the toughest of rapids. For sheer speed, they fold back their legs and flex their muscular body up and down, using their tail to steer.

Strangely enough, young otters have to be "introduced" to the water. The female usually ferries the reluctant pups out into deep water and then leaves them, returning to shore to watch. In no time, they are performing the graceful acrobatics that otters are famous for. These stunts also help otters catch fish, dive for crayfish, and outsmart frogs. On land, otters can outrun people by humping their body, a little like an inchworm in high gear.

In various parts of the world, humans take advantage of the fact that otters will sometimes take turns "driving" fish toward each other. As far back as 618 AD, people in the Tang Dynasty would train otters to catch fish or drive schools of fish toward their nets. Otters are still being used as fishing partners in parts of Asia.

Look for river otters: in the water, shooting the rapids, floating on their back, swimming under water or ice, or dog-paddling. Look for a small, sleek head creating a "V" of ripples in its wake. Also watch for them sliding or running along the borders of streams, lakes, or other wetlands in forests. They may travel up to 3 miles overland in search of food or new water-ways. Active throughout the year at any time, but especially dawn to midmorning and in the evening.

Look for dens: in the crevice of a rocky ledge, under a fallen tree, in an abandoned beaver lodge or muskrat house, in dense thickets along shore, or dug into the bank. In the summer the opening is above the water, and in winter they use an opening below the water.

Look for tracks: in a two and two pattern, 3½ inches wide, especially noticeable in mud. The inner toe of the hind paw points out to one side.

Look for belly slides: in mud or snow, sometimes 25 feet or longer. Trails lead off from these slides, and vegetation may be disturbed in a 5-foot-diameter circle where the otters have rolled on the ground. In the winter, they may dive under the snow and tunnel for awhile before coming back up. Even on level ground, they run and slide, run and slide, forming a dot-dash trail with 2 to 4 bounds, then a 5–15-foot-long trough, then more bounds.

Look for scent stations: where otters regularly leave droppings and scent. Areas may have twisted up tufts of grass where scent is deposited. Droppings may be irregular or filled with fishbones, depending on diet.

Listen for: chirps, grunts, whistles, snarls, and squeals. While swimming, family members will call back and forth with bird-like chirps. A surfacing otter blows and sniffs loudly.

WATER SHREW

At home in most watery environments, the water shrew seems to prefer cold, rocky, log-strewn streams running through woodlands. Here, the most aquatic of our shrews dives, swims, floats, runs along the stream bottom, and most amazingly, runs along the top of the water! Observers have seen these tiny, half-ounce water shrews scamper as far as 5 feet across the water before dipping under. Beneath each foot, there seems

Water shrew.

to be an air bubble trapped in the fringed, bristling hairs between the toes. Like the water strider (a spidery insect), the shrew is held aloft on this bubble atop the surface tension of the water.

When underwater, the shrew swims with all four feet, as if running. Part of the challenge is to stay submerged, because air trapped in the shrew's fur gives it remarkable buoyancy. Large, webbed hind feet propel it to the bottom, where it need only shift position slightly to begin running along the streambed. Here it probes with long, pointed snout to uncover the larvae of aquatic insects such as caddisflies, as well as snails and leeches. On land, it is just as hungry for beetles, bugs, and the larvae of flies.

This tiny animal's tremendous metabolism requires it to eat its entire weight in food each day just to remain alive. It is eaten, in turn, by hawks, owls, big fish, and snakes. Animals with more discriminating palates tend to pass on shrews because of their unpleasant taste.

Look for water shrews: running alongside or swimming in streams. They can look silvery underwater because of the sheath of air trapped in their fur. When on land they use runways under protective coverings such as bank overhangs, fallen debris, and logs. You can consider yourself fortunate if you see a water shrew; they're very secretive.

Look for nests: balls as large as 4 inches in diameter, made of vegetation including sticks and leaves, hidden in streamside debris or burrows.

Look for tunnels: under fallen leaves, about an inch wide. Tunnels in the snow become visible when the upper layer melts. They look like someone dragged a stick randomly across the snow.

Listen for: highpitched squeaking from the depths of the bankside vegetation.

105

NORTHERN WATER SNAKE

A canoe might be your best vantage point from which to see this heavy-bodied water snake. As you glide by, search among the tangled roots, overhanging branches, and downed logs that rim the river. If one of the long, twisted roots slithers into the water, you've found your snake. Watch as it swims from you, its head and body just barely below the surface.

Human ignorance and learned fear of snakes may be the greatest threat to the water snake. Unfortunately, its colorful brown, red, tan, and black bands, as well as its love of water, cause many to assume that this harmless snake is a water moccasin, a more southerly snake with a venomous bite that can be deadly. Moccasins simply don't live in the northwoods, and yet many innocent water snakes lose their lives due to mistaken identity.

This snake is an important part of the river food chain, pursuing slow-moving fish, frogs, toads, and salamanders. In turn, it provides food for big fish, herons, minks, raccoons, and red-shouldered hawks—but not without a fight. When cornered, a water snake will flatten itself so that it appears bigger, and repeatedly strike its enemy with tiny, needle-sharp teeth, releasing a foul-smelling fluid from an opening in its undersurface (cloaca). Although there is no venom behind the bite, its performance can be frightening enough to give predators second thoughts.

Look for northern water snakes: swimming in slow-moving, unpolluted rivers, or basking on logs, overhanging branches, or tree roots at the river's edge. They are common under bridges and near dams and spillways where rocks provide refuge. Older individuals are a dusky beige color until their skin gets wet and the pattern emerges again.

In the fall: when they move to rocky crevices or streambanks to hibernate, look for snakes crossing highways.

Northern water snake.

WOOD TURTLE

The wood turtle has definite ideas about its choice of prime real estate. It is usually found only near lazy, slow-moving streams with sandy bottoms and over-hanging broadleaf trees. Where conditions are just right, a large group or colony of wood turtles may be present.

In the spring, wood turtles perform a curious court-ship dance. The male and female walk slowly toward one another with their necks extended and their heads held high. When they are within 8 inches, they begin to swing their lowered heads from side to side, a movement that could go on for 2 hours. Finally, they move to the stream to mate. The female leaves the water to lay her eggs, digging a basin-like pit in the sand with her hind feet, and filling it back in with tamped-down dirt.

During the summer, wood turtles roam in nearby hardwood forests and meadows during the day, for-aging for insects, fruit, moss, and mushrooms. They are also fond of soaking up the morning sun on a log in the middle of the stream. Below them are aquatic foods they will also eat: mollusks, tadpoles, and fish.

Perhaps because they spend some time negotiating on land, wood turtles have been found to do well in laboratory maze-learning tests. Strangely enough, the wood turtle has also been credited with being the only turtle that can climb; one observer reported a wood turtle ascending a chain-link fence! Also among its distinctions is the ability to make a teakettle whis-tle while courting, rare among turtles.

Wood turtles used to be more numerous than they are now. They suffered a decline after much of their habitat was destroyed and because of over-collecting by biological supply houses. They are now protected in many parts of our area and recognized as an en-dangered species in Minnesota.

Look for wood turtles: swimming in rivers, plod-ding along the banks, or roaming nearby broadleaf woods and meadows during the summer.

Don't disturb nests: in covered pits in open sand or gravel, not necessarily near water.

In the winter: turtles hibernate in holes in muddy riverbanks and bottoms, under leaf litter near a stream, or in abandoned muskrat burrows. When hibernating on the bottom of a stream, they absorb oxygen through tissues at the base of their tail that are richly supplied with blood vessels in gill-like fashion. When on land, they breathe through lungs.

Listen for: a subdued, teakettle whistle associated with sexual activity in the spring.

Wood turtle.

Canada geese.

MARSH

Even with your eyes closed, it's easy to tell where you are. The air is heavy, humid, and pulsing with sound. Hoards of insects wriggle from the surface of the water and buzz around you on new wings. From every direction, red-winged blackbirds exclaim their forceful "o-ka-leeee!" At your feet, an American bittern explodes with a sucking sound, and a black rail trails away with a series of chirps. Farther out, an American coot splatters to a landing in the lily pads, and a pied-billed grebe among the cattails squawks like a horn. If you like what you hear, wait until you open your eyes! A marsh is as rich and full of wildlife as it sounds.

What Is a Marsh?

A marsh is a shallow basin with 6 inches to 3 feet of standing water throughout much of the year. Its trademark is the nearly shore-to-shore growth of herbaceous (soft-stemmed) aquatic plants—those with leaves emerging above the water, submerged below, or floating on the surface. Most conspicuous are the cattails, bulrushes, and water lilies. This shallow dish of plants, animals, insects, microorganisms, and water is as productive as a tropical rain forest.

1. *Marsh Wren*
2. *American Bittern*
3. *Eastern Mud Turtle*
4. *Yellow-headed Blackbird*
5. *Red-winged Blackbird*
6. *Sora*
7. *Virginia Rail*
8. *Muskrat*
9. *Pied-billed Grebe*
10. *American Coot*
11. *Mink*
12. *Bur-reeds*
13. *Arrowhead*
14. *Water Lilies*
15. *Rushes*
16. *Pickerelweed*
17. *Cattails*
18. *Sedges*
19. *Speckled Alder*
20. *Pussy Willow*
21. *Aspens, Birches, & Alders*

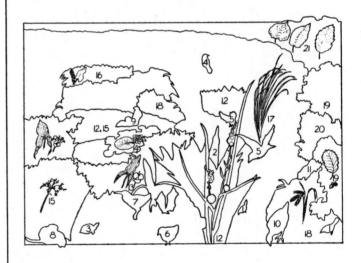

Origins

A marsh forms in any basin that will hold water long enough to allow water-tolerant, soft-stemmed, rooted plants to germinate and survive. They often start in shallow basins and flat outwash plains left by glaciers; others crop up at the edges of lakes or slow-moving streams; and still others take over after sedge meadows flood, or when lakes and ponds silt in.

Viewed from above, the classic basin marsh resembles a bull's-eye, with concentric rings of vegetation closing in on an inner circle of open water. The outer ring, near shore, is a dense collection of tall and short stalks: cattail, bulrush, arrowhead. Where the water is deeper, the flat pads of water lilies create a floating isle of green. Beyond that and into the center, the water is still thick with plants, some rooted and others floating free.

Marsh plants grow in the depth of water to which they are best adapted. **Submergents**—plants that live totally underwater—can live in the deeper sections of the marsh, as long as the sun's rays can filter down to them. They often have finely segmented leaves and are adapted to take in nutrients and water through their bodies. **Floating-leaved plants** (e.g., water lilies) expose great pads of green to the sun, and send down "runners" to root themselves in the muck. In shallow water near the shore, **emergent plants** are rooted in the bottom, but send up light-seeking, air-adapted leaves on stems and stalks that emerge above the surface. **Free-floaters** buoy themselves with air-filled tissues, and dangle their hairy roots in water of any depth. Finally, suffusing the water with a St. Patrick's day green are the millions of simple plants (the algae) that are **suspended** in the water.

These plants play musical chairs from season to season as the water level in the marsh drops or rises, or as herbivores, such as muskrats, uproot some of the cattails and open up pools of water. In extreme cases, a large population of muskrats can strip the marsh of its vegetation. At another extreme, a drought may dry up the pools, exposing the muddy bottom to the sun. Plant and animal remains along the bottom now begin to decay, providing nutrients for the thousands of seeds that have become buried over the years.

When the sun hits this cracked, muddy seedbed, a carpet of green plants shoots up, and the competition begins. The plants are all adapted to survive best at different water depths. If water returns to the marsh, deep-water plants will survive in the center, and the shallow emergents will survive at the edge. If water doesn't return, sedges and grasses will make the strongest comeback, and the marsh may become a meadow; or, in certain areas, it may turn into a sphagnum bog, and then slowly convert to forest.

The Incredible, Edible Cattail

A cattail seedhead is the very symbol of the marsh. This "punk" may carry 250,000 seeds, each with its own flossy parachute. These seeds are spread far and wide by wind, currents, and animals, and it may be months before they land on a mud flat that is sunny and moist enough to allow the seed to germinate. They grow at a phenomenal rate, providing food, nesting materials, and protection to many marsh inhabitants. Cattails also "travel" by sending out a horizontal stem (called a rhizome) that starts a new clump of cattails not far from the parent. This clone radiates out in a circular fashion, creating a colony that is made up of just one plant.

In the autumn, before the upper stalks of the cattail plant die, their nutrients are are rerouted to the fleshy rhizomes rooted in the mud. These storage pantries remain very much alive beneath the ice of a winter marsh, relying on dead, hollow stalks to "snorkel" air down to the roots. Rhizomes provide a kick-start of energy for hurtling spring growth, unless, of course, muskrats discover them first.

Muskrats and cattails are an inseparable pair. Muskrats feed on stalks and seedheads as well as on the fleshy tubers. They also use cattail stalks to build their jackstraw houses, which become lifesavers against winter winds and predators. When food supplies

114

dwindle, the muskrat can gnaw at the very walls of its edible abode.

When cattails abound in the marsh, muskrat populations can also explode. This can lead to a stripping of the marsh, followed by an echoing crash in the muskrat population. Under balanced conditions, however, muskrats actually provide a service by cutting some cattails and opening areas of the marsh. Migrating flocks of waterfowl are special recipients of this service. You can watch flocks on any autumn day, wheeling high over a marsh, and then funneling down by the hundreds to rest on the open patches of water.

Value to Wildlife

To migrating waterfowl, the marsh is a good place to refuel before heading south. Many will return to the marsh to breed. Here they find a lush environment, complete with fast-growing plants and plenty of decomposing bacteria to break down dead matter and quickly recycle nutrients. In many cases, a marsh is a rich oasis in comparison to nearby uplands, producing a superabundance of plant, animal, and insect life.

Recognizing these rich resources, many opportunistic animals and birds have developed modifications that enable them to exploit these riches. For instance, they swim and wade, are able to hover, dive, and take off in restricted places, and can perch on vertical stems. Marsh wrens and yellow-headed blackbirds balance neatly with a foot on each of two stalks. Other marsh-ready "gear" includes webbed feet, extra down, or water-resistant fur. They have also adapted to nest in dense congregations, without having to worry so much about the assortment of land predators they would find in the uplands.

It is probably not advantageous to be completely dependent on the marsh, however, because some marshes can dry out and disappear. The most flexible species seem to be adapted to the edge of the marsh, where they can retreat to the upland habitat if the wetland does dry out.

Wildlife Action

Stand at the edge of the marsh where you begin to sink into the saturated soil. Behind you, wood ducks and northern orioles nest in the trees. Swamp sparrows and common yellowthroats sing from nearby thickets. At your feet, rails slip stealthily between grasses, minks leave prints in the dark, turtles climb landward to lay eggs, and bitterns feed on rodents, snakes, and frogs. In the shallows, the green-backed heron jabs at a school of tadpoles and young salamanders. Look among the cattails for tail-wagging marsh wrens, perching blackbirds, and paddling muskrats. Look for bulbous-eyed frogs lifting the lids of water lilies, lashing out tongues to catch insects dozing there. Farther out in the water, American coots and mallards up-end for plants, and the pied-billed grebe builds its incredible floating nest. Muskrat lodges form a special microhabitat of their own on which Forster's terns nest, plants grow, and spiders and insects crawl.

PIED-BILLED GREBE

Just as you get your binoculars properly focused, the pied-billed grebe is likely to disappear from your sights without a ripple, seemingly swallowed by the water it sits on. The "water witch's" sorcery is actually a change in its specific gravity. By squeezing air from its feathers, the grebe shrinks in volume, but remains the same in mass. This enables it to overcome its buoyancy and literally sink into the water like a submarine. Once underneath, the grebe swims with its wings and huge lobed feet to the edge of the marsh, where it resurfaces amid the vegetation. In dangerous waters, the grebe will patrol with only its eyes and nostrils held above the water.

The pied-bill is as awkward on land as it is swift and graceful in the water, however. Like all diving ducks, the grebe's legs are placed well back on its body for maximum thrust, a design that makes standing up a precarious sport. When hurried, the grebe often pitches forward on its belly and scrambles along with both wings and feet, as if swimming. Thankfully, most of its time is spent in the water, hunting for aquatic insects, fish, snails, crayfish, and frogs.

One curious habit grebes have is that of eating their own feathers when grooming. One possible explanation may be that the feathers filter out sharp bones and shells of fish and crustaceans, which grebes swallow whole. Rather than risking a trip through the digestive tract, these hard bits are coughed up in a feather-coated pellet.

Pied-billed grebe.

Look for pied-billed grebes: submerging in the open water, reemerging in the cattails at the edge of the marsh, or running atop the water for take-off. The marsh must be large enough to provide a generous "runway" of open water, and deep enough to cover a grebe when it sinks out of sight. They arrive early in spring, often before the ice is out. Adults will carry chicks on their backs, and dive with them too! Though rarely on land, they do climb onto lily pads and shores sometimes to preen and sun themselves.

Look for nests: in a well-concealed, floating mass of dead marsh vegetation, usually built over shallow water and anchored to the stems of adjacent marsh plants. If not floating, the nest is built up from the bottom of the shallows, with enough plant material to fill a bushel basket. The nest is a foot in diameter and rises only a few inches above the surface of the water. Grebes cover their nests with sodden vegetation when they leave them, possibly to protect the eggs from predators.

Listen for: a series of hollow "cow-cow-cow" notes.

AMERICAN BITTERN

Thoreau called this bittern the "genius of the bog," perhaps referring to its brilliant knack for imitation. When the bittern thinks you have seen it, it will turn its striped breast towards you, raise its bill skyward and compress its wings against its sides, becoming, quite convincingly, one of the marsh reeds that surround it. The vertical lights and shadows blend seamlessly with the bittern's striped plumage, and when a breeze bends the reeds, the bittern sways too. If you turn your eyes away for a moment, you'd be hard-pressed to once again pick out the impostor.

If you close your eyes and listen, however, a booming "oong-KA-chunk!" is likely to confirm the bittern's presence. One version of its call is a good imitation of an old-fashioned water pump being cranked, and the other sounds just like a wooden stake being driven into mud; hence the nicknames "thunder-pumper" and "stake-driver." The power of the calls comes from a thick-skinned patch on the male's neck that balloons out when he calls, serving as a bellows to amplify the sound. The male uses the call from spring into summer as a warning to rival males and an invitation to potential mates.

The bill that the bittern uses so well in its illusion is equally effective when capturing food. Practicing the wade-and-wait method of fishing, the bittern stands patiently in the water, or imperceptibly advances step by step until it spies a likely dinner. Flashing from a freeze, its javelin-like bill grabs frogs and fish in the blink of an eye. Occasionally it will travel to a meadow to dine on meadow mice, lizards, small snakes, and grasshoppers.

Look for American bitterns: wading in the shallows of the marsh, or hiding in the dense vegetation. When standing rigid, the bittern can look like an old stake, a dead limb, or a stump projecting from the water. When nearly stepped on, the bittern will spring up awkwardly, wings flopping and legs dangling, finally gathering itself for a rapid flight.

Look for nests: on the ground in dense, dead stalks of last year's cattails. The nest is a practically flat platform of dead stalks a foot or more in diameter, on the ground, floating, or raised a few inches above the water. By the time the eggs hatch, new green growth has grown up to conceal the nest.

Look for "runways": two opposing trails in the cattails near the nest. Watch the female leave the nest via one trail, and approach via the other to help keep the nest location a secret.

American bittern.

Listen for: "oong-KA-chunk" or "pump-er-lunk" repeated several times, audible for ½ mile, at any time of day or night in breeding season, but mostly before sunrise and after sunset. Calling bitterns pump their heads and necks violently, as if in a coughing fit. The sound is ventriloquistic—it informs other bitterns without giving away the bird's exact location to predators.

RED-WINGED BLACKBIRD

In the spring, the flashing red epaulets of these blackbirds seem to adorn nearly every other stalk in the marsh. The males are singing for all they're worth to attract mates (often two or three) and to stake a claim to a nesting territory. Research indicates that female blackbirds evaluate potential males not on the basis of their physical traits but on the quality of the territory that they have secured.

Although we normally associate blackbirds with marshes, they may not have originally nested here. In many ways, they differ from true marsh birds that have adapted specifically for this habitat. When in danger, for instance, blackbirds do not camouflage themselves in the marsh grasses as rails and bitterns do; instead they fly away.

Blackbirds may have originally been denizens of upland fields, and moved to marshes because competition was less intense here. Marshes provide them with a good supply of aquatic insects, a supply that is renewed each day when new insects emerge, harden, and fly away. The flexible blackbirds also use upland sites near the marshes to catch these escaping prey, and take advantage of the crop of weed seeds in spring and autumn. Redwings are now thought to be the most numerous land birds in North America, with a fall population of around 400 million. Their success is not because they have specialized in one habitat, but because they are able to use many rich environments.

Look for red-winged blackbirds: (males) singing from the tops of cattails to defend territories during

GAPING
Redwings get some of their food by "gaping"—inserting their closed bill into a stalk, a flower, rotting wood, or the soil, and then opening it. This exposes insects that are not visible on the surface.

119

the breeding season. Later in the summer, you'll find flocks feeding on weed seeds in upland fields. Watch as they return to the marsh at night to roost. In late August, they return to marshes during the day for protective cover while they are molting. In late September they leave for the uplands again before migrating.

Look for nests: made of grasses woven into deep, firm baskets and attached to reeds, rushes, or cattails above water. Nests are occasionally built on a tussock of grass or in a bush or small tree, typically within 6 feet of ground or water. They also nest in upland fields, in dense grass, alfalfa, or clover.

Listen for: loud, musical "o-ka-leeee" repeated at intervals, a "chack" call, and a whistled alarm note. If you listen very carefully beside a marsh, you may hear the female ripping strips of cattail leaves to use in her nest. Another indication of the blackbird's recent arrival to the marsh is a nesting accident that evolution has not yet found a cure for. Blackbirds sometimes attach their nests to two or more stalks of growing vegetation. When one stalk outpaces the other, the nest may be overturned, spilling out and ruining the eggs. This occasional mishap doesn't seem to slow blackbirds however, and in spring, the marsh is alive with nestlings which, though they cannot yet fly, spend their days crawling from blade to blade, well-protected by the dense cover of the marsh.

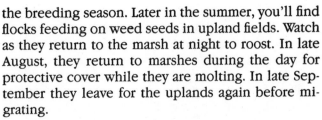

Red-winged blackbird.

MINK

In bright light, the hairs of the coveted mink's fur are iridescent. It's as if each chocolate brown hair is a prism, reflecting back red, blue, and green, and shimmering with an overall bluish tint. It takes 75 of these animals to make one full-length coat. Only 10 percent of these pelts are caught in the wild today, however; the rest are farmed on mink ranches.

Although they are in the same family, minks can't climb as well as martens, nor swim as well as river otters, nor aim their musky scent as well as striped skunks. They are not as precisely adapted as those

120

creatures are, but rather, appear to be a composite of all of them. Like weasels, they twine their serpentine body around their victim while delivering a lethal bite to the nape of the neck. Like otters, they watch for fish from along river banks, then dive to overtake them. Like skunks, they communicate with scent from their musk glands.

Their search for prey on land and in water keeps them constantly on the move. Males travel twice as far as females, and may make a circuit that takes 5–7 days to complete. Along the way, the mink will rest in a number of dens, favoring abandoned muskrat houses. One sure way of commandeering a muskrat den is to devour the occupants, which minks will do when given the chance.

Because of their taste for muskrat, the Indians used to say, "mink and muskrat: bad friends." Actually, mink prey on muskrat most often when the latter are young or weak because of disease, overcrowding, weather, stress, or starvation. Muskrats are most susceptible when good habitats become crowded or scarce, and they must relocate to areas with less food and cover. In good habitat, and in full health, a grown muskrat is a formidable enemy that minks rarely tangle with. Minks also eat mice, rabbits, birds, fish, frogs, salamanders, crayfish, clams, and insects. This wide range of quarry allows the mink to "switch" when one prey item becomes scarce.

Minks themselves have few predators, except for hunters, trappers, and an occasional carnivore or raptor. They are tenacious fighters, and are usually difficult to kill.

Mink.

Look for minks: at dusk and dawn, prowling the shorelines of marshes and streams, especially where there are logs, debris, and other forms of cover. They hunt mainly at night, but in wilder areas, you're likely to see minks out during the day too. In early summer, you may see a family of minks traveling in a single file, looking like a long, undulating serpent. They are curious, and are likely to be watching you as you watch them. You can keep them curious by squeaking or chirping. In winter, you may even see minks swimming under the ice!

Look for dens: in "borrowed" muskrat houses, brush piles, natural cavities in logs, under tree roots or rock ledges, or inside 8–12-foot-long burrows in stream banks. Minks borrow or dig these burrows, creating as many as five entrances above water level. Look also for plunge holes built straight down from the surface, leading 2 or 3 feet to the chambers below. Mink sometimes store their prey in dens.

Look for tracks: 1-1⅜ inches long, in the soft mud of a shoreline. The tracks of a hunting mink may lead from a hole in the bank to a muskrat house to a hole in the ice. Minks will also slide in the snow, creating troughs 4–6 inches wide.

Look for droppings: in piles outside dens. They are slate-colored, bluntly cone-shaped and segmented, made of dirt, hair, fur, feathers, and bones.

Look for fish: left on the ice with holes bitten in the back of their head.

Smell for: a repugnant odor left by mink as a territorial marking, a courting signal, or a show of alarm. Minks discharge scent with a lot less provocation than skunks do.

Listen for: chuckling, defensive screams, hissings, and warning squeaks.

MUSKRAT

"Le rat muske" is an animal equipped for underwater life. Its gear includes a wetsuit of waterproof fur, a sleeve of trapped air for buoyancy and insulation, and lightly webbed hind feet that act as flippers. Like other diving mammals, the muskrat's physiology allows it to "breathe" oxygen from its own tissues, tolerate high levels of carbon dioxide, and control the amount of body heat it loses and gains by regulating its blood flow. Last but not least, the muskrat sports fleshy, furry lips that can close behind its gnawing front teeth to seal its mouth for underwater dining.

What it hasn't come equipped with, the muskrat

engineers. To build its haystack house, it cuts down large patches of cattail stalks, heaps them up on the marsh floor, and binds them with mud. When the dome is high enough, the builder dives to the bottom and chews its way up inside to create a dry, protected cavity above the water surface, hidden from the eyes of aerial predators. It also builds several smaller feeding houses where it rests and feeds during the day.

When ice caps the marsh, muskrats dive down "plunge holes" to forage underwater for roots, stems, and tubers. They may even eat part of their home-made shelters to help them survive! As a way of extending their range under the ice, muskrats pull or push balls of vegetation through holes in the ice to form small hollow shelters known as "push ups." These spots are used as feeding and breathing stations during under-the-ice swims.

Muskrat populations seem to fluctuate in cycles of 8 to 10 years. Sometimes a drought will devastate muskrats temporarily, but the new flush of vegetation on the exposed soil creates conditions that may lead to a population "explosion" within a few years after deeper water returns. This large population may eventually eat itself out of house and home. When this happens, part of the population will be forced into poorer habitats, making them more vulnerable to starvation and predators. Flooding, freeze-outs, disease, and human trapping also take their toll on muskrat numbers.

Despite these risks, muskrat populations can usually bounce back. They are not picky eaters, and, when plants are not available, they will feed on animal fare such as mussels, snails, crayfish, fish, and frogs.

Look for muskrats: in marshes at least 3–4 feet deep—deep enough not to freeze all the way down—with little or no current, consistent water levels, and vast stands of cattails interspersed with open water. Look for their V-shaped wake and their tail snaking behind them or arcing out of the water. They are much smaller than beavers, and have a thin tail instead of flat "paddle" tail. On land they bound and gallop, usually following established runways. When harvesting cattails, they stand on their hind feet and cut off 5–10-inch sections. They're active at night, but you can see them during the day too, especially at twilight throughout the year.

Look for lodges: domes built of marsh vegetation, as large as 4 feet high and 8 feet wide, in the middle or along the edges of the marsh. When abandoned, these lodges house minks, and are used by turtles, raccoons, American coots, and Canada geese. Lodges are built between August and October.

Look for tracks: in pairs, separated by a stride of 3 inches. The hindprint, 2–3 inches long, is twice as long as the foreprint. The skinny tail may drag between prints.

Look for feeding houses: similar to lodges, but less than half the size. In the summer, you may see muskrats perched outside these houses, on platforms built for feeding.

In the winter: look for "push-ups," small lumps of vegetation at openings in the ice. These are smaller than feeding houses. Watch for motion as muskrats visit these for feeding and for air.

Look for feeding debris: such as floating rafts of cut cattails or piles of mussel shells on the bank or on feeding platforms.

Look for burrows: in banks, sometimes used for lodging instead of grass domes. Look for canals in

Muskrat.

the marsh vegetation radiating away from the burrow, or paths on the bank that lead to the burrow.

Listen for: a loud splash when an alarmed muskrat dunks into the water and warns its comrades of your presence. Young muskrats may squeal, but adults are usually quiet.

*Red-winged
blackbird
proclaiming his
territorial rights.*

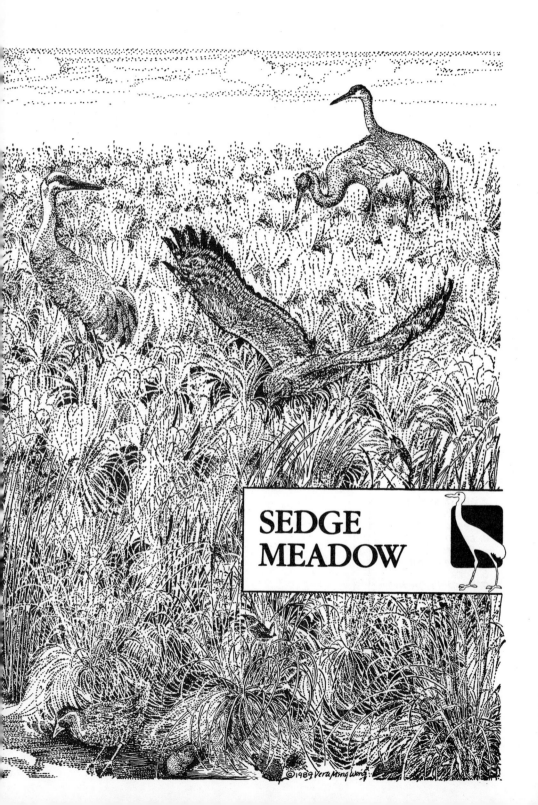

SEDGE
MEADOW

©1989 Vera Ming Wong

A warm, salmon-colored glow sinks over the sedge meadow at sunset. Scarcely an hour before, animals scurried for cover as sheets of rain and thundery winds rippled across the fields of sedge and grass. Now, a hard-to-locate, wavering sound drifts down from the clearing sky above as a common snipe resumes his circling courtship flight. Northern leopard frogs grunt and snore loudly as they float spread-eagle in swollen pools. From scattered willows, chattering sedge wrens renew their territorial claims. Hidden among the bulrushes, an American bittern pounds out a deep, resonant "oong-KA-chunk, oong-KA-chunk."

Suddenly this peculiar chorus falls silent. Wrens slip from their perches and scurry along the ground, the bittern freezes in place, and frogs submerge in the murky water. Seemingly out of nowhere, a northern harrier has appeared, cruising low over the vegetation. Rising abruptly, it hovers for an instant before dropping to the grass with yellow talons outstretched. Just as quickly it is airborne again, clutching the limp form of a meadow vole that soon will be eagerly fought over by five downy harrier chicks.

What Is a Sedge Meadow?

A sedge meadow is a wet, springy peatland covered mostly by grasslike sedges and fed by minerals washing in from surrounding lands. The soil beneath your

1. *Sedge Wren*
2. *Meadow Vole*
3. *Northern Leopard Frog*
4. *Le Conte's Sparrow*
5. *Common Snipe*
6. *Sora*
7. *Sandhill Cranes*
8. *Short-eared Owl*
9. *Northern Harrier*
10. *Spotted Joe-pye-weed*
11. *Panicled Aster*
12. *Swamp Birch*
13. *Slender Willow*
14. *Rushes*
15. *Sedge Tussock (Hummock Sedge)*

feet may be a peat made of partially decomposed plants, or a muck, which is more completely decomposed. Both are saturated, because the surface is at or only slightly above the water table. Open pools of water are common in the spring because of flooding.

Origins

Sedge meadows occur along the edges of lakes and streams, or in extinct glacial lakebeds where there's plenty of water percolating through the soil or collecting in shallow basins. Sometimes a marsh will turn into a sedge meadow as it becomes drier.

In some ways, sedge meadows resemble open bogs. Like bogs, they are treeless peatlands, dotted with clumps of low shrubs. The peats of a sedge meadow, however, are made up of partially decayed sedges and grasses instead of sphagnum moss, and the shrubs are broadleaf rather than needleleaf. Sedge meadows contain more nutrients than bogs and are not as acidic. Bogs and sedge meadows can border one another and sometimes intermix in a complex landscape known as a patterned peatland.

Sedge meadows are fragile habitats, sensitive to human-caused and natural disturbances that alter their moisture supply and delicate chemical balance. Road construction, drainage projects, peat mining, or nearby beaver dams may transform sedge meadows into shrub thickets, tamarack swamps, or dry grassy meadows.

Unfortunately, many people see such damp places as relatively useless and empty and have remained unaware of the effects that habitat alterations may have on these wetland meadows. The uncommon species that thrive here do so because the meadows offer a unique mixture of terrestrial and aquatic environments, a blend of dense cover and open space not found in human-caused habitats.

The Invincible Sedges

A good way to identify the grasslike sedges is to remember that "sedges have edges;" when you twirl them between two fingers, you'll feel that sedge stems have three flat sides, while grass stems are smooth cylinders. Many species of sedges grow in tussocks, which are clumps of aerial stems arising from a horizontal runner called a "rhizome." To start another tussock, they send out a rhizome for as much as a foot and then sink it into the sedge mat. Tussocks come up year after year and live to an old age. The mass of dead leaves and the matted roots and rhizomes that are added to the soil each year tend to create a fibrous peat—the perfect growing medium for the sedge.

Unlike most plants which sprout in spring, new sedge shoots sprout in late summer and remain green as they endure a winter locked in snow and ice. These tiny green shoots are ready to resume vigorous growth as soon as the ice thaws, giving sedges a competitive edge over many other wetland plants.

Sedges owe much of their success to their ability to withstand the up-and-down water levels that are characteristic of their habitat. Even when the sedge meadow is flooded, their aerial leaves are usually long enough to extend above the water. When water levels drop, these same leaves have the ability to fold up to conserve moisture.

Sedge root systems are also ready for anything. When water-logged, sedges depend on oxygen stored in large air spaces in their shallow, fibrous roots. When these same roots are exposed to the air during dry spells, they have rigid structural cells that help them hold their shape. In the meantime, long taproots take over, extracting water from saturated zones 6–8 inches below the surface.

Nutrients Are Where You Find Them

Along with sedges, you'll find plenty of grasses, forbs, and shrubs that are also adapted to the feast-or-famine conditions on the sedge meadow. Bluejoint reedgrass, red-stemmed aster, spotted joe-pye-weed, and swamp birch are all common associates of sedges.

Sweet gale, a woody shrub that grows in dense patches, is one of the most valuable players in this community, thanks to the warty nodules that cover its roots. Special bacteria that colonize these nodules are able to convert airborne nitrogen into a form useful to plants. Here on the sedge meadow, where plant nutrients are continually buried in layers of peat and washed away by runoff waters, this nitrogen source helps maintain the fertility of the soil. Try rubbing the leaves or fruit of the sweet gale to release its spicy odor—a wonderful surprise, especially in winter.

The fascinating, animal-eating bladderworts can be found drifting in the organic slurry of sedge meadow pools. Bladderworts are free-floating plants that actively bag their nitrogen in the form of tiny animals that swim by them. Their traps are hollow, bladder-like chambers that grow on feathery sprays of underwater branches. These bladders are "set" when the walls absorb all the liquid from inside the chamber, thus creating a vacuum. When an unsuspecting mosquito larva or even a drifting duckweed leaf brushes against bladderwort's sensitive trigger hairs, a hinged, one-way door springs open, sucking in water and the helpless victim within the blink of an eye. "Sensing" the chemicals of a victim within its walls, the bladder begins to exude digestive juices, and then slowly absorbs its prey. As the chamber walls absorb the liquid within, they form a vacuum again, and are soon ready to gulp down more prey.

Value to Wildlife

Most sedge meadow dwellers are secretive, spending most of their time concealed within the rank growth of sedges, grasses, and rushes that characterize this habitat. These grassy tangles provide elevated nesting sites preferred by sedge wrens and Le Conte's sparrows. Arctic shrews, meadow voles, and other small mammals forage for insects or seeds in this thick vegetation, but must constantly be on alert for aerial attacks by northern harriers or short-eared owls. Semipermanent ponds rich with algae and microorganisms offer late-developing tadpoles the sheltered water and food they need to mature into adult northern leopard frogs.

Wildlife Action

Bring boots and insect repellent, but by all means, go explore a water-soaked sedge meadow. As you walk, watch for sedge wrens that may step away from you or common snipes that may flush. Watch the tops of small bushes or tall stalks for singing common yellowthroats or swamp sparrows. In pools of open water, look for mallards and teals dabbling, or leopard frogs floating spread-eagle, especially at breeding time. On mud flats around the open water, keep an eye peeled for sandhill cranes. Up above, watch for the circling flight of the common snipe, and, closer to the tops of the sedge, be alert for the tilting, V-shaped form of a northern harrier (day) or the glide of a short-eared owl (dusk). Along the edges of the sedge meadow, watch for predators or other animals coming to drink.

SANDHILL CRANE

A great winged form erupts from the yawning expanse of sedges, spreading a large shadow on the meadow below. With a few powerful strokes it is aloft, long neck and bill stretched out like a spear, legs like stilts trailing behind. As it angles its 7-foot wingspan, it begins to arc, gain altitude, and call with a plaintive trumpeting that booms and ricochets over the wetland. The sandhill crane—"wildness incarnate"—looks and sounds for all the world like a pterodactyl come to life.

"Nature's airplane" can soar upon thermals (columns of warm rising air) for hours and hours, traveling 600 miles at a stretch without stopping or resting. When it finally descends from the clouds, it lands forcefully, dampening the recoil by running a few steps and backstroking with its wings.

The sheer size of the cranes contrasted with the featureless sedge meadow makes their courtship dance all the more spectacular. You may see a pair perform, or sometimes, an entire flock will dance for hours. They begin by circling slowly and bowing their head to one another. One, two, then many cranes will begin to spring up, 15–20 feet in the air, with their

Sandhill crane

132

wings thrown back for balance and their legs gracefully dangling beneath them. Sometimes they will
whirl completely around as they bound, and then
stop to bow again. When near the nest, they may
uproot sedges and plants and throw them over their
shoulders with their bill. The cranes' dance of courtship is an unforgettable gift of the sedge meadow.

Look for sandhill cranes: in damp, low-lying
meadows at sunset, especially where there are mud
flats around open water. In the early morning, the
birds move to drier upland fields, which may be ½
to 12 miles away from the sedge meadow. Here they
feed until midmorning, returning to the wetter area
to rest and preen. Mid-afternoon, they return to the
upland feeding area again where they eat rootlets,
insects, grains, berries, mice, frogs, lizards, and snakes.

Despite their large size, sandhills may be tough to
spot because their blue-gray coloring blends perfectly with the greys and browns of the sedge. Also
see the "hotspots" section for staging areas where
cranes gather before migrating.

Look for nests: in knee-to-shoulder-high vegetation, tall enough to reveal only the head and upper
neck of a standing crane. They build islands of sticks,
mosses, dead reeds, and rushes that lift the nest up
above the shallow water. The nest itself may be more
than 5 feet wide.

Listen for: a chorus of "garooo-a-a-a" calls trumpeting down through as many as 2½ miles of sky (on
migration flights). The sounds are amplified by the
coils of the crane's extra-long windpipe. A loud rattling call is used to marshal the troops for migration.
"A rook-crook-crook" seems to mean "safe feeding
here."

SEDGE WREN

Sedge wrens are named for the wet meadows they
inhabit. Their close relatives, the marsh wrens, prefer
cattails or vegetation characteristic of marshes, but
sedge wrens find everything they need to survive and
raise young within the dense jungle of sedge.

They attach their nests to sedge stalks early in the season, and as the sedge grows taller, so does the nest, until it is raised 2–3 feet above the ground and well above any water that may flood the site. Male sedge wrens build a number of "dummy" nests near the real nest, perhaps as a way of confusing potential predators. Parent sedge wrens are secretive, and will never fly directly to or from a nest for fear of leading predators to their young. Instead, they will land some distance away and walk stealthily towards the nest under cover of sedges.

When flushed, the elusive sedge wren will skim low and straight along the pointed tips of the sedges, then duck suddenly out of sight again. If they see you first, they are likely to simply creep away, mouse-like, among the stems.

Sedge wren.

Look for sedge wrens: singing atop small bushes, weeds, or stalks early in the morning, at twilight, and at night. Look for flushed sedge wrens flying along the top of the sedges. Part the sedges and you may find them stepping away from you. They are one of our tiniest birds; only hummingbirds are smaller.

Look for nests: typically 2–3 feet up, suspended in sedges, globular in shape, and extremely well built. Fresh green sedges may be woven on the outside of the nest, and a canopy of sedges may hide the nest from above. Unlined dummy nests may be nearby. Also, these wrens sometimes nest in loose colonies, so you may find more than one breeding pair in the area.

Listen for: "tip tip tip a trrrrr," increasing in tempo as it decreases in pitch. Reportedly sounds like a bag of marbles being rattled.

LE CONTE'S SPARROW

Le Conte was a medical doctor, a bird enthusiast, and a friend of John James Audubon, who named this sparrow after him. Though it is secretive, you'll be rewarded for your patience by a glimpse of this sub-dued but beautiful bird of chestnut, gray-black, and

134

soft beige. Its coloring blends well with the tangles of dead sedges where it spends most of its time.

Because it is not easy to flush, the Le Conte's sparrow has gained a reputation as a "stink bird" among quail hunters who hunt with dogs. Evidently, the dogs are easily distracted by this sparrow's secretive movements in the sedges, and will often point at them or otherwise lose interest in the quail hunt.

Look for Le Conte's sparrows: occasionally singing atop a small willow or tall weed. You'll seldom see them flying, and when you do, look quickly, because it's only a short trip and then back into the sedges.

Look for nests: on or slightly above the ground in dry borders of sedges, concealed under tangles of dead stems. The grasses and rushes used to build the nest are interwoven with standing stems.

Listen for: "reese, reese" thin, husky, and insect-like.

NORTHERN HARRIER

Chances are you'll see this slender raptor overhead, since it spends 40 percent of its day flying, covering about 100 back-and-forth miles a day. It keeps a tireless vigil over wetlands and meadows, skimming only 10–30 feet above the waving stems, searching for rodents, shrews, rabbits, frogs, snakes, or even insects moving in the sedges.

Le Conte's sparrow.

These "marsh hawks," as they were once called, are thought to have better hearing than many birds of prey because their owl-like, disk-shaped faces funnel sound toward their ears. Short-eared owls, which are also adapted to open habitats, are equipped with similar features, including a ruff of face feathers, ultrasensitive ears, and a low quartering flight.

Like the short-eared owl, the northern harrier is also able to "hover," poised and flapping in the air above its victim, before diving down to pluck the morsel skyward. If it overshoots its target, it simply somersaults back to make the strike.

135

Northern harrier.

Watch closely as the male, with a tiny vole dangling from its talons, mounts higher and higher in the air, circling and crying out. You may hear a return cry from a female, perhaps tending a nest in the sedges. She will emerge and rise up to meet him halfway, and both birds will perform aerobatic twists and turns at this meeting. Finally, the male will drop his offering, and the female will lunge for it, racing it to the ground if need be, and snatching it just before it lands. The young learn this aerial "food pass" soon after they can fly and receive food from parents in this way.

The courtship flight is another aerial wonder. The male dives from a height of 60 feet to within 10 feet of the ground, swooping upward at the last minute. When he reaches the peak of his rise, he will stall, somersault or roll his body and descend again, repeating these U-shaped flights 25 to 70 times in a row.

Look for northern harriers: flying low over sedge meadows or along the borders of open water. They hold their wingtips up when skimming, similar to the "V" of a turkey vulture, and have an obvious white patch at the base of their tail. Also look on the ground where they devour prey, and where they roost, often in groups of up to 50. Though most prey is captured on the ground, they have been known to pluck rodent nests from the sedges, shake them out in mid-air, and swoop to catch the tumbling contents.

Don't disturb nests: on the ground, or built up as high as 18 inches above the water on a stick foundation, sedge tussock, or willow clump. Nests are typically 13–20 inches across and 3–10 inches deep. They may be placed near the nests of other northern harriers (as close as 200 yards).

Listen for: a "kee-kee-kee-kee" when on the nest, or a sharp whistle. Usually, they are silent.

COMMON SNIPE

The common snipe has many nicknames, most having to do with the peculiar winnowing sound it makes in flight. Newfoundland fishing communities time the inland migration of lobster by these flights: "When the snipe bawls, the lobster crawls." Alaskan Indians referred to snipes by a name that meant walrus, because the winnowing reminded them of a walrus "blowing." In Germany, the bleating snipe is called "goat of the bog," and in Sweden, the people once believed that snipes were whinnying horses that had been transformed into birds!

Actually, the winnowing is caused by a combination of air rushing by the stiff tail feathers and the slow quivering of the wings as a male snipe performs his courtship diving. He rises high into the air and then slants diagonally toward the ground, wings raised and tail spread. He repeats this performance again and again to gain the female's attention. Females may also perform this display as a way to distract nest predators. Another courtship display is a peaceful float toward the ground with legs dangling and wings arched behind the back. Just before touching down the snipe will regain altitude, sometimes turning a somersault before drifting, leaflike, down again.

Snipe bills are specially adapted to probe and explore the mucky organic soil in which they find their meals. The tip of the bill is made of honeycombed cells attached to highly sensitive nerve fibers, derived from the same type of nerve that serves our eyes, eyelids, forehead, and nose. The tip is pliable as well, so that the top jaw can bend up to snatch an earthworm underground without opening the whole length of bill. The skull, in turn, is compacted and reinforced to withstand the strain of all that probing.

The snipe's coloring also enables it to survive by simply freezing and blending perfectly with the brown-and-gray-streaked sedge jungle. The chick's natal down, streaked with blacks, browns, and reds, and tipped with white and silver, blends in with the mosses and lichens often found near the nest at that time of year.

Common snipe.

Look for common snipes: on moist organic soils, probing for aquatic insects, earthworms, crustaceans, or the seeds of marsh plants. They also glean insects from the surfaces of plants. A good place to look is on flat, muddy banks that have been trampled by tracks. There is evidence that snipes force earthworms to wriggle into sight by stamping the muddy soil with their feet. At dawn and twilight, look overhead where a snipe may be circling and diving, or hovering and drifting.

Look for nests: on dry ground, concealed by sedges and other vegetation, sometimes on a tussock or in a slight depression lined with sedge stems.

Listen for: a haunting "who-who-who-who-who" of air over feathers as a snipe descends from a circling flight. When flushed, they fly up in a crazy, zig-zag flight uttering a raspy "scaipe." Listen for "kak-kak" when they are perched on a fence post or feeding on the ground.

SHORT-EARED OWL

This lover of open places is one of the few owls that you can see during the day. Especially active at dawn and dusk, short-ears ply the air just above the sedges in a back-and-forth hunting style reminiscent of the northern harrier's. You'll be able to pick out this owl even from a distance because of its habit of hovering on beating wings just before it drops down for the kill.

Short-eared owl.

You can also identify short-eared owls by listening for a flapping or fluttering noise like a small flag whipping in a strong breeze. This sound is made by the short-eared owl during its courtship flight. Coming down from a high circling, the owl arches his wings back and then forward, touching them together under his breast, as if applauding his own aerial acrobatics.

The short-eared owl is able to match its reproductive strategies to local availability of food. If the vole population crashes, the owls may move elsewhere, or, if they stay, they won't produce as many young. Even when the clutch of eggs is large, some of the owlets inevitably disappear, often eaten by their stronger siblings. This insures that whatever food is available goes towards rearing those young that have the greatest chance of surviving to adulthood.

Look for short-eared owls: at twilight as they move out over wet or dry fields for a night of feeding. They usually fly low, legs dangling, and they hover for a moment before dropping down on their victims. They normally perch, eat, and nest on the ground. When mice and voles are abundant, you may see a group of owls feeding in the same field. If you're close enough (through good binoculars), you may catch a glimpse of their brilliant lemon-yellow eyes.

Look for nests: on the ground in weeds, or beneath bushes in a shallow, sedge-lined depression. An owl that is trying to lead you away from its nest will fly around you and then drop down far from the nest, squealing and with wings outstretched as if in great pain. If you follow, it will rise, fly farther, and drop down again, effectively luring you from the nest.

In the winter: look for groups of owls roosting on the ground in open fields, or, if the snow is deep, under the cover of conifers.

Listen for: a clapping together of wings that sounds like the fluttering of a flag in the wind. The courtship song is a series of toots repeated 15 to 20 times, resembling the barking of a small animal.

NORTHERN LEOPARD FROG

In early spring on the open waters of a meadow pond, a convention of leopard frogs sprawls across the surface, calling to one another with a rumbling snore. By the first week in June, their eggs have been laid and the adults are climbing back into the waving fields of sedge.

Meanwhile, thousands of tadpoles are undergoing the rigors of pond life. A tadpole nibbles the tip of a delectable green stem only to find it is the young, soft-bodied form of the diving beetle, equipped with vice-like jaws to hold the tadpole fast. This fixes an immovable feast for the larvae of the dragon-fly, which eats every part of the captive tadpole except the intestines. Other insect enemies of the tadpole include "backswimmers," water bugs, and leeches.

The tadpoles that survive will transform into frogs in mid-summer (it may take 2 years). They'll stay close to the shores of the pond to keep from drying out in their first year. As you walk along the banks of a pond at this time, hundreds of frogs will pop like corn kernels at your feet. They are sitting in small clearings of wet soil called "forms" that they make by pushing aside dead vegetation. These frogs face their own set of predators—water snakes, turtles, birds, weasels, raccoons, minks, and fish are all fond of leopard frogs.

Both adult and young frogs migrate to the deep water of rivers or lakes to spend the winter, piled up in large numbers along the banks or on the bottom beneath logs and rocks. If they winter in water that is too shallow, they risk running out of dissolved oxygen, or being encased in ice if the pond freezes straight through.

Look for northern leopard frogs: leaping in all directions as you flush them out of a summer sedge meadow. In the early spring and fall, look for them in and around ponds. Young leopard frogs stick closer to open water, and will not move as far into meadows as adult frogs. When you pick up a leopard frog, it may squirt a stream of liquid that has a disagreeable odor.

Look for eggs: in shallow water, laid in globular, black masses of 4,000 to 6,500, sometimes attached to twigs.

In the winter: frogs hibernate along the banks, piled on the bottom of lakes and rivers, or in caves. They sometimes emerge during warm days.

Look for "forms": small, bare patches of soil surrounded on three sides by a ½-inch-high, horseshoe-shaped ridge of dead sedge stems. Frogs push the sedges aside to form a resting spot.

SEDGE
MEADOW

Listen for: (April–June) a drawn-out, rattling snore, a loud chuckle, or a rapid croak that sounds like rubbing your wet finger along the surface of a taut balloon. They sing profusely when you pick them up, and have been known to "purr" when their back is stroked.

Northern leopard frog.

© 1989 Vera Ming Wong

SHRUB SWAMP

At the sunlit edge of a glassy-calm beaver pond, the moose trail you are following comes to an abrupt end. An abandoned dam of gnawed aspen branches and mud still stands, now thickly overgrown with tufts of tall grass. Water spills over the low spots, fingering into brooks that meander through the dense shrub swamp below. With your eyes, you try to follow the water that snakes around, under, and through the tight weave of speckled alder stems. As you watch, a woodcock negotiates the labyrinth, stopping to probe at the base of the alders, pulling a fat earthworm from its bed. You look up. The flat palm of a moose antler flashes above the thicket, catching the last of the day's light. As you step in to get closer, the soft, black muck confiscates your brand new sneaker . . .

What Is a Shrub Swamp?

A shrub swamp is a wetland thicket dominated by 10–15-foot-tall speckled alder and pussy willow shrubs. Ferns, tall asters, sedges, and wildflowers may grow beneath these dense thickets. The soil is a wet muck, made up of well-decomposed plant and animal remains. There are often streams trickling through the swamp, and occasionally, the area may be flooded.

1. Yellow Warbler
2. Common Yellowthroat
3. Alder Flycatcher
4. American Woodcock
5. Star-nosed Mole
6. Moose (cow and calf)
7. Cinnamon Fern
8. Sensitive Fern
9. Skunk Cabbage
10. Arrow-leaved Tearthumb
11. Turtlehead
12. Narrowleaf Meadowsweet
13. Smooth Gooseberry
14. Speckled Alder
15. Pussy Willow
16. Red-Osier Dogwood
17. Marsh Fern
18. Sedge
19. Goldenrod

Origins

Shrub swamps develop in lowlands such as drained beaver ponds, old sedge meadows, old marshes, or around the edges of lakes and streams. Unlike acidic peat bogs, shrub swamps are likely to be alkaline, with rich muck soils that are fertilized and aerated by moving groundwater and streams. Speckled alder, the most abundant shrub in the swamp, further improves the real estate.

Speckled alder invades with abandon, forming an impenetrable thicket of contorted, reddish-brown to purple-black branches that can be taxing to walk, or rather, to climb through. Rough bedstraw, virgin's bower, and other trailing plants clamber over alder's white-speckled, woody stems. Wedged among the alders are tall, wispy willows and squat clumps of red-osier dogwood. Patches of skunk cabbage sprout from the rich muck, hiding dozens of posthole-deep hoofprints made by moose.

Alder swamps are likely to remain shrubby as long as water is moving through them. In cases where the thickets have invaded burned-over lowland conifers, trees may eventually return. Other lowland trees such as black ash or red maple could also invade if the swamp starts to dry up somewhat. For the most part, however, as long as the shrub swamp stays swampy, speckled alder will rule the roost.

The Speckled Alder Story

Speckled alder enriches the soil wherever it grows; its lumpy root nodules harbor bacteria that extract nitrogen from air in the soil and make it available to the plant. Alder distributes this important plant nutrient throughout the swamp by producing a bumper crop of leaves that blanket the floor of the swamp each fall. This mulch makes the shrub swamp an especially productive place. A diverse assortment of herbs thrives under alder's semi-open canopy.

Alder expands its empire by sending up new shoots from underground stems, or by "layering," a process by which a branch that touches the soil sends down roots and begins a new plant.

The weight of winter's first wet snowfall often bows over pliable young alder stems, creating a hidden maze of air pockets under the snow. Beneath these snow-laden branches, a snowshoe hare can pass winter's coldest days shielded from biting winds, hidden from its predators, and supplied with tasty young plant shoots within close reach.

Finally freed of their snow burden by the intense spring sun, resilient alder branches arch toward the light, thus producing the sprawling shape so characteristic of this shrub. As a new crop of fragrant, wrinkled leaves emerges, alder thickets become a preferred haunt of female moose, which seek complete seclusion before giving birth to their spindle-legged calves.

What's A Swamp Without Cabbage?

Long before its broad leaves are unfurled, skunk cabbage pokes its maroon-colored hood or "spathe" out of circular holes melted in April's crusty snowcover. Using energy stored for months in starchy, tuberous roots, each plant generates enough heat not only to melt leftover snowbanks, but to maintain summerlike temperatures inside the spathe on subfreezing swamp mornings. This is critically important, because each spathe incubates a spadix, a club-shaped cluster of tightly-packed, cold-sensitive blossoms. The insulating walls and curved design of the spathe allows eddies of warmed air to circulate around the developing flowers, insuring the development of another generation of skunk cabbage seeds.

These tiny islands of dependable warmth are exploited by a number of insects. Honeybees will stop to warm themselves within the folds of a skunk cabbage spathe between pollen-gathering visits to nearby pussy willows, another early bloomer found in alder swamps. Hungry spiders occasionally lurk inside these sheltered chambers, patiently waiting to ambush nectar-feeding flies that are drawn to the musky odor of skunk cabbage blooms.

Value to Wildlife

Shrub swamps play an important role in the lives of many wildlife species, but few depend exclusively on these dense stands of alder and willow throughout the entire year. During the growing season, the dense, 10–15-foot shrubs provide a cool, moist refuge for many species, including moose that are with calf. Star-nosed moles and shrews often build their "highways" under or on the ground beneath the shrubs. Above, songbirds feather their nests in the leafy branches. In the winter, bent-over alder branches form snug tunnels for snowshoe hares.

In the fall, alder catkins provide seeds for common redpolls and black-capped chickadees, while white-tailed deer and ruffed grouse eat the twigs and buds. Willows are often tall enough to stick up through the snow and provide buds for ruffed grouse, as well as twigs and bark for browsing mammals. In the summer, moose and snowshoe hare both pass by the ubiquitous alder in favor of the more palatable willow. (Willow leaves contain the chemical that aspirin is made from.)

Most animals avoid skunk cabbage because its leaves contain a noxious chemical defense. Black bears can tolerate these oxalic acid crystals, however, and feed liberally on skunk cabbage in the spring. American woodcocks probe the moist earth nightly with sensitive, pencil-thin bills in search of an earthworm meal. Rarely seen, amphibious star-nosed moles are surprisingly adept at pursuing prey in the tiny rivulets and streams.

Wildlife Action

In the shrub canopy, look for acrobatic redpolls and chickadees dangling upside down as they pry tiny seeds from alder catkins. Look in the branches of alders for warblers and other feeding birds. Watch perches at the edge of thickets to see alder flycatchers hawking for flying insects. Look on the ground for surface runways of star-nosed moles, the nests of

mourning warblers, or holes left by woodcocks probing for worms. Watch for the backs or antlers of moose
feeding, calving, or cooling off in pools in the summer.

AMERICAN WOODCOCK

Close up, a woodcock's plumage is a portrait of camouflaged beauty—its several shades of cinnamon
feathers look like a collage of colored leaves on the
forest floor. Indeed, much of their protection from
aerial predators comes from their ability to freeze and
blend seamlessly with their habitat. They also are
equipped with huge, backset eyes that enable them
to watch for predators from any direction, even when
their beaks are buried to the hilt in muck.

Woodcocks spend much of their time face down
like this, devouring their own weight in earthworms
each day. Their beaks are serrated and flexible at the
tip and so they can grasp their prey underground.
The tip is also ultrasensitive and is thought to function like an underground antenna, able to detect the
movements of earthworms a short distance away.

The best places to find woodcocks, not surprisingly, are also the best places to find earthworms.
Earthworms seem to favor moist, mucky soil that is
high in nitrogen. Aspen and alder thickets fit the bill
nicely (no pun intended) because the leaf litter they
produce has a high nitrogen content, and bacteria on
alder roots actually fix nitrogen in the soil.

Woodcocks use these moist, fertile areas for raising
young, daytime resting, and for hunting earthworms
and other soft-bodied insects in the early evening.
About ½ hour after sunset, they move into drier upland fields to feed and roost for the night, returning
to the swampy thickets come morning. In hot weather,
woodcocks like to loaf under the shade of dense
needleleaf trees.

After their food and daytime cover needs are met,
the next most important habitat to a woodcock is a
courtship arena—a forest opening with small scattered alders or aspens. The trees around the clearing
must be low enough to allow the woodcock room to
escape quickly. High over these openings the male

performs his sky dance to advertise his willingness to fight for and mate with a female. He begins on the ground with a gurgled "tuko" and then a nasal "peent peent" call. Next he circles wide above the clearing, creating a musical twitter as the air rushes past his accelerating wings. At the peak of his flight he warbles and then drops, like a leaf floating to the ground. He'll repeat this flight several times until a female alights next to him, signaling her willingness to mate.

This beautiful bird is extremely vulnerable to pesticides that poison earthworms and then accumulate in woodcocks. They are also affected by the draining of wetland habitats on which they depend.

Look for American woodcocks: probing for earthworms in swampy soil, moving into upland fields ½ hour after sunset, or performing springtime courtship flights in clearings at dawn and dusk. A brooding woodcock will stubbornly sit on her nest, so long, in fact, that you can easily study her—that is, if you can see her.

American woodcock.

Look for nests: in cup-like depressions on the forest floor or in small openings, within 50 yards of an edge. Nests are usually lined with dead leaves and rimmed with twigs. The female will only reluctantly leave her brood, and will then try to lure you away by flying low with her legs dangling and tail held low.

Look for feeding holes: in the mud, about the size that a pencil would leave.

Listen for: a gurgling "tuko" and "peent peent" before the courtship flight, or the twitter of wings as the male circles overhead. Other calls include a scolding "cac-cac-cac-cac," quacking, "wick-wick-wick," a cat-like call when flushed, and a hawk-like "keeee."

ALDER FLYCATCHER

No matter how careful you are, moving through the alder swamp is a noisy business, and this regular resident is likely to hear you coming. It usually shuns an audience, but you may see it retreating before you, moving with short flights from perch to perch. Stand still for a while and watch this flycatcher sally out for a quick meal, skimming low over the tops of the bushes in a long, zig-zag flight punctuated with the seizing and snapping up of wasps, beetles, bees, and flies.

If you can't find the bird, look for its beautifully built nest. From the outside it looks shoddily made, with scraggly strands of grasses and shiny fibers hanging down. Inside this silvery gray cup is a fine lining of light yellow grasses, neatly trimmed and carefully molded.

Look for alder flycatchers: singing from the tops of bushes, or snatching insects from the air. These flycatchers prefer edges between brushy areas and clearings.

Look for nests: typically 3–4 feet up, suspended in the fork of a low bush or sapling. The birds return from migration late, and start nesting when bushes are already leafed out.

Listen for: "fee-be-o" accent on last syllable, often slurred so that it sounds like "free-beer."

Alder flycatcher.

COMMON YELLOWTHROAT

From almost any moist tangle of vegetation, the highway-robber mask of the male yellowthroat is likely to peer. By no means restricted to the shrub swamp, this warbler is just as comfortable wherever there is low dense cover with water nearby. Wherever they are, they polish off large quantities of leaf-destroying insects including cankerworm and fall webworm caterpillars. One observer saw a yellowthroat down 89 aphids in 60 seconds!

The yellowthroat has the energy and nervous movements of a wren. When intruders (you) enter their territory, they will fuss a bit, repeating a characteristic "tscick" of disapproval. They will sometimes sound off with a vigorous outburst of song to announce that their privacy has been invaded.

In breeding season, the male performs a shallow looping flight display, rising 25–100 feet, giving sharp calls as he ascends. At the peak of his flight, he lets out a jumble of highpitched notes, then descends quietly back to the alders.

Look for common yellowthroats: lurking in the grass, weeds, or bushes of a marshy spot. You can tell when the female arrives in the breeding territory because the male stops singing for awhile and concentrates on following her. Look for the display flight described above.

Look for nests: well-hidden, on the ground among weeds, sedges, or shrubs, in grassy tussocks, or sometimes in shrubs or briars, no higher than 3 feet up. The nest has three layers of successively finer grasses. Female yellowthroats are close nest sitters.

Listen for: "witchery, witchery, witchery," and an alarm chip with a peculiar, husky quality. Also listen for their jumbled flight song.

Common yellowthroat.

YELLOW WARBLER

A female yellow warbler leaves her eggs for just a moment to catch herself a caterpillar. While she's gone, a female cowbird deposits one of her own eggs in the warbler's nest, and rolls one of the warbler's eggs over the rim and onto the ground. If the new egg goes undetected, the warbler pair may raise the young cowbird, often to the detriment of their own young.

Many warblers are plagued by the cowbird, but the yellow warbler is especially harassed. Fortunately, this warbler has evolved a way to retaliate against cowbird meddling. Upon returning to her nest to find the alien egg, a yellow warbler is likely to build a new nest floor on top of the eggs, thus burying them in a basement too cool for hatching. She will match the cowbird's persistence, building as many as six new nest floors if need be, one on top of the other. The conspicuous height makes this phenomenon worth looking for.

Look for yellow warblers: gleaning caterpillars, beetles, and lice from branches of small trees (up to 40 feet), or chasing neighboring birds. Males perform

151

a circling display to defend their territories. Two adjacent defenders will fly into each other's territory, then circle back to their own, performing a kind of "pushing contest" in the air. Look for the female with bits of white fluff in her beak during nest-building. This is one of the easiest warblers to approach with a camera.

Look for nests: typically 3–8 feet up in the fork of a sapling, shrub, or tree, where there is plenty of concealing cover, tall singing posts, feeding areas in trees, and a nearby stream. Silky seed filaments are intricately woven into the nest.

Listen for: a bright and musical "sweet-sweet-sweet, sweeter-than-sweet." The male may sing more than 3,000 times daily during peak season.

Yellow warbler.

STAR-NOSED MOLE

The bootsucking muck of the swamp suddenly bubbles, and a lump beneath the surface begins to force its way across, buckling the rug of soil ahead. The lump pauses, and a lid of muck is pushed up and heaved aside. From the hole pokes a pointed snout festooned with 22 pink, fleshy, quivering tentacles. The tentacles move, shaking off dirt and seemingly testing the outside air. At the center of this rosette sit the nostrils of the star-nosed mole.

The star-nosed mole goes to great lengths to keep this nose clean, even dunking it in water occasionally. With the help of its tentacles and the multitude of sensing hairs on its face, hands, feet, and tail, the nearly blind star-nosed mole feels its way through the swamp. It uses its broad, flipperlike forepaws to build two types of tunnels: shallow ones used to catch insects and worms in warm weather, and deeper ones used to forage in the winter, rest, and rear young. When tunneling downward, the mole kicks dirt back with its hind feet. When a load has accumulated, it turns a slow half somersault and pushes the dirt back up, forming a lumpy molehill on the surface. To keep dirt out of its nostrils, it curls its fleshy feelers inward.

Some of its burrows open directly into water, for this mole relishes water and is a strong swimmer. Streambeds are often plowed up by star-nosed moles looking for the waving bodies of annelid worms anchored on the sandy bottom. They graze on fields of these worms, grasping them at one end and sucking them up like a kid with spaghetti.

Surprisingly, this small worm-hunter has more teeth (44) than most other mammals on this continent (except the opossum), including wolves, bears, and wild cats. Its broad jaw and convoluted teeth can crush the bodies of not only worms, but also mollusks and crustaceans such as crayfish. To fuel their high metabolism and tunnel building efforts, these moles give their jaws a workout—they consume 50 percent or more of their weight each day!

Unlike their other mole relatives, star-nosed moles spend a lot of time on the surface or in very shallow tunnels due to the high water tables of their habitat. Their aboveground excursions leave them vulnerable to hawks, owls, and other predators that can stomach their somewhat unsavory taste.

Look for star-nosed moles: especially on wet and cloudy days, running along the recessed surface runways that connect their underground tunnels. At night, they forage aboveground for earthworms, slugs, snails, and small bits of plant food. Look also in the water where they swim in a zig-zag fashion. They are active year-round, and appear to spend more time swimming in winter than in summer!

Nests are underground: 3–12 inches below the ground surface but above the high-water line. Shrews enlarge a section of tunnel, usually in a natural rise (e.g., knoll), and fill it with dry grass and leaves. You may also find grass nests on the ground under logs.

Look for ridges: formed by their burrowing in shallow tunnels. The ridge may stop suddenly as the mole burrows deeper, then reappear as the mole surfaces again. Moles will redrill their tunnels if they collapse, perhaps because the soil is still loose along the old routes, and provides a path of least resistance.

Star-nosed mole.

Look for molehills: pushed-up soil in mounds as much as 2 feet wide and 6 inches high. These are formed when moles build their deep tunnels for rearing young, resting, and winter foraging (in the summer, when surface soil is unfrozen, moles forage in shallower tunnels). Molehills are most apparent in spring and fall when their builders are cleaning out and repairing tunnels.

Look for droppings: irregularly curved and left in or outside of runways.

Listen for: the shrill cries of nestlings in ground nests. Adult moles are rather quiet.

MOOSE

It's a heart-thumping shock the first time you happen upon a half ton of shaggy, shovel-antlered moose. Your heart needn't pound in fear, however, because moose, for all their bulk, are mild-mannered vegetarians, more interested in nipping the stalk of a water lily than in charging you. Nevertheless, it usually makes good sense to give moose a wide berth, especially during the rut, or whenever a mother is with her calf.

Female moose have a notoriously close relationship with their calves, protecting them for up to a year and a half before she must drive them off to make room for the new season's calf. This protection makes a difference in winter, when deep snow makes it difficult for young moose to run from predators.

Born tiny, young moose grow at a staggering rate, gaining 75 pounds in the first 9 weeks. To fuel this spurt of growth, they depend on their mother's milk, butting eagerly at her udder to get the flow going. Mom will take only so much of this badgering before she walks away, often trailing a stubborn calf still attached to her nipple. When very young, calves may mistakenly follow other females, or even humans. This may be why the mother blanketly repels all intruders that get near her calf.

Moose do best where a forest is just coming back after being cleared by fire, logging, pest outbreaks,

ANTLER ALLURE

Male moose use their 75-pound, 7-foot-wide antlers to attract females and to fight with other males. The antlers are designed so that the business end of their tines points forward when the buck bows its head, while the flatter portions act as shields to catch the opponent's antlers.

154

or the industry of beavers. They feed voraciously on the tender shoots of broadleaf trees such as quaking aspen, paper birch, sugar maple, American mountain-ash, willows, red-osier dogwood, and beaked hazel. To get at the leaves, they may straddle saplings and walk forward, bending them down to moose height. In the summer months, they prefer a wet swampy area where they can wade for sedges, horsetails, rushes, pondweeds, and other aquatic plants. They frequent the inlets and outlets of lakes where water is shallowest. In the winter, they may move to older, mixed woods where there is a bit more cover. They eat an amazing 50 to 60 pounds of browse a day, an appetite that makes them dependent on habitat that is open enough to encourage young growth.

Deer also thrive in this open moose habitat. In fact, deer populations exploded after logging opened up the northwoods. As the deer multiplied in these areas, moose mysteriously declined. Many of the deaths were found to be caused by a brain parasite that deer carry, one that is harmless to deer but fatal to moose. Since the 1940's, however, moose populations have gradually rebuilt and stabilized, especially in areas where deep snows give the long-legged moose an advantage over deer.

Look for moose: browsing the shrubs, especially at dawn and dusk, or wading in swampy wetlands to get sodium-rich aquatic plants. In a sea of vertical shrubs or trees, look for the horizontal line of deepest shadow, crowned with a rack of antlers. Males are usually alone and females are usually with a calf. If you come between a female and her calf, she may lower her head, flatten her ears, raise the hair on her neck and back, and flare her nostrils—simply her way of shaking her fist. That's your cue to bow out quickly.

Look for tracks: large cloven prints, up to 6½ inches long, in posthole-like depressions in snow or in wet mud along lake trails.

Look for scats: in a pile; they look like deer or porcupine pellets, but are much larger. In the summer, look for cow pies or clumped pellets, indicating a softer more succulent diet.

OPENING A RESTAURANT

Moose owe a debt to the beaver, porcupine, and even to the spruce budworm. These and other organisms damage trees and create clearings that are full of the moose's favorite saplings and shrubs: aspen, paper birch, sugar maple, mountain-ash, willows, red-osier dogwood, and beaked hazel. In the summer months, they prefer a wet swampy area where they can wade for sedges, horsetails, rushes, pondweeds, and other aquatic plants. They even relish grasses in clearings, getting down on their knees to graze.

In September and October: rutting males thrash their newly hardened antlers against trees to remove the shedding velvet. They stalk the woods, bellow, and fight for territory and females at this time. You may be lucky enough to glimpse a galloping moose, moving at 30–35 mph.

In the winter: moose move in small groups to yarding areas of heavy cover, preferring mixed stands where they feed on needleleaf and broadleaf twigs and bark. Look high on the trunk for large teeth marks.

Look for wallows: A wallow is a urine-soaked patch of mud that bulls make while rutting and that both sexes roll in as part of their mating behavior. Females will stretch out on a wallow to claim it, and a rival female will work tirelessly to get her to leave.

Listen for: gutteral grunts and moans made by males during the rut. Females will grunt to their calves. To attract a moose's attention, pour a bucket of water over the side of your canoe to imitate a urinating moose, or one that is dripping into the water after wading.

Moose.

Blackberries.

©Vera Ming Wong 1989

OPEN BOG

© Vera Ming Wong 1988

It's as if you're on the surface of another planet. The ground beneath you dimples and quakes, bouncing back with each footfall like a giant trampoline. Knee-high mounds of living plants grow directly on top of dead ones. They shimmer with shades of pink, red, olive, and rust. Some of the plants have tough, leathery leaves lined with a nap of wooly hair. Others are delicate, with arrestingly beautiful blossoms. Only a few animals can stomach these plants, but many of the plants survive by eating animals! A strange new world awaits you. Pull on a pair of hip-high waders and become a bogtrotter!

What Is A Bog?

A bog is a spongy mat of wet, nutrient-poor, acidic peat. Atop the peat is a continuous carpet of sphagnum moss dotted with bog-hardy plants and shrubs. Although there are no streams feeding into the bog, a pond of dark water may be at its center. The peat closest to this pool may quake under your feet, because it is actually floating! In a ring around the perimeter of the open bog, black spruce and tamarack are commonly standing guard.

Origins

Many of the bogs in the northwoods have already celebrated their 10,000th birthday. They were born

1. Four-toed
   Salamander
2. Lincoln's
   Sparrow
3. Arctic Shrew
4. Palm Warbler
5. Southern Bog
   Lemming
6. Eastern Ribbon
   Snake
7. Mink Frog
8. Black-backed
   Woodpecker
9. Labrador Tea
10. Bog Laurel
11. Leatherleaf
12. Bog Rosemary
13. Blue Flag
14. Round-leaved
    Sundew
15. Trailing Arbutus
16. Pitcher Plant
17. Rose Pogonia
18. Calopogon
19. Cottongrass
20. Tamarack
21. Black Spruce
22. Sphagnum Moss
    Peat
23. Underwater

160

when the last ice age ended, developing in kettle-shaped lakes where abandoned ice chunks had finally melted. The lakes were isolated in their kettles; no water drained from them, and no new streams entered. This seclusion made them perfect sites for bogs.

As the main glacier wasted away and the margin retreated north, most of the tundra-loving plants that had been growing nearby moved northward with it. A few of these arctic plants remained behind, however, in and around the kettleholes where temperatures tended to be lower than in the surrounding uplands. They played a part in the formation of bogs—a process that is still going on today in the quiet eddies of streams and the protected bays of modern lakes.

It happens gradually. Sedges begin to grow along the shore, weaving an interlocking mat with their roots. Slowly, the mat extends out over the water like a shelf. Sphagnum moss, low-lying needleleaf shrubs, and wildflowers grow amid the sedges, and, as they die and accumulate, the mat begins to deepen. In time, the spreading mat may cover all but a small pool of open water at the center.

The water is usually the color of strong tea, because it has, in fact, been steeping in the remains of its own plants for many years. Decay is agonizingly slow in cold northern bogs. Instead of being recycled like leaves on a forest floor, the dead bog plants simply accumulate. Living mosses pile on top of the dead ones, and the roots of sedges and needleleaf shrubs help hold the mat together. Everything is loosely entwined, so that stepping in one spot can make other parts of the bog quake.

The deepening mat eventually extends down to the lake bed and, under its weight, the compressed plant remains are slowly converted to peat. As the rug of peat becomes thicker and firmer with age, it becomes an inviting place for the seeds of black spruce and tamarack to take root. Eventually (if no fires occur), a bog forest rises from this grounded mat. (See Semi-open Lowland Needleleaf and Closed-canopy Lowland Needleleaf Forest. And remember, your local bog may go through changes that differ from those described here. Nature doesn't always follow the rules of "classical succession.")

A Touch of the Arctic

The open bog has some of the toughest and most tenacious plants in all of the northwoods. This reputation is hardly surprising, however, given the peculiar trials they face every day.

PERCHED BOGS
A bog may continue to pile up on itself until the mound of living and dead plants is perched above the water table. When the mound grows so high that the sphagnum can't hold water against gravity, it stops growing.

Take the temperature for example. Bogs are the cold storage tanks of the northwoods. The insulating mat of peat, sometimes several feet deep, keeps the sun from warming the water below. Chilly air from the surrounding uplands often sinks into bog hollows, further lowering the temperature and producing frost even in summer. As a result, roots of bog plants can be slightly frozen as late as July, while up above their leaves are experiencing 100-plus-degree-F temperatures. This is one reason why most plants can't survive bog life, and thus, why the competitive advantage rests with the arctic holdouts that still reign here.

In addition to being cold hardy, bog plants, like their arctic and desert counterparts, must be able to conserve water. Why is water so carefully guarded, you might ask, when the plants are literally perched on a lake? The answer, again, lies in the coldness of a bog. During chilly spring, fall, and certainly in winter, plants have a hard time absorbing water through their roots. At the same time, their leaves may be releasing water vapor into the air in the process of making food (photosynthesis). Because they can't replace the water they lose, bog plants suffer desert-like conditions, and are in danger of drying out.

Bog plants counteract this in many ways. Most of them are low to the ground, so that their leaves are covered with snow for most of the dangerous drying period. Exposed leaves are covered with a tough, waxy material that cuts down on moisture loss and discourages browsers as well. Just under the surface of each leaf is a layer of stiff cells that help prevent wilting. The pores through which they lose water vapor are hidden on the undersides of the leaves, sunken into deep pits, or smothered with dense wooly hair. As a way to further shield these pores from drying winds, many of the leaves curl down over the edges.

The Giant Sphagnum Sponge

Ironically enough, the plants themselves contribute to making the bog a difficult place to live. The sphagnum that spreads across the lake absorbs 25 times its own weight in water, and thus, effectively blocks circulation and drainage. (Native Americans, realizing its absorptive prowess, used dried sphagnum for diapers! Test this by squeezing the live moss. It will "exhale" air, and if you submerge it, it will refill with water.)

The trapped, stagnant water soon loses most of its oxygen and becomes brown with humic acid, a by-product of plant decay. Sphagnum adds to this acidity by releasing ions into the water around it, thus discouraging competitors and making room for more sphagnum.

This acidity, along with a lack of oxygen, makes life difficult for the tiny organisms that would normally decompose plant remains. As a result, the bulk of the plants simply sink to the bottom of the lake intact, piling in deepening layers of peat. It's no wonder that logs, boats, and even human bodies can remain perfectly preserved for decades in the vault of a peat bog!

Preserving these plant bodies, however, locks up the nutrients that would normally be made available through decay. Without this recycling of nutrients, the acid bog quickly becomes an impoverished place. The sealed system relies primarily on rain, dust, and minute ground seepage for nutrients, an allotment that most plants would find too meager. The competitive edge rests with plants that are adapted to make the most of this precious commodity.

INSIDE SPHAGNUM
Sphagnum moss plants have balloon-shaped cells. Their transparent cell walls are reinforced with spiral bands that keep the cells from collapsing.

Getting By with Fewer Nutritients

Many bog plants, for instance, are evergreen; they hold onto their leaves (and their nutrients) for 2, 3, even 4 years. Just before they shed them, they are able to reroute the leaves' nutrients back into the plant, where they will be used to make new tissue. Because evergreens stay green throughout the year, they are able to make food in early spring and late fall, as well as during sunny winter days.

Some bog plants, such as orchids and heaths (e.g., leatherleaf), have fungi that live around their roots and help them extract nutrients from the peat. Plants such as sweet gale have round nodules on their roots filled with special bacteria that make nitrogen available to the plant. Other plants, called accumulators, simply hoard all the nutrients they get for future use. By evolutionary design, they can tolerate large quantities of nutrients that would kill other plants. When leaves from these accumulator plants fall, they add toxic amounts of this nutrient to the soil, killing off other seedlings that try to invade.

Believe it or not, there is a bright side to nutrient deficiency. A lack of nitrogen causes tannins to concentrate in plant leaves. These tannins are toxic to browsing deer and moose, and may also help prevent attacks from disease-causing fungi and bacteria.

Plants That Eat Animals

Perhaps the most amazing adaptations to bog living are those of carnivorous plants. They have partially solved the problem of nitrogen scarcity by capturing animals, mainly insects, that venture into the bog. Two of the most common animal-eaters are sundews and pitcher plants.

Sundews sparkle. They have upright hairs on their leaves, each tipped with a drop of sticky fluid that ensnares and stupefies insects that land there. These tentacles gradually curl around the body of their victim, bathing it in digestive juices, so that the plant can later absorb the liquefied meal.

164

Pitcher plants lift their innocent-looking vases of red and green leaves to the sky. Drawn by their fragrance, insects often land on the graceful lip of the vase. Downward pointing hairs funnel the visitor into the pitcher, where spangles of sticky, easily removable platelets wait. The victim collects gobs of these on its legs as it tries to escape, and winds up tumbling down the smooth neck of the pitcher—a one-way ticket to the pool of rainwater in the bottom. Its final resting place is among the hairs at the very base, where glands exude enzymes to digest it, and thin-walled cells absorb it.

Even in the inhospitable bog, opportunity abounds for some organisms. For example, some insects spend their entire lives in the rainwater of the pitcher plant; apparently immune to the toxic juices, they survive by sharing the feasts that "drop by." Some spiders spin webs across the opening, and treefrogs wait (sometimes falling in themselves), all for the sake of an easy insect meal.

Value to Wildlife

Bog animals confront the same problems that bog plants do. The water-logged peat is acidic, cold, and low in oxygen. Most burrowing animals such as arctic shrews, southern bog lemmings, and meadow voles stick to the upper, somewhat drier layers. They build their runways along the sides of sphagnum hummocks and nest within or atop hummocks. Short-eared and great gray owls patrol these hummocks, hoping to catch one of these mammals unaware.

The openness of a bog makes it ideal for aerial hunters, but provides little cover for large animals. Browsers that do brave the bog must pick around the unpalatable heath shrubs. Berry connoisseurs will find blueberries and cranberries to their liking, however, and a bumper crop may entice fall migrators to stop here. During spring stopovers, the gruff, rattling calls of migrating sandhill cranes may pierce the usual deep silence of the bog. Some ground-nesting sparrows and warblers that are more commonly found in open fields may also nest here.

BOG LIGHT
Will-o'-the-wisp, or ignis fatuus, *is a phenomenon of ghostly flame reportedly seen over bogs and marshes at night. This spontaneous combustion may occur when methane gas, a byproduct of the decay process, bubbles to the surface and ignites on contact with oxygen.*

Only a few amphibians, such as the four-toed salamander and mink frog, can tolerate the highly acid conditions of a bog. Some of the more common reptiles, such as garter snakes and painted turtles, may also be spied here. Most swimmers with gills, such as fish and tadpoles, steer clear of the bog; besides the low oxygen content, the brown humic acid in the water can actually damage their gills.

Wildlife Action

Look in dry hummocks of sphagnum for the cave-like nests of warblers and sparrows, the tunnels and runways of voles, shrews, and lemmings, as well as signs of occasional bogtrotters such as foxes, minks, weasels, lynx, and snowshoe hares. In hot weather, look for visiting black bears. Watch the edge between an open bog and a shadier spruce-tamarack forest for species that may breed in one and feed in the other, such as hawks and owls. Look in the water for salamander young, and listen for the breeding sounds of mink frogs.

PALM WARBLER

You're stepping carefully from sphagnum clump to sphagnum clump, when suddenly you hear a rustling on the bog floor. Out steps a dull-colored bird, gliding in a graceful walk, body tilting and tail wagging with each step.

Before nesting season and in the fall, you'll usually see more than one, because palm warblers tend to flock together along with other ground-feeding birds in groups of 6 to 10, or sometimes as many as 50 at a time. Flocks are especially conspicuous before they depart for their tropical winter haunts in Florida, Cuba, and the West Indies. In these areas, where the name "palm warbler" has context, these birds are common or even abundant in the landscape. Palm warblers are one of the first warblers to return to their northern breeding grounds, often arriving while the nights are still crisp and the lakes still skimmed with ice.

Voracious insect eaters, palm warblers have been known to eat up to 60 insects a minute. They feed

Palm warbler.

166

Pitcher plants lift their innocent-looking vases of red and green leaves to the sky. Drawn by their fragrance, insects often land on the graceful lip of the vase. Downward pointing hairs funnel the visitor into the pitcher, where spangles of sticky, easily removable platelets wait. The victim collects gobs of these on its legs as it tries to escape, and winds up tumbling down the smooth neck of the pitcher—a one-way ticket to the pool of rainwater in the bottom. Its final resting place is among the hairs at the very base, where glands exude enzymes to digest it, and thin-walled cells absorb it.

Even in the inhospitable bog, opportunity abounds for some organisms. For example, some insects spend their entire lives in the rainwater of the pitcher plant; apparently immune to the toxic juices, they survive by sharing the feasts that "drop by." Some spiders spin webs across the opening, and treefrogs wait (sometimes falling in themselves), all for the sake of an easy insect meal.

Value to Wildlife

Bog animals confront the same problems that bog plants do. The water-logged peat is acidic, cold, and low in oxygen. Most burrowing animals such as arctic shrews, southern bog lemmings, and meadow voles stick to the upper, somewhat drier layers. They build their runways along the sides of sphagnum hummocks and nest within or atop hummocks. Short-eared and great gray owls patrol these hummocks, hoping to catch one of these mammals unaware.

The openness of a bog makes it ideal for aerial hunters, but provides little cover for large animals. Browsers that do brave the bog must pick around the unpalatable heath shrubs. Berry connoisseurs will find blueberries and cranberries to their liking, however, and a bumper crop may entice fall migrators to stop here. During spring stopovers, the gruff, rattling calls of migrating sandhill cranes may pierce the usual deep silence of the bog. Some ground-nesting sparrows and warblers that are more commonly found in open fields may also nest here.

BOG LIGHT
Will-o'-the-wisp, or ignis fatuus, *is a phenomenon of ghostly flame reportedly seen over bogs and marshes at night. This spontaneous combustion may occur when methane gas, a byproduct of the decay process, bubbles to the surface and ignites on contact with oxygen.*

Only a few amphibians, such as the four-toed salamander and mink frog, can tolerate the highly acid conditions of a bog. Some of the more common reptiles, such as garter snakes and painted turtles, may also be spied here. Most swimmers with gills, such as fish and tadpoles, steer clear of the bog; besides the low oxygen content, the brown humic acid in the water can actually damage their gills.

Wildlife Action

Look in dry hummocks of sphagnum for the cave-like nests of warblers and sparrows, the tunnels and runways of voles, shrews, and lemmings, as well as signs of occasional bogtrotters such as foxes, minks, weasels, lynx, and snowshoe hares. In hot weather, look for visiting black bears. Watch the edge between an open bog and a shadier spruce-tamarack forest for species that may breed in one and feed in the other, such as hawks and owls. Look in the water for salamander young, and listen for the breeding sounds of mink frogs.

PALM WARBLER

You're stepping carefully from sphagnum clump to sphagnum clump, when suddenly you hear a rustling on the bog floor. Out steps a dull-colored bird, gliding in a graceful walk, body tilting and tail wagging with each step.

Palm warbler.

Before nesting season and in the fall, you'll usually see more than one, because palm warblers tend to flock together along with other ground-feeding birds in groups of 6 to 10, or sometimes as many as 50 at a time. Flocks are especially conspicuous before they depart for their tropical winter haunts in Florida, Cuba, and the West Indies. In these areas, where the name "palm warbler" has context, these birds are common or even abundant in the landscape. Palm warblers are one of the first warblers to return to their northern breeding grounds, often arriving while the nights are still crisp and the lakes still skimmed with ice.

Voracious insect eaters, palm warblers have been known to eat up to 60 insects a minute. They feed mainly on beetles, ants, caterpillars, gnats, mosquitoes, flies, and mayflies, capturing their prey on the ground or on the wing.

Look for palm warblers: on the ground, searching for insects, or, near migration, in a flock of sparrows, chickadees, vireos, creepers, and warblers. Look for their characteristic up-and-down tail pumping.

Look for nests: on the ground, often at the base of a small tree or shrub. They're made of grass with shredded bark, lined with feathers and rootlets.

Listen for: a rapid series of thin lisping notes, "thi, thi, thi, thi, thi."

ARCTIC SHREW

Imagine a tiny cylinder of fur and tail scurrying tirelessly through the moss of the bog floor, sleeping only in snatches, and eating round-the-clock to replenish the energy lost in its excessively frenzied life. Shrews have relatively little body mass with which to produce heat, but they have a vast expanse of skin from which it can radiate. Fueling this inefficient furnace is a 24-hour-a-day job.

The struggle to keep warm intensifies in winter. Shrews often travel beneath the surface of the snow, joining the community of animals that use the relatively warm, still corridors between the snow and the ground (see The White Habitat, page 12).

Even when its body is resting, the pointed snout of the shrew is in motion, sniffing for the scent of prey or enemy. Shrews feed mostly on animals that they find in their runways, such as earthworms, insects, snails, centipedes, salamanders, etc. Because they only carry reserves for an hour or two, frequent meals are crucial. For all their fierceness as predators, shrews are extremely high-strung and subject to death by sudden shock. When frightened, their heart rate can skyrocket to 1,200 beats a minute. Only 20 percent of all shrews born will live longer than 4 months. Many are captured and killed by predators, but, because of bad-tasting secretions released by their skin glands, they are rarely eaten.

Arctic shrew.

167

Lemmings live most of their lives in the darkness of snug tunnels 6–12 inches beneath the surface of the bog. To shuttle between tunnel entrances, lemmings use the same trails over and over until shallow ruts become worn in the moss. As they travel, they clip and gather plant food. It's during these above-ground sojourns that they are often picked off by predators such as owls, hawks, weasels, snakes, foxes, and minks. The scarcity of prey species in the bog makes the lemming an essential link in the food chain of this habitat.

Look for shrews: running between their hiding places under logs, bark, leaves, or in underground tunnels dug by moles, mice, and other shrews.

Look for nests: on or under the ground, protected above by a log, rock, or stump. Nests are globes, 3 inches across, made of shredded leaves.

Look for droppings: in and around runways. They are tiny and corkscrew-shaped.

Look for runways: in and through the moss, about an inch in diameter. When the top layer of snow begins to melt, look for meandering trails in the snow.

Look for tracks: in muddy runways or on the top of the snow. Look for drag marks made by their tails and ridges in the snow made by tunneling shrews.

SOUTHERN BOG LEMMING

Bog lemmings are voles, mouse-like rodents with a shortened tail. They live in a complex of tunnels carved 6–12 inches below the surface of the bog. These tunnels are chambered to provide areas for nesting, feeding, and storing cut grass for winter. Occasionally you may see lemmings surface and race along "runways" or ruts in the bog that connect the various entrances to their subterranean homes.

The lemmings' favorite foods are bog plants such as sedges, leatherleaf, blueberries, and the starchy roots of various herbs. In turn, predators such as owls, hawks, weasels, snakes, foxes, and minks all make meals of the bog lemming.

Look for southern bog lemmings: in runways between their tunnel entrances. Dig around in the moss near the roots of dead conifers to expose these runways.

Southern bog lemming.

Look for nests: in summer, a ball of shredded grass, 3–5 inches across, built high in a sphagnum clump. Nests are also built in underground tunnels.

Look for cut grass stems: 2–3 inches long, in piles lining the runways.

Look for droppings: in runways or nests. Pellets are greenish and the size of small grains of rice.

Black bear.

©1989 Vera Ming Wong

SMALL WOODLAND
OPENING/EDGE

Standing atop a boulder that was dropped by a glacier more than one hundred centuries ago, you gain an unobstructed view of this quiet, grassy clearing in the upland forest. With white rumps flashing, five northern flickers flush from an ant mound and scatter in all directions for the protective shelter of the dense forest nearby. Immediately you scan the sky for signs of a swooping hawk, but instead hear the soft rustlings of a red fox patrolling a patch of bracken fern. Stepping lightly onto the anthill, he sniffs at stab holes made by the flickers' probing beaks, then deposits a pile of blueberry-filled feces on the bare soil. Satisfied with his territorial claim, he trots on, following an oft-traveled route along the brushy border where field and forest merge.

What Is a Small Woodland Opening/Edge?

A small opening is a clearing 1–3 acres in size covered by a layer of permanent sod. "Permanent" means that it remains grassy, rather than converting to forest as shrub-sapling openings do (see page 201). For wildlife, the most important feature of this habitat is its perimeter—the edge between forest and clearing.

1. Ruby-throated Hummingbird
2. Eastern Chipmunk
3. Eastern Cottontail
4. Northern Flicker
5. Eastern Garter Snake
6. Orange Hawkweed
7. Red Bat
8. Red Fox
8a. Red Fox Pups
9. Broad-winged Hawk
10. Large-flowered Trillium
11. Wild Strawberry
12. Largeleaf Aster
13. Solomon's Seal
14. Violets
15. Sugar Maple
16. Shelf Fungus
17. Chokecherry
18. Woodchuck
19. Smooth Sumac
20. Serviceberry
21. Beaked Hazel
22. Bracken Fern
23. Aster
24. Columbine

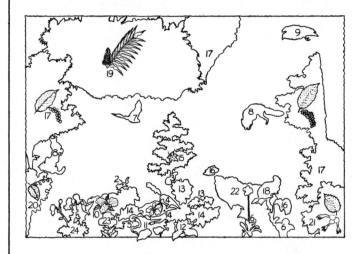

Origins

Some small woodland openings in the northwoods owe their existence to human use and settlement around the turn of the century. In a few you can still see the outline of a crumbled log foundation, the angular timbers buried under decades of matted bluegrass and dried bracken fern fronds.

The settlers who carved these clearings in the forest usually owned horses and cattle. Their constant trampling and heavy grazing favored the growth of sod-forming grasses on the densely compacted soil. Bales of hay hauled in to feed the livestock contained the seeds of many non-native plants that rapidly colonized the disturbed ground. Hop clover, common yarrow, oxeye daisy, and a variety of exotic grasses still persist today in places occupied years ago by logging camps or wilderness farmsteads.

Besides human disturbance, physical and biological forces have also helped to create openings. Once an area is opened by fire, wind, or insects, for instance, the climate in that opening changes. Because there is no canopy to shade the ground or to slow air circulation, the soil heats up and dries faster. If the soil is light or sandy, and especially if it has been burned badly, it may not have enough nutrients or be able to hold enough moisture to satisfy tree seedlings. In openings where a sod layer becomes established, tree seedlings may have an even slimmer chance, because of the competition from grass roots that are better able to absorb moisture from the surface soil. In openings where bracken fern is abundant, the shade and competition, as well as several tons of leaf litter per acre may also inhibit tree seedlings. In other openings located in low spots or "frost pockets," the frequent frosts on clear summer nights stunt and kill all but the most cold-hardy plants.

A Fertile Zone of In-Between

An "ecotone" is a place where the vegetation of two distinct plant communities overlaps. Of the nearly 400 species of birds, mammals, amphibians, and reptiles found in the northwoods region, nearly half are

WHAT'S A FROST POCKET?

"Frost pockets" are dips in the landscape where cold air becomes trapped and causes frost to form, even on relatively mild nights. It works like this. When the sun sets, objects on the ground give up their heat, causing the layer of air just above the surface of the ground to become chilled. Cold air is heavier than warm air, and so, if there is a slope, the cold air from the uplands tends to roll downhill into the frost pocket. In many cases, these low temperatures discourage plants other than grasses and hardy weeds.

closely linked to the field-forest ecotone! Here animals have access to a greater variety of food and cover than would be found in either community alone, and they benefit from the structural diversity offered by a combination of the two communities.

For instance, red bats roost under the loose bark of large forest trees by day, but feed on the wing in nearby clearings each evening. Indigo buntings glean tiny seeds from the ground in grassy fields, nest in the protective cover of dense shrubs, and sing incessantly from exposed perches near the top of young saplings. White-tailed deer and moose browse extensively in woodland openings, nipping off tender young sprigs of chokecherry and quaking aspen, and coming in spring to feed on the early-greening grasses and other herbaceous plants.

For all its advantages, a woodland edge also has its drawbacks. Sharp-eyed hawks and egg-eating mammals frequent field-forest borders and clearings because of the abundance of nesting songbirds. Edge environments also attract the brown-headed cowbird which, instead of building its own nest, secretly deposits its eggs in the nests of many other birds.

Value to Wildlife

Small openings offer many of the amenities of large openings—grassy nest sites, plentiful seeds and insects, between-season foods for grazers such as deer, openness for aerial hunters, good sites for burrows, etc. (see Large Field, page 185). The difference is that with a small opening, protective shelter (the forest) is always close at hand, even from the very center of the field. Contrast this to a large field which a wary animal may not want to cross for fear of being caught by a predator. The edge of the forest serves as an important escape route, as well as being a habitat in its own right.

The grassy vegetation in a woodland opening is also a unique offering. Deer tend to feed in openings regularly, especially in the spring and fall. In the spring, they find some of the first plants "greening up," and in the fall, when forbs and other summer foods are becoming scarce, deer look to openings for grasses and sedges.

Wildlife Action

A stroll along the brushy fringe of a small woodland opening is usually a pleasant and productive wildlife watching experience. The hollow tapping of woodpeckers echoes from the surrounding forest. Nervous songbirds dart about, repeatedly scolding you for passing too near the shrub that shelters their downy, fledgling young. With lightning quickness, a smooth green snake slithers off the sun-warmed surface of a fallen snag and vanishes in the matted grass. Fresh dirt, excavated the night before, lies scattered around the cool, dark mouth of a woodchuck burrow. White-tailed deer trails crisscross in all directions through damp bluegrass and fragrant hop clover, inviting you to choose one and follow.

RUBY-THROATED HUMMINGBIRD

Audubon was amazed by this "glittering fragment of the rainbow," the only bird species that can hover and fly backwards with its aerial "oars." Engineers who have studied the hummingbird's wings claim they are surprisingly similar to the rotors of a helicopter.

When hovering, the wings cut a figure-8 in the air. By tilting the plane of their wings backward slightly, they can move up and back. By tilting them downward, they zoom forward, getting power and lift both from their downstroke and their upstroke. Their sternums are large and deeply keeled, flanked with 8 ribs, instead of the usual 6, which probably helps minimize the stresses of flight.

The engine that runs these wings is equally amazing. Hummingbirds must refuel every 10 minutes or so to support a heart that beats 1,260 times a minute, and breath that comes and goes 250 times a minute. The energy output for a hummingbird is 10 times that of a person running 9 miles an hour. If a 170-pound man led the life of a hummingbird, he would burn 155,000 calories a day, and evaporate about 100

Ruby-throated hummingbird.

175

pounds of perspiration an hour. If he ran out of water, his skin temperature would reach the melting point of lead, and he would eventually ignite.

Despite the demands of staving off starvation, hummingbirds are able to accumulate enough fat (2.1 grams) to carry them non-stop in their migratory flight across the Gulf of Mexico. All in all, they migrate more than 2,000 miles every year.

Wherever they go, hummingbirds look for flowers that offer them a supply of small insects and a source of nectar. In return, the hummingbird may unknowingly transport pollen picked up on its bill to each plant it visits, thus sometimes acting as a pollinator.

Of the 31 species of plants that rubythroats are known to visit regularly, 19 have been specially adapted to appeal to a bird, rather than to an insect pollinator. In true hummingbird-adapted plants, the flowers are usually red and tubular, reinforced against piercing, and shaped to accept long bills and tubular, brushy tongue tips. They usually have large reservoirs of nectar that reward their pollinators. The time of blooming, lack of scent, and size and shape of the flower has evolved to discourage other types of nectar lovers, such as bees, that may not be as efficient at delivering the pollen.

Look for ruby-throated hummingbirds: hovering at the sunlit edges of forests where there are plenty of flowers, especially red ones such as salvia, trumpet creeper, and jewelweed. In the spring, look for the male hummingbird on his courtship flight, arcing back and forth over a female waiting on a branch. The arc is so exactly drawn in the air that it looks like he is riding on a suspended wire.

He is showing off his shimmering red "gorget," or throat patch. Unique laminated structures on the feathers of this throat patch scatter light waves, causing the iridescent ruby effect. The same phenomenon produces the swirling colors on a soap bubble. Also look for hummingbirds at tree trunks that have been drilled by sapsuckers; they will be feeding on the insects attracted to the sap from these holes. Watch for hummingbirds bathing in the puddles trapped on large leaves. Fond of water, they will often streak through the spray from a waterfall or a suburban sprinkler.

Look for nests: typically 10–20 feet up, in the saddle of a drooping limb, overhanging a trail or a waterway, and exposed to the surface below. No more than 2 inches across, built of bud scales bound with spider silk, the nest looks like a knot on the branch until you look inside and see two pea-sized eggs.

Listen for: the audible whir of their wings in flight. Males and females seem to disagree often, and their squeaky, high-pitched bickering can easily be heard.

NORTHERN FLICKER

Northern flicker.

The flicker is a classic example of an edge species. While it needs the forest's large trees for roosting, nesting, drumming, and cover, it also needs open areas for ground foraging. The flicker is our only woodpecker that feeds on the ground, pecking at the soil in hopes of turning up its favorite dish, ants. Its long, extendible tongue is powerfully muscled and covered with a sticky substance that helps collect the ants quickly. According to one observer's records, an enthusiastic flicker finished off no less than 5,000 ants at one feeding!

Unlike many woodpeckers, the flicker's bill is curved and relatively weak. When digging their nest cavities, they look for the punkiest wood of dead or dying trees. They also find dead limbs on which to drum to advertise territory or attract a mate.

The flicker courtship ceremony is a drawn-out drama of head bobbing, plume display, and competition with other displaying males. Later in the breeding season, females take their turn as the aggressors. You can tell males from females because males have a black "mustache"—a streak extending back from either side of their bill—and females do not.

Look for northern flickers: probing for ants, ground beetles, and other insects in short grasses at the edges of clearings, especially where snags or dying trees are still standing. They also like open, parklike woodland where they'll forage for wild fruits.

Look for nests: in cavities 2–90 feet up (typically 10–30 feet) in dead or dying trees 12 inches or more in diameter. Nest trees are often at forest borders next to fields for feeding. Look for fresh wood chips at the base of a tree that has several holes in it. Flickers return to the same tree year after year, digging out a new nest each time. Starlings often usurp flicker nests.

Listen for: a far-carrying "woika woika woika" call, a high-pitched "tierr," a long roll of drumming on a hollow limb, or warbling as adults leave the nest. Tap on the nest tree and listen for the buzzing of young flickers inside.

RED FOX

The red fox, though secretive, is actually common in the northwoods, especially where humans have staked a claim. The patchwork landscape created as people clear parcels of land is made to order for the red fox. Clearings provide plenty of grass-nipping voles, and woodlots between clearings provide safe travel lanes.

Solitary for much of the year, foxes spend a good deal of time zigzagging back and forth across this patchwork in search of small rodents, insects, birds, berries, and carrion (foxes are called the "everything eaters"). They mark the areas they visit with urine, feces, and scent from their musk glands. These markers send messages to other foxes about territory, identity, well-being, food eaten, passage of time, and things we can't even guess at.

Red fox.

The elaborate use of scent is a luxury that adult foxes can afford because they do not have any large predators to hide from in the northwoods besides humans. Human hunters have learned to use dogs to follow the trail of scent that foxes leave.

The fact that foxes have been successful despite hunting and trapping pressure is due in part to their notorious wariness. Before a fox will approach an object, such as a baited trap, it will circle it carefully, studying it from all angles and sniffing the breeze for

178

clues to its identity. Only the most careful trapper can out-fox that discriminating nose.

Voice, like scent, is another form of communication. During the breeding season, the ordinarily quiet males engage in territorial disputes that include 15-minute screaming matches. Wide-mouthed and inches apart, the foxes deliver blood-curdling screams until one fox backs down and skulks away. Males and females may also confront one another. Opponents often stand on their hind legs facing each other, with their forepaws on each other's shoulders in a pushing contest. Because they are bloodless and ritualized, these fights rarely result in injury or death. This method of diffusing aggression helps foxes and many other animal species live longer.

During the day, red foxes rest in thickets or in long grass, favoring sunny spots in fields or south-facing slopes in the winter. They sleep lightly and are alert to any new sounds or smells. Foxes make nervous and extremely cautious parents, and in a populated area it is not unusual for a mother fox to move her pups to one or even two new dens before they grow up.

Young foxes do not develop their red coat until they are about 10 weeks old. For the first month of life, spent mainly in the darkened den, they are a smoky charcoal color. At about 5 weeks, their coat turns a sandy buff color, which camouflages well with the apron of sandy soil at the entrance to the den. Young fox pups spend their days playing on this apron, practicing the stalking, stiff-legged, arching pounces that they'll later use to catch prey hidden in the grasses or beneath the snow.

Look for red foxes: trotting along the edges of woods at dawn and dusk. At 6 mph, they seem to float along, "light as thistledown on their feet." They'll also run, if need be, at an average of 28 mph. Foxes are mainly night-hunters, but you can see males staking out territory and chasing females during the day in late winter. Watch for females hunting during the day when hungry pups are in the den. Try kissing the back of your hand (sounds like a squealing mouse) to lure a curious fox to investigate. The best spot for fox-watching is facing the entrance to a den where young will play in the sunlight. Watch with binoculars though, because too much disturbance will cause the female to move the family—a costly use of her energy.

Look for dens: at the edges of woods and fields, on a dry slope with sandy, loamy soil, often near water. There are sometimes several entrance holes, 10 inches in diameter. Dens may have an underground tunnel system of more than 25 feet. Study the apron of dirt at an abandoned den to find bones of prey, hair, feces, and tracks.

Look for tracks: at the entrance of dens, in the snow, or along regularly used fox trails. Foxes put one foot in front of the other, producing a dotted line with four claw marks per paw and an occasional brushing of a dragged tail. Domestic dog tracks are similar, but not as straight-lined. Pet dogs also tend to romp through deep snow, wander, and "play" more, a function of having no enemies and no need to hunt their own food. The fox conserves its energy by taking the line of least resistance: along ridges, the wood's edge, and paths of shallow snow. It has been noted that the fox's track is straight when traveling between two points, wandering when hunting, and circling when it is about to bed down.

Also look for tracks at "water jumps," places where foxes regularly jump across streams and scramble up the other side. A fox's trail in the snow may lead you to the site of a kill, or to a mound (6–12 inches across) where a cache of uneaten meat is stored. In January and February, fox tracks in the snow will come in pairs, crisscrossing and intertwining, signaling the travels of a mated pair.

Look for bedding sites: in overgrown ditches, thickets, long grass, or tangled tree roots. Look also for sunny spots where a winter-active fox can warm up.

Look for scat, urine, and fur: at conspicuous points along a fox trail such as elevated bare ground, a gap in hedges, or the edge of fields. The scat is twisted, 2 to 3 inches long, pointed at both ends, and

THE ART OF LEAPING

Engineers have known for years that the most efficient takeoff angle for any projectile is 45 degrees. Guided missiles achieve their longest flights when aimed at this angle. Foxes have come to the same conclusion through years of natural selection. Their average takeoff angle is exactly 45 degrees, corrected of course, if the prey is up close, or if the fox is standing in loose sand and needs extra "umphf" to launch itself.

contains hair and bone chips, unlike that of domestic dogs. Also look for balls of fur that foxes remove with their teeth while grooming. Foxes will sometimes bury food under snow and then mark the spot with urine.

Smell for: the skunky odor of fox urine lingering in the woods in January and February, when foxes court and set up territories. Frightened foxes also exude a heavy musk. Sniff at the den entrance to get the full bouquet of fox.

Listen for: "wo-wo-wo," the yelling bark issued by the male when traveling and staking his territory in late winter. A mated pair traveling together will trade softer yaps to keep in contact with each another. A night-splitting shrieking is probably the screaming match of two fighting foxes.

RED BAT

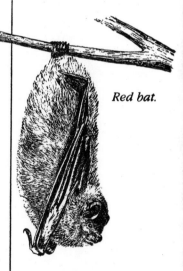

Red bat.

When we think of bats, we think of caves, not trees. It's sometimes surprising, then, to see this common, tree-dwelling bat hanging, not from stalactites, but from leafy branches. Their daytime, upside-down sleep is a deep one in which their body temperature and metabolism drop way down. Curled in a ball, with a thick, handsome cape of fur around them, red bats are able to withstand wind, rain, and extreme changes in temperature.

When they wake, hunger sends them out to the field for their evening forays. As they fly, they send out a constant stream of ultrasonic pulses, taking a fix on insect prey by "listening" to the waves that bounce back to them. They'll also fan out their hairy tail membrane to net larger insects in their path.

Solitary for most of the year, red bats form loose groups to migrate south for the winter. They apparently travel great distances over water, because there are records of exhausted red bats landing on ships in the ocean far from shore.

Look for red bats: foraging in openings and over water in early evening, or on dark, cloudy days. They are most active on warm, humid nights. They will often ply the same 100-yard stretch over and over, looking for moths, beetles, flies, and other flying insects. They roost in trees and shrubs (often on the ends of lower branches) where leaves offer some concealment and protection from weather. The roosting areas are open from below, and the bat's yellow-red coloring is obvious against the green leaves.

Look for a female: roosting in branches with young bats clinging to her fur. If disturbed, she may abandon her roost, struggling to fly with as many as four young attached to her fur! Please be quiet and unobtrusive when around roosts!

WOODCHUCK

The "bulldozer" can bury itself from sight in a moment, clawing out earth with its front paws, ejecting it with its hind paws, chiseling past stones and through roots with its strong teeth, and pushing loose soil from tunnels with its head. This digging machine builds burrows up to 40 feet long and 4 feet deep, removing as much as 700 pounds of soil from one burrow! Escape routes to the burrow are drilled straight down from the surface, so the woodchuck can drop quickly away from enemies—namely humans, dogs, and red foxes. It shares its burrow with other small mammals when hibernating, simply sealing off its sleeping chamber and allowing others free rein of the rest.

After a winter of sleeping nose to tail, breathing only once every 6 minutes, and rationing its own fat, the groundhog wakes up famished. When it first emerges, it often has difficulty finding the succulent plant parts that it needs (1½ pounds a day) and may return to the den, whether it sees its shadow or not. The tradition of watching groundhogs on February 2 comes from the European belief that hedgehogs and badgers could predict the weather. If they emerged on a sunny day and saw their shadows, 6 more weeks of nippy weather was on its way.

Look for woodchucks: during the day along forest-field borders, waddling away or plunging down escape holes. They commute along well-worn run-

ways to favorite meadows, where they eat alfalfa, clover, and grasses. (They don't "chuck wood;" the name probably reflected their use of wood piles for shelter.) Watch for them basking in the sun atop a mound, squatting at the entrance to their burrow, or standing up on their haunches for a better view.

Look for burrows: identified by a fresh mound of dirt at the flattened oval entrance. From here it dips down and then up to the nest chamber which is situated "up-tunnel" to prevent flooding. Scattered on the surface above the burrow are "plunge holes"— entrances without mounds that give woodchucks instant refuge. Overland trails connect most entrances.

Look for tracks: in sandy portions of the field or at entrance mounds. Four toes on the forefoot and five on the hind, about 2 inches long.

Listen for: a shrill whistle followed by a low churring sound when there's danger. Hence the name "whistle pig."

Woodchuck.

©Vera Ming Wong
1988

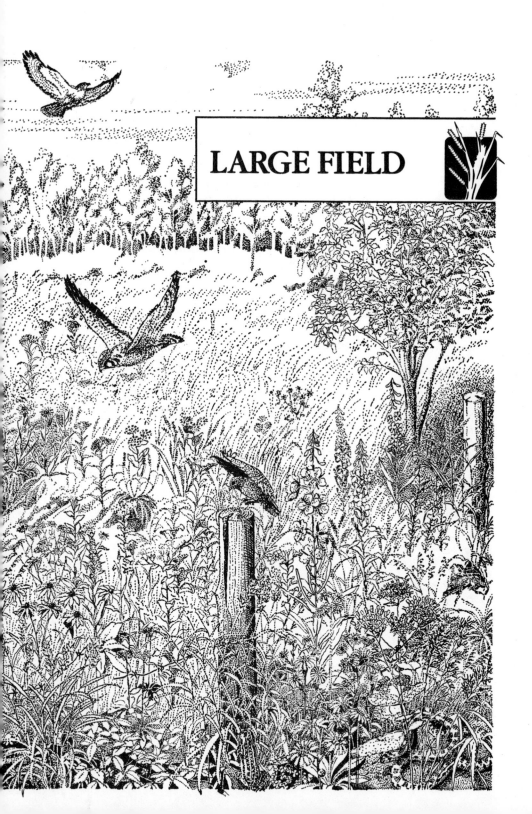

LARGE FIELD

Billowy cumulous clouds parade across a hazy August sky. A red-tailed hawk floats up into them, turning circle after circle above the broad, gently rolling grassland. Her keen eyes inspect a several-hundred-acre meadow below dotted with aging, charcoal-stained stumps. These weathered monuments, so apparent to a soaring raptor, are often hidden from our earth-bound view by a sea of swaying grass and bracken fern. Over the years the barkless stumps have become crusted with lichens and riddled with the tunnels of wood-boring insects. If you look carefully, you're likely to see the century-old scars of a logger's axe still etched there.

What Is a Large Field?

Large fields are openings larger than 3 acres, covered by a layer of permanent sod. They usually remain grassy rather than convert to forest the way shrub-sapling openings do. No more than 30 percent of the area is covered by trees. Their openness makes these fields especially attractive to aerial predators (and wildlife watchers), and their workable soil is attractive to burrowing mammals.

Origins

Red-tailed hawks and the field-dwelling creatures they hunt are common in the northwoods today as a result

1. *American Kestrel*
2. *Eastern Bluebird*
3. *Smooth Green Snake*
4. *Meadow Voles*
5. *Northern Shrike*
6. *Red-tailed Hawk*
7. *13-lined Ground Squirrels*
8. *Common Mullein*
9. *Fireweed*
10. *Black-eyed Susan*
11. *Milkweed*
12. *Butterflyweed*
13. *Chokecherry*
14. *Rice Grass*
15. *Hedge Bindweed*
16. *Bluegrass*
17. *Badger*
18. *Gopher Snake*
19. *Quack Grass*
20. *Aspens*
21. *Orange Hawkweed*
22. *Pearly Everlasting*
23. *Poverty Grass*
24. *Goldenrod*

of the widespread clearcutting of stately red and white pines around the turn of the century. Catastrophic fires, fueled by acres of logging debris, were common in the early 1900's. In areas where the soil was only a thin, sandy scalp atop glacial bedrock, these fires caused lasting damage. The intense heat destroyed not only the aboveground vegetation, but also the underground root networks and seeds. This laid the sandy barrens wide open to colonization by the wind-scattered seeds of grasses and forbs.

In other logged clearings, plows followed the saws and kept the land open for years. Eventually, many farms on poorer soils were abandoned.

Decades later, you can still find treeless, grassy fields, looking much like they did only 10 years after the fires or the farms. Why have shrubs and trees been unable to reconvert these areas into forests? The answer is in the invasion strategies of grasses, ferns, and other meadow plants.

Cornering the Market

Cool-season grasses green up early each spring, long before frost-sensitive bracken fern. They are well established by the time the dependable warmth of summer coaxes the bracken fronds to unfurl. The nearly unbroken canopy of grass and bracken intercepts much of the incoming sunlight before it can reach any sun-loving tree seedlings that might have taken root. Thirsty bracken and grass roots also soak up scarce moisture and compete with seedlings for much-needed nutrients.

Over the years, decomposing grass blades accumulate, producing a dense sod mat that physically prevents tree seeds from anchoring their taproots in the soil below. And each winter a blanket of snow packs another layer of brown bracken corpses atop the ever-deepening sod mat.

Some resourceful forbs, such as hawkweeds, goldenrods, and asters, manage to infiltrate the sod mat, using horizontal underground stems to spread across the field. They also employ a potent chemical defense against potential competitors. Their leaves contain water-soluble compounds called phenols. As rain hits the decaying leaves, the phenols are washed into the soil. Pioneering trees, already struggling to gain a foothold in the dense mats of grass and bracken, wither and die when their roots incorporate these poisons into their systems.

Value to Wildlife

Large fields differ from small openings in ways that are important to wildlife. The center of a large field is farther from the woodland edge than the center of a small opening. Thus, species that need a ready getaway to woody cover will find it safer in small, rather than large, openings. However, for species that profit from a large, open foraging area, such as hawks and many seed-eating birds, a large opening is more appealing. The large size also helps support sufficient numbers of prey species such as meadow voles.

Burrowing species, such as badgers, find plenty of room to dig complex underground networks in a large field. Also, species that are adapted to prairie environments, such as upland plovers and sharp-tailed grouse, are quite at home in these large abandoned meadows. They tend to feed on the grasses themselves, or on the insects and mammals that eat the grasses.

In the spring, fields are among the first areas to "green up," providing deer and other grazers with succulent grasses and forbs. Fields provide grazing and sunning for many species of snakes and toads as well.

Wildlife Action

There is action above, in the form of soaring hawks and meandering songbirds. The hawks are focused on minute movements in the grass: a grasshopper alighting, a ground squirrel peeking out of a burrow, or a green snake winding its way through the grasses. Concealed beneath the wind-tossed lavender and yellow blossoms, a sharp-tailed grouse hen and her brood probe the dried grass, uncovering juicy insects that the young birds eagerly devour. Look carefully in the

A LONG SHELF-LIFE
Many old-field invaders hitched a ride with colonists from Europe, and then released millions of tiny seeds on our soil. Even when crops were growing on the surface, the soil held its treasure of "weed" seeds—some 7,000 per square foot of soil down to plow depth. The secret of these seeds is their ability to remain viable for decades. In fact, there is a record of a mullein seed that actually sprouted after being buried in the foundation of a medieval church for 650 years!

shadows of the grasses for the well-disguised 13-lined ground squirrel standing straight up outside its tunnel entrance. Look for signs of other burrowing animals in disturbed patches of sod, where entrances or exit holes may be visible.

RED-TAILED HAWK

You train your binoculars on what at first looks like a speck, traveling a slow and lazy circle, almost out of sight. It spirals down until you see its wings, and then suddenly, the wings fold and the form drops, traveling an unbelievable 120 mph toward the field. It fills your lens with the shape of one of our largest hawks. Swooping up from the ground is another hawk, a female, that turns onto her back mid-air and presents her talons to the approaching divebomber. Seconds before collision, the male checks his flight, the female rights herself, and they fly off in tandem, executing turns, spirals, and dazzling dives together. Occasionally, another breeding pair will join the first to create a true aerial circus.

When defending their range, however, the resident pair makes sure trespassing hawks spend as little time as possible in their 80–200 acre territory. They simply escort them on the flight out, not giving them a chance to perch and get too comfortable.

Redtails often hunt from high in the air, relying on their eyesight to detect scampering mice 100 yards below. Their eyes are huge, occupying as much space in their head as their brains. Hawk watchers at lookouts such as Hawk Ridge will often "borrow" the sight of a captive redtail to help them locate migrating hawks. The "helper" hawk will train one eye on any movement in the sky, even that of hawks too far away to be seen with human eyes. Researchers suspect that this monocular vision might function like an adjustable telescope, with a zoom effect achieved by muscular action on the lens. These muscles are designed for rapid refocusing in flight so the hawks don't lose sight of their prey or crash into obstacles. They even have a special second eyelid that periodically cleans and moistens this special instrument.

Red-tailed hawk.

The red-tailed hawk's diet includes a menagerie of organisms—from large insects to half-grown rabbits. One key to its success is its ability to switch foods to whatever is plentiful, be it mice, chipmunks, squirrels, amphibians, reptiles, nestling birds, or carrion.

Look for red-tailed hawks: soaring high above grasslands, flying low for hunting, or perched atop a utility pole or in a tall tree at the edge of the woods. Look for them traveling with red-shouldered and other hawks on migration flights, especially on cold days with prevailing northwesterly winds. They need large trees for nesting and perching. Their home range may be as large as 2 square miles.

Look for nests: 35–90 feet up in the tallest tree along the edge of the woods, or in a lone tree in a field. The nest is a flat-topped dish, 30 inches wide, made of sticks and "marked" in early spring with a fresh green branch.

Listen for: a highpitched steam-whistle scream, "tsee-eeee-arrr." While waiting for parents to return with food, the young can be noisy.

EASTERN BLUEBIRD

The bluebird, which, as Thoreau said, "carries the sky on its back," has become a symbol of happiness and harmony. At nesting time, however, the bluebird's life is anything but harmonious. They must compete for a limited number of suitable nesting cavities with other cavity nesters, chiefly starlings and house sparrows (both introduced to this country), tree swallows, and wrens. Unlike woodpeckers, the bluebird's bill is not strong enough to peck out a cavity, so they must depend on holes that rot naturally in a trunk. The scarcity of natural cavities was among the factors that has caused bluebird numbers to decrease. Indiscriminate use of pesticides such as DDT also threatened songbirds such as the bluebird.

Luckily, public response to the bluebird's plight has been impressive. DDT has been banned, and thousands of nest boxes have been built on public and private land, prompting a partial recovery in the last 25 years.

Eastern bluebird

190

You may notice that these artificial nests are sometimes placed in pairs. This is done deliberately to take advantage of the guarding instincts of birds other than bluebirds. A pair of early nesting tree swallows will take over one of the boxes before bluebirds arrive in the spring. They'll aggressively defend their nesting area against any other birds of their kind, thus keeping tenants out of the nearby box. Since bluebirds are a different species, and therefore not seen as a threat, the swallows allow them to nest in the box without harassment.

Although this "reservation" system helps boost the number of possible nesting sites, the competition for these sites is still keen. Female bluebirds that can't find cavities of their own lay eggs in the nests of other bluebirds. This would seem to explain the belligerent stance that nesting females take against other female bluebirds. It takes energy to raise young, and if the payoff for the individual comes only in passing on its own genes, raising another bluebird's young can be seen as a waste of energy.

Look for eastern bluebirds: on perches, or dropping to the ground to feed on caterpillars, grasshoppers, crickets, and beetles. Favorite feeding areas typically have poor soil and sparse ground cover. They also hunt for insects in the air and on leaf and branch surfaces. Best habitats are open areas that have plenty of nearby perches and dead trees with low cavities. In fall, they wander the countryside in groups before heading south. Likely to be lured by premature warm weather, many die in early spring frosts.

Look for nests: typically 5–12 feet up in natural cavities, woodpecker holes, holes in fence posts, or wooden bird boxes. Here are specs so you can build your own: a box 8 inches in height, with a floor 5 inches by 5 inches and an entrance hole 6 inches above the floor and 1½ inches in diameter. Fasten the box 5–10 feet above the ground and place another box 20–25 feet away.

Listen for: a liquid, musical "turee" or "queedle" when bluebirds are flying overhead.

HELPER BIRDS

An example of the "selfish gene" at work in bluebird populations is the phenomenon of helper birds. Young bluebirds of the first brood may hang around to help their parents feed the next brood. By caring for their own siblings, they are indirectly safeguarding some of their own genetic material.

AMERICAN KESTREL

American kestrel.

The small, pointed wings and tapered tail of the kestrel make it look like a three-pointed star, but its lightning-quick movements make it seem more like a meteor. The kestrel can easily outmaneuver most birds, and can often be seen harassing birds by flying circles around them, rising above them, and then divebombing them in classic falcon style.

The jay-sized kestrel hunts from an exposed perch, and will also skim the grasslands, often at great heights, in hopes of spotting dinner. When it keys in on something moving, it will seem to back up over the spot, hover on beating wings, and then drop down for the morsel. A feet-first approach is used to snag grasshoppers and other large insects, while a headlong dive signifies capture of a mouse or snake. When it realights on its perch, watch for its characteristic tail-pumping motion.

Unlike most falcons, this species has adapted to the presence of humans and has been known to frequent even downtown areas, roosting on office buildings and preying on the abundant house sparrow population. In the wild, "sparrow hawks" (a common name but a misnomer) seek out sparrows only when the supply of grasshoppers, snakes, mice, or other rodents is low.

The kestrel is uniquely and richly colored. On the back of its head it has markings that look like a beak and two eyes—a "second face" which may repel would-be predators or mobbing songbirds.

Look for American kestrels: hunting from an exposed perch, or flying over an adjacent field, hovering over their next meal. Downtown skyscrapers may harbor kestrels, as do telephone wires along roadways, especially in the fall during migration.

Look for nests: typically 35 feet up in a natural cavity or one that has been abandoned by a flicker or pileated woodpecker. They will also nest in cliff faces, under the eaves of old buildings, or in human-made nest boxes.

Listen for: a shrill "killy, killy, killy" as the kestrel scolds intruders. They are especially noisy in late summer when family groups travel together.

BADGER

For the animal called "nature's steam shovel," digging is a way of life. Badgers dig to find food, to build their homes, to avoid enemies, to house their young, and to weather winter. They dig so frequently, in fact, that digging can almost be called their major means of locomotion.

Naturally, their bodies are designed for earth-moving. They actually flare from pointed nose to wide jaws to stout, triangular body, forming a wedge that works its way through the soil. As the badger probes and pushes, protective ear hairs and eye membranes seal off sensitive tissues from dirt. When a badger is caught out of its burrow and needs to lay low, it can flatten its wide body, looking like a throw rug with legs.

Its premier tools are the muscular forelegs and the long, sickle-shaped claws of its forefeet. These claws come equipped with pressure sensors that have not been found in any other mammal and are thought to be used to identify objects it encounters while digging. They work at high speed, loosening dirt and passing it back to the broad hind feet, which express it out the hole in a 5–8-foot plume. In less than 3 minutes of furious digging, a badger can "disappear" into the earth, exerting a force against hard soil that can amount to thousands of pounds per square inch.

Badgers hunt underground, patrolling their own burrows (in which other rodents sleep, travel, or hibernate), or digging tunnels to intercept other burrows, hoping to find the owners at home. The jaws and teeth of the badger are incredibly powerful, easily crunching through muscles and bones with only one bite.

THE BADGER'S BADGES

Researchers speculate that the badger's bold markings may have evolved to warn other animals that the badger is fierce and ready to defend itself. Other theories are that the stripe divides the form of the badger in two, thus confusing predators such as the golden eagle, which may not be able to add the two halves together. The white stripe may also help badgers recognize one another at night or in the darkness of their burrows.

Badger.

Coyotes and badgers have an up-and-down relationship. A badger may attack and kill coyote pups, and likewise, a group of adult coyotes occasionally take down a badger. In some ways, however, a live badger can be more valuable than a dead one. While digging for dinner, badgers have been known to flush a ground squirrel or mouse to the surface, where a well-placed coyote can enjoy the windfall.

Look for badgers: at twilight as they emerge from their burrows to hunt. Occasionally you may see them aboveground during the day, but not often.

Look for dens: built into the side of a knoll or on a flat grassy field. The entrance is wider than it is high and strewn with a fan-shaped mound of dirt. When young badgers are in the den, you may find hair mixed in the dirt at the entrance.

Look for tracks: pigeon-toed with inch-long claws, especially evident in the mound of dirt at the den entrance.

MEADOW VOLE

In a world without natural checks and balances, a meadow vole and her offspring could produce a million descendants if they bred throughout the year. With each of these voles consuming 60 percent of its body weight in grass each day, our large field habitat might look very different indeed.

In reality, the average vole lives only 2–3 months, long enough to produce only two or three litters. The fact that they can survive that long is a tribute to their ability to elude the hundreds of hungry eyes looking for them. The number of predators that depend on voles for their mainstay is impressive, making the meadow vole a prime source of energy in the field community.

In addition to filling the stomachs of a great many predators, meadow voles fill a special consumer niche in the meadow. They eat the grass blades and stems, while mice prefer the seeds and fruits, and shrews eat the invertebrates (e.g., insects). Because they eagerly eat even introduced plants, voles have adapted

NICKNAMES
STICK
The badger became Wisconsin's mascot not because it is especially abundant here, but because the miners that extracted lead and zinc from the state's early mines were called "badgers."

Meadow vole.

194

well to almost every agricultural change we throw at them. They prefer the open land of our fields; thus, we unwittingly boost their numbers and hasten their spread.

Meadow voles may construct as many as 4½ miles of runways per acre. As they create and maintain these 1-inch-wide trails, they are also nourishing themselves by eating the grasses they clip. (Researchers estimate that 10 voles in a 100-acre meadow could polish off 11 tons of grass a year.) Arched grasses form a roof over the runway that protects the vole from overhead hunters. Other rodents use these covered runways for safe travel. In the winter, voles tunnel under the insulating blanket of snow.

Meadow vole numbers tend to swell every 3 or 4 years. When a field gets crowded, some of the voles begin to disperse into adjacent habitats, while others remain. Which animals go, which ones stay, and why, are riddles that researchers are still unraveling.

Look for meadow voles: darting across an open area on their way to another runway, or surfacing briefly atop the snow before tunneling under again. They are active both day and night, but peak activity times are dawn and dusk.

Look for nests: balls of dried grasses, 6 inches in diameter, under boards, rocks, logs, and in runway tunnels.

Look for tracks: ⅝–½ inch long. The pattern varies, but when jumping, the tracks are 2–4 inches apart.

Look for runways: 1-inch-wide paths at the base of grasses, sometimes rutted into the soil. Arched grasses usually form a roof over the runway. Look for 1½-inch-wide holes in this roof, most easily seen in spring when grasses are matted down from a winter of snow. Starting at the hole, part the grasses carefully to "unzip" the roof and expose a network of runways tunneling through the grass.

In melting snow: look for meandering trails, 1½–2 inches wide. These are snow tunnels with the tops melted off.

EXTENDED FAMILIES
Without nature's checks and balances system, vole populations could easily explode. One well-fed laboratory vole had 17 consecutive litters before her first birthday, resulting in 83 offspring and 78 grandchildren!

Look for gnawings: at the base of shrubs and small trees in meadows.

Look for skulls: of meadow voles in the undigested pellets of hawks and owls (especially red-tailed hawks and great horned owls, which may eat 2 or 3 of these voles a day).

Listen for: highpitched squeaks, uttered in fights or in distress. Although you can't hear them, meadow voles are thought to emit ultrasonic sounds that bounce off the grassy sides of their runways. Nestlings may emit these sounds to their mother, or adults may use them to respond to threats.

13-LINED GROUND SQUIRREL

For this mammal that spends half its life in a deep, subterranean sleep, its underground habitat is as important as its aboveground one. These squirrels dig complex burrows to hibernate in and then scatter the dirt with their feet so as to leave no trace at the entrance. The foyer of their tunnel runs straight and then jogs in an "L" shape, a feat of evasive engineering. The "L" acts as a security system against badgers that prey on 13-lined ground squirrels. Badgers need clear space behind them to expel the dirt that they generate when they dig. When hunting badgers hit the crook in the "L," they may read it as a dead end and become discouraged. For extra security, ground squirrels plug the entrance to their hibernation chamber before retiring.

Once asleep, curled in a ball with head between legs, the ground squirrel won't fully wake up for another 5 or 6 months. During this time, its heartbeat will drop from its normal high of 350 beats to a low of 5 beats per minute. Its breathing will drop from 50 breaths a minute to 4, and its temperature will drop to that of the air around it. With no sustenance except the fat stores it built up in the autumn, the ground squirrel will lose up to 40 percent of its weight. Although this hibernating nearly depletes them, it is actually a good way to survive during a season when the climate is demanding and the food supply is low.

When it finally stumbles awake in the spring, the squirrel will be famished, and chances are good that food will not yet be readily available. At this time, the squirrels depend on the stash of seeds, grains, and nuts that they buried last autumn.

For summertime survival, the evasive ground squirrel relies on its camouflage and on keeping a low profile in its grassy runways. When it does stand in its "picket pin" posture for lookout duty, it is completely motionless. Its stripes help to scramble its outline shape in the eyes of airborne predators. And when it senses danger, it heads for one of the strategically placed escape hatches leading to its extensive burrow system below. These precautions are important in areas where, for instance, the ground squirrel makes up 25 percent of the northern harrier's diet.

Thirteen-lined ground squirrels moved northward as people did, following the roadsides and utility rights-of-way, colonizing cut-over lands and clearings. They are another example of a wild animal expanding its natural range as humans created favorable habitat for it.

Look for 13-lined ground squirrels: standing like surveyor's stakes or running for their escape hole. After they disappear, wait a moment, and there's a good chance they'll poke their heads back out in curiosity. They are most active in sunny weather during mid-morning to late afternoon, and may be seen hunting insects (they have a passion for grasshoppers) by pouncing and pinning them down with their forefeet.

Look for dens: by following a ground squirrel as it disappears down a hole. There is no dirt around the entrance of a burrow so it is hard to detect unless the ground squirrel leads you to it.

Listen for: a bird-like whistle or "churr" in high key, descending in pitch.

13-lined ground squirrel.

SMOOTH GREEN SNAKE

On the roadway ahead of you lies a blade of fluorescent green grass, freshly cut, and, wait—moving! These snakes of the grasslands are a brilliant, tropical, satiny green. They blend so well into a field of real green blades that it's easy to miss them. You're more likely to spot them during warm summer or fall rains when they often cross highways, standing out in high contrast to the black asphalt.

If you pick a docile green snake up, it may discharge a fluid, but rarely will it bite. Look for the black tip on its long, pink tongue. Because they eat great numbers of insects such as caterpillars and grasshoppers, green snakes are very susceptible to insecticide poisoning.

Look for smooth green snakes: on roadways during warm spring and fall rains, or under boards or rocks in grassy fields. Just before they molt, their skin may be bluish instead of green. Their underbelly is pure white. When they die, smooth green snakes also turn bluish.

Look for nests: in rotting logs and under boards in June.

In the winter: smooth green snakes hibernate in deserted ant hills, sometimes with other species of snakes.

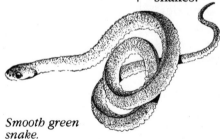

Smooth green snake.

Gray fox pup.

SHRUB-SAPLING OPENING

©Vera Ming Wong 1988

From the shade of a deep wood, you come blinking into a sunny opening. You can smell the tang of ripe berries and the spiciness of new green leaves. Vigorous shrubs cover every square inch, jockeying for position, moisture, and nutrients. Scores of birds and rodents roam beneath this thorny tangle, avoiding the occasional hooves of white-tailed deer and moose that have come to nibble at the shoots and fruits above their heads. Even higher, hawks and owls patrol the skies, waiting for a reckless mouse or vole to dash into view. Bears paw at old stumps, or sit to strip blueberries with their lips, teeth, and gums. Songbirds flit from bramble to bramble, plucking juicy berries from their stalks. Out of this seeming chaos, a tall, straight forest will someday rise, ushering in a whole new complement of birds and animals.

What Is a Shrub-Sapling Opening?

A shrub-sapling opening is a regenerating forest, coming back 3 to 12 years after logging, fire, or other disturbance. You'll find dense shrubs up to 10 feet tall, and in some cases, a well-developed layer of herbaceous plants underneath. There may also be broadleaf saplings such as aspens, paper birch, pin cherry, and other trees that do well in full sunlight.

1. Indigo Bunting
2. American Goldfinch
3. Rufous-sided Towhee
4. Gray Catbird
5. Brown Thrasher
6. Song Sparrow
7. Ermine
8. Blue-spotted Salamander
9. White-tailed Deer
10. Largeleaf Aster
11. Starflower
12. Hedge Bindweed
13. Quaking Aspen
14. Chokecherry
15. Paper Birch
16. Sugar Maple
17. Pin Cherry
18. Bracken Fern
19. Bush-honeysuckle
20. Serviceberry
21. Smooth Solomon's Seal
22. Corn-lily (Clintonia)
23. Beaked Hazel
24. Wild Sarsaparilla
25. Red Raspberry

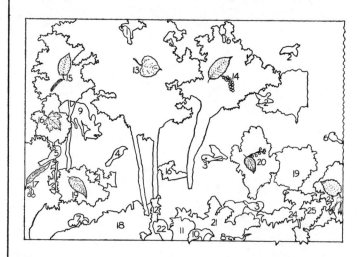

Origins

There are many ways to clear a forest. Beavers flood them, diseases weaken them, winds flatten them, insects digest them, humans harvest them, and fires reduce them to ashes. The result is the same: a patch of land once shaded by branches is now bombarded by sunlight. There are no leaves to block the force of rains, and when the rains subside, the sun heats up the soil, and water drains away or evaporates. Onto this surface, winds blow seeds from surrounding forests. Old seeds, rootstocks, or stumps from the previous forest may also begin to sprout. As these plants poke up, animals begin to graze, insects descend, diseases infiltrate, and the competition for dominance begins.

A shrub-sapling opening is a moment in time, a bridge between the demise of one forest community and the dawn of another. The kind of forest it will become depends on soils, climate, what kind of forest was there before, how the opening was created, and the actions of humans, fire, insects, and disease. In the meantime, it is a unique community in its own right, serving the needs of a multitude of species.

Colonizing Plants— The Soil Stabilizers

On severely charred land, the fast-growing fireweed is often the first colonizer. Fireweed has narrow leaves that expose little surface area to the blazing, moisture-robbing sun. Bracken fern, with its 10-inch-deep roots, can also spring to life from the ashes of a fire. If the fire is not too hot, the roots of perennials such as wild sarsaparilla, largeleaf aster, sweet-fern, bunchberry, and wintergreen will survive and send up a new flush of growth. These are joined by vigorous shrubs such as beaked hazel, bush-honeysuckle, and red-osier dogwood.

These plants help rebuild the soil by returning organic nutrients to the soil when they die. This mulch eventually becomes humus—a looser, richer soil that lets air and water travel down to plant roots. The improved soil also benefits tree saplings that are also vying for space, sun, and the limited amount of water in the top layers of soil.

Trees—The Opportunists

One of the most famous fire "chasers" is jack pine. Many of its characteristic humpbacked cones remain sealed until intense heat (from the sun or a fire) forces them to open. They are extremely tolerant of poor soils, and will thrive in dry conditions that would put great stress on most trees. Their short, compact shape provides tough resistance against the winds that whistle across openings, and their roots do a herculean job of holding down the sandy soil.

Some jack pine cones remain sealed until the heat of a fire opens them.

On better soils, the classic northwoods pioneers are the quaking and bigtooth aspens. Aspens have cornered the market on colonization because they attack from not one, but two angles. They can come in as lightweight seeds (3 million to the pound), blown from more than a mile away on light, downy fluff. Or they can emerge, phoenix-like, from the roots of aspens that were cleared from the site. This "suckering" can result in more than 20,000 new aspen sprouts per acre in only one year. Because they are fed and watered by a fully formed root system, these sprouts can grow at a rate of 4 feet a year for several years before slowing down. Because each sucker is a genetic duplicate of its parent root, a clump of aspens in an opening may all belong to the same "clone" (a group of genetically identical trees). In the Rockies, where aspens have been suckering for generations, one clone may cover as many as 100 acres. Here in the Lake States, clones range from 1/10 to 1 acre.

Aspens are not alone, however, in their ambitious scramble to recover recently cleared forest land. Although they shade out some forbs and grasses, aspens still have to contend with an assortment of versatile shrubs and vines that are also adapted to invade openings.

Shrubs—The Versatile Invaders

Beaked hazel has even more ways to reproduce itself than aspens do. In addition to seeds and sprouting,

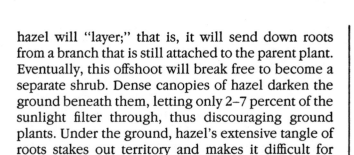

hazel will "layer;" that is, it will send down roots from a branch that is still attached to the parent plant. Eventually, this offshoot will break free to become a separate shrub. Dense canopies of hazel darken the ground beneath them, letting only 2–7 percent of the sunlight filter through, thus discouraging ground plants. Under the ground, hazel's extensive tangle of roots stakes out territory and makes it difficult for other root systems to squeeze moisture out of the soil.

Hazel is among the many shrubs that not only endure but are actually rejuvenated by fire or animal browsing. Hawthorn is another; as it's browsed, it becomes compacted in a tight crown, discouraging future browsers.

The tight crown of hawthorn is a real haven for many species of birds and mammals that hide and nest within, protected from many predators by their thorny patron. Tree seedlings that can stand the shade are also protected from browsing and will grow up through the hawthorn, often overtopping and shading out their fortress. Wild grape vines climb the bushes and trees around them to gain access to light.

Value to Wildlife

The shrub-sapling opening is an all-you-can-eat stop for many kinds of wildlife. Deer mice and southern red-backed voles invade in great numbers, searching for seeds. Insect-eaters such as shrews head for decaying limbs and stumps, where bark beetles and ants abound. Hazels produce nuts with beak-shaped or frilly husks that are a favorite treat for chipmunks, bears, and squirrels. White-tailed deer, snowshoe hare, and moose browse hazel twigs, and ruffed grouse eat the catkins. Aspens are a staple of these same species, and can become both food and building material to the industrious beaver. Flowering shrubs such as dogwoods attract delectable insects with their blossoms. These later yield berries that are popular with songbirds and grouse.

More than 100 species of birds and mammals are known to feed on brambles (e.g., red raspberries,

WELCOME GUESTS
In addition to being fruitful for wildlife, openings are also beneficial to the forest itself. The birds that flock to openings are helpful, for instance, in keeping populations of plant-eating insects at a manageable level. This "peace-keeping" force is but one of the many free benefits that come from a sunny opening.

blackberries), making these shrubs (*Rubus* spp.) the major providers of wildlife food in eastern North America. Fruits provided by chokecherry, pin cherry, and blueberry are also at the top of wildlife's summer menu. The berry-eaters "return the favor" by carrying the seeds they swallow to other places and "planting" them along with their droppings.

Much of the appeal for wildlife is that these foods can be gathered in relative safety. If trees have been toppled by wind, floods, insects, or disease, the landscape is a rough jumble of decaying trunks and branches. As shrubs grow up around these ruins, they provide not only food but also shielded nest sites, nest-building materials, a wind-screen, cool shade, enriched soils, and flowers that attract insects.

Patchy shrub-sapling openings have the openness that aerial hunters need, along with the scattered cover that makes travel safe for shy birds or scrambling rodents. When a snag remains, the opening becomes prime real estate for perching birds and cavity nesters. The fact that openings always come with edges makes them even more attractive to wildlife such as broad-winged hawks that use both forests and openings.

Wildlife Action

Get into the thick of things. Wear pants and a long-sleeved shirt to pick your way through thorny thickets. Get down on the ground and search for runways in the grass, burrowed ridges, rodent-chewed twigs, and camouflaged nests. Sit in the tangle of opulent berry brambles and wait for songbirds, small mammals, or even bears coming in to feed. Old stumps are another good place to search for ant-eating flickers, the dens of weasels, or scent stations of foxes. Deer may come like clockwork to browse at dawn or dusk. Watch for hares on their hind legs, reaching for a tempting fruit. Look above for circling birds of prey and below for broods of ruffed grouse and American woodcock. Look near rotting logs to find snakes and salamanders, and watch your footing for toads.

AMPLE HARVEST
A study in Texas found that plants growing in openings produced 7 times more twig growth and 32 times more fruit than the same species growing under the shade of a forest canopy. No wonder wildlife like it here!

AMERICAN GOLDFINCH

At sunset, you may be lucky enough to see a flock of goldfinches swirling into the branches of a tree roost like a bright yellow banner. These colorful birds spend most of the year (except the breeding season) feeding and traveling in flocks of 10 to several hundred birds. You can recognize them by their undulating, bouncing-ball flight, and by the way the flock moves from feeding site to feeding site. They "leapfrog" along, the birds in the back flying over the leading birds again and again.

In the springtime, while other birds are straining to feed hungry nestlings, goldfinches seem to be just enjoying the season. Their parenting responsibilities won't begin until later in the summer, when their favorite nest-building material—thistle down—becomes available. The silky down parachutes that burst from thistle seed husks are used to line the goldfinch nests. The female shapes this lining with her breast, and weaves it tightly with her bill and feet—so tightly, in fact, that the nest will hold water! As a finishing touch, she rolls a caterpillar cocoon over the outside of the nest to form a webby binding. Once the eggs are laid, she rarely leaves the nest, depending on the male to bring most of her food.

One of the advantages of nesting so late is that full-sized leaves are available to shield the nest from predators' eyes. Also, many weeds have gone to seed by that time, providing the main entree for goldfinches.

*American
goldfinch.*

Right before nesting, goldfinches gather in groups of a dozen or more for a "festival" of song that seems to be associated with pairing. Once they are paired, the flocks break up and males will begin to fly courtship displays over their mates and over potential nesting areas. One of the two courtship flights is a deep, roller-coaster flight performed while singing and circling 50 to 80 feet above the female. The other is a flat flight in which the male flies with slow, deep wingbeats, ending in an explosive call.

Look for American goldfinches: near thistles, on the ground, in low shrubs, or hanging on the seedheads of weeds. Sometimes 2 or 3 goldfinches will alight on a stalk and bend it under them with their weight, riding it to the ground and stripping it of its seeds. Also look for circling courtship flights. When they first arrive in spring, flocks visit American elms for their seeds, then move to common dandelions in June, and later, feast on seeds of bachelor's-button and common evening-primrose. They also dine on insects and buds.

Look for nests: in a fork formed by 3 or 4 upright branches, or on a horizontal limb, typically 4 to 40 feet up in a shrub or tree. Late in the summer, watch for the male circling overhead. When the female calls to him, he will drop down to feed her, and you will find the nest. Its inside diameter is only 2 inches, and the rim is usually whitewashed with droppings because the young hang over the nest to defecate.

Listen for: "per-chic-o-ree, per-chic-o-ree." In the fall, they repeat a call over and over that sounds like weeping. The young follow their parents in the air at this time calling "chipee, chipee."

RUFOUS-SIDED TOWHEE

Ahead of you on the trail is a loud rustling, as if a circus of squirrels is performing in the leaves. When you reach the sound, you may be amazed to find that this is a one-bird show. Rufous-sided towhees search for insects, seeds, berries, and acorns by stirring up leaves and scattering debris with their feet and bills.

Rufous-sided towhee.

If you get too close, a towhee will explode out of the shrubbery with a flourish, and land in cover away from you. If it is a female returning to her ground nest, she will never fly to the nest directly, for fear that you will follow her. Instead, she'll land at least a foot away and then creep towards the nest under cover of the tangles. If you happen to get too close, the rusty, brown-headed towhee will stand her ground and fan her tail as if to hide her nest. If all else fails, she'll limp away, seemingly injured, to divert your attention.

Look for rufous-sided towhees: kick-foraging on

208

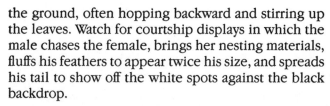

the ground, often hopping backward and stirring up the leaves. Watch for courtship displays in which the male chases the female, brings her nesting materials, fluffs his feathers to appear twice his size, and spreads his tail to show off the white spots against the black backdrop.

Look for nests: in a slight depression so that the rim of the nest is flush with the ground. The nests may also be built up to 5 feet from the ground in a brushy tangle.

Listen for: "drink-your-teeeea, drink-your-teeeea" or its namesake call "tow-hee" (sounds like the proverbial "tweet"), which is used to express alarm or to maintain contact between two mates. To find feeding towhees, listen for rustling in the leaves.

GRAY CATBIRD

True to its name, the catbird seems to have a natural curiosity. If any type of bird in its area sounds a distress call, the catbird is usually the first to investigate. As it rushes to the scene, it stirs up all the other birds in the area as well.

Also like a cat, the catbird may sing at night, especially between midnight and dawn. It not only sings its own songs (never repeated twice), but can also imitate most birds in the neighborhood. Interspersed in this jumble of bird songs you'll hear the catbird's convincing "mew" for which it is named.

Gray catbird.

Look for gray catbirds: feeding on fruit-bearing shrubs or kicking aside leaf litter on the ground in search of insects. They are especially fond of forest edges, and are ravenous feeders when there is an insect outbreak. Look for the male on a low perch, singing with tail and body held low. During the amorous days of courtship, the male will strut around with wings outstretched and plumage raised to show his chestnut patches underneath. Try luring an inquisitive catbird out by imitating its mewing sound.

Look for nests: well-hidden in low, dense thickets; small, bushy trees; or tangles of vines, typically 5 feet up. The nest is so deeply cupped that all you'll see of the incubating female is her perpendicular tail and head thrown back. Favorite nesting bushes include hawthorn, wild grape vines, and multiflora rose. They often choose a site that is shaded by a layer of leafy branches 10–30 feet above the nest.

Listen for: a catlike mewing, or a potpourri of imitations of other bird songs, sung during the day and sometimes at night. The catbird, unlike its relative the brown thrasher, doesn't repeat its own song phrases. If you listen carefully, you'll hear the catbird inadvertently give clues as to where its nest is hidden. If you are near the nest, it will mew, but when you are next to the nest, it will become more secretive and give a short, throaty "kwut, kwut, kwut."

SONG SPARROW

Song sparrows are aptly named. From early spring through the dog days of summer, in the noon heat and in the darkness of night, these sparrows pour out their message in song. The males typically have 8–10 distinctly different songs, with up to 200 variations for each song. During a typical performance, the sparrow will vary a song 6 or 8 different ways, then move to a second tune, with all its variations, then continue with a third and so on. An entire sequence, without repetitions, can take several hours.

Females are apparently impressed by this virtuosity; they show a preference for males with many songs. Among themselves, males use song to distinguish neighbors (which are tolerated as long as they stay in their territories) from intruders. In order to recognize its neighbors (up to 7 of them at a time), a song sparrow must become familiar with as many as 70 songs—quite a feat of memory! If an unfamiliar bird enters its area, a sparrow will challenge it by fluffing its feathers, raising one or both wings, and singing, often for more than an hour. If the intruder flees, it is probably a male. If it stays and calls "eee, eee," it is a female, and the pair will probably mate.

When shopping for the ideal habitat, sparrows look for water which they can drink and bathe in. In lieu of ponds or puddles, song sparrows will improvise

Song sparrow.

by splashing up moisture from wet leaves and grass. They prefer low, wet areas, with plenty of sunlight and elevated perches for singing.

Look for song sparrows: in grassy weed patches or shrubby growth, feeding on insects, weed seeds, and fruits. The male sings from a perch and is never far from his ½–1½-acre territory. Watch for swooping flights during which the male will "buzz" the female, singing loudly as he passes. Young can be easily spotted when they first learn to fly because they follow their parents in the air, fluttering their wings and begging for food.

Look for nests: on the ground or up to 4 feet up in barberry, eastern redcedar, speckled alder, Canada yew, or other shrubs. Song sparrows may produce two broods of young a season, building the first nest on the ground and subsequent nests higher up as cover vegetation grows. Multiflora rose and red raspberry are favorite nesting sites.

Listen for: their basic song, which sounds like "Madge, Madge, Madge, put on your tea kettle, ettle, ettle," repeated as many as 300 times an hour, day or night.

BROWN THRASHER

The name "thrasher" may refer to the way this bird rummages in the leaf litter with its long, curved bill, thrashing leaves this way and that. Or it may allude to the way it thrashes large insects against a branch or a rock before eating them. Or perhaps it's the way it thrashes soil-choked roots against the ground to clean them for nest lining. Its real notoriety lies not in thrashing however, but in singing.

Brown thrasher.

With its lusty, powerful voice, this "mockingbird of the north" endlessly improvises and mimics other bird's songs. It is an accomplished singer in its own right, however, and more of a musician than its close relative the catbird. You can get a sense of where a brown thrasher's territory is by watching which perches it uses when it sings. It will move from perch to perch during the nesting season, drawing a fence of sound around its territory.

Look for brown thrashers: rummaging on the ground in dense, woody thickets for insects, berries, and acorns. The males sing from perches to attract mates and advertise territory. Look in the dust near roadways where thrashers often take dust baths.

Look for nests: on the ground under thickets or typically 2–7 feet up in shrubbery such as greenbrier, gooseberry, hawthorn, honey locust, wild plum, and barberry. Nests are 1 foot wide and layered with twigs, dead leaves, and soil-choked roots. The inner lining is made from roots that have been cleaned of soil. To find a thrasher nest, look for a pair that has been collecting nesting material and follow them.

Listen for: twice-repeated phrases along with mimicry of other birds' songs. Listen for a loud, smacking call signaling that an intruder, namely you, is in the area.

INDIGO BUNTING

The indigo bunting, named for its rich and changeable plumage, is actually black in color; it has no blue pigment. It is the diffraction of light through the structure of the feathers that causes the bird to appear a brilliant tropical blue, and in other lights, to look green.

This bunting is best suited to an edge habitat, with brushy cover for nesting and nearby tall trees for singing. Clearings created by logging have opened up large new areas of habitat, and allowed the bunting to move farther north. The irrepressible bunting sings throughout the day, working its way from the bottom to the top of the tree until on the top, in full blazing sun, the male pours forth its song to would-be intruders and to females.

Look for indigo buntings: on branches, leaf surfaces, or bare soil, feeding on insects and weed seeds. The males typically sing from the top of tall trees. They are sometimes abundant near rivers and streams.

Indigo bunting.

212

Look for nests: in weeds, brambles, or in the fork of a shrub or low tree, typically 3 feet above the ground. The cup-shaped nests are· made of twigs, broadleaf forbs, grasses, and bark shreds.

Listen for: "zwee, zwee, zwee, zorry, zorry, tsu, tsu" with each phrase given first in high pitch then repeated in a lower pitch. Notes are widely spaced and leisurely.

ERMINE

"If this creature was as large as a cougar, nobody would dare venture out of doors," commented one Idaho biologist, referring to the weasel's reputation as "ounce for ounce and tooth for tooth, the fiercest and most efficient predator on earth."

Indeed, weasels are immensely well-suited to catching and killing prey. The ermine is long and thin, like "a furry snake with legs." This serpentine body is quick, agile, and able to follow its rodent prey down into narrow burrows and runways.

Despite its slender build, a weasel can overcome an animal twice its size and can outmanuever a snake. Quickly and lethally, a weasel wraps its tubular body around its victim, hugs it tightly with its forelegs, and, with its large canine teeth, bites at the base of the victim's neck or at the jugular vein. Its most notorious weapon is its spunk, which will prompt a weasel to take on an animal 30 times its size, especially if it's standing between the weasel and its dinner.

For the weasel, this aggressive, predatory nature is a survival tool, especially in cold weather. Because of its short fur and unusually long shape, a weasel loses a lot of body heat, and thus needs up to twice as much energy as other mammals of its size. In addition, the tubular weasel can't roll into a ball for warmth like other mammals. The best they can do is coil into a flattened disc.

To repay their energy costs, males need to consume almost half their own weight in meat every day. Females need two-thirds of their own weight in order to nurse 8–10 hungry pups for the 3 months before they can fend for themselves. Given these demands,

Ermine.

213

it's not surprising that males have evolved to be larger than females. The males can overpower prey that is too large for the females, while the females can enter burrows that are too small for the males. This way, they are not always competing for the same foods.

Ermine in its winter coat.

Ermines hunt mainly at night, usually traveling no more than 800 feet from their den, but covering up to 3½ miles in a zigzag search for prey. They investigate every crook and cranny, smelling and listening, while evading the larger four-footed carnivores and birds of prey that feed on them. Many of their enemies are too big to follow them down escape holes that weasels can fit into. If away from a burrow, they can also climb trees or swim to get away.

By the time snow is on the ground, the weasel has traded in its brown coat for a white one that blends perfectly with its surroundings. Only the tip of its tail is dark, and this too is a survival tool. Enemies can spot the dark tail tip from the air and will aim for it, often missing the well-camouflaged body. When spring comes, the white hair falls out and brown hair grows back in. This change is triggered by hormones that seem to respond to the lengthening daylight hours.

Look for ermines: bounding with back arched and extended, arched and extended, like a speeding inchworm through the underbrush. When its nose is bent to the track of some prey, the weasel can be oblivious, even to the prey itself doubling back beside it! Ermines nap in burrows, often lined with the bones of former occupants that were surprised and eaten in their den. Try squeaking or whistling to entice a hiding weasel to peek out and investigate.

Look for dens: in burrows, stumps, rock piles, or log piles, lined with the "trophies" of the hunt—bones, fur, feathers, or dried meat that the weasel stores for its next meal. They tend to layer their nests—fouling them, then layering with grasses, then fouling them again.

Look for tracks: less than 1 inch long, and not quite as wide. The longer hindprints are placed in or in front of the foreprints. A running ermine may show a 20-inch stride, but the normal gait is 12 inches.

Look for scat: long, slender, black or dark brown droppings on a prominent object such as a rock, stump, or log in the trail. The droppings are tapered at one end and may be segmented. Look for bits of bone or hair.

Look for pellets: of regurgitated fur.

Smell for: a skunk-like musk discharged at the slightest provocation, or to mark territory. Females release their scent to entice a male to mate with them.

Listen for: a characteristic, rapid "took-took-took," an enraged hiss, squeal, or shriek.

WHITE-TAILED DEER

Some frosty autumn morning, try moving as quietly as you can to a secluded spot with a good view of a small woodland opening. Carry with you the sawed-off antlers of a buck. When all is quiet, rattle the antlers against each other, imitating the sound of two bucks meshing their antlers in a fight over a doe. If you are lucky, you may prompt a real buck to come and investigate. (Don't overdo it, however. Luring the same deer several times is harassment.)

Before the arrival of the loggers, the northwoods were heavily timbered, broken here and there by fire-caused openings. White-tailed deer were here, but not in great numbers. As people opened up the forest and turned back the successional clock, deer thrived on the influx of young leaf-bearing saplings and bushes. Deer eat between 6 and 8 pounds of succulent leaves, twigs, buds, and bark per day in the summer. They'll also snack on grasses, forbs, mushrooms, and roots.

As long as the food supply was plentiful, adult deer had little to fear from their four-footed predators, thanks to their well-engineered bodies and cautious behavior. Deer's legs are long and agile, enabling them to bound 8 or more feet from a standstill and clear obstacles that their enemies can't. If need be,

RELAXING
OVER DINNER
The deer's habit of chewing its cud (they have 4-chambered stomachs like cows) may have developed as a precaution against predators. Cud-chewers can concentrate on gathering food quickly, and then retire to dense cover to rechew and digest it at their leisure.

deer can even swim to get away. When cornered, they can strike at predators with their sharp hooves.

Their eating habits also help to minimize their exposure to predators. When they are in the open, usually at dawn and dusk, they eat large quantities of food quickly, then get to cover as soon as possible. Here, they have the leisure to chew their cud, i.e., regurgitate the food into their mouth and chew it thoroughly.

Tiny fawns elude predators by being nearly odorless and covered with a coat that is dappled to help break and camouflage their solid outline. For further protection, mothers keep their two fawns in separate locations to reduce the chance of both being found by hungry carnivores.

Whitetails have also evolved adaptations to help them survive severe northwoods winters. After putting on a layer of fat in the fall, their metabolism slows down, allowing them to survive on a smaller amount of food. They grow a heavy winter coat formed of hollow hairs that, like vacuum bottles, have an insulating core of air. As their succulent summer and fall foods become scarce, they switch to a diet of woody twigs and white-cedar boughs.

When the snow depth approaches 16 inches, they move in groups to winter yards, usually to northern white-cedar swamps. In addition to dense cover (which reduces heat loss) and food, they find strength in numbers. Their activity in close quarters packs down a network of trails which, in turn, increases mobility. Because there are so many deer in one place, each individual has a smaller chance of being the one eaten, and the group has a better chance of confusing a predator. And, because other deer are watching for danger, they can spend more energy finding food and less on surveillance.

Its swift flight, deceptive camouflage, acute sense of smell and hearing, and uncanny ability to "dissolve" into the woods make the whitetail a challenge to human and non-human hunters alike. These qualities symbolize a creature that has adapted ingeniously to fit into its habitat.

Look for white-tailed deer: in shrubby feeding grounds at dawn and dusk. During the day look for them bedding in heavy stands of timber. They rarely venture into open grassy areas during the day, but you may find them there at dawn and dusk or at night. Deer frequent these areas, especially in the spring, to feast on the flush of early green growth. When a deer raises its tail to horizontal, it is probably about to bound, leaving with a goodby wave of its white tail. The flash of white may warn other deer of approaching danger.

In the winter: look in lowland, northern white-cedar swamps where packed-down trails and abundant tracks will be obvious. The ideal winter yards are those that are near shrubby or young aspen forests that provide some supplemental browsing.

Look for deer beds: a body-sized "dent" on the leafy forest floor, on high ridges, on south-facing slopes in the sun, or on packed snow. Look for nearby tracks, browsed twigs, or a pile of 20 to 30 small black droppings with one pointed end. In the summer, droppings are softer, like cowpies.

Look for tracks: on deer trails (worn-down runways) between bedding places, feeding openings, and sources of drinking water. Deer place their hind feet in or near the prints of their forefeet. Tracks are wedge-shaped and point in the direction of travel. When following tracks, be sure to glance behind you periodically. Deer that have spotted you will often circle back to where you have just walked to get a whiff of your scent.

Look for deer-bitten twigs: along regularly used deer trails. Sometimes after a severe winter, you can see a browse line along the bottom branches as high as a deer can reach. Deer leave a ragged cut on the bitten twig, whereas rabbits slice a clean 45-degree angle.

Look for antlers: shed from December to March. The number of spikes and the size of the antlers tells how healthy the buck was, but not necessarily how old it was. Experts can age a deer by checking the

THE SEARCH FOR SALT

Why do large browsing animals seek aquatic plants when they are starved for salt? The sodium count in aquatic plants may measure 10,000 parts per million, while salt in woody browse may be only 10 parts per million.

amount of wear on its teeth. Shed antlers are hard to find because they are calcium-rich and quickly eaten by mice and other small rodents.

Look for "scrapes": In the fall, deer's antlers become hard, their necks double in size, and they go looking for a mate. At this time they leave extensive messages in the form of scent-marked branches and scrapes—bare patches of ground that they have pawed up and urinated on. These bulletin boards are read by rival males and potential female mates. Look for scrapes below limbs that deer have already rubbed against or licked. A scrape is a good place to "rattle up" a buck.

Look for "bark rubs" and "velvet": In the late summer, the deer's antlers become hard and shed their layer of blood-rich velvet skin. This process must itch, because deer rub their antlers on the trunks of small trees and shrubs to help remove the velvet. Sometimes you can find frayed strips of dried velvet fluttering in the breeze near the worn-away bark of rubs. These rubs may also carry scent marks left by the enlarged scent glands on the buck's forehead.

Listen for: the snorting of a startled deer, or the bleating of a fawn.

White-tailed deer.

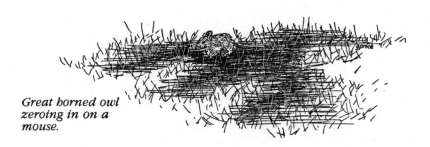

*Great horned owl
zeroing in on a
mouse.*

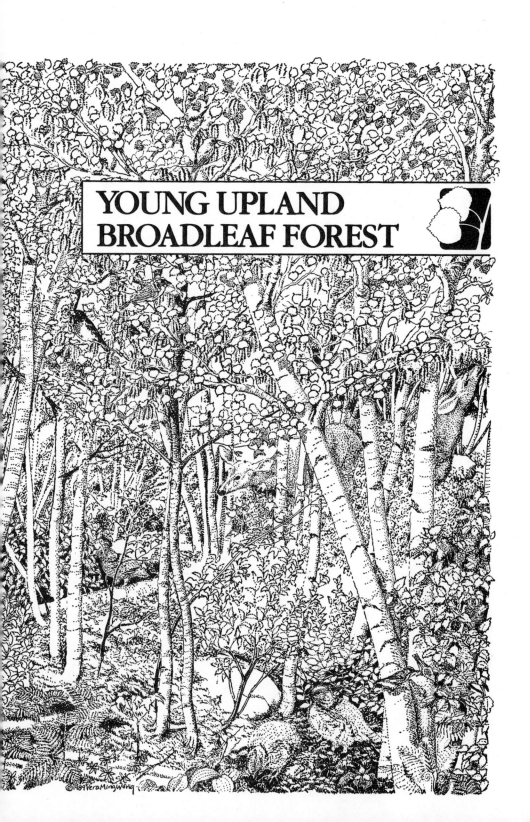

YOUNG UPLAND
BROADLEAF FOREST

©1989 Vera Ming Wong

A ruffed grouse, standing portrait still amid the tall, thin aspens, is nearly invisible. The trees are packed closely enough to discourage aerial predators, such as northern goshawks, from swooping in to take a look. But they are far enough apart to let a cautious doe step among them. The aging, rotting trees of a more mature forest are absent here, and the canopy is lower. These young trees are still in the throes of a struggle that began 12 or more years ago, when the first inhabitants sent their leaves up to the sun. Because of the keen competition, most of the trees you see today will not be here in another 30 years. Only the better positioned and healthier specimens will persist as this youthful forest passes into maturity.

What Is a Young Upland Broadleaf Forest?

A young upland broadleaf forest is 12 to 30 years old, with closely spaced, pole-sized trees from 10 to 30 or more feet tall. You'll find quaking and bigtooth aspens, paper birch, and pin cherry—sun-loving trees called "pioneers" because they colonized the land cleared by logging and fires. Beneath them grow shrubs and herbaceous plants that can exist in their shade.

1. American Redstart
2. Least Flycatcher
3. Chestnut-sided Warbler
4. Rose-breasted Grosbeak
5. Ruffed Grouse
6. White-tailed Deer
7. Paper Birch
8. Quaking Aspen
9. Red Maple
10. Chokecherry
11. Beaked Hazel
12. Bracken Fern
13. Bunchberry
14. Sweet-scented Bedstraw
15. Canada Mayflower
16. Largeleaf Aster

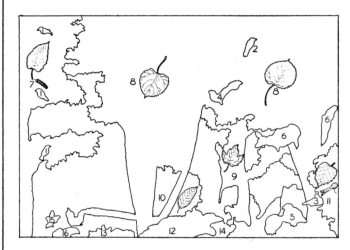

Origins

More than 100 centuries ago, when the glacier scraped the landscape bare and then retreated, the modern northwoods began. Since then, the starting whistle has blown again each time the forest has been cleared by wind, fire, chainsaws, or insects. Such was the case after the widespread logging and fires that transformed the landscape at the turn of the century. Today, aspen, birch, and other forest "pioneers" recolonize land that has been abandoned by farmers, logged, or otherwise cleared of vegetation.

Sugar maple, American beech, and American basswood are also broadleaf trees, but they, unlike the aspens, do not require full sun to get started. In the Lake States, these northern hardwood trees generally spend their early years under the shade of taller "nurse" trees instead of standing alone as young upland forests. The best examples of *stand-alone* broadleaf forests under 30 feet tall, therefore, are the aspen-birch type, which we will concentrate on here.

The Bright-Light Pioneers

Aspens are opportunists. Every 3–5 years, when they have bumper crops, they release their cotton-tufted seeds in such abundance that the seed flight resembles a snowstorm. These seeds are fragile, however, and very few of them encounter the conditions they need to germinate.

More commonly, aspens take over disturbed sites by sprouting from their roots, a process known as "suckering." Like the dandelions in your yard, each aspen tree that is cut down is capable of producing many more. Their roots radiate like spokes laying just under the soil surface. Every 6–9 inches, there is a group of tissues capable of sprouting when conditions are right. If, for instance, the original forest is removed and the soil is heated sufficiently by the sun, a bristling thicket of new aspens may shoot up. Because they are nourished by a large, established root system, they can grow 3 or 4 feet in just one season, easily outdistancing their competitors.

Paper birch is another efficient colonizer of disturbed land. This species sprouts prolifically from stumps, and can also develop from seeds. The lightweight seeds (1.5 million to the pound), with tiny wings on either side, are packaged to fly.

Pin cherry, also called fire cherry because of its habit of coming up after fires, often grows along with aspen and birch. The cherries it produces are a wildlife favorite.

Value to Wildlife

Young upland broadleaf forests are prime feeding grounds for browsing mammals. Deer and moose select tender saplings within reach and strip them of their leaves. (Deer prefer aspen suckers that are less than 1 year old.) Beavers, hares, and other mammals eat the bark, twigs, and leaves of aspens. Ruffed grouse consume aspen leaves as well as a variety of berries and seeds. The closely-packed trees also offer grouse a safe haven from sudden attack by goshawks or other avian predators.

Wildlife Action

In a young forest, much of the action revolves around the canopy and understory rather than the trunks, because the trees are not old enough to attract insect eaters and cavity nesters. Look in the leafy branches for songbird nests, and watch for birds and mammals nipping leaves and browsing twigs and buds. Don't forget the lower layers where berry pickers and seed eaters can be seen picking up food. Animals may use the trunks for rubbing their antlers (deer) or eating the bark (porcupines and beavers).

RUFFED GROUSE

The ruffed grouse is a bird of contradictions. For instance:

• It is called the king of game birds because of its elusive and wily getaways, yet at times, it seems tame enough to touch.

• The dignified ruffed grouse typically walks most

places, but, when startled, it can accelerate to 50 mph in almost no time.

- It is adept at swerving and maneuvering in the densest of aspen thickets, and yet in the "fall shuffle" (when the young move on to find their own territories), juvenile grouse are famous for smashing through windows in reckless flight.

Although frequently studied, the ruffed grouse has many mysteries that biologists haven't been able to explain. How, for instance, can the female grouse know which eggs to roll out of the nest after a week of brooding? Yet she does, and without fail, rolls out only those eggs that are infertile.

In this and many other ways, the ruffed grouse is a classic success story. Researchers have found that these birds will eat more than 600 different species of plants and half that many insects. They hunt for fruits, berries, mushrooms, acorns, and occasionally, even snakes and frogs. The reward for this flexibility is a dependable food supply, even when the branches are bare and the harshest winter snows have buried the forest floor.

Their bread-and-butter winter foods are the buds and catkins (male reproductive parts) of aspen. Aspen also meets the bird's need for cover at different stages of its life. In the shrub and sapling stage, aspen provides ideal hiding cover for hens and chicks. Young, pole-sized forests are perfect for winter and breeding cover because they're open enough to provide good visibility for the grouse, but dense enough to provide protection from predators. More mature stands of aspen are valued for winter food found at the tips of branches.

Anyone who has walked near a grouse in hiding knows about their explosive getaways. With the help of their powerful, rounded wings, they flush like a rocket straight up out of the brush, curving into an arc, and then slanting into even deeper brush a few dozen yards away. Photographers and hunters become hikers as the retreating bird goes farther into hiding. And if grouse are memorable for this aerial slalom, they are equally notorious for their drumming.

WHY DO ASPENS QUAKE?

According to an American Indian legend, aspen was the only tree that did not humble itself by bowing to the ground when the Great Spirit visited. As punishment for its arrogance, the aspen is now condemned to tremble each time the wind blows.

Of course, scientists have their own theory. They suspect that the trembling occurs because the stalk that attaches the leaf to the twig is flat rather than cylindrical. It tends to catch and spill the wind like a sail, thus causing the leaf to flutter.

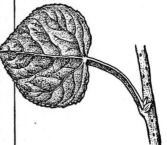

The male ruffed grouse chooses his drumming log carefully: usually a large, moss-covered log in a forest glade that is open enough for the grouse to see predators at his level, but with a ceiling of upper branches to shield him from aerial enemies. Often there are branches or old roots sticking up on one end of the log for extra protection. Once the ruffed grouse finds a log to his liking, he is likely to return to it spring after spring.

Early in the morning or evening, the grouse will climb up on the log, brace with his tail, and position his feet, looking much like a sprinter getting into starting chocks. He then spreads back his cupped wings and begins a few slow, powerful forward strokes. These strokes accelerate quickly until the grouse's beating wings become a blur of motion. Each outburst lasts for about 10 seconds, and is repeated every 5 minutes or so.

The muffled kettledrum sound you hear is actually a series of sonic booms created by air rushing in to fill the tiny vacuums created by these strokes! Some people have described it as distant thunder, or the dull throb of an engine. Indeed, the grouse must agree, because there are reports of grouse coming into farmer's fields to follow tractors that are making a drumming sound. Someone chopping wood with an axe may also attract a curious ruffed grouse.

The drumming display is both a challenge to competing males and an invitation to potential mates. When approached by another male, the grouse fans his tail like a turkey and stiffens his ruff (a feathery collar), nearly hiding his head. With red eyebrows bristled and wings dragging, he walks slowly and deliberately toward the intruder, wagging his lowered head faster and faster. Throughout the frenzy of head shaking, the grouse hisses in a beat similar to that of drumming. This usually discourages the rogue, and the victor returns to his log for more drumming. If the approaching grouse is female, the male will switch to a gentle mood that usually precedes mating.

Look for feeding ruffed grouse: on the forest floor or on logging roads, pecking and scratching like chickens. Ruffed grouse are more numerous in some years than in others. Every 10 years or so they decline in number, and then slowly rebuild over the next 10 years.

Look for nests: on the ground, in shallow, leafy depressions against the base of a stump, or under an overhanging branch, fallen log, or clump of bushes.

In the winter: look for signs of burrow roosts under the snow. Grouse dive in with wings folded, so there's not much sign of entrance. Eventually, their breathing will melt a small hole in the snow. When leaving, they burst straight up and into flight, and you can sometimes see wing marks from their take-off left in the snow. Also in the winter, you may see grouse by a roadside picking up grit that they use to digest their food. Grouse tracks will show the furry combs they grow on the sides of their toes to help float them over the snow. Try following these tracks.

Look for dusting depressions: an inch or more deep, in sand or ant mounds. Here, grouse spread dust on themselves, an action that may flush out parasites, or perhaps improve the insulating qualities of the birds' plumage by absorbing excess oil and moisture and fluffing up their feathers. Look for grouse feathers in the dust wallows.

Look for drumming logs: on upper slopes or ridges in the forest that are open at ground level, but have a ceiling of branches to shield the grouse from hawks and owls. You may find a pile of curved, grey-white droppings, 1–1¼ inches long, beside a log showing signs of wear. Look for matted-down moss and bare earth around the log where leaves have been fanned away by powerful wing strokes.

To flush a grouse: walk quietly toward likely grouse cover. The grouse will fly up and dive ahead into deeper cover. Make a lot of noise approaching this spot and then stand still. The grouse will be puzzled when the noise stops, and after a while, it will be unnerved enough to flush again to find refuge elsewhere.

Ruffed grouse.

a low throbbing or woofing sound lasting about 10 seconds, repeated every 5 minutes or so. The best time to listen is dawn to 7:30 a.m. and late afternoon and evening. To sneak up on a drumming grouse, move forward when the bird is drumming and can't hear your approach. Freeze during the silent intervals and move again when drumming starts.

LEAST FLYCATCHER

The smallest of our flycatchers utters its distinctive "che–BEC" call with a jerk of its head and a twitch of its tail. In courtship season, the male repeats this war call up to 60 times a minute as a territorial display. Challengers to his territory or mate must meet him in an airborne fight. The victor will chase off the interloper with a triumphant "che–BEC," thus warning other males that might have similar ideas.

Unlike other flycatchers that choose topmost branches for their lookouts, the least flycatcher typically haunts the open spaces in the lower one-third of the canopy. It hunts its prey from the wing, sallying out after insects it spots from its vantage point in the branches. With a click of its bill, it snaps up winged game that includes at least 67 kinds of beetles, as well as bees, wasps, and even dragonflies. Young, dense stands of broadleaf trees provide the cover it needs when stalking this low-level hunting ground.

Least flycatcher.

Look for least flycatchers: on the wing in the lower one-third of the canopy, or sitting upright in the lower branches watching for its next meal.

Look for nests: typically 7–35 feet up, compact and deeply cupped, wedged in an upright fork or crotch or firmly affixed to twigs rising from horizontal branches, often in a tall, spindly tree. An underpinning of spider webs holds the structure together.

Listen for: a loud, vigorous "che-BEC" repeated incessantly. Also listen for the clicking of the bill when the flycatcher snags an insect in mid-air.

AMERICAN REDSTART

In its South American wintering grounds, the redstart's brilliant dashes of red and orange have inspired the name "candelita," or "little torch." Whether in the act of hawking insects or on a display flight, the redstart's shoulders, wings, and tail do seem to light a flame in the leafy gloom of a dense young forest.

American redstart displaying.

Watch for this flash of color when the males perform their semicircular display flights, in which they stiffen their wings and stretch out their tail to show off their plumage. These flights are designed both to attract mates in springtime and to announce their territorial rights. Other birds that contest this right are often attacked, pecked, and driven out in startlingly short order.

Like the least flycatcher, the redstart also uses the lower one-third of the forest canopy for its nesting and feeding. Because it builds its nest in the branches of slender saplings, it is free of some of the enemies that plague ground nesters.

Look for American redstarts: in the lower story of dense, wet forests. Watch for their characteristic habit of dropping down suddenly to snap up an insect victim, then fanning their colorful tail from side to side. Their flight is airy and loose, like a leaf cradling in the wind. They are active feeders.

Look for nests: 4–30 feet up in upright crotches, forks, or clusters of twigs rising from a horizontal branch on a tree or shrub. Nests are well-made, deeply cupped, and felted. In the arduous act of building one of these nests, one observer watched a female redstart make nearly 700 trips.

Listen for: "chewy-chewy-chewy, chew, chew, chew."

ROSE-BREASTED GROSBEAK

The male rose-breasted grosbeak, with its rose-red patches on breast and underwings, is one of our most conspicuous birds in early May before the trees leaf out. Males are not only colorful at this time, but feisty as well, engaging in battles with competing males. Much of the warfare is waged on the wing and is accompanied by penetrating screams and a blizzard of flying feathers.

Once mated, the male settles down to share nesting responsibilities with the female. The parents take turns feeding the young, carefully crushing insects in their large beak and removing the hard-to-digest wing covers. This dual-parenting is somewhat unusual, given the attention-grabbing color of the male grosbeak. Many brightly colored birds avoid their own nests, for fear of attracting predators.

The grosbeak's diet is half seeds and fruits and half insects. Their specially formed jaws have two ridged, horny mounds that serve as "anvils" for cracking fruit pits and nuts.

Rose-breasted grosbeak.

Look for rose-breasted grosbeaks: at the edge between tall forest trees and dense high shrubs. The grosbeak uses all of the forest, floor to top canopy, for feeding, resting, and breeding. Look for them in all ages of broadleaf forests.

Look for nests: loosely woven, saucer-like, in a crotch, fork, or on a horizontal branch, typically 10–12 feet up.

Listen for: the metallic "clink" of their call note.

CHESTNUT-SIDED WARBLER

Although it is one of our most common birds today, the naturalists of the early 19th century rarely saw the chestnut-sided warbler. Audubon, in all his travels, saw only one. The subsequent clearing and abandoning of farmland, however, has created more of the young, open type of habitat which this warbler thrives in.

Like others in the wood warbler family, chestnut-sided warblers dine primarily on insects. They meticulously comb the entire canopy of small trees or shrubs in search of these leaf-eaters. Sometimes you will see them poised like hummingbirds to get at insects under a leaf or hopping along branches for

those on top. One observer reported a chestnut-sided warbler devouring 22 gypsy moths in only 14 minutes.

Look for chestnut-sided warblers: along edges of woodlands and feeding in low vegetation and trees under 35 feet. This warbler will sit concealed in the leaves and let you come close before it moves away, often to another nearby branch.

Look for nests: in a fork in a low bush, small sapling, or briar, usually 2–3 feet from the ground.

Listen for: "pleased/pleased/pleased to meet-cha," an emphatic song that sounds like a sentence.

Chestnut-sided warbler.

© 1989 Vera Ming Wong

MATURE UPLAND BROADLEAF FOREST

Maple-Beech-Birch Forest

There's no place like a broadleaf forest in the fall. Sunlight sifts through the rustling canopy and dapples the leaf-strewn forest floor. The leaves are aflame with reds, oranges, and yellows—pigments unmasked as the green chlorophyll fades away. The trees are shutting down for the winter while the wildlife are busy stuffing themselves for a southern flight or stocking up for the snowy days ahead. The rolling taps of woodpeckers and the excited "whirrrrrrr" of squirrels fills the air. The sharp snap of twigs and the rich, humic smell of decomposing leaves accompany you wherever you walk. Under the fallen leaves, and at the tips of the balding branches, the makings of spring growth lay waiting.

What Is a Mature Upland Broadleaf Forest?

The mature forest is more than 30 years old, with trees that are 30 or more feet in height. More than half of them are broadleaf trees, growing in a solid canopy that shades the cushion of leaves below your feet. Older trees are beginning to break down, letting sunlight into gaps. The understory may be lush or sparse, depending on the type of community you are in. The most common broadleaf communities in the northwoods are the aspen-birch community and the northern hardwoods (sugar maple dominated) type.

1. Red-eyed Vireo
2. Four-toed Salamander
3. Ovenbird
4. Scarlet Tanager
5. Pileated Woodpecker
6. Eastern Chipmunk
7. Pileated's nest hole
8. Broad-winged Hawk
9. Gray Fox
10. Spring Beauty
11. Violets
12. Large-flowered Trillium
13. Downy Solomon's Seal
14. White Baneberry
15. Sugar Maple
16. American Beech
17. Yellow Birch
18. Eastern Hophornbeam (Ironwood)
19. Red-berried Elder (Elderberry)
20. Striped Maple (Moosewood)

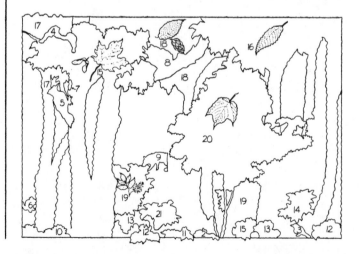

234

Origins

The complex, intricate world of the broadleaf forest
is something really new under the sun. The first woody
prototypes to raise their branches and sink their roots
into the earth looked like large ferns, and maintained
their green canopy throughout the year. Later,
needleleaf trees dressed the shores of the ancient
oceans, but they didn't drop all their leaves every year
either. It wasn't until much later that the first broadleaf, leaf-dropping tree came on the scene. This "deciduous" idea (from the Latin for cut or fall off) was
a daring concept. To drop all your leaves each fall
meant you'd have to invest a lot of energy to recreate
them come spring. As it turned out, this shedding-
and-leafing-out cycle was quite a successful formula.

By shutting down for the winter, these trees were
able to survive farther north than they ever had. Without their porous leaves, the trees were sealed and no
longer giving up water vapor to the air. Thus, when
cold winters held water captive in snow and ice, the
trees were able to survive the "drought." They benefited doubly when their fallen leaves began a second
career as a nutritious, moisture-holding mulch.

The energy in this mulch helps trees recreate themselves each year. Long before a deciduous tree drops
its leaves, it fashions a whole new set of miniaturized
leaves for next year. These lay curled in waxy buds
that are heavily fortified against cold, drying winter
winds. Come spring, these buds are ready to catapult
into growth, nourished by nutrients in the soil and a
storehouse of starches packed in the roots and in
horizontal "rays" in the trunk.

All in all, the deciduous idea was a good one, and
when the glacier melted from the northwoods less
than 10,000 years ago, there were plenty of leaf-dropping trees to the south, ready to spread northward.
They tended to concentrate where the glacier had
laid down the makings of deep, well-drained soils.
You are likely, for instance, to find broadleaf trees on
hills where the glacier deposited a great pile of silt
and rubble.

The broadleaf forest has expanded in the Lake States, thanks to a continual round of disturbances including fires, and of course, the ravages of logging at the turn of the century. Loggers sheared the great pines from the land, and subsequent fires left massive clearings. Here, second growth trees got their start; some were needleleaf trees such as jack pine, but most were pioneering, sun-loving broadleaf trees such as aspen and birch.

Aspen-Birch Forest

Before the northwoods were logged and settled, aspens covered a smaller area than they do today. Because of human intervention in the forest over the past century, the fortunes of quaking and bigtooth aspen, referred to as "popple" by many northwoods residents, have greatly improved. Mature aspen-birch stands now constitute roughly one-third of our northern forests. Manufacturers of forest products are scrambling to develop new technologies that can make use of this super-abundant wood resource before it is too late.

In fertile soils, aspen-birch stands mature quickly (50–60 years), and just as quickly, the aged trees begin to disintegrate. Their trunks become riddled with heartrot, and as their inner wood weakens, tree-hugging conks erupt on the bark. This aging forest, which is "decrepit" to a logger, is prime real estate for cavity-nesting wildlife. The best trunks are not available for long however, falling victim to the rasps of wood-boring insects, the ambitious threads of fungi, and finally, to the shove of overwhelming winds. Once on the ground, the logs provide handy cover for many species.

In and among the downed logs, the future forest begins to form. Ironically, however, it is not another generation of aspen that is growing there. The sun-loving qualities that enable aspen to rapidly colonize disturbed sites limit their ability to persist in the long-run. Aspen seedlings can't get started in their parents' shade. Instead, shade-tolerant trees such as balsam fir and white spruce or sugar maple, American basswood, and American beech grow slowly under the

SUN AND
SHADE
LEAVES
A plant's leaves—its solar collectors—are shaped or positioned differently, depending on where they are in the canopy. Those that grow in the shady understory present their leaves to the sun in a single, non-overlapping layer. Their leaves tend to be thin but large, thus maximizing the amount of sun-trapping surface area. Trees in the overstory may have two kinds of leaves in their upper and lower canopy. Leaves in the sunlit tops tilt like louvers to escape the full heating and drying effects of the sun. The leaves below are facing up to receive the sun that filters through. A single large
continued on next page

236

aspens and birch. If no disturbances reopen the canopy, these trees may eventually outlive the aspens and birches, and, in effect, take over the stand.

Maple-Beech-Birch Forest

Young sugar maple seedlings can remain nestled on the floor of a mature aspen-birch forest for years, growing slowly until a windstorm or the death of an old tree creates a gap in the canopy above. The sudden, available light triggers several years of rapid growth. Sapling maples lean into the gap and stretch their branches toward the sky, refilling the void in the canopy with green maple leaves.

Once established, a maple forest may dominate a site for hundreds of years. The shady, moist conditions created under mature trees encourage the growth and reproduction of yet more maples. An individual tree may live as long as 400 years, producing many large crops of winged fruits. Spiralling to the ground at the same time as leaf-fall, the seeds in the maple "keys" become partially buried in the accumulating litter. This litter is built up by a yearly leaf fall that can average 2 tons per acre. These leaves drop to the ground still highly enriched with minerals. Nourished in this fertile blanket, thousands of maple seedlings may carpet the ground. When a break in the canopy occurs (e.g., when a tree falls), these seedlings will shoot up to fill the gap.

Sugar maple is the common denominator in the northern hardwood forests of our region; the accompanying species change as you travel east to west or north to south through the region. For instance, American basswood is abundant in Minnesota, but decreases to the east. Yellow birch is most plentiful in northern Wisconsin and in Michigan's Upper Peninsula, but occurs less frequently elsewhere. American beech and eastern hemlock, common in the Lower Peninsula of Michigan, both disappear from forests as you travel westward through Wisconsin into Minnesota. Some of these differences are caused by variations in climate and geology. In other cases, it may be that the migration after the glacier is still occurring, and some species have not made it west yet.

broadleaf tree can have as many as 6 million of these tilting, micro-adjusting leaves. Trees accomplish this fine tuning with the help of growth compounds called auxins. Auxins cause tissues to grow on the shaded side of the stalk so that the leaf actually bends toward the light. (Think of how houseplants on your windowsill behave.) When one side is "done," auxins switch to the other side so that growth flips the leaf around.

237

*Millions of maple
keys "helicopter" to
the ground at the
same time as leaf
fall. Nourished by
the blanket of de-
caying leaves, the
seeds will produce
as many as 4,000
seedlings per tree.
Look for islands of
these small maple
seedlings rising like
domes from sunny
gaps in the forest.
The seedlings near-
est the center will
be tallest, tapering
off at the edges
where the oppres-
sive shade once
again darkens their
chances for growth.*

Value to Wildlife

This forest is as multi-layered as an onion, with wild-life species populating each and every vertical layer. From the moist burrows of red-backed voles to the sunny treetops of the warblers, this diverse habitat harbors a great zoo of wildlife species.

In dense forests, prey species such as grouse and voles find good cover from the eyes of aerial preda-tors. Nocturnal animals, such as bobcat and fox, bed down in the underbrush during the day, sleeping near the nests of ground-dwelling species such as oven-birds. Moisture-loving insects, amphibians, and rep-tiles lurk among the leaves and fallen logs. For pred-ators with keen hearing, such as great horned owls, the top layer of dry leaves magnifies every sound and helps them locate their next meal. Other foods in-clude the succulent herbs of spring (in sun-filled gaps), the seeds, berries, acorns, and beechnuts of autumn, and the tree trunks full of overwintering insects.

Aged trees and those with disease or injury are often pocked with natural cavities. Because of the wood strength of hardwoods such as maple, these old snags may remain standing for years, providing room and board for woodpeckers and nest sites for flying squir-rels, owls, wood ducks, raccoons, nuthatches, and other tree-dwellers.

Wildlife Action
Aspen-Birch Forest

Check the light-filled treetops for red-eyed vireos and migrating warblers. You can usually find them by lis-tening for their often-repeated songs. Scan the white, peeling bark of birches and the smooth, greenish or gray-white trunks of aspen for bark-gleaners like the hairy woodpecker. Keep an eye out for sudden move-ments in the open spaces just below the canopy, places where flycatchers forage and hawks patrol. Dead and downed trees offer cover for many small mammals, reptiles, and amphibians. During the win-ter months, search trees for porcupines, which oc-casionally doze as well as feed on branches in the bare canopy.

Aspen-Birch Forest

©1989 Vera Ming Wong

Maple-Beech-Birch Forest

Wildlife is plentiful and often easily seen in maple-beech-birch forests. Watch for songbirds flitting through the dense, multi-layered canopy. Look in the forked branches for leaf nests of squirrels or the stick structures of hawks. Hollows in large trees may shelter owls or pileated woodpeckers. Look for excavated chips, pellets, whitewash, or bits of down around the base of large nest trees.

Listen for the tell-tale rustle of dry leaves, then find the squirrel, chipmunk, or sparrow responsible. A snapping twig in the underbrush might also signal a fleeing deer or an approaching fox.

OVENBIRD

Next time you are in a hardwood forest, try sitting quietly on a log. Before long, a resident ovenbird is likely to poke out of the brush to investigate. It will come daintily forward on pink legs, putting forth its head with each step like a miniature chicken. If you come too close to the ovenbird's domed nest, a panicky female is likely to limp ahead of you, dragging a bogus broken wing to distract you from her eggs. This ruse is a matter of survival for ground-nesting birds such as the ovenbird that are vulnerable to four-footed predators. Despite their efforts, many oven-

1. *Blue-spotted Salamander*
2. *Least Flycatcher*
3. *Downy Woodpecker*
4. *Yellow-bellied Sapsucker*
5. *Ruffed Grouse*
6. *Long-tailed Weasel*
7. *Snowshoe Hare*
8. *Sweet-scented Bedstraw*
9. *Bunchberry*
10. *Sweet-fern*
11. *Wild Sarsaparilla*
12. *Quaking Aspen*
13. *Paper Birch*
14. *Balsam Fir*

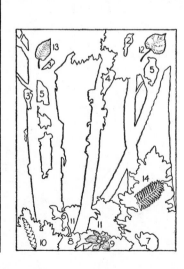

birds will lose their first brood of young to a woodland enemy.

Because they prefer to nest deep in the interior of forests, ovenbirds do best where there are large, uninterrupted tracts. If forests are too fragmented, predators or nest parasites that roam the edges may have ready access to the ovenbird's nest.

Look for ovenbirds: poking about on the ground, turning leaves over in their search for snails, slugs, earthworms, caterpillars, and spiders. They may also be perched in a low branch to sing and observe. They need densely canopied, mature forests. Try imitating their call or squeaking like a wounded bird to draw three or four curious ovenbirds.

Look for nests: of domed leaves that look like miniature dutch ovens. They are on the ground in openings, but are extremely well-concealed beneath a mound of leaves. The female is such a close nest sitter that you may nearly step on a nest before she'll leave.

Ovenbird.

Listen for: a loud staccato "teacher" repeated 5 to 15 times in the afternoon or at nightfall. Ovenbirds deliver a pleasing jumble of notes while flying, followed by the characteristic "teacher." Like the voice of a ventriloquist, the ovenbird's voice is hard to place. To locate the bird, walk past the sound and then return to it.

BROAD-WINGED HAWK

Broad-winged hawks are best known for their spectacular migrations along the Atlantic Coast and the Mississippi River. The hawks travel together in loose flocks that look like undulating streamers in the skies. Hesitant to cross the Great Lakes, these flocks skirt along the shorelines, congregating at geographical "bottlenecks" like Hawk Ridge in Duluth, Minnesota. Here, binoculared birders can watch tens of thousands of broadwings pass overhead in a single day.

To conserve energy on their trek to South America, broadwings employ a unique form of transit that takes

241

advantage of the natural currents of wind and temperature. With wings outstretched, these living sailplanes circle upward in a rising column of warm air called a thermal. Once they have reached a height where the air starts to cool, they begin a long diagonal glide downward, as if on a giant sliding board, to the base of the next thermal, which may be miles away. Thermal to thermal they go, covering great distances with little energy. Groups of hawks circling in a thermal are called "kettles." These kettles can sail high into the atmosphere until, from the ground, they look like a swarm of bees.

Until recently, shooting these elegant aerial acrobats from points like Hawk Ridge was a popular fall pastime, a way to dispose of so-called "varmints." Now hawks are protected by law and stopover spots are sanctuaries rather than shooting galleries.

Broadwings feed on small mammals, snakes, frogs, etc. Thanks to their phenomenal eyesight (8 times better than ours) they can screen and recognize distant objects in great detail. Broadwings typically hunt from perches, waiting silently for the least movement. When something stirs on the forest floor, the hawk will twitch its tail, cat-like, and begin to sway excitedly back and forth on the branch. At precisely the right moment, it will drop on its unsuspecting prey, talons out and wings folded for speed. It will return to the perch with its meal, skinning it before eating.

Look for broad-winged hawks: alongside highways or old unused forest roads, perched one-third of the way down from the top of the tree. Also look for hawks wheeling above the treetops of extensive, shady broadleaf or mixed forests. They are rarely found in open country, in pure needleleaf forests, or near human dwellings.

Broad-winged hawk.

Look for nests: in the crotch of a large tree, next to the trunk, typically 24–40 feet up. These loosely built, stick-and-twig platforms are 14–21 inches in diameter, often the repaired remains of a hawk, crow, or squirrel nest. Hawks are secretive during breeding so you may have to follow the sound of a parenting bird or a crying nestling. Watch as the female brings bits of greenery to the nest, perhaps to cover food scraps or droppings that litter the nest.

In September: look for flocks of migrating hawks, especially after a cold spell and when the winds are from the south or northwest. Peak viewing around the Great Lakes is in mid-September. See the "Hotspots" section on page 347 for the best viewing opportunities in your area. After good flight days, look in the branches for stragglers that are taking a night off.

Listen for: an ear-piercing alarm whistle that sounds like branches creaking in the wind. Also described as a wrong-way screech of chalk on a blackboard. A scuffle on the forest floor may be a broad-winged hawk pouncing on its next meal.

RED-EYED VIREO

This plain-clothes vireo makes up for what it lacks in color with a persistent and enthusiastic song. Even in the heat of a summer's day, when all other birds are laying low, or when its mouth is crammed with caterpillars, the vireo sings, for a daily total, according to one patient observer, of 22,197 outbursts!

Red-eyed vireo.

They have been called "preacher birds" because their lilting phrases sound like a preacher asking a question, pausing for the congregation to answer, and asking a question again. The male and the female seem to be listening to one another constantly. If the male stops singing, the female will leave the nest and fly to him. He may feed her, and she'll return to the nest when he begins to sing again.

His performances are often punctuated by time-outs for insect snacks. Vireos glean the branches and leaves tirelessly, looking for caterpillars, moths, beetles, wasps, bees, and ants. They are well-hidden in their drab olive plumage, and aptly equipped with a somewhat heavy, slightly crooked beak to capture and hold their prey. Just before fall migration, their diet changes to take advantage of the ripening crop of berries and fruits.

Look for red-eyed vireos: at the outer edges of the

uppermost canopy, gleaning insects from the under-sides of leaves. They prefer forests where there is a continuous canopy and a thick undergrowth of sap-lings. Vireos glide rather than hop from branch to branch.

Look for nests: 2–60 feet up (typically 5–10), often in a tall shrub or small tree, suspended in a V-fork of a horizontal limb, towards the outer edges of the canopy. The miniature basket of woven bark fibers is strengthened with bits of bark and paper wasp nests. After wrapping the basket with cobwebs, the vireo camouflages it with lichen and sews it to the tree with the silk of cocoons, where it may last for years. Female vireos are close nest-sitters.

Listen for: a constant song with a rising inflection at the end of each phrase. Sounds something like "You-see-it—you-know-it—do you hear me? Do you believe it?"

SCARLET TANAGER

Thoreau called the scarlet tanager "a surprisingly red bird, a small morsel of Brazil." Indeed this tan-ager seems attired for the tropics, but when motion-less in the uppermost canopies of our hardwood for-ests, it blends in perfectly with the shifting lights and shadows of the leafy woods.

Though we may pass the "firebird" by, female tan-agers undoubtedly take note, responding to the male's wing-spread display with a whistle. At the end of the summer, when its breeding plumage has served its function, the male will molt, turning in his firey reds for a yellow-green coat that will blend with the jun-gles of his tropical wintering grounds.

Scarlet tanager.

The scarlet tanager's appetite for caterpillars, wood-boring beetles, oak-leaf rollers, and moths has earned it the name "guardian of the oaks." One observer watched a scarlet tanager finish off 600 small gypsy moth caterpillars in less than 15 minutes!

Look for scarlet tanagers: on the outer tips of the topmost branches, or on dead, bare tree limbs. After a soaking spring rain, look for tanagers poking around

244

on the forest floor for insects that may have washed off leaf surfaces. They also feast occasionally on soft fruits in shrubs.

Look for nests: well out from the trunk on a horizontal branch, typically 20–35 feet up. usually shaded from the eyes of hawks above but open to the ground below. The shallow nest of twigs is so loosely built that you can often see the eggs right through the bottom.

In the spring: migrating tanagers will often return to the same grove of trees each year, filling the branches with dazzling color.

Listen for: a loud, bright warble undercut with harsh humming notes. Its call note is a nasal "chip-churr" similar to the robin's. Tanagers are true ventriloquists; it helps to walk past the sound, then return to locate them.

PILEATED WOODPECKER

Most people who see these firey-headed "logcocks" don't soon forget them. Pileateds are as large as crows and have wings that span up to 30 inches. They are the straightest flying of the woodpeckers, gliding soundlessly from trunk to trunk on ebony wings lined with a flash of pure white. Leading the way is a powerful, spearlike bill surrounded by a crest of gleaming scarlet.

With this bill, pileateds carve great rough-hewn rectangular holes into tree trunks. As they work, they shower the ground beneath them with chips as large as a human hand. To withstand all this pounding, the pileated's brain is encased in air, and its skull is heavily fortified. The whole operation is powered and stabilized by massive neck muscles. After breaking through solid wood, the pileated feasts on the ants, grubs, and other insects living in the softer, decayed wood inside the trunk. They also use their bill to rip sheets of bark off dead trees in search of beetle larvae, which they lap up with their sticky, fringed tongue. By breaking up these trees, pileateds hasten their decay and their eventual return to the soil.

Pileated woodpecker.

245

Pileateds are great ant eaters; one naturalist found 2,600 ants in a single stomach! By listening carefully, pileateds can "hear" which trees are infected by black carpenter ants that infiltrate a tree from its base and penetrate upward, eventually killing the tree. Somehow, pileateds can locate the colonies even in winter when the ants are dormant and motionless.

Each year, with rare exceptions, pileateds carve new cavity nests. Their old ones are then available for other hole nesters such as owls, squirrels, and wood ducks. Other insect eaters profit from their work as well, feeding at holes that their weaker bills could not have made.

Instead of singing to announce its territory or attract a mate, the pileated drums on the tree trunk, tapping out a rolling tatoo that is a sound signature of this species.

Look for pileated woodpeckers: in extensive, dense forests, especially where storms or insect attacks have killed trees. Look for them on large-diameter trunks, or occasionally on the ground pecking at fruits or routing ant hills. Their winter staple is carpenter ants in trees that have heartrot. Despite its size, the pileated is evasive and difficult to spot without careful stalking.

Look for oval nest holes: 3 or 4 inches wide, typically 45 feet up in a large-diameter (14+ inches) trunk or limb, usually dead, often near water. Nest trees that have been used year after year will be honeycombed with holes.

Listen for: an accelerating, rolling tapping on the trunk, repeated often. Pileateds will often "sign off" before roosting for the night. Also listen for flicker-like "whucker whucker whucker" calls, and a bugle call to greet the dawn. The sounds of excavation can be heard more than ½ mile away on a calm day.

GRAY FOX

Gray foxes are the only dogs that will regularly climb trees, thanks to sharp, curved claws that help them grab hold with their forepaws, then boost themselves up with their hind paws. Once aloft, they may wait on a limb overhanging a travel lane to ambush prey that pass underneath. Or they may help themselves to eggs, nestling birds, or squirrels that they find in the branches. Gray foxes also use trees to escape enemies, den in cavities, stand lookout, or to simply laze away a summer's day.

Gray fox.

On the ground, they follow their nose, zigzagging back and forth until they smell a potential meal. They prefer rabbits, mice, or voles, but they'll also go after northern bobwhites, grouse eggs, reptiles, plants, fruits, nuts, insects, and carrion. In times of plenty, gray foxes will stuff themselves to the limit, becoming very fat.

To communicate with one another, foxes leave urine or scat at "scent posts," usually next to prominent objects such as rocks, posts, or tree trunks. This may help in marking the extent of their territories.

The gray fox was originally a more southern species, but has expanded into the north in recent decades. Some authors speculate that this may be due to the increase in rabbit and rodent populations following the clearing of forests for agriculture. Others contend that the trend in converting abandoned farms to woodland has attributed to the fox's return.

Look for gray foxes: on brushy hillsides hunting at twilight, night, and occasionally during the day. They like to rest in dense thickets, or sun themselves on large rocks, limbs, or in the crotches of trees. When pursued, a gray fox will take to a tree or duck into an earthen burrow. When traveling, they often follow an open trail or an old road. Look for their grizzled gray coat and black-tipped tail. You can sometimes call them by squeaking like a mouse (kiss the back of your hand), a sound they can hear at 100 feet.

Look for dens: under rock ledges, in hollow logs or tree cavities, and occasionally in another animal's abandoned burrow. Several converging fox trails usually signal a den nearby. Look for well-worn trails used by the pups.

Look for tracks: in a single dotted line. The proverbial fox trot is a loping 3–4 mph, but when galloping in a rocking-horse gait for short bursts, a fox can manage 28 mph.

Look for droppings: left at "scent posts" or at communal fox "latrines" on the tops of rocks or in openings. Droppings look a little like a domestic dog's, only smaller, narrower, individually creased, and tapered at one end. Scats are often along trails or road edges.

Listen for: a hoarse, raspy bark repeated 4 or 5 times. Gray foxes also emit an assortment of whining growls, screams, and caterwauling, especially when fighting.

FOUR-TOED SALAMANDER

Along the water's edge, a drama is unfolding. Wriggling furiously and then stopping to gather strength before wriggling again is one of 50 four-toed salamander young hatching from their egg mass. They are dangling from exposed plant roots as high as 7 inches above the still pool below. After much effort to free itself from its siblings, the tiny salamander will plop into the water to spend the first 6 weeks of its life. Eventually, it will lose the gills it needs for water life and climb onto shore to begin life as a land-dwelling adult.

Chances are you won't find a four-toed salamander in a hardwood forest if there are no ponds, springs, or bogs about. Likewise, you won't find them near water unless a heavily shaded broadleaf forest is close at hand. Their breeding activities require water shaded by leafy branches.

The four-toed is the smallest salamander in the Lake States and our only land-dwelling one with less than five toes on each foot, hence the name. Their tails are compressed right where they join to the body and it is here that they break off so easily, just by pressing against something (like a predator's jaws, for instance). A frightened salamander will curl its tail over its body as if offering this piece in exchange for a clean getaway. Often the predator is left with just the wriggling tail, and thus distracted, seldom sees the escaping torso. The salamander will grow a tail back shortly.

Look for four-toed salamanders: near ponds, pools, or swamps within broadleaf forests. Look in sphagnum mats, beneath leaf litter, or around rotting logs. This tiny salamander, no more than 3 inches long, is also one of the most difficult to spot because of its secretive, nocturnal nature and its cryptic coloring. Finding one is a rare treat for amateur and specialist alike.

Look for eggs: hanging in a cluster from mosses at the water's edge, 2–7 inches above water. Communal nesting may occur, with as many as 1,000 eggs laid in one spot. Up to four females will stay with the eggs. If you are lucky enough to witness a hatch, you will see tiny, fully formed salamanders in their aquatic stage dropping to the water below. Eggs may also be laid among decayed leaves.

In the winter: they hibernate in the decaying roots of trees.

*Four-toed
salamander.*

YOUNG UPLAND NEEDLELEAF FOREST

©Vera Ming Wong 1989

The day is hot and still, a scorcher. The thrum of flying insects builds, peaks, and quiets as you approach the young jack pine stand. The densely crowded trees close their ranks to you. As you peer into the darkness beneath the scraggly canopy, you catch sight of quick wings opening, closing, then gliding onto another needled branch. Inside, the shaded air is several degrees cooler, and the sandy soil is covered by a bed of fragrant needles. You can hear, but not see, a small bird picking through the litter in search of insects. With precise, dignified steps, a spruce grouse leads a covey of young under a low-lying shrub.

What Is a Young Upland Needleleaf Forest?

A young upland needleleaf forest is 12–30 years old, densely populated with trees that are 10–30 feet tall. In places, the shade is so intense that shrubs and ground plants are sparse. More often, these areas will have a savanna look, with numerous small openings interrupting the tree coverage. Most young needleleaf forests you'll see, especially in sandy areas, will be jack pine combined with oak. You may also see stands of young red pine, white pine, white spruce, and balsam fir.

1. *Magnolia Warbler*
2. *Kirtland's Warbler*
3. *Wintergreen*
4. *Bush-honeysuckle*
5. *Trailing Arbutus*
6. *Ram's Head Orchid*
7. *Low Sweet Blueberry*
8. *Northern Pin Oak*
9. *Red Pine*
10. *Jack Pine*

Origins

How do upland needleleaf stands become established in nature? Here in the Lake States, eastern hemlocks, white pines, and balsam firs and white spruces grow up slowly under the protective shade of broadleaf forests. They bide their time and eventually dominate when the "nurse" forest begins to decay. Occasionally, however, needleleafs are the first invaders in an upland area. Red pines, for instance, will sometimes seed along thin-littered lakeshores or on a burned-over island where competition is light. Balsam fir and white spruce may also take over a cleared area, but only when soil and moisture conditions are just right. But for the most part, in uplands, young natural needleleaf stands are the exception rather than the rule.

Today, there is only one species of needleleaf that consistently takes over disturbed sites across all of our region: the jack pine. Jack pine's success is due to adaptation, tolerance, and its ability to have withstood and even profited from the firey aftermath of the logging era.

During that brief half century, 7 million acres of pines were shorn from the northwoods, leaving a layer of logging slash that stood hip deep in places. This duff burned mightily in post-logging fires, killing most of the red and white pine seeds. Jack pine, which keeps a portion of its seeds locked up in resin-sealed cones, was now in a position to succeed. The fire not only melted the resin and released the seeds, but also prepared the soil and opened up the canopy for the sun-loving jack pines. With few competitors to stop them, jack pine came in like "hairs on a dog's back." Today, jack pine is a major player in our Lake States forests, second only to aspens.

It's dominance is in danger, however, because of a different kind of human attention. With our modern means of fire control, devastating wildfires are quickly contained, and there are fewer acres of the fire-cleared seedbeds that jack pines prefer. All across our region, mature jack pine cones are sealed up tight, waiting for a fire that may never come. Instead, they may be replaced by other shade-tolerant trees that are now growing under their boughs. To repeat another generation, jack pines need the very thing that helped them become established in the first place—a hot fire.

To provide for species such as the Kirtland's warbler that depend on young jack pine stands for nesting, the Forest Service now sets controlled burns to encourage jack pine regeneration. In addition, many acres of young pines, especially red pines, are planted by various land management agencies.

Value to Wildlife

The young pine forest is a brief, transitional stage, and only a few species are actually adapted to make their homes in this in-between forest. Many of the animals that visit may actually prefer younger or older forests, but will spend time here as well.

In the densest sections of forest, they find cool shade, a few ground plants, and a variety of burrowing mammals, snakes, salamanders, and insects. The lack of sun prunes away the lower branches, and opens the interior. At the outer perimeter, where sun keeps the branches green all the way to the ground, birds find a safe travel corridor from forest floor to treetop.

In some areas, the young forest won't be so dense, and ground plants will receive more sun. Small openings may be sprinkled throughout, and these too have "curtains" of green at the edges. Black bears often feed in these openings and rest in the shady thickets.

In the winter, a young needleleaf stand provides protection from wind and snow, and may offer food for browsing birds and mammals.

Wildlife Action

Pay special attention to the perimeter of the forest and the edges of interior openings, where green branches extend all the way to the ground, providing a curtain of safe travel to the Kirtland's (in Michigan) and the magnolia warbler. Wildlife may be seen crossing the small clearings scattered throughout the stand. In the shady sections, watch for ground-nesting birds, burrowing rodents, toads, salamanders, and snakes. In the winter, look around edges and inside for browsing visitors such as snowshoe hares, spruce grouse, porcupines, moose, and white-tailed deer.

KIRTLAND'S WARBLER

Of all the species in this book, the Kirtland's warbler has by far the rarest habitat. Its requirements for breeding are stringent, and where these are not met, the Kirtland's song will not be heard. The breeding population of the endangered bird, censused each summer, has fluctuated little since the early 1970's, averaging 206 singing males. All of these have been limited to a 60-mile-wide area in Michigan's lower peninsula.

Kirtland's warbler.

Here, the Kirtland's finds the young jack pines (and some red pines) that it favors for nesting and insect hunting. In an ideal stand, the trees are 5.6 to 16.4 feet tall, the crowns are touching or nearly touching, and the soil is sandy and porous so that heavy rains drain quickly rather than flooding the Kirtlands' nests. Grasses, sedges, and blueberry bushes provide protection for the eggs, while low pine branches provide a safe place for the female to hunt insects.

Fires seem to create the habitat that Kirtland's prefer most. The intense heat pops open the jack pine cones and releases their seeds, while the fire clears away vegetation so that the seedlings have few competitors. Because these post-fire thickets are dense, they tend to appeal to Kirtland's more than those seeded in or replanted after logging.

Even the most ideal haven is a temporary one, however. When the trees grow taller, they lose their lower branches, and the vegetation beneath them may change. Unfortunately for the warbler, the fires that could begin the cycle again are routinely squelched by modern fire-fighting forces.

Another threat to the Kirtland's survival is the invasion of their nests by the brown-headed cowbird. The female cowbird does not build a nest of her own. Instead, she watches the Kirtland's warbler build its nest, and then, when the owner is away, she hurriedly lays her own eggs there. Even though the hatchling cowbirds are ten times the size of warbler chicks, the warbler feeds them as if they were her own.

Within 3 days, the cowbirds are as big as the mother warbler, and are demanding a staggering amount of food. In a nest with two or more of the larger birds, the smaller Kirtland's hatchling has no chance of surviving. Because cowbirds are relative newcomers to the northwoods since the Europeans settled, the invaded warblers have not yet developed defensive strategies.

To help protect and increase the numbers of Kirtland's warblers, nearly 133,000 acres have been set aside for Kirtland's warbler management in and around the Huron-Manistee National Forest. Timber harvests, controlled burning, and planting are used to maintain or create the young forests these warblers prefer. A U.S. Fish and Wildlife Service program to trap and kill cowbirds in the area has also been successful. Nests are now producing an average of 2.76 fledglings per nest, as against the 0.81 fledglings per nest produced before cowbirds were controlled.

Look for Kirtland's warblers: along the edges of young jack pine stands in Michigan. If you are interested in seeking out the Kirtland's warbler, contact the U.S. Fish and Wildlife Service in Grayling, Michigan, to find out about escorted trips at certain times of the year. Note: Kirtland's warblers are listed as an endangered species, and under the Endangered Species Act of 1973, it's a Federal crime to harass or kill them.

Listen for: a short, loud, persistent song with a clear, liquid quality. It can be heard up to ½ mile away.

MAGNOLIA WARBLER

This brilliantly colored, yellow-and-black-jacketed warbler is part of the wood warbler family, often called the butterflies of the bird world. You will understand why if you ever come across one of these bright wonders in the relative gloom of a dense woodland. They look like they have been painted onto the branches with an artist's brush.

The magnolia warbler's colors serve a reproductive

purpose first and foremost. The male's brilliant plumage combined with his virtuoso singing enables him to compete for the female's attention so that he can mate and ultimately pass on his genes to a new generation of warblers.

Spring is a time of great activity in warbler woods, as the birds return from their wintering ground in Mexico or Central America. High above the Gulf of Mexico, tropical storms and battering winds take their toll on the thousands of flocks.

Soon after the survivors arrive, the female chooses a site and begins to build a nest, with the male singing for all he's worth to defend their newly staked territory from invading birds. The pair becomes especially busy filling the gaping mouths of the new hatchlings. A pair in Maine was seen feeding its young a beakful of insects an average of once every 4 minutes! In addition to feeding, the pair will continually clean the nest, carrying fecal sacs away, and killing insects, such as biting ants, that attack the helpless chicks. It's a busy 12 days before the young are on their own.

The name magnolia comes from Alexander Wilson, the ornithologist who first sighted this migrator in magnolia trees in Mississippi. In the northwoods, you're likely to see it flitting about the lower branches of small needleleaf trees, where it gleans the bark, twigs, and leaves for spiders, caterpillars, plant-lice, and other insects. Some of the insects that it removes from the trees are ones that strip the leaves or damage the bark of the young pines.

Magnolia warbler.

Look for magnolia warblers: in the lower branches of small evergeens. As it moves, it often fans its tail so you can see its characteristic white band on a black background.

Look for nests: usually less than 15 feet from the ground. They are flimsy, loosely built affairs attached to the branch with a bit of spider webbing. Attention is given to the lining, which is made with fine black rootlets, grasses, and hair.

Listen for: "weeta-weeta-weeteo;" the male elaborates on this for his versatile mating song.

MATURE UPLAND NEEDLELEAF FOREST

©Vera Ming Wong 1987

White Spruce/Balsam Fir Forest

The shade, the evocative fragrance, and the hush make a cathedral of the towering pines. You enter, ease out of your backpack, and flop down on the mattress of needles. Just as your eyes begin to adjust to the shade, you feel something raining down from above: well-chewed parts of a pine cone! The tiny rainmaker (a red squirrel) suddenly broadcasts his displeasure at your choice of a daybed. He flicks his tail, gives a loud, ratcheting chirrrr, and runs back and forth as if in a rage. A gray jay, its curiosity aroused, appears on a nearby tree to get a good look at you. He too starts a metallic calling. A welcoming committee? Knowing better, you gather your backpack and head back to the trail, creating peace once again in the needleleaf forest.

What Is a Mature Needleleaf Forest?

Mature needleleaf forests have an overstory taller than 30 feet, and a cushion of fallen needles underfoot. Many of the trees are 30 years and older. Their lower trunks are often clear of branches, creating a lofty canopy effect. In pine communities, the undergrowth varies depending on the site. Where the sun can penetrate, you may find blueberries, bracken fern, grasses, and woody shrubs. In white spruce-balsam fir communities, you'll find a well-developed tall shrub layer,

1. *Brown Creeper*
2. *Evening Grosbeak*
3. *Red Squirrel*
4. *Red-breasted Nuthatch*
5. *Porcupine*
6. *Red Baneberry*
7. *Oakfern*
8. *Corn-lily (Clintonia)*
9. *One-sided Pyrola*
10. *Twinflower*
11. *American Fly-honeysuckle*
12. *Paper Birch*
13. *Mountain Maple*
14. *American Mountain-ash*
15. *Balsam Fir*
16. *White Spruce*
17. *Redbelly Snake*

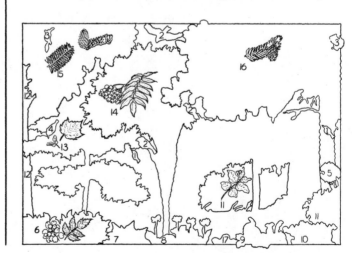

a poorly developed low shrub layer, and a ground layer of mosses.

Origins

Needleleafs, also called conifers, evergreens, or soft-woods, flourished millions of years before broadleaf trees, shrubs, grasses, and wildflowers appeared on the earth. Conifers, in fact, were the first trees to inhabit dry land. (The fern trees, their predecessors, were in swamps.) It's no wonder, then, that spruce, fir, and tamarack were the first trees to reinhabit the northwoods after the glacier's retreat. Their ability to survive the near tundra conditions that existed close to the ice cliff gave them a great advantage. Pines followed suit, and up until 100 years ago, they covered 7 million acres of the northwoods. Today, all that's left of the "tall pines" are some scattered survivors and a phantom forest of stumps under the leafy boughs of their successors.

Though they are not quite as extensive as they once were, you can still find spruce-fir forests and pine forests in the uplands of the Lake States. We're lumping them together here because they attract and support similar kinds of wildlife. They also have adaptations that all needleleaf trees have in common, developed long ago, long before broadleaf trees evolved into being.

White Spruce/Balsam Fir Forest

The spruce-fir forest typifies the northwoods scene that most of us carry in our imaginations: shady green spires, snowy-barked birch, and a loon silhouetted on a lake. This is the classic boreal forest, a cold climate type that circles the northern hemisphere and dips down into our area from the vast forests of Canada.

Foresters call it a "climax" or self-sustaining forest, which means it replaces itself tree by tree until a major disturbance, such as fire, logging, or a windstorm opens up the canopy. The resulting flood of sunlight gives pioneer trees such as aspens, birches, and jack pine a chance to move in. Once their canopies cast enough shade, fir and spruce seedlings begin to grow again—a forest within a forest.

Eventually, the needleleaf trees rise above the short-lived aspens and birches to again become dominant. In this way, the climax forest reestablishes itself, with an occasional generation of "nurse" trees in between.

Pine Forest

Our other type of needleleaf forest, the pine forest, does not bounce back as easily after a major disturbance. Red and eastern white pines need just the right combination of full sun, bare soil, and enough seeds to get started. For at least 6,000 years before the settlers came, periodic fires had created perfect seedbeds, and adjacent forests had supplied the seeds.

It took loggers less than a century to level the tall pines, and after fires spread through the remains, there were few seed trees left to regenerate the land. Aspen and birch quickly invaded the openings and shaded out the pine's chances of recovery. Public outcry over loss of the pines prompted a tree-planting movement in the early 1900's. Eastern white pine seedlings were imported from Europe along with an exotic disease called white pine blister rust. To this day, blister rust plagues efforts to restore the eastern white pine to its former prominence.

Red pine is also finicky about its growth needs, and came back naturally in only a few places. Most of the mature red pine forests that you see today in the Lake States are those that were either spared the axe or planted as seedlings by the Civilian Conservation Corps in the 1930's.

Jack pine, a stubbier but tougher tree, was often ignored by the loggers. The fires that followed the harvest didn't damage its heat-resistant seeds, and acres of jack pine sprang up in the ashes. Today, jack pines depend on frequent fires to release the seeds from their resin-sealed cones.

The Needleleaf Strategy

Needleleaf trees are remarkably hardy. They inhabit some of the harshest environments in the world, from crags in the clouds to dunes in the desert. Here in

the northwoods, their adaptations to cold and snow allow them to cope with long winters and short growing seasons. Instead of dropping all their leaves each fall the way broadleaf trees do, needleleaf trees hold onto their needles for 2–3 or even 6–8 years. Even though a certain percentage of the needles reach the end of their cycle each year, those that remain on the tree outnumber those that fall off. This everpresent canopy allows the trees to stretch the short growing season, making food early in the spring and late into the fall.

In the winter, the tree goes into cold storage, and its sap is usually immobilized. A waxy coating on the needle-thin leaves cuts down on the amount of moisture escaping from the pores. This is essential when frigid temperatures freeze soil water, creating a virtual Sahara for tree roots. The snow that bunches up on the branches actually helps to insulate the needles and further plug any leaks. Finally, needleleaf branches slope gracefully downward so as to handle the snowload without breaking.

Beneath the ground, a shallow spreading root system can anchor needleleafs on even the thinnest mantle of soil. They are also able to get by on a thin offering of nutrients, making a go of it even in sandy or acidic soils. One of their secrets to success is a relation with certain types of soil fungi. These fungi grow in harmony with needleleaf trees, wrapping thimbles of cottony thread around the end of each root tip. These threads act as auxillary roots, extracting nutrients out of even the poorest soils, and making them available to the tree. In return, the tree supplies the fungus with vital chemicals that cause it to multiply vigorously. Without this fortunate arrangement, many sites would be closed to needleleaf trees.

Other adaptations, such as the ability to live through periodic fires, also hold certain needleleafs in good stead in the northwoods. For instance, the pulpy bark of mature red and white pine scorches, but doesn't burn, and is thick enough to keep much of the heat away from the sensitive tissues underneath. The buds at the tip of young trees are surrounded by a thick tuft of long needles that burns slowly and at a low heat. By the time the tuft is consumed and the bud is exposed, the fire is likely to be past.

Even needleleafs have their Achilles' heel, however. Human logging, human-set fires, and human-imported diseases managed to nearly wipe out the great forests of red and white pines that once ruled the landscape. Jack pine healed some of the scars, but most sites were taken over by broadleaf trees. Today in the Far North, under the shadow of these broadleaf "nurse" trees, spruce and fir forests are quietly making a comeback.

Value to Wildlife

The ingenious evergreen needle that enables conifers to withstand winters is the same needle that limits the kinds of wildlife you see here. These needles fall off when they become overloaded with resin, and they pile up for years before finally breaking down. This slow decay keeps nutrients locked up in the needles instead of returning them to the soil. In turn, the nutrient-poor soil attracts few ground plants (except mushrooms, which deer relish) that wildlife can eat.

The needles themselves are appetizing to only a few species of birds, and even these birds prefer the young tender shoots if they can get them. Needleleafs do have some insect fans, however, and they come in swarms. Needle-chomping caterpillars attract a whole gamut of birds from wood warblers to thrushes. Conifer bark is sometimes nibbled on by moose, but probably more for the lichens and mosses on it rather than the bark itself. Porcupines strip the bark to get at the sweet sapwood underneath.

The most popular part of a needleleaf tree is its seeds, and some species, such as red and white-winged crossbills, have evolved special equipment for extracting these nutritious tidbits from their cones. Seed-eating rodents such as southern bog lemmings, meadow voles, mice, and squirrels supply a bonanza of meals for woodland hawks and owls. In chance openings in needleleaf forests, blueberries and hazelnuts may attract bears, foxes, and some birds.

Pine Forest

Wildlife Action

Look above you. In mature needleleaf forests, most of the wildlife action is in the treetops where there's more cover, food, and light than there is on the ground. Some birds are hunting for insects on the needles, and, in the process, helping to slow the buildup of harmful pests such as the spruce budworm. Other insect-eating birds are foraging under the bark of infested trees. And many species, both birds and mammals, are looking for the seed-filled cones that are the unique fare of needleleaf forests.

BROWN CREEPER

This slender bird is often seen spiraling its way up a tree trunk as if it is unzipping the bark. Actually, it is searching for insects and their eggs hidden in the cracks and crevices of the bark. Halfway up, it will flutter to the ground, move to the base of a neighboring tree, and begin its upward spiral again.

The brown creeper is specially outfitted for climbing and dining on trunks. Razor-sharp, oversized claws help it cling to the bark while it probes for insects with a thin, conveniently curved bill. For balance and leverage, it props itself up with a long, rigid tail. Even its protective, bark-brown coloring is in keeping with its tree-trunk life.

1. Brown Creeper
2. Red Squirrel
3. Evening
   Grosbeak
4. Eastern White
   Pine
5. Red Pine
6. Balsam Fir
7. Paper Birch
8. Beaked Hazel
9. Shinleaf
10. Canada
    Mayflower
11. Blueberry
12. Bush-
    honeysuckle

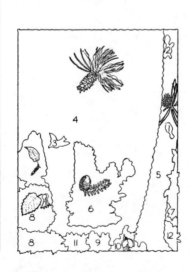

Look for brown creepers: hitching along trunks and sides and undersides of limbs. They creep up the trunk in a spiral and then fly to the base of the next tree and begin again.

Look for nests: concealed behind loosened strips of bark, 5–15 feet up on the trunks of dead trees, usually pines. Spider webs are used to line the nest.

Listen for: A highpitched lisp as it works the tree trunk, or a warble—thin and descending.

Brown creeper.

RED-BREASTED NUTHATCH

This tree-trunk gleaner has a better idea. Instead of traveling upright on the trunk like woodpeckers and creepers do, the red-breasted nuthatch works its way down the trunk headfirst, feasting on insects and their eggs that its right-side-up colleagues missed. Nuthatches move jerkily, angling down the bark and winding around even the tiniest branches to reach cones dangling at the tips. With a needle-sharp beak, they deftly pry the scales open and pluck out the nutritious seeds.

The name nuthatch comes from the bird's habit of wedging seeds or nuts in the crotch of a tree and hammering them open with its powerful beak. They'll sometimes store these morsels in holes in the trunk, sealing them in with tiny pieces of bark, then returning to them later.

Clever as they are, nuthatches have never learned to be wary of humans, so they make good subjects for study. If you watch them fly into and out of their nest cavities, you'll soon discover why males may get "sticky" in early spring. As a way to discourage predators, nuthatches smear the entrance to their nests with glistening tree sap, and, in the process of leaving and returning, they manage to smear themselves as well.

Look for red-breasted nuthatches: in the tops of tall pines or spruces, or along trunks, all year long. Nuthatches may be common one year (especially in the winter), and uncommon the next, depending on food supplies to the north of us. If needleleaf seed

Red-breasted nuthatch.

crops fail in Canada, large numbers of nuthatches may migrate here in search of food.

Look for nests: typically 15 feet up, in cavities of rotted stumps or dead branches, either borrowed from a woodpecker or pecked out of a tree themselves. They prefer trees that are at least 12 inches in diameter for nesting.

Listen for: a tinny "yank yank."

EVENING GROSBEAK

The Chippewa Indians called this bird "Paushkundamo," which means berry-breaker. In fact, the grosbeak's powerful, cone-shaped beak is perfect for breaking into berries, the winged seeds of maples, and the fruit of boxelder and ashes. To a grosbeak, the juicy flesh of a berry is just packaging to be unwrapped and discarded; the real treat is the seed within. Grosbeaks also consume large numbers of needle-chomping spruce budworms, which cause nearly 3 million dollars worth of damage to needleleaf forests in the Lake States each year.

The evening grosbeak is perhaps best known for its colorful, noisy visits to bird feeders in the winter. Handouts at feeders have enabled these birds to survive the winter and breed farther north than they would have naturally. This is just one example of how humans can alter the range and habitats of wild species.

The "evening" in the name is due to the mistaken impression that grosbeaks are nighttime singers. Actually, they are most active during the day.

Evening grosbeak.

Look for evening grosbeaks: feeding on buds, fruits, and seeds, or picking insects off branches. Look for forests that have been infested by spruce budworm, one of the grosbeak's favorites. Grosbeaks are common at feeders in the winter, and are especially partial to sunflower seeds.

Look for nests: a shallow cup of loosely woven twigs and moss 20–60 feet up in needleleaf trees.

Look for feeding debris: the light wings of empty maple fruits and the rejected skin and pulp of berries.

268

In the spring: watch for the courtship ritual of the evening grosbeak, performed on the ground. The female asks to be fed in this dance, posturing much like nestling grosbeaks do. The male feeds her, and then dances with his bill and tail up, breast almost touching hers, wings dropped but spread wide and vibrating.

Listen for: a series of short, musical whistles.

RED SQUIRREL

If you like high-speed chase scenes with plenty of dizzying climbs, free-fall leaps, and lightning-fast footwork, go watch a red squirrel defend its territory. Traveling up to 15 miles per hour, this tiny acrobat will chase an intruder high and low, leap treetop to treetop, and dive if it has to, grabbing branch after branch to break its fall. Few intruders, except for the equally agile marten (a predator), can make it look this easy.

Red squirrel.

That's because the red squirrel's body is specially built for treetop travel. Five strong and flexible toes enable it to scramble over and under even the tiniest twigs. When climbing, its tail acts as a balance pole, and as a rudder when sailing through the air. Its eyes are specially adapted for viewing vertical (tree-shaped) objects, which helps it judge the distance between trees. To supplement its sharp vision, special "sensing" hairs along its body allow it to tell a branch from a twig, and to avoid either with great dexterity.

A red squirrel, always on the lookout for trespassers, never travels far along the ground without climbing a tree to get a better view of its surroundings. If this seems overly protective, consider that it is guarding a winter's worth of food in its 600-foot-wide territory. This hidden larder may contain an incredible 14,000 cones, mushrooms, nuts, and other foods stored on the basis of their perishability. Soft foods such as mushrooms are stored on branches to dry, while cones are buried in hollow stumps and logs where it's moist (if allowed to dry out, the cones

269

would open and release their seeds). This ingenious storage scheme allows the red squirrel to remain active and well-fed during all but the coldest days of the winter.

Look for red squirrels: scampering along their "highways" in the branches or along the forest floor. They are quite visible and active during the day. In the winter, watch as they rediscover their buried cache; they can smell cones buried 12 inches below the surface.

Look for nests: in natural cavities or abandoned woodpecker holes. When tree holes are unavailable, they will build globular, leafy nests 1–2 feet in diameter, in treetops or next to the trunk. They often line these nests with strips of easily shredded bark (look for worn sections on tree trunks). Less commonly, they nest in borrowed ground burrows. A good way to find a nest is to follow a red squirrel with nesting materials in its mouth.

Look for tunnels: built in the snow to connect their caches of food to resting and eating places.

Look for signs of feeding: piles of pine cone scales stripped off to get at the seeds. Red squirrels usually have a favorite stump or knoll that they perch on to eat. The pile of debris around this perch accumulates into a "midden," which may be several feet high after generations of squirrel use. In the winter, red squirrels tunnel through this well-insulated midden.

Listen for: a scolding, ratchet-like "cherr." If you ignore this warning, the red squirrel will bark, stomp its feet, flick its tail, and angrily leap from perch to perch as if in a rage.

PORCUPINE

Armed with 30,000 bristling and barbed quills, porcupines can afford to take life at a leisurely pace. They are slow but confident climbers, and spend much of their time in the uppermost branches of trees, browsing succulent leaves and sweet inner bark or just dozing in the sun. Less at home on the ground, they

meander when they walk and are easy to catch up to. You'll want to keep a respectable distance though, because direct contact with porcupines can be unpleasant.

Contrary to popular wisdom, porcupines do not shoot their quills or throw them like darts. When approached, a porcupine simply turns its back and swats with its tail to drive dozens of quills into its opponent. These stiff, modified hairs are loosely anchored at the porcupine end, and tipped with hundreds of minute, overlapping barbs at the other. Once embedded, they penetrate through an inch of flesh each day, being drawn in deeper each time the victim's muscles contract. Needless to say, the porcupine has few enemies. Its arch foe, the fisher, is quick enough to flip a porcupine to get at its soft, quilless underbelly.

Porcupine.

"Porkies" live on twigs, leaves, bark, and ground plants in the summer, and the inner bark of softwoods and hardwoods in the winter. Also, as resort owners in the northwoods are well aware, "quill pigs" have a passion for salt. Salt on ax handles, canoe paddles, wooden porches, and even road salt on tires can entice porcupines to gnaw, often causing much damage.

Look for porcupines: hunched in a ball at the top of a tree, or waddling through the forest. They are more active by night than by day.

Look for their dens: in a rocky cave, burrow, or hollow log or tree.

Look for droppings: like brown beans spilling from their dens. In well-used dens, these fibrous droppings can build up and even crowd out the owner.

Look for signs of feeding: small branches and green-needled twigs on the ground under a tree where the porcupine is feeding, especially in winter. The chewed twig will be cut off at a diagonal and have tiny parallel rows of bites. Also look for bright, barkless patches on tree trunks or broad gnaw marks on buildings, canoe paddles, and anything else made of wood.

In the winter: look for porcupines sitting on or draped over branches high up in trees. Sometimes, 5 or 6 will hole up in an old building for the winter, going on foraging expeditions when hunger strikes.

Smell for: the musky scent of porcupine urine with which they mark the entrance to their den, the base of their favorite feeding tree, and the trails they follow in between.

Listen for: vigorous sniffing as the porcupine searches for food or senses danger. They also snort, bark, cry, and whine. A frightened porcupine may chatter its teeth. Listen for a low-pitched meow during mating, or a high-falsetto wooing song. Their courtship display includes a circle dance, nose rubbing, and face touching.

REDBELLY SNAKE

The redbelly is a woodland snake, most at home under logs and litter on the forest floor. Don't let the bright flash of red underbelly frighten you; unlike some colorful snakes, this one is quite docile, and rarely attempts to bite humans or predators. If you pick one up, it may exude a musky smelling liquid, signaling only that it is afraid.

Some reports suggest that the redbelly snake "plays possum" when in danger, i.e., it stiffens straight as an arrow, flips over, and exposes its bright red belly as a warning to would-be predators. As soon as the threat is past, the "stiff" slithers nonchalantly back into the underbrush.

Female redbellies give birth to 2 to 14 live young in August or early September. During late September and October, offspring and adults migrate by the hundreds to hibernaculas (usually abandoned ant mounds) where they will spend the winter in a deep sleep with other snakes, including garter and smooth green snakes. Still groggy when they emerge in the spring, redbellies are vulnerable to predators such as broad-winged hawks.

Look for redbelly snakes: under logs, boards, stones, and bits of debris along forest edges. They

A TONGUE FOR A NOSE
When snakes flick their tongue out, they are picking up chemical particles of scent from the air or from the surface of objects. When they reel their tongue back in, the forked tips fit into paired cavities on the roof of their mouth; these lead to scent-sensitive Jacobson's organs, which are lined with sensory cells like those in our nose. By pressing their tongue to the trail, these reptilian bloodhounds are able to track down predators, prey, or possible mates.

**MATURE
UPLAND
NEEDLELEAF
FOREST**

may also be seen crawling across roads on warm summer nights or after rain.

Look for hibernating snakes: in abandoned ant mounds from fall to March or April.

Redbelly snake.

MATURE UPLAND
MIXED FOREST

A southern flying squirrel makes a three-point landing on a bed of birch leaves. A ruby-crowned kinglet sings incessantly from the top of a spruce tree. From where you stand you can see them both, denizens of two very different forests. The kinglet is accustomed to the cold-climate needleleafs of the North, and the flying squirrel is suited for the more temperate broadleaf forests to the south. Yet here they fly past each other, sharing different patches of the same mixed woodland.

What Is a Mixed Forest?

In this book, when we say "mixed" forest, we're referring to a mixture of broadleaf and needleleaf trees (about half and half) growing together. Most of the trees are older than 30 years and taller than 30 feet. The mature mixed forest has a dense, closed canopy overhead, with a cushion of leaves and needles underfoot. The shrub and ground cover is sparse or lush depending on how much light the canopy lets in. In some stands, the trees may be old, and some may be leaning or toppled.

Origins

Because the northwoods is a meeting place for the two worlds of north and south (see "A Transition Forest," page 5), it supports plants from both areas.

1. Red-backed
   Salamander
2. Black-throated
   Green Warbler
3. Solitary Vireo
4. Northern
   Goshawk
5. Ringneck Snake
6. Fisher
7. Northern Flying
   Squirrel
8. Large-flowered
   Trillium
9. Large-flowered
   Bellwort
10. Rose Twisted-
    stalk
11. Club Moss
12. Starflower
13. Downy
    Solomon's Seal
14. Wild
    Sarsaparilla
15. Serviceberry
16. Mountain
    Maple
17. Yellow Birch
18. Sugar Maple
19. American Beech
20. Eastern
    Hemlock

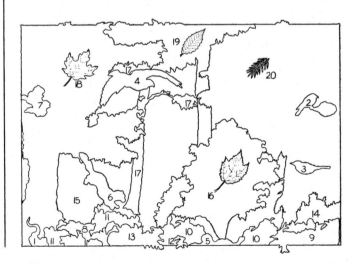

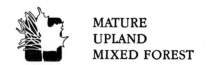

The lineup includes the spruces, balsam firs, and tamaracks of Canada, as well as the sugar maples, eastern hemlocks, paper birches, and American beeches to the east and south. Also characteristic of the northwoods are the majestic red and white pines, and the stubbier, hardy jack pines.

The trees that make up any one mixed forest change as you move north to south or east to west across the northwoods. The northern part of our region has a greater proportion of the Canadian species, which peter out somewhat as you move south, where maples and oaks begin to take over. In the eastern portion of the Lake States, sugar maple-beech-hemlock forests are prominent. As you move west into western Michigan and northern Wisconsin, however, American beech disappears and yellow birch becomes an important part of the mixture. Farther west into Minnesota, eastern hemlock and yellow birch drop out and white pine and American basswood come into the fore.

Some biologists observe that the northwoods is becoming more of a mixed forest all the time. Trees that can grow well in shade (e.g., sugar maple, balsam fir) have found extensive nurseries under the boughs of quaking and bigtooth aspens that cropped up after the logging era. Now that this aspen is reaching maturity, maple-dominated mixed forests are coming of age. This broadleaf-needleleaf combination offers a unique smorgasbord of habitats to a rich complement of birds, mammals, amphibians, and reptiles.

Who's Forest Is It Anyway?

Step into a fragrant, sundappled glen and look around you. You can't hear it or see it, but a fierce competition is occurring. Plants at all levels, from the giant supercanopy eastern white pine to the running clubmosses at your feet are fighting for space, nutrients, moisture, and lifegiving sun. A few species of trees tend to excel in such contests, and are called dominants.

Dominant trees are those that have the most influence over the rest of the plant species: they create shade or let in sun, influence temperature, humidity, and by the needles or leaves they shed, they affect the makeup of the soil. Needleleaf trees tend to dominate on sandy or boggy sites, creating conditions that attract wildlife of needleleaf habitats. Broadleaf dominants hold sway on rich, moist soil, and they too create their own communities. In some places, however, broadleaf and needleleaf trees share the dominant position. These are the places we refer to as mixed forests.

Types of Mixed Forests

One type of mixed forest occurs when a small patch of needleleaf forest is right next to a patch of broadleaf, which is next to another patch of needleleafs. This patchwork mosaic may be seen as a mixed forest.

A second type of mixed forest occurs at the junction of two large, pure forests, where one type gradually blends into the other. Here, sloping needleleafs may mingle side by side with spreading broadleaf trees in a more heterogeneous mix.

Yet a third type of mixed forest occurs when one type of tree species is growing up underneath the canopy of another type. Here, a canopy of aspen may be nursing a budding balsam fir stand in its shade. Or, if the soil is right for hardwoods, sugar maple and yellow birch may be climbing up under a canopy of 200-year-old pines.

Under Your Feet

Whatever the composition, the interplay of softwoods and hardwoods creates a unique habitat. When needles and leaves fall together, they prompt decomposers to produce organic compounds that are not present when either is alone. These in turn provide energy for new decomposers that produce a type of organic layer (humus) unique to mixed forests. This humus, in turn, favors new kinds of plants that are rare or not found in pure stands.

278

Value to Wildlife

Mixed forests are ecologically the richest on the continent. The diverse plant forms, ages, and vertical and horizontal contrasts provide a broad array of food and cover for wildlife, allowing many species to coexist. Local disturbances, such as fire, windthrow, or an insect outbreak, can create an even more diverse tapestry. When a large spruce tree topples, for instance, it lets in a shaft of sunlight that encourages an aspen root to sprout. This fresh growth adds a new dimension and makes the habitat attractive to a new set of birds and mammals. These chance occurrences also prevent a single species or group of species from dominating a mixed forest.

In mixed forests, wildlife species have both broadleaf and needleleaf trees at their disposal. They may nest in one and feed on prey associated with the other. There is an assortment of refuge sites and food provided by the diverse mix of plant species types. Generalists do well here, as do species that are adapted to one type, but are flexible enough to use both to their advantage. Because of their sheer variety, mixed forests support one of the most diverse communities of birds and mammals in North America.

Competition among wildlife species is especially keen in mixed forests because the competitors represent the best of the harsh northern forests pitted against the most adaptable of the southern species. Many of them, like the plants that draw them to this area, are at the outer limits of their ranges. The dynamics of their coexistence is one of the things that makes the northwoods a special place.

Wildlife Action

Use the same techniques you would use to find wildlife in mature needleleaf or broadleaf forests. Watch the litter for voles, snakes, salamanders, and four-footed predators. Berry-producing bushes are good places to find songbirds and birds that will stay the winter. In the summer, most birds are looking for insects, either on the leaves and needles of the canopies, or on the trunks and branches of mature trees.

Dead and rotting trees provide a special source of bark beetles, ants, and other insects that comprise the "wrecking crew" in the decay process. Also look for the cavity nests of woodpeckers, owls, nuthatches, and squirrels in old, large diameter trees. The branches of the tallest trees are good places to look for hawk nests. Birds that spend the winter here, including chickadees, woodpeckers, and nuthatches, can be found on trunks and branches, probing for dormant insects and insect eggs. On needleleaf trees, look for crossbills excavating seeds from the cones.

NORTHERN GOSHAWK

A ruffed grouse struts out of the shadows, stiffens each proud feather, and climbs onto the drumming log. As he touches his wings together behind his back, an unearthly silence falls, as if the forest is drawing its breath. Into that silence roars a clap of aerial thunder, a blue-backed bullet of a hawk with outstretched talons trained dead on the grouse's back. A brief squeeze quiets the terrified bird, and it is suddenly hoisted high into the treetops by one of our largest and fiercest winged predators, the northern goshawk.

Goshawks are built for the chase. They are tireless pursuers, matching the movements of even their quickest prey, twist for turn. They can throw themselves right or left with their long tails, and can drop, rise, or weave expertly around obstacles, even when traveling at high speeds. Unlike many other hawks, goshawks will follow airborne prey into dense forest thickets, and run after them if need be. Upon returning to a feeding perch with its prey, be it crow, red squirrel, chipmunk, or rabbit, the goshawk will often tear off the prey's head before eating it or presenting it to its mate.

Northern goshawks are among the most frequent copulators in the northwoods, mating 500 to 600 times for each clutch of eggs! Researchers theorize that frequent copulation may reinforce social bonds between mates. Another theory says that the more a male mates with a particular female, the better his chances are of being the one to father her offspring,

Northern goshawk.

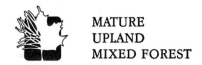

especially if there is a chance that she is mating with other males while he is away from the nest. The frequent mating may increase his confidence in his paternity, and thus assure the female that he will be around later to help care for the young.

Look for northern goshawks: feeding in bushy openings in the interior of remote and heavily forested areas. Goshawks can also maneuver in dense forests for prey. Look for mated pairs performing a display flight about 40 minutes before sunrise.

Look for nests: in the interior of heavy woodlands, in a crotch of a hardwood tree, close to the trunk, or out on a limb, 20–60 feet up.

Listen for: a loud, goose-like "kak-kak-kak-kak" when disturbed.

SOLITARY VIREO

The solitary vireo shuffles sideways along a branch, head tilted to one side, stalking caterpillars. When it sights one, it will dash out to capture it, then tenderize it with a few blows from its heavy, slightly hooked bill. Above this bill sits a pair of white "spectacles" adorning a sleek, blue-gray head.

Solitary vireo.

The solitary is the first vireo to migrate north each spring, arriving at the leading edge of a host of small warblers and other migrants. During the summer, these vireos become more solitary, remaining hidden in their treetop haunts.

You may hear them, however, whistling their sweet, slurred phrases even while wandering in search of prey. In breeding season, two male birds will sing against each other, echoing phrases back and forth in a show of territorial rivalry. A courting male will sing low songs to a female he is following, all the while bobbing, bowing, and fluffing out his yellow flank feathers to impress her.

Also noteworthy is the fact that vireos have evolved a strategy to defeat cowbirds that lay their eggs in vireo nests. Instead of hatching and raising the foster young, vireos simply cover up the eggs and lay their own on the new nest floor.

Look for solitary vireos: feeding at the base (close to the trunk) of horizontal branches and dead stubs, most often in the lower to middle canopy. They prefer forests that have dense understories as a result of openings in the canopy.

Look for nests: typically 4–12 feet up in the middle of a small needleleaf, hanging like a cup from the forked end of a horizontal branch, or from two side-by-side twigs extending from a small sapling.

Listen for: a slow series of sweet, slurred phrases of 2 to 6 notes or an occasional burst of 15 to 20 warbled notes.

BLACK-THROATED GREEN WARBLER

The lazy, murmuring song of this warbler conjures memories of summer, and is unforgettable once it is heard. The trick after hearing this melancholy songster is to find it in its treetop haunts, where it tirelessly scours the branch tips for leaf-eating insects. Its feeding area is usually a few branches down from the top of a conifer, just below that of the blackburnian warbler and above that of the lower-roaming magnolia warbler.

A good time to catch this warbler in action is in early spring, before the leaves hide its colors from view. It usually arrives in mass migration, and if you catch it right, the branches may be alive with warblers. They group again in fall to move to southern climes for the winter. Despite their small size, these warblers fly clear across the Gulf of Mexico to reach their low-lying wintering grounds in Mexico and South America.

Look for black-throated green warblers: 10–50 feet up, between the sunlit tops and lower branches of needleleaf trees, close to branch tips, and usually on the borders of forests. These warblers are attracted to the dripping water of streams.

Look for nests: deeply cupped, bound with spider webs, nestled 15–20 feet up on a drooping branch of a needleleaf tree (common in hemlocks).

Black-throated green warbler.

Listen for: a thin, buzzy "zee-zee-zee-zoo-zee" or a lazier "trees trees murm'ring trees."

FISHER

The fisher is a type of weasel, with a sleek, muscular body, an arched back, and a pointed, alert face. Its short, strong legs and sharp claws help make it one of the fastest tree-climbing animals in North America. Most of its time is spent on the ground rather than in trees, however, traveling a circuitous hunting route that may be 60 miles in length and take as long as 2 weeks to cover. Needing 1½ pounds of food a day, fishers have become efficient predators of snowshoe hares, squirrels, mice, shrews, game birds, and even the all-challenging porcupine!

Fishers have learned that the best way to eat porcupine without getting a snout full of quills is to catch a porkie in the open, usually on its way between den tree and feeding tree. This way, the porcupine has less occasion to nose into a crook or cranny from which it can brandish its rump of quills. Fishers wage a frontal attack, skillfully dodging the porkie's tail and biting its face until it is dead or bewildered. Then the fisher deftly flips its dinner and digs into the soft quilless belly, peeling back the armored skin like a true gourmet.

Not long ago, it was next to impossible to see a fisher in the northwoods, even though they had at one time been rather well-distributed. In 1920, when a luxurious fisher pelt would sell for $345, trapping pressure rose to a fever pitch. Along with the wholesale destruction of vast tracts of prime fisher habitat, fisher numbers were greatly reduced. Today, thanks to protection and reintroduction efforts, these fascinating mammals have made a comeback in many areas.

Look for fishers: climbing along fallen logs, brushpiles, or downed treetops. They prefer forests with a continuous canopy overhead and conifer swamps nearby (the haunt of their main staple, the snowshoe hare). They will often travel along watercourses, the tops of ridges, or old logging roads. They

Fisher.

are active day and night, all year round, except for the coldest winter days.

Look for dens: in hollow trees, logs, ground holes under boulders, or in abandoned beaver or muskrat houses.

Look for destroyed cavity entrances: where hungry fishers have torn apart rotten trunks to get into other mammals' nests.

In snow or mud: look for tracks, 1½–2¼ inches in diameter, in which all 5 toes show (only 4 toes show in dog and cat tracks). Fishers often bound, and paired tracks will be up to 16 feet apart when the trackmaker is moving at top speed.

Listen for: a soft "tcheek tcheek tcheek" when contented or curious. They will also hiss, snarl, spit, and growl, arching their backs like annoyed cats.

NORTHERN FLYING SQUIRREL

Flying squirrels are common in the woodlands around us, often as numerous as gray or red squirrels, yet few people stay in the forest late enough to see them. The flying squirrel circus begins at twilight when these tiny acrobats launch from their nests, gliding on their body-sails to a soft, soundless landing below.

Northern flying squirrel.

A unique cape of flesh and fur allows the flying squirrel to glide distances of 150 feet or more through the forest. This web of skin stretches from the fore to the hind legs, so that when the squirrel is spread eagle, it looks like a rectangular sheet stiffened at the edges with cartilage. The squirrel steers by adjusting its limbs and flat, featherlike tail, and by changing the tension in this gliding membrane. For a soft landing, it lifts its tail and uses the cape as an air brake. Scurrying quickly to the other side of the trunk, it flicks its tail, giving the illusion of having gone in the opposite direction.

The flying squirrel's night vision is improved by large, wide-set eyes that can scope a wide field of vision and let in lots of light. Before taking off, squirrels will often bob their heads, perhaps to take two or more readings which they use to triangulate, or pinpoint, their landing site. They also rely on muscle memory; that is, they memorize their most frequently used routes through the forest and glide along these familiar pathways by rote. These sophisticated adaptations make flying squirrels the fastest squirrels in the northwoods.

Flying squirrels are nimble on their feet as well as their "wings." Watch as one negotiates to the end of a tiny twig, then dangles upside down, using its hindpaws as grappling hooks while grabbing for nuts with its forepaws. They seem to be able to tell rotten nuts from good ones just by hefting them, presumably calculating the weight of the nut relative to its volume. They also rotate nuts and feel the outsides with their teeth to locate any soft, wormy spots.

Other favorite foods include: seeds, flowers, fruits, fungi, and lichen in the summer; stores of conifer seeds and mushrooms cached during the busy fall; and insects, birds' eggs, nestlings, and carrion. In spring, they feast on the tender buds of aspen, alder, and pussy willow. In other parts of the country, researchers report that flying squirrels feed on the soil-dwelling fungi that are associated with tree roots. Because these fungi actually help tree seedlings survive, the squirrel's role in spreading them (through droppings) is a welcome one.

Look for northern flying squirrels: at twilight anytime of year, when the bark of trees 6 feet away becomes hard to see. Stand in an area where you have located a nest during the daytime. Squirrels will become adjusted to a dim light from a flashlight, or a porch light near a feeder that they frequent. Look for the orange-red reflection of their eyes. Watch for their diagonal flights (they move somewhat faster than leaves fluttering to the ground), or for their straight downward spiraling flights. Look along the forest floor, where they may be digging for fungi, or excavating stored nuts. During the autumn hoarding frenzy, you may be able to catch a glimpse of them during the day. In addition, in early summer, when nestlings are learning to glide, the branches may be alive with squirrels on "practice runs."

SHOPPING FOR THE RIGHT NUT

At rest, flying squirrels can pucker in their fleshy parachute with a muscle, allowing them to be nimble on their feet. Watch as one ventures out on a branch, using its hind legs like grappling hooks, freeing its paws to grab buds, nuts, and berries clustered at the tip. Before eating, the squirrel turns the nut in its paws, hefting it the way a conscientious shopper hefts fruit, and feeling with its teeth for possible worms and imperfections. If the nut passes muster, the squirrel will use its lower incisors to slice open a neat hole and scrape out the meat. What it doesn't eat, it will cache in a variety of underground, underbark, and inner-tree hiding spots.

Look for nests: in cavities of trees, often an abandoned woodpecker hole lined with finely shredded vegetation. They may also build nests of leaves on branches or in the middle of "witches' brooms" (abnormal, bunched branching in the canopy). Squirrels often use many nest sites: one for eating, another for raising young, etc. They will also settle in artificial duck boxes.

In the snow: look for "sitzmarks," where squirrels have made a 4-point landing, or a drag mark of 1½ feet which shows a more leisurely, gradual descent. As it bounds along the ground, its tracks are connected with a line from the cape of skin.

Look for gnaw marks: on sugar maple bark where the sweet-toothed flying squirrel may have tapped into some sap. Also, smooth, elliptical openings on one side of a nut are trademark signs of flying squirrel feeding. Mice open many holes, and other mammals leave rougher-toothed edges.

Listen for: a "chuck chuck" sound similar to that of other squirrels, or a quiet "tick" as they land on trunks. Also listen for a tap-tapping as squirrels pound nuts into hiding places (bark crevices) with their front teeth.

REDBACK SALAMANDER

This salamander is completely terrestrial, that is, it lives on land away from wet areas, and does not resort to wetlands even for breeding. This is somewhat unusual, when you consider that the redback has no lungs. The young are born with large gills that disappear a few days after hatching. From then on, they must absorb oxygen through their skin.

To help transfer this oxygen, salamander skin must always be kept somewhat moist. They do best in humid, heavily shaded areas that have a good amount of moist leaf litter on the ground, with plenty of decaying logs, stumps, or rocks that they can hide beneath. They are equally at home in broadleaf and in needleleaf forests.

In our region, redbacks make up a large percentage

of all salamander numbers. Not only are they an important food source for shrews, snakes, and birds, but they also eat their share of small insects, larvae, earthworms, snails, slugs, spiders, and especially mites.

Breeding starts in the fall and continues in the spring. Males lay a jelly-like mass containing sperm in front of the female being courted, and she picks it up with her cloacal lips. (The cloaca is an all-purpose opening on her underside.) Eggs are laid in grape-like bunches and hung by a gelatinous stalk from the roof of the nesting cavity which is most often the inside of a rotting log. The female guards these eggs for up to 2 months, defending them from predators and coating them with her own skin secretions to keep them from drying out or becoming moldy. She goes through this demanding ritual only once every other year. The young hatch as miniature replicas of the adults; there is no free-swimming phase as with other salamanders.

Look for redback salamanders: by turning over logs, stones, rocks, bark, moss, and leaf mold, or by looking within rotting logs or stumps. They are most active at night and may be found roaming the forest floor. On rainy nights, they even climb tree trunks and shrubs in search of food. They are rarely found under birch logs, perhaps because of a chemical in birch that disagrees with them.

Redback salamander.

Look for nests: in cavities of rotting logs or in rock crevices. They suspend their bunch of 3–14 eggs from the roof with a gelatinous stalk.

In winter: redbacks hibernate 15 inches or more below the ground, in rock crevices, or deep within the labyrinth of decaying root systems.

RINGNECK SNAKE

There's no mistaking the brilliant yellow ring around this snake's "neck." Their underbellies are yellow as well, with a lively smattering of black spots. When you hold a ringneck, drops of saliva will appear at the corners of its mouth. Though the snake itself is docile, this foul, pungent musk tends to remain with you for a long while.

Adapted for woodlands, ringnecks require lots of shade and the cover afforded by rotting logs and deep leaf litter. They are particularly partial to dark, moist hillsides, and occur farther north than almost any American reptile. Female ringnecks lay up to 10 eggs in rotting logs, often ones that have an outer shell of bark that is still intact. If possible, they choose a log that is warmed by the sun for part of the day. More than one female may lay eggs in the same log.

Their preferred foods are earthworms, sowbugs, slugs, beetles, redback salamanders, frogs, green snakes, and redbelly snakes. They seize their prey with gaping jaws, then swallow them live, letting digestive juices in their stomachs do the rest of the work. In turn, birds and other snakes feed on ring-necks.

Look for ringneck snakes: by exposing their hiding places beneath flat rocks or under the bark of fallen trees. (Be sure to put the rocks back!) Look early in the evening along unused forest roads. This nocturnal and secretive snake hibernates in groups for the winter.

Look for eggs: in a moist cavity in a rotting log that is exposed to the sun.

Ringneck snake.

Ruffed grouse.

©1989 Vera Ming Wong

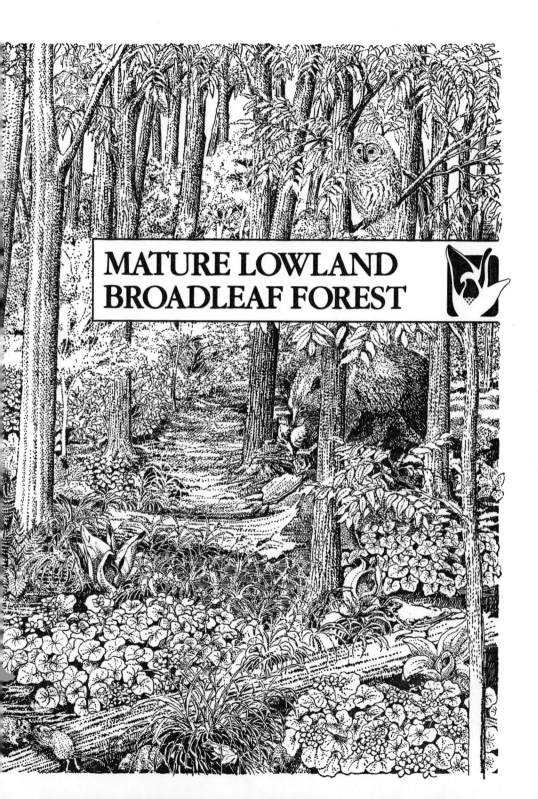

MATURE LOWLAND BROADLEAF FOREST

Isolated pockets of lowland broadleaf forest border the lakes, streams, and bogs of the northwoods. During the spring thaw, slender black ash trees stand leafless in pools of chilly, black meltwater. Around them, red maples are dressed with the deep, brief crimson of new leaves. Below, in the warmth of the sun's rays, ferns unroll their delicate green fiddleheads amid a cluster of waxy-yellow marsh marigold blossoms.

What Is a Mature Lowland Broadleaf Forest?

It's shady and moist, but there are open pockets in the canopy where the sun can reach the clumps of shrubs and ferns. The soil beneath your feet is muck or peat, and may be covered with water during parts of the year. Typically, a stream or a river runs through the forest. Many of the trees are older than 30 years, taller than 30 feet, and some may be starting to rot and topple. Characteristic species are: red maple, black ash, and a few American elms.

Origins

Red maple and black ash persist in conditions that most broadleaf trees would find intolerable. They are anchored in muck or peat that can often be acidic and relatively mediocre in terms of nutrients. And in

1. *Wood Frog*
2. *Woodland Jumping Mouse*
3. *Red-shouldered Hawk*
4. *Black Bear*
5. *Barred Owl*
6. *Veery*
7. *Skunk Cabbage*
8. *Marsh Marigold*
9. *Cinnamon Fern*
10. *Yellow Birch*
11. *Red Maple*
12. *Black Ash*
13. *Speckled Alder*
14. *Red-osier Dogwood*
15. *Black Willow*

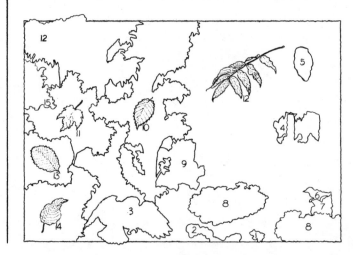

the spring, their shallow roots are often covered with cold meltwater. Yet the lowland hardwoods survive, and a whole community of birds, mammals, reptiles, and amphibians survive along with them.

Balsam poplar, balsam fir, and yellow birch are among the other trees found in the broadleaf swamps of the Lake States. Before 1970, American elm was commonly found in these stands, but during the past 2 decades this tree has been attacked and killed throughout the northwoods by Dutch elm disease. The disease is spread by elm bark beetles; as they move from tree to tree, the beetle larvae carve out feeding tunnels under the elm's bark where the fungus grows and reproduces. Although some surviving elms can still be found in the region, you are likely to find only half-collapsed, decaying snags or young elms in most lowland broadleaf forests.

What comes after the lowland hardwood swamp? In Michigan, northern white-cedar can move in. But more commonly, on sites where the soil drainage improves, upland broadleaf trees may find it inviting. This succession tends to be very slow, however.

The Burly Black Ash

Black ash itself is far from burly—it has a characteristically slender, graceful shape. When browsed by a deer or moose, a young black ash will shoot upward, as much as 5 feet a year, thus putting its crown above the heads of hungry herbivores. But when grown in supersaturated soils, the mature trees do get "burly." Burls are large, round tumors that develop on the trunk. They form when thwarted buds inside the tree begin to send out shoots that branch and curl around inside the wood. Though bound by the bark, these growths eventually swell outward. When cut open, the wood inside the burl looks braided and swirled, producing the "curly ash" veneer that is prized by cabinetmakers.

Value to Wildlife

The lowland broadleaf understory is strikingly different than that found in a lowland needleleaf forest

293

(see page 317). Here the canopy is rather open so that direct sunlight often reaches shrubs and herbaceous plants below. This open layer is used by hawking birds (e.g., flycatchers) that perch on a branch and sally out to catch insects on the wing. Cavity nesters also have a heyday in lowland hardwood swamps. Because the trees are nestled away from winds, many half-rotting and broken-topped trunks stay upright for years, providing the hollow hideaways that cavity dwellers such as wood ducks and raccoons need. Speckled alder, red-osier dogwood, and pussy willows grow in tall, dense clumps that provide cover in the summer and food in the winter for small birds and mammals. A rich assortment of ferns, sedges, and grasses thrive in the cool, moist groundlayer and offer much-needed shade for heat-sensitive species such as the four-toed salamander. The grass here is among the first to green up in the spring, and is heavily used by black bears.

Wildlife Action

Visibility is fairly good in lowland broadleaf stands, but wildlife here can be elusive. Look for wildlife near the ground, where fallen logs and tangles of brush offer cover and where cool, humid conditions provide relief from the summer sun. Fallen logs will be good sources of insects for mammals, snakes, salamanders, and frogs. Watch snag trees with tattered bark and decaying wood. Bark-gleaning species will be probing for hidden insect larvae here. Check high in the largest snags for nesting owls or perching hawks and in the smaller ones for cavity-dwelling woodpeckers. Canopy openings are used by fly-catching birds. Watch for white-tailed deer that may come to browse red maple twigs.

BARRED OWL

The teetering, barkless old snag is riddled with holes and dusty with beetle drillings—peak condition for a barred owl hangout. From here the owl will scream like a human, bark like a dog, hoot up a storm, court a mate, fledge a brood, and search for food. When it

senses an unsuspecting mouse, frog, bird, or snake, it will leave the snag, lifting on heavy, soundless wings, and glide faultlessly to the forest floor. A quick squeeze of talons and a buoyant swoop brings the owl and its dinner back to the safety of the perch.

The barred owl has a wingspan of nearly 4 feet, and by fluffing out its feathers, it can appear much larger than it actually is. Like all owls, the barred has eyes with tremendous light-gathering qualities, the secret weapon of an accomplished night hunter. These sensors also enable the owl to negotiate through dense forests without colliding with low-hanging vegetation. Owls hear through long slits on either side of their disk-like face. Because one ear is slightly higher than the other, the owl can take two "readings" on a sound and triangulate to pinpoint movement in total darkness.

Barred owl.

At night, the barred owl hunts the same area that the red-shouldered hawk hunts during the day. Because they are not in direct competition for food, these birds coexist amicably, even building nests in close proximity. Occasionally, the owl (usually a cavity nester) will even make use of an old hawk's nest to lay its eggs.

Look for barred owls: at dusk, perched on dead branches or stubs of decaying trees, watching for prey. Owls with young may hunt during the day. Try calling them to a nearby perch by making mouse-like squeals (kiss the back of your hand) or by playing tape recordings of their strange chuckling and hooting sounds. It's also rather easy to imitate their hoot.

Look for nests: up to 80 feet high in cavities of trees at least 20 inches in diameter. A telltale sign is a strand of gray down fluttering from a hole. A barred owl nest may be used faithfully for as many as 25 years.

Look for pellets: beneath roosting sites. Pellets are masses of indigestible bones, hair, and feathers that the owl coughs up. If pellets are moist and shiny (fresh), the owl may be nearby. Allow pellets to dry and then examine them for telltale signs of prey, such as whole skulls.

"Who cooks for you? Who cooks for you all?" accent on the "you." Also makes laughing, hissing, barking sounds, especially loud during February and March (the "months of madness") when they are courting, and thus calling more often.

RED-SHOULDERED HAWK

Besides their beauty and grace in flight, the thing to remember about red-shouldered hawks is their feet. Like all birds of prey, these hawks kill by grabbing and piercing their prey with their talons, which makes their feet crucial to their survival. However, red-shouldered hawks have small, weak feet compared with other birds of prey. This explains why they specialize in small prey such as frogs, mice, shrews, grasshoppers, spiders, small snakes, and a few birds. Rather than being at a disadvantage because of their feet, they are probably better adapted than other hawks to hunt small prey, and thus, have found a lucrative niche.

Red-shouldered hawk.

Red-shouldered hawks tend to stay out of the open country where red-tailed hawks soar, keeping to river-bottom woods where this smaller game is abundant. Their beautifully mottled coloring blends well with the lights and shadows here, enabling them to remain undetected until the final swoop towards their woodland prey. Barred owls also use these wet forests, hunting at night when the red-shouldered hawk is asleep.

With its lusty "kee-yer, kee-yer, kee-yer," the red-shouldered hawk is sometimes called the singing hawk. Its flight consists of rapid wingbeats followed by a brief sail, and although it doesn't soar regularly, you may see one circling high into the sky during breeding and migration. In the autumn, particularly late September, some red-shouldered hawks will join flocks of southward migrating hawks.

Look for red-shouldered hawks: on perches overlooking rivers, swamps, or the "kettlehole" ponds where they get most of their food. They also skim along the treetops on hunting flights. In spring, breeding pairs will circle high above the nest area. Watch for the male to divebomb into the trees screaming.

Look for nests: 30–60 feet up, placed in a crotch near the trunk. Nests are bulky stick-and-twig platforms 2 feet in diameter lined with bark strips, lichen, green twigs with leaves, and sometimes "decorated" with a tent caterpillar nest or the nest of a red-eyed vireo. Occasionally hawks will use an abandoned nest of another hawk, squirrel, or crow. Leaving their nests, these hawks will first swoop down in a graceful curve, then slowly veer up and out of the trees. Returning to the nest, they fly in low and glide up at the last moment.

Look for bits of down: sticking out around the edges of nests or on the branches below the nest.

Look for feeding debris: such as the discarded skins of frogs. Some frog skins are poisonous, so the red-shouldered hawk neatly peels back the skin of all frogs it eats.

Listen for: a downward slurred, whistle-like "kee-yer, kee-yer." They are noisy and conspicuous in the spring during courtship and while defending their territories.

VEERY

At dusk, an ethereal song drifts from the understory and seems to "breathe the spirit of the dying day" (ornithologist Edward Howe Forbush). Another naturalist, Arnold Bent, claimed that the veery's call was a song of intertwining circles, like the sound you would hear if you whirled a weighted string around your head. When two of these ventriloquists alternately call, they can sound like a waterfall, blending with the running water often found in veery country.

The veery can afford to call attention to himself with his song, however, because he is so well camouflaged in the dense shrubbery and tangled forest floor on which he forages for insects and fruits. In some cases, birds that are flamboyantly colored tend to have less distinctive voices, perhaps because they

SUPERHUMAN SIGHT

Hawks are able to discern details from soaring heights because of the one million visual receptor cells they have in their eyes (that's five times more than humans have). Most of these cells are found on the upper half of their eye, where images from the ground register when they are in flight. When perching hawks have to focus on something over their head (such as another hawk flying by), they often turn their head almost upside down.

Veery.

297

advertise and communicate with color instead of with sound. Many birds that are difficult to spot, like the veery, have more distinctive, notable songs that they use to attract mates, deliver warning calls, or defend their territories. (The relationship between color and song differs from species to species, however; like most natural phenomena, there is no hard and fast rule.)

Look for veeries: turning leaves over on the ground, feeding in dense shrubbery, or running swiftly in alarm. Veeries are found in the lower canopies of cool, moist swamps, and their preference for willow-lined rivers and swamps has earned them a nickname of "willow thrush."

Look for nests: on or near the ground, in low shrubs, or on top of a mossy hummock, a clump of shoots, or tangled vines. They're made of twigs, grasses, and leaves.

Listen for: a downward spiraling song that sounds like "veery" repeated over and over.

WOODLAND JUMPING MOUSE

Hopping along the forest floor like a miniature kangaroo, the woodland jumping mouse is able to make an impressive getaway in a quick series of 2–3-foot bounds. Its secret is in its long hind feet, which have well-developed toes and muscles for maximum "lift" over and above obstructions. When pursued, the jumping mouse can traverse 8 feet in a single leap! When not alarmed, the jumping mouse usually creeps through vegetation, looking for bonanzas of seeds, insects, wild fruits, and underground fungi. Unhampered by its long tail and bounding hind feet, it can even climb low bushes to feast on fruit.

Autumn is a time of gorging to store away internal reserves of fat for the 6-month hibernation ahead. Because they don't bury food, these mice must feed off their own fat, using up nearly a third of their total weight over the winter.

Look for woodland jumping mice: along moist forest borders, the shores of streams, or in an under-

Woodland jumping mouse.

story of ferns, grasses, and shrubs that has rocks, logs, and brush piles for cover. When frightened, they may drum their tail on the ground. You may see them during the day, especially when it's drab or rainy, but they're most active at night. They need loose soil for burrowing.

Look for nests: a globe of grass in an underground chamber, usually about 4 inches below the surface of the ground or under a log or stump. Burrows may be up to 5 feet long, with plugged openings that leave no traces to tip off hungry weasels and striped skunks.

WOOD FROG

The frog with the robber's mask occurs farther north than any amphibian or reptile in North America. So far north, in fact, that its range penetrates the Arctic Circle. Part of its survival strategy is to winter in shallow depressions below the ground, blanketed by dead leaves and snow. Despite this insulation, sub-freezing temperatures sometimes reach the frog in its refuge. After a few days of frigid cold, wood frogs do what we would do: they begin to freeze. Their eyes become opaque, their lungs and hearts stop working, their organs get cut off from oxygen and nutrients, and finally, their bodies stiffen.

Wood frog.

But when warmer weather comes, these frozen frogs do something we humans could not: they thaw out alive! The secret is glucose. Glucose is a "cryoprotectant," a chemical that makes sure that ice crystals only form between cells, not within them, so that delicate cell walls are not damaged by expanding ice crystals. If need be, wood frogs can manufacture glucose by breaking down glycogen (a carbohydrate stored in the liver) at a rapid pace. This raises the concentration of glucose in their blood to about 60 times its normal value. While this would cause a diabetic reaction in many animals, it doesn't seem to bother the wood frog.

Those that make it through the winter emerge early and breed explosively, often before the ice is fully off the ponds. All the wood frogs in the pond will lay their eggs together, forming a globular mass of about

299

3,000 eggs just below the water's surface. The dark, light-absorbing color and jelly coating of the eggs give them needed protection from the frigid pond water. The tadpoles are also remarkably tolerant of the cold and mature more rapidly than other frogs do. This allows them to reach adulthood faster so they are less vulnerable to late spring cold spells, the drying up of temporary ponds, or the jaws of larger pond-dwelling organisms.

After breeding, wood frogs head back to the woods, where their grayish-green-to-brown coloring blends nicely with the mottled shadows of the leafy or needle-strewn litter. Although you may find wood frogs hopping in the forest, they'll never be far from the flat embankments along the ponds that they need for survival. Studies have shown that wood frogs will follow the receding shoreline of a drying pond and resort to the moist leaf litter only when the water is gone. Their most important requirement is enough shade to provide high humidity and cool air. Wood frogs also need hummocks and piles of brush in which to escape from predators such as garter snakes, birds, and minks.

Look for wood frogs: hunting insects along the shaded edges of woodland ponds, most often facing the pond. They often seek cover in piles of grass, hummocks, or leaves instead of fleeing to the water.

Look for eggs: laid early in the spring in a communal mass of jelly attached to underwater twigs, or floating free on the pond bottom. Occasionally, a female frog will become entrapped in the mass and die.

In the winter: frogs hibernate under moist forest floor debris or in flooded meadows.

Listen for: a chorus of sharp, rasping clacks, almost like the clucking sound of ducks. They are commonly heard around ponds in the spring during breeding season.

Gray wolves chorusing.

SEMI-OPEN LOWLAND NEEDLELEAF FOREST

© 1989 VeraMing Wong Inc.

In the crisp October dawn, a lacy frost etches the drooping, waxy leaves of labrador tea. Nestled on a bed of pale green moss, ripe cranberries sparkle in the early morning light. Energetic boreal chickadees inspect the boughs of scattered conifers for late-season insects paralyzed by the night's chill. A gray jay abandons his favorite lookout atop a ragged black spruce and glides noiselessly to a nearby tamarack. Landing awkwardly, he jostles the branches, unleashing a confetti of golden needles to the moss below.

What Is a Semi-Open Lowland Needleleaf Forest?

The ground beneath your feet is a jumble of hummocks and spongy sphagnum. Scattered throughout are small clumps of stunted spruces and tamaracks, even the oldest of which are usually less than 20 feet tall. Between these clumps are plenty of open glens with mosses, heaths, and wildflowers. The water table of the "muskeg" is close to the surface, and though there is no standing water, your sneakers will probably get wet as you walk.

Origins

Semi-open lowland conifer forests, also called muskeg bogs, are open bogs that have begun to fill in

1. *Boreal Chickadee*
2. *Olive-sided Flycatcher*
3. *Connecticut Warbler*
4. *Tennessee Warbler*
5. *Nashville Warbler*
6. *White-throated Sparrow*
7. *Gray Jay*
8. *Leatherleaf*
9. *Small Cranberry*
10. *Pitcher Plant*
11. *Yellow Lady's-slipper*
12. *Arethusa*
13. *Low Sweet Blueberry*
14. *Labrador Tea*
15. *Swamp Willow*
16. *Bog Birch*
17. *Swamp Birch*
18. *Tamarack*
19. *Black Spruce*

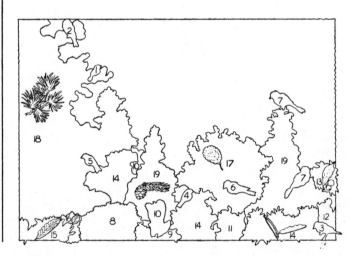

with some isolated trees and thickets. (For more about how open bogs form, see page 160). Black spruce is the most common of these trees, and is joined by the eerily beautiful tamarack. A number of heath shrubs, mosses, and wildflowers accompany them.

The roots of all these plants are entwined for mutual support, spreading in a complex net throughout the floating mat of peat. Thus, when you walk in one part of the bog, you may see trees some distance from you tilt in response. Many semi-open forests remain sparsely forested for years, reopened occasionally by a ground fire. However, some bog forests proceed to the next stage (see page 317), in which the bog is completely forested in one continuous canopy of green.

Slow, Stubborn Growth

The semi-open bog forest, like the bog, truly tests the mettle of the plants and animals that live here. The surface is a tangled mat of mosses and heaths atop layers of dead plants that have not fully decayed. These compressed mats are called peat. The peat is often saturated with cold, acidic water that is starved for oxygen, and thus untenable for many decay organisms. Without active decay, plant bodies stack up, and few nutrients are fed back into the system. The top mounds of undecayed peat may become dry and brittle during droughts, providing perfect tinder for smoldering fires.

Despite these adversities, a handful of black spruce and tamarack rooted in the spongy peat live a gnarled life on the muskeg. They tend to sprawl, and their growth is so slow that a century-old tree may stand less than 10 feet tall. This small stature can be a blessing however, protecting them from blasting winds that could overturn a taller target.

Black spruce avoids the water-logged lower layers of the mat by growing roots straight out—horizontally—from its trunk. These shallow roots fuse into "I" beams of incredible strength to keep the spruce from toppling. When the mosses begin to choke up too high around the trunk of the spruce, or when periodic floods inundate its roots, the spruce responds by "layering." Layering means that the tree grows roots from the undersides of its lowest branches, especially when these branches are weighted down to the ground with snow. When these roots take hold, buds on the branch become leader shoots, and a new tree begins to grow upward. Sometimes you'll see an old spruce that has layered many times, and is now surrounded with one or two concentric rings of living trees.

Under their branches, feather mosses drape themselves on hummocks, awaiting raindrops that hang briefly from branches, and then drip down laden with nutrients they have absorbed from the leaves. Beyond the shade of the canopy, the hardier sphagnum takes over again, relying on plain rainwater and dust for its sustenance.

Black spruce are sometimes attacked by dwarf mistletoe, a leafless, parasitic plant that saps nutrients from its host. Mistletoe-infected spruce aren't hard to find—just look for "witches' brooms," compact balls of branches in the canopy that are often caused by the mistletoe infection. When triggered by a gust of wind or a sudden jolt, ripe dwarf mistletoe berries fire off sticky seeds that may carry up to 50 feet before they land and infect a neighboring tree. Red squirrels, gray jays, and other animals that may nest and forage in brooms accidentally spread the mistletoe seeds which they have picked up on their fur or feathers.

Tamarack, the only northern conifer to shed all its needles each fall, grows best on sunny, wet sites, sometimes far out on bog mats. Early each spring, soft tufts of pale green needles emerge from warty tamarack twigs (the warts are actually short shoots). Turning a misty bluish-green as summer progresses, these wispy needles cast little shade. Bog birch, swamp willow, and various heath shrubs grow in clumps under its open, airy branches.

306

Survival Lessons

Roughly a dozen species of heath plants, all low shrubs or trailing vines, share unusual adaptations for success in this harsh environment. Heath leaves are tough, leathery, and often almost needle-like, with waxy surfaces or dense woolly undersides to help conserve water. Each winter, these leaves must resist freezing and, in summer, temperatures on the partially shaded bog may sizzle to over 100 degrees F. Heath plants beat the nutrient scarcity on muskegs by being evergreen—holding onto their leaves instead of expending precious energy to grow new ones each year.

Despite their numerous similarities, bog heaths differ strategically in the times that they flower. Leatherleaf blooms earliest, followed in turn by bog rosemary and bog laurel, then velvetleaf blueberry, labrador tea, small cranberry, and finally by creeping snowberry. Many ecologists believe that this progressive flowering is the heaths' way to make sure their pollen is delivered to the right address. If they all flowered at the same time, pollinating bumblebees might visit one species of flower, then carry their pollen to an incompatible flower, thus wasting pollen, which is very expensive, energy-wise, for the plants to produce. This way, only one species blooms at a time, so bees can't help but make the right delivery.

Value to Wildlife

The semi-open bog forest differs from the open bog in one important way—it has trees. The branches of spruce and tamarack are nesting, perching, and food-gathering sites for squirrels, hawks, owls, jays, wrens, flycatchers, warblers, and chickadees—all species that also frequent upland conifer forests. The random groupings of trees provide the occasional cover that moose, deer, lynx, and bobcats need to safely cross the bog. The trees also shed branches that become home to shrews, garter snakes, and four-toed salamanders. Shrubby willows below the trees provide nesting sites for warblers, and berry-bearing bushes

THE EXCEPTION TO THE RULE
Tamaracks are the only conifers in the northwoods that are not evergreen. Each autumn, their delicate sprays of green turn yellow and fall to the ground. Unlike evergreens, which must protect their needles from drying winter winds, tamaracks don't need rigid cells or waxy coatings on their needles. That's why their needles are so soft and pliable.

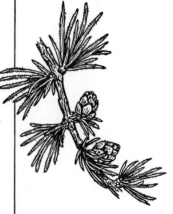

CULTURAL ROOTS
Indians once used the fibrous roots of tamarack to bind together birch bark canoes and to stitch wounds. The black resin that oozes from its trunk was known as "lumberman's chewing gum."

attract hungry fall visitors. The mossy hummocks between the trees provide cave-like tangles for dens, tunnels, and runways of snowshoe hares and burrowing mammals. Some songbirds also feather their nests in these hummocks.

Wildlife Action

Look in dense spruce boughs for nervous red squirrels clipping spruce cones and gray jays caching bundles of food. At the base of the trees, shrews and voles unearth and devour overwintering larch sawfly young. Be careful not to disturb the moist lairs of snakes and salamanders under fallen branches and logs. Growing in the shelter of tamaracks, shrubby willows conceal crouching snowshoe hares, and the nests of Connecticut and Nashville warblers. Watch the open patches, too, for the spring courtship displays of spruce grouse or for the passing of silent hunters such as the great gray, saw-whet, and hawk owl.

GRAY JAY

The gray jay may be one species you don't have to seek out. If you are camping in needleleafs, chances are good that the gray jay, or "camp robber" as the loggers knighted it, will be around to see you. These bold pilferers will take anything they can get their beaks around, whether they have a use for it or not. Bacon from the pan, chunks of freshly caught fish, table scraps, matches, cigarettes, pencils, the bait from a trapline, or the very food from your plate. They are said to have a special fondness for baked beans!

They've also made themselves fairly unpopular with hunters because of their early warning alarm system. When a hunter appears, the gray jay sounds a warning call from its lookout far above, thus allowing any animals in the area to escape.

When they're not making off with your food, they find their own in the form of insects, fruits, seeds, buds, lichen, birds' eggs, and even small mice. As their Latin name suggests (*Perisoreus* means heapup in Greek), gray jays cache what they don't eat for future use. They've developed an effective method of binding the small pieces together with their thick saliva and then gluing these packets to trees and branches for safekeeping.

In the spring, you may be fortunate to find a female leading her new hatchlings on a foraging expedition. Using the branches like the rungs of a ladder, the clan explores the tree from bottom to top, then parachutes gently to the base of another one.

Look for gray jays: feeding on the ground, or gleaning insects from branch and leaf surfaces.

Look for nests: typically 5–12 feet up in the crown of a low tree or lower down, near the trunk or branchtips. The nest—large, bulky, and made of twigs, strips of bark, grasses, and dry moss—is held together with spider webs and cocoons. It has a deep cradle, and the rim is smaller than the base to fit snugly about the female's body, thus trapping heat for the clutch of 3 to 4 young. This heat-conserving technique is a special adaptation to a cold environment, much needed for this early nesting (March and April) bird.

Listen for: "whee-ah, chuck-chuck." They also scold, scream, and whistle. Commenting on their vocal variety, some people have said that any strange noise in the northwoods could be attributed to the gray jay.

Gray jay.

BOREAL CHICKADEE

Boreal chickadees are the ones with brown derbies that accent their brown coats and black bibs. They are also one of the few tiny birds that are able, amazingly enough, to handle the rigors of a northwoods winter. As the temperature drops, their heartbeat rises, so that on a sub-zero day, an active feeding bird can be expected to clock more than 1,000 beats per minute, up from a low of 500 when asleep. Chickadees are also fast and agile, able to change their flight direction in three-hundredths of a second, wings humming at 30 strokes per second.

To gather enough in a short winter's day to fuel their internal furnace, they must stay incredibly active. Despite bitter cold, you will see them at work, poking into bark crannies for cocoons and dormant insects, searching for seeds in needleleaf cones, and hanging upside-down from snow laden branches. Before the snow flies, these chickadees "squirrel" away bits of food along the underside of branches. This way, when food along the top of the branches is sealed away by a mantle of snow, they can raid their own stores to stay alive.

They are particularly fond of lowland needleleaf forests because of the abundance of decaying trees that usually exists here. These cavity nesters prefer trees that have soft heartwood and hard exterior layers and bark.

Look for boreal chickadees: searching along the branches for insects. Their habit of hanging upside-down will help you identify them.

Look for nests: 1–10 feet up, in cavities of decaying trees that are firm outside and soft inside. They may excavate several holes before choosing one, or they may use an abandoned woodpecker hole. Look for the female bringing food to the young, reportedly at a rate of 24 times an hour.

Boreal chickadee.

Listen for: a slow, drawling "psik-a-zee-zee-zee" in a weak, husky voice that slurs downward at the end of the phrase. When alarmed, a single chickadee will sound a sharp chattering note that sends all nearby birds to cover. Although this bird assumes a certain risk by calling attention to itself, it may be rewarded at another time when a different chickadee sounds the alarm. As some researchers have suggested, the maxim in the bird world seems to be "the bird you save today may be the one that sounds the alarm call tomorrow." When a predator such as an owl is actually spotted, the entire flock will join in a shrill, penetrating chorus. For the owl, it becomes difficult to locate any one bird in the midst of all that racket.

WHITE-THROATED SPARROW

The white-throated sparrow has many nicknames, most of them referring to its evocative, melancholy, and memorable song. The "Canada bird" is also called

310

the "nightingale" because it sings freely at night and even as it migrates, which is unusual.

The whitethroat is mainly vegetarian, feasting on many weed seeds, including the noxious (to humans at least) ragweed and knotweed plants. When the young hatch and are begging to be fed, the parents' diet switches to proteins, and they gather beakfuls of insects as quickly as they can. When the young depart, it's back to seeds and berries.

Look for white-throated sparrows: scratching on the ground to uncover food or singing from a perch among lower branches.

Look for nests: well-concealed in a brush pile, under a fallen limb, in a grassy hummock, a mat of dead branches, or under a bracken fern. The nest is usually placed at the edge of a clearing and at a particular angle from a nearby perch, which may provide a lookout before the bird returns to the nest. After perching, the wary parent will fly to the ground some distance from the nest and run to it. They exit running as well.

Listen for: a whistling "Old Sam Peabody, Peabody, Peabody" repeated frequently. Some folks hear "Oh sweet Canada, Canada, Canada." These sparrows may sing at night.

White-throated sparrow.

OLIVE-SIDED FLYCATCHER

"Quick, three beers" is a common song in tamarack swamps, and a distinctive signature of the olive-sided flycatcher. The singer is most likely to be sitting on its favorite perch on a high, dead branch overlooking an opening. From here the flycatcher can patrol its territory, chase intruders, and dart out to snatch a winged meal. Because its pinnacle is close to the sun and far above the shadows, olive-sided flycatchers are one of the first birds to herald the sunrise, and the last to sing at sunset.

Most everything the flycatcher eats can be taken in the air, and most of its meals are from the ant-wasp-bee group of insects. Besides these, it also eats flat-headed borers, which damage spruce trees.

If you happen to walk near a tree containing a fly-

Olive-sided flycatcher.

311

catcher nest, you'll have an opportunity to see this bird at close range. First the flycatcher will scold you with its three-note alarm. Like a geiger counter, the closer you get, the more agitated it becomes, darting nervously, swooping once or twice over your head. If you ignore the warning, the flycatcher may attack, screaming, snapping, and nearly striking. Not surprisingly, few species attempt to nest in the vicinity of a flycatcher's nest.

During the 3 weeks that young flycatchers are in the nest, parents feed them insects. The yellow-orange mouth linings in the young trigger the parental response and show the parents where to place the food.

Look for olive-sided flycatchers: perched upright on bare branches at the top of tall needleleafs.

Look for nests: far out on horizontal branches high up in needleleaf trees (15–50 feet). These twiggy saucers are shallow and rather small for the size of the bird.

Listen for: "quick, three beers," a loud ringing call that carries a long distance. Also listen for the triumphant call of a hunting flycatcher returning to its perch after a tasty, flying meal.

Connecticut warbler.

CONNECTICUT WARBLER

The name Connecticut warbler is a misnomer on many counts. First, although it was named for its place of discovery, it is rarely seen in Connecticut, except en route to South America for the winter. Second, the last part of its Latin name is *agilis*, named by noted ornithologist Wilson, who claimed that the bird is "more than commonly active, not remaining for a moment in the same position." Actually, the Connecticut warbler is very careful and deliberate in its movements. It walks instead of hops and will perch for a long time, staring through its spectacle-like white eye rings.

Still and well-camouflaged among the grave-like moss mounds of the bog forest, the Connecticut warbler can remain perfectly hidden from sight, flushing at the last minute, just as you are about to step on it.

312

Look for Connecticut warblers: walking secretly on and around mossy hummocks. They are well-camouflaged and may be difficult to see. In the fall, they put on a lot of fat in preparation for their southward journey.

Look for nests: on the ground, deeply cupped and sunken into sphagnum moss hummocks. The rim of the nest is flush with the top of the mound.

Listen for: a loud, shrill, yet pleasing "beecher, beecher, beecher" or "chippy, chippy, chippy, chipper."

TENNESSEE WARBLER

Speaking of misnomers, the Tennessee warbler neither breeds nor winters in Tennessee. It was discovered there, and hence its name.

Audubon saw only three Tennessee warblers in his life, and now, because they are so abundant, especially at migration time, it appears that this species may have benefited from the wholesale clearing of forests for logging and agriculture. For the Tennessee is a bird of openings, favoring boggy swales in the North, and upland openings in other parts of its range. In its winter home, it shows a preference for coffee plantations, repeating its preference for open woods, where tree crowns are not quite touching.

Tennessee warbler.

Researchers in Panama have observed that migrating Tennessee warblers have a unique way of establishing a pecking order. They struggle for the right to be the first to feed on the nectar of one of their favorite flowers, the combretum. The dominant bird then becomes "war painted" with the brilliant red pollen of the flower. This stain announces that he is the dominant bird, so that other birds do not waste energy challenging his right to that feeding spot. Lesser birds quickly defer.

This insect eater eats small insects that its tiny, precise beak is perfectly adapted to handle. Birds larger than the Tennessee are not interested in these minute meals. In addition to insects, the Tennessee has been known to pierce grapes and drink the juice.

Look for Tennessee warblers: in flocks in the tree-tops (up to 40 feet) in the spring "warbler wave." They are abundant again in the fall, feeding in the weed tangles and hedgerows.

Look for nests: well-hidden under sedge tussocks or on the ground under a small shrub. Nests are deeply cupped and made of a coarse, grasslike sedge.

Listen for: a loud, persistent, three-part, chipper-ing trill and little "yeaps," which announce its passage from treetop to treetop.

NASHVILLE WARBLER

In our area, Nashvilles are most abundant in late September when birds that have been breeding in Canada gather with our flocks for their trek to Mexico and Central America. At this time, many needleleaf habitats are fairly alive with birds, many of them Nashvilles, searching among the thick dried weedtops for insect fuel for their long-distance flight.

The Nashville eats vast quantities of leaf-destroying caterpillars, plant lice, locusts, and to our delight, mosquitoes. East of us, the Nashville resides in old fields and open needleleaf woods. Like many of our open-country and shrub-loving birds, the Nashville profited when settlers cleared the land.

Look for Nashville warblers: in the lower story of the forest, hovering on beating wings to snatch a morsel from a leaf. Look for them singing from the top of a small tree.

Look for nests: on the ground, well-concealed in the side of a hummock of sphagnum moss. Stoop down and look under overhanging vegetation. If you happen to flush a brooding female, she will feign injury to distract your attention from the nest.

Listen for: a loud, ringing "che-see, che-see, che-see" or a chippering, starting slowly and then accelerating and increasing in volume.

Nashville warbler.

Marten.

©Vera Ming Wong 1988

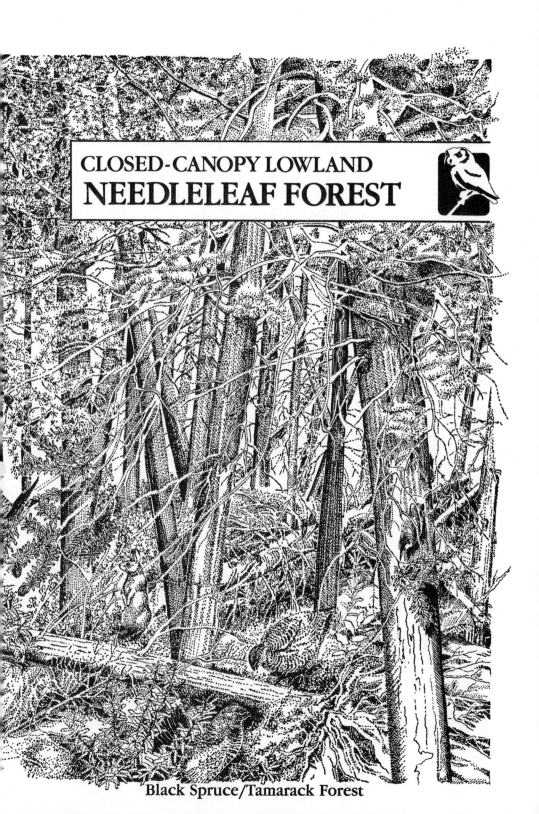

CLOSED-CANOPY LOWLAND
NEEDLELEAF FOREST

Black Spruce/Tamarack Forest

On clear spring mornings, a dense layer of low-lying ground fog blankets everything. Beads of condensed water drip from tamarack needles and dangle from spider webs. Only the tall spires of black spruce and balsam fir trees rise above the thick, chilly mist. Within the network of interlaced branches, the tufted ears of a lynx twitch, then disappear. A few leaps ahead, a snowshoe hare beelines for refuge, negotiating the moguls of moss at top speed. As predator and prey fade into the overgrown shadows of the bog forest, your imagination races after them.

What Is a Closed-Canopy Lowland Needleleaf Forest?

From a distance, this forest of needleleaf trees looks flat-topped, as if it's been sheared by giant clippers. Inside, the overstory is dense, up to 60 feet high, letting little light in. Trees grow so closely together that fallen trunks and branches often become snagged before they reach the ground, forming a chaotic tangle of brush and trees. Stumps, logs, pits, and mounds lay hidden beneath an unstable carpet of mosses. Acidic black water oozes from the sphagnum as you walk. Interlaced branches and unsloping terrain challenge you to keep your bearings as all directions begin to look alike. Depending on the site and ecological history, dominant trees are black spruce, tamarack,

1. *Brown Creeper*
2. *Porcupine*
3. *Red Squirrel*
4. *Lynx*
5. *Evening Grosbeak*
6. *Snowshoe Hare*
7. *White-breasted Nuthatch*
8. *Spruce Grouse*
9. *Great Gray Owl*
10. *Black Spruce*
11. *Tamarack*
12. *Labrador Tea*
13. *Leatherleaf*
14. *Sphagnum Moss*
15. *Lady's-Slipper*
16. *False Solomon's Seal*

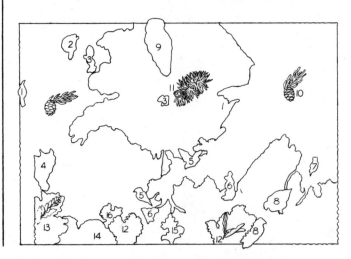

northern white-cedar, or balsam fir. A muskeg, open bog, or some other type of wetland may adjoin this forest.

Two Varieties of Lowland Forest

While equally impenetrable to human travelers, **black spruce bogs** and **northern white-cedar swamps** differ in several important ways.

In spruce bogs, acidic groundwater moves at an extremely slow rate through spongelike, saturated peat. Peat is composed of many layers of not-yet-decomposed plants and plant parts. (The water in the bog forest is too acidic and cold to support the organisms that normally cause decay.) Acid-tolerant, needleleaf heath plants dominate the understory.

In northern white-cedar swamps, the water that trickles through is neutral or slightly alkaline and carries higher concentrations of important plant nutrients. As a result, understory plants more typical of fertile woodlands are found here, as are several lovely, but rare, orchids.

Origins

Black Spruce/Tamarack Forest

Black spruce sometimes grows in pure stands, but is more often seen growing together with tamarack. Unlike the sparsely treed muskeg bog (see page 302), these forests have a continuous canopy of densely packed trees. Few understory plants, other than mosses, can survive their deep shade. Pure tamarack forests are a bit brighter, because of the sparse foliage on the branches.

In both forests, sounds are muffled by deep cushions of sphagnum and feather mosses and by wisps of old man's beard lichen draped from branches. Beneath the mosses, well-preserved twigs and charcoal fragments many years old confirm that fires do occasionally claim these bog forests. In unusually dry years, smoldering ground fires may eat their way through layers of dried-out peat, killing off trees and shrubs at their roots. Burns tend to eliminate tamarack, but black spruce can reestablish itself after fire.

Located high in spruce crowns, beyond reach of the flames, clusters of persistent cones may continue to shed seeds gradually for as many as 4 years after ripening.

Black spruce is heavily utilized for pulpwood. Our society consumes paper products at an annual rate equivalent to ⅔ acre of forest per person, much of which comes from the lowland forests of the U.S. and Canadian northwoods. When these forests are harvested, wildlife species specially adapted to survive here usually disappear as well, replaced by species adapted to openings. When undisturbed for many years, black spruce-tamarack forests may eventually be followed by northern white-cedar swamps.

Northern White-Cedar Forest

When an old spruce, weakened at its base with heart-rot, finally snaps and falls to the ground, it begins to prepare the way for the future development of a northern-white-cedar-dominated forest. The fallen trunk slowly begins to decay and become incorporated into the mossy mat. Compared to the rest of the nutrient-poor bog, the rotting log, which is blanketed with water-soaked sphagnum, is a fertile seedbed. It may harbor some white-cedar seeds left by cone-harvesting red squirrels or by late fall windstorms. When spring arrives, the raised log sites are the first to emerge from the melting snow, and often remain perched above standing water. Studies have shown that these linear nurseries supported 75–85 percent of all white-cedar seedlings in one forest, although they occupied only 16 percent of the forest floor. Such places are also ideal nurseries for the everpresent bunchberry, a cluster of showy lady's-slippers, or the delicate blossoms of goldthread.

White-cedar is sometimes called "arborvitae," a name derived from the French word "l'arbre de vie," meaning tree of life. Though its life is long, the arborvitae's growth is slow, so slow that the twisted base of century-old individuals is sometimes only 6 inches thick. Four-hundred-year-old trees are frequently found in undisturbed swamps, and one

Northern White-Cedar Forest

©1989 Vera Ming Wong

gnarled Minnesota Methuselah is believed to be more than 1,100 years old!

In spite of spreading roots, these old white-cedars tilt and lean on the spongy peat of the swamp. Continuously growing toward sunlight, their trunks acquire distinctive sweeping curves after years of gradual tipping. When a cedar is uprooted suddenly by the wind, branches thrust into the moist peat take root. Other skyward-pointing branches are transformed into new trunks. The original trunk, buried under deepening layers of moss, eventually dies, but in its place stand several vigorous replacements—arborvitae, tree of life!

Although they are most likely to follow a spruce-tamarack forest, white-cedars will also invade shrub swamps after wildfires or water-level changes. As they mature, they form a tightly knit canopy that keeps rain and sunlight from reaching the lower levels. Black spruce and tamarack seedlings do poorly in the deep shade and drier conditions found below, but balsam fir is shade-tolerant enough to make it. Sometimes, after white-cedars are harvested or badly browsed, balsam fir or even swamp hardwoods such as black ash will take over a stand. It's more likely, however, that an undisturbed white-cedar swamp will persist for generations.

White-cedar swamps were among the last forested

1. Northern Saw-whet Owl
2. Golden-crowned Kinglet
3. Northern Parula
4. Black-backed Woodpecker
5. White-tailed Deer
6. Southern Bog Lemming
7. Showy Lady's-slipper
8. Naked Miterwort
9. Dwarf Raspberry
10. Goldthread
11. Red Currant
12. Cinnamon Fern
13. Black Ash
14. Balsam Fir
15. Northern White-cedar

habitats to be cut during the logging spree at the turn of the century. Extremely resistant to decay, cedar heartwood was used for fenceposts, shingles, and canoes before other durable materials became available. By the mid-1900's, cedar stands were reduced by roughly 75 percent. Regeneration of these stands can be difficult, especially where large numbers of deer browse the saplings.

Value to Wildlife

Black Spruce/Tamarack Forest

Few animals make their homes here, and those that do capitalize on what limited abundance this forest has to offer. Spruce grouse, for instance, feed on conifer needles and on the tough, leathery leaves of heath plants. Early greening grasses are important to hungry bears emerging from their dens. Some songbirds and squirrels pry seeds out of the tiny spruce cones. Others search for insect larvae that bore into the shaded, half-rotting trees. For others, the dense tree canopy is a source of temporary shelter from winter winds or the eyes of roving predators. For small mammals, the sphagnum provides good burrowing turf, and these mammals, in turn, provide a source of energy for owls, hawks, and other predators.

Northern White-Cedar Forest

Winter weather conditions beneath a dense cedar canopy are moderate compared to those found on open bogs or in upland forests nearby. Less snow accumulates on the ground, biting winds are greatly reduced, and nighttime temperatures often remain higher. Wildlife find not only shelter, but also plenty to eat in these swamps. White-tailed deer strip white-cedar branches clean as high as they can reach, creating easily visible browse lines. Moose eat large quantities of young balsam fir and some cedar. Snowshoe hares nip off smaller bits of foliage passed over by larger herbivores. Red squirrels eat the buds, while porcupines girdle the thin-barked cedar stems. In the summer, these swamps support a host of small insect-eating birds. Larch sawfly, a needle-eating insect

WITCHES' BROOMS

Those brushy clumps of distorted branches in the canopy are known as "witches' brooms." In black spruce, they are most often caused by dwarf mistletoe, a parasitic plant that sinks its roots into the branches. This invasion presumably upsets the balance of growth hormones in the spruce, causing scores of dormant buds along the branch to start growing. This cluster of new branches and twigs weakens the tree by usurping an unfair share of nutrients and water. Fungi can also cause brooming in spruces and firs. Look for the yellow-orange rust (fruiting bodies and spores) on the twigs in these brooms. Pines and other needleleaf trees in dense forests may develop "stimulation brooms" when they are suddenly exposed to sunlight. Look for these masses in trees that are next to a new road or logging operation.

that is occasionally present in large numbers, will add to the diet of many swamp birds.

Wildlife Action

Perhaps the best way to observe wildlife in the bog forest is to find a freshly fallen log at the edge of a clearing, sit down, and wait quietly for things to happen.

Black Spruce/Tamarack Forest

Warblers, kinglets, and chickadees scour spruce and tamarack boughs for insect larvae. Cones are investigated by red squirrels and seed-eating birds. Northern parula warblers conceal their nests within pendant clumps of lichen. Three-toed woodpeckers chisel off patches of spruce bark. Roving black bears may strip away much larger sections of bark to chew on the soft, sweet sapwood beneath. Compacted pathways in the soft sphagnum mat reveal travel routes used by snowshoe hare or small southern bog lemmings.

Northern White-Cedar Forest

Check around the shaggy, twisted bases of white-cedars for wood chips scattered by pileated woodpeckers as they carve out huge rectangular holes in search of carpenter ant colonies, or for fresh sprays of white-cedar leaves clipped and dropped by red squirrels. Look for browse lines left by wintering deer.

GREAT GRAY OWL

With a body that stands 2½ feet tall, and a tail that flows another foot or more below its perch, the great gray owl is simply huge. It is also beautiful, crowned with a solemn, circular face of muted grays. Perched on a branch overlooking a prime meadow vole runway, this uncanny hunter is the picture of concentration, leaning forward as much as 45 degrees, eyes riveted to the blank, motionless snow below. You can often sneak up close to an owl that is locked in its hunting trance, mainly because it's not tuned in to you. It's listening for something far below the range of your hearing—the scurrying or calling of a rodent under the snow.

Owls' ears, actually openings behind their facial disks, are slightly offset, one higher than the other. The "soundings" they receive from each ear are different enough to help the owl triangulate to find the source of the sound, even as it scrambles by at top mouse-speed. Minute sounds are amplified by a covert of stiff feathers that form a kind of trough around each ear.

At the first audible footfall, the owl will spread its wings, all 5 feet of them, and sail silently from its perch. The edges of a great gray's wings are frayed so as to mute the sound of the wind whooshing by. It hovers on these wings for a moment to pinpoint its prey and then drops to the snow, plunging in with sharp, curved talons. More often than not, it emerges with a rodent dangling from one foot, killed by the squeeze of powerful muscles attached to its talons.

Owls can also be seen diving face downward from on high. Within a hair's breadth of the snow, they flip around and thrust their feet down, often disappearing deep into a drift. By extending their legs below the length of their bodies, they actually extend their hunting range to reach prey 18 inches below the surface.

Great grays eat their prey whole, on the spot, then return to their perch to digest. In the summer, one owl will eat at least four mice a day; in the winter, when demands on survival are greater, it will kill and eat all it can find.

A male will bring a female an offering of a freshly caught rodent at the beginning of the breeding season. By accepting the gift, she begins a strong pair bonding. The male will continue to bring meals all during courtship, egg laying, incubation, and later, to feed hungry nestlings. Some researchers suggest that the number of mice or lemmings the male brings early in the season has some effect on how many eggs the female will lay.

When conditions are good, reproductive success may be high, and the owl population will rise a bit. If several years of this are followed by an abrupt drop

Great gray owl.

in rodent populations, the owls may be forced to move away from their breeding grounds. In unusual years, owls travel hundreds of miles, sometimes appearing in unlikely, semi-urban places. These migrations are called "irruptions."

Look for great gray owls: perched on low branches in spruce-tamarack swamps, black ash swamps, or nearby dense mixed woods. They can also be found in open country near lowland needleleafs. In winter, you may see them walking or running on top of the snow, kept aloft by "snowshoes" of dense feathers on each foot. They like to sunbathe in higher branches, sitting for hours with their eyes closed and their face turned toward the sun. Like many birds, owls use oil from their glands to dress and clean their feathers. When this film of oil is exposed to the sun, it is turned into vitamin D. When the owl preens its feathers with its bill, it picks up this enriched oil and ingests this needed vitamin.

During the day, look for roosting owls in the crotch of a branch, flattened against the trunk of a tree. They fold their facial disks into a vertical line that matches the stripes on their breast. Both look like the scars of an aspen tree, and help the owl disappear against its background. The feathers at the sides of their head and neck have diffuse patterns and are semitransparent. When light passes through them, they tend to blur, both in photos and in real life.

Look for nests: large stick structures, 8 to 65 feet up in islands of aspen or tamarack amid a sea of black spruce. They often use the abandoned nests of ravens, crows, or hawks.

Look for plunge holes: where an owl dove into the snow in search of prey. Look for the crescent-shaped marks of folded wings hitting the snow, and the faint lines of spread wings where it hoisted itself out. You may see the impression of the tail and a drop of the prey's blood.

Look for whitewash: white, crusty splashes of waste on branches below active nests. Owlets eject this waste over the rim of nests.

Listen for: a series of 10 or more melancholy hoots, getting faster and softer at the end. Its warning cry is a series of double notes repeated up to a hundred times in a row. When threatened, owls will snap their bills—forcing the lower part of the bill against the upper to make a loud clicking sound.

SPRUCE GROUSE

Spruce grouse are truly birds of the wilderness. Humans are a relatively new element in their environment, and they have not yet had time to develop a strong fear of us. Unfortunately, we have tended to take advantage of their tameness; the first hunters who found that a spruce grouse could easily be clubbed or snatched from its perch quickly named it "fool hen."

Today, we can appreciate the spruce grouse's trusting nature for the wonders that it allows us to witness. At breeding time, the male struts and displays his tail and breast plumage like a miniature tom turkey. The display begins with an upward flight on short, cupped wings that are specially shaped for these fast takeoffs rather than sustained flight. Reaching a peak in his flight, the grouse will "drum" the air with his wings, then flutter to the ground or to another perch. The eery whirring sound is made by beating the wings rapidly in the air, and it serves to attract female grouse and to warn other males to "Stay out, this is my turf!"

Spruce grouse.

Once he's got an audience (a prospective mate) the male will shake loose his feathers so that they stand on end to expose an underlayer of color at his eye, breast, and under his tail. With wings drooped, head held high and back, and tail feathers fanned and raised straight up, the grouse will strut for hours to impress the female. These performances are best seen in early morning or evening in a clearing in the swamp.

Although young grouse are fed a generous diet of insects, adults are more interested in plant leaves, seeds, and summer berries, switching to needles and buds come fall. Once on this needleleaf diet, their flesh tastes much like turpentine, a far cry from the delectable taste of a summer, blueberry-fed bird.

Come winter, grouse sport their cold-weather plumage, which includes fluff right down to their claws. These feathers double the size of the grouse's feet, turning them into snowshoes that allow the birds to float on top of soft snow.

Look for spruce grouse: perched on low branches or picking their way over the forest floor, usually alone but sometimes in family groups.

Look for nests: hidden in a ground hollow under a clump of overhanging vegetation at the base of a tree trunk. A brooding female is so well-camouflaged that you may step on her before she will move and risk giving away the location of her nest.

Look for courting grounds: in small openings in needleleaf swamps. You can often find a spot in the moss that has been flattened or covered with green, segmented droppings. At the edge of the clearing, you might find a low, exposed branch that is worn in one spot where a displaying male repeatedly perches.

Listen for: a noisy whirring (drumming) or fluttering of wings from a branch, log, or from the air. A rustling sound, like sandpaper rubbing as the male fans his tailfeathers. Low hooting, clucking, hissing, or squeaking.

NORTHERN PARULA

Northern parula.

Parula is a form of the Latin word for "small, small bird." Despite its tiny size, you can often get a good binocular fix on a parula because it tends to feed out in the open at the tops of trees. Most commonly you'll find it hanging upside-down, like a chickadee, gleaning beetles, inchworms, and plant lice from needles and twigs.

The parula suspends its nest in a sling of "old man's beard," or *Usnea*, the mossy, pale green lichen that dangles from spruce branches. Its preference for this lichen keeps the parula closely tied to habitats such as upland and lowland spruce forests where *Usnea* is abundant.

Look for northern parulas: picking insects from branches, twigs, and needles—often hanging upside-down.

Look for basket-shaped nests: swinging from the tip of a branch, anywhere from 6–100 feet up. The nest is made of grass, bark, and vegetable fiber, and neatly hidden in a suspended "purse" of old man's beard lichen.

Listen for: a buzz that rises up the scale.

BLACK-BACKED WOODPECKER

When motionless, this woodpecker's coat of black renders it almost invisible against the charred bark of burnt trees. This camouflage may have been especially effective in the days when frequent fires blackened the northwoods swamps. Today, it also works well against the darkened bark of old or dead tamaracks and black spruces.

Notoriously persistent, the blackback will often work in the same place for as long as 10 minutes, filling the woods with the sound of its hammering. Methodically turning its head side to side, as if listening for grubs, the bird slants its beak under the bark and chisels away patch after patch. It continues until the whole trunk is debarked, exposing a road-map of bark beetle tunnels and holes made by borers. With a sticky, brush-tipped tongue, the blackback laps up its reward of grubs (immature bark beetles), weevils, borers, or ants.

Black-backed woodpecker.

They also use their beaks to chisel out nesting holes, often stripping enough bark from the tree to leave a conspicuous white ring around the entrance. Some researchers believe that this ring may act as a marker to help the returning bird find its nest among the dark tree trunks.

Look for black-backed woodpeckers: clinging to the trunks of dead or fire-scarred trees, especially where some bark has already been removed. They seem to prefer trees that are beginning to die (needles turning brown) or that have recently died (needles falling off). There may be a choice insect that lives under the bark only at this time, leaving the tree after it has been dead for a while. These woodpeckers often return to the same tree day after day, and may even return after a season in migration!

Look for nest holes: typically 5–12 feet up on the trunk. The entrance is strongly beveled at the lower edge, forming a "door-step" that is characteristic of the species. There may be a white ring of stripped bark around the entrance. It sometimes nests in live trees that are soft with decay inside. The hard outer surface makes it more difficult for predators, such as black bears, to claw their way into the nest.

Look for patches of white on trunk: where black-backed woodpeckers have scaled off the bark. Also look for fallen bark chips on the ground.

Listen for: a sharp "kip" or a scolding rattle. It also has a soft, wooden call that is said to resemble the "cluck" used in New England to start a horse. Like all woodpeckers, the blackback also has its own sound "tattoo," a hammering pattern that distinguishes it from other species.

GOLDEN-CROWNED KINGLET

This kinglet is one of the smallest and most maneuverable birds in the needleleaf forest. It is constantly in motion—tacking back and forth, shadowing flies in flight, or hovering like a hummingbird on invisible wings. Watch closely as it races by, stops on a dime, and snatches a caterpillar with a movement that's often faster than the eye can see. When it does pause, it may land rather close to you.

In the winter, some kinglets will stay in the north-woods, joining flocks of brown creepers, woodpeckers, chickadees, and nuthatches. These mixed flocks can hunt over a large area, and thus find more food sources than individuals could on their own. Also, flocking gives the group more "eyes" to spot and avoid potential foes.

Look for golden-crowned kinglets: en route to or from the upper limbs of trees. Their favorite foods are insects on the wing or on needles, branches, twigs, and tree trunks. Watch for their characteristic wing-flicking, open and closed, as they hop from twig to twig.

Look for nests: woven into a dense cluster of twigs in the horizontal limbs, typically 30 to 60 feet up. These bulky nests are made of moss and spider webs and lined with fur and feathers for warmth.

Listen for: a song that starts high, then drops to a staccato chatter. The golden-crowned kinglet is not as melodious as its near relative, the ruby-crowned kinglet.

Golden-crowned kinglet.

SNOWSHOE HARE

Humans might have easily copied the design for snowshoes from the hind feet of this northern hare. They are long and heavily furred, with a wide spread of toes to keep the hare aloft on soft snow. Snowshoe hare tracks are common in the northwoods; look for habitually used areas where hare traffic has thumped down highways in the snow.

Their snowy coloration is another adaptation to northwoods winters. By the time the snow flies, hares have lost their brown summer coat and grown a white one that allows them to freeze still against the heavy drifts, virtually disappearing from sight.

For further protection, hares stick to areas where they can be shielded from airborne predators such as great horned owls. The dense-canopied needleleaf swamps fit the bill nicely, especially if their second favorite habitat, the shrub swamp, is adjacent. Hares will also seek out young broadleaf forests where they binge on the tender parts of leafy trees. In the summer, succulent grasses and forbs make up most of their diet.

Although their traditional enemies are lynx and bobcats, these hares seem, at times, to be their own worst enemies. Every 10 years or so, their prolific populations undergo a boom and a bust. During the boom, a virtual army of hares fills the needleleaf swamps with tracks and signs of feeding—stripped bark and nipped buds. Their collective appetites work against them, as they literally eat themselves out of house and home. A study in Alaska suggests that the shoots coming back on these severely browsed saplings may contain "defensive" chemicals that are unpalatable to hares. Eventually, this reduction in food supply takes its toll, and soon hares are fewer, weaker, and more prone to predators.

In the meantime, lynx and other animals that eat hares have been experiencing a heyday, growing in numbers to match the plentiful food supply. When the hare population begins to crash, often to a twentieth of its former size, the predators crash as well. The roller coaster goes up again, however, when the vegetation recovers, and there are fewer predators to threaten the growing hare numbers.

Look for snowshoe hares: in brushy understories during the day. When flushed and chased, hares almost always circle back to where they started. Their busiest hour is just before midnight when they can be seen clipping vegetation along their trails, or stretching and rolling in dust wallows to remove ticks. Their springtime mating antics are worth watching. A jumping, dancing procession of males may chase a female until she faces them off, standing upright and drumming her hind feet. In squawking battles with one another, the males leapfrog each other, trying to kick the opponent as they go by. They are easiest to spot between their brown and white phase, when they are pinto-colored.

Look for nests: in a packed-down depression under a log; in a sheltered area of grass, brush, or low trees; or even in an entrance to an old woodchuck burrow.

Look for trails: chewed through vegetation or stomped out in snow, serving as a network of highways across the home range. Other animals also use these packed-down travel routes, so be on the lookout for tracks.

Look for matted vegetation: or "forms" where hares rest during the day. These 6–8-inch-wide

Snowshoe hare.

332

depressions are often next to a natural feature that offers protection, such as a log, rock, or grass tuft.

Look for the browse line: on trees and saplings, a level below which woody vegetation is retarded. The line shows how high the hares could reach, standing on hind feet on top of snow, to browse bark and buds.

Listen for: thumping, low chirps, snorts, grunts, or the shrill, bleating cry of a hare in trouble.

LYNX

In a trail stomped down by the hare's snowshoe feet, the lynx slinks along, head lower than shoulders, muscles rippling under a thick warm coat. It climbs up an inclined log along the trail to watch and wait. Its eyes, placed far apart on its head, act like binoculars to pick out the ghostly form of a white hare against a matching snowdrift. Before too long, the hare dashes below, and with a few powerful bounds, the lynx's huge paws reach the hare and hold it down for the kill.

The lynx is especially effective at night, when special light-sensitive rods in its eyes give it extraordinary vision (lynx means lamp). The iris muscles that control pupil diameter react quickly to sudden darkness, and a special reflecting layer in the retina further intensifies visual images. Any light that passes the first layer without being absorbed is bounced back through again, doubling the electrical signals that the lynx receives. These mirror rods cause the "nightshine" you see when a light shines in a cat's eyes.

For a medium-sized cat like the lynx, the hare is a perfect prey: small enough to overcome, but large enough to fill its 3-pounds-a-day meat requirement. If the lynx depended entirely on small mice or voles, it would spend most of its energy collecting enough to fill its stomach. A lynx will eat about 200 hares a year, and, like any economy based primarily on one crop, the lynx's welfare is tied to the hare's welfare. Thus, lynx are dragged along on the hare's roller coaster cycle of crash and resurgence every 10 years or so.

LYNX-EYED
The term "lynx-eyed," meaning keenly sighted, comes from a European belief that lynx could see through walls. They can't, of course, but they can see in very dim light.

Look for lynx: hunting along snowshoe hare trails at night, or during the day in wilder areas. They climb up logs to scout and may snooze there on cool days. They don't like to exert themselves in hot weather because of their heavy coat. Twice as large as house cats, lynx can be recognized by their muttonchop style ruffs, their long ear tufts, and their 4-x-4-inch feet that look like "furry floormops." They do have the curiosity of a house cat, though, and trappers use this to lure them with bits of colored thread or shiny objects.

Look for dens: in hollows created by upturned tree roots or bent-over branches. Also look in cleared areas in the midst of thickets, among rocks, or in hollow logs. Lynx prefer to nest in extensive, unbroken forests far from human activity.

Look for tracks: 4-x-4 inches, in swamp mud or the dust of roads. The hindfoot looks like a tailed snowshoe. Stiff winter hairs on the bottom of its feet cover the toepads and remove the detail from the tracks.

Look for "cairns": a pile of droppings displayed on stumps, anthills, etc., to advertise the cat's presence in that range.

Look for eyeshine: the green shine of their eyes in car headlights.

Listen for: caterwauling of male cats at breeding season. This long, plaintive cry was described by John Burroughs: "If a lost soul from Hades had been given a few hours freedom, but had to be back at the striking of midnight, it might let off such a heartbreaking moan as I heard."

Lynx.

334

WIDE-RANGING WILDLIFE

Some species make their living by visiting a mixed bag of habitats, from the soggiest wetlands to the sandiest uplands. Because they show up everywhere, they are familiar to anyone who spends much time in the northwoods. The fact that they can survive in many different habitats is an adaptive trait, acquired through the rigors of natural selection. Their flexibility enables them to find enough food, space, cover, and water to survive and to pass on their genes to offspring.

Other species in this chapter are "area-sensitive" species: those that need large areas of uninterrupted habitat to roam in. Summer homes, roads, and farms often slice up these expanses, inviting more development, and curtailing the area's usefulness to wide-ranging species such as wolves. Realizing this, land managers have an opportunity to propose (with the public's blessing) measures that would reroute development so as to keep these sanctuaries whole.

GREAT HORNED OWL

It is said that almost any living thing that crawls, flies, hops, slithers, or runs eventually falls prey to the insatiable appetite of the great horned owl (even musky shrews and skunks!). Below one nest, a biologist counted 120 fairly fresh bodies of black rats, with their skulls open and only their brains eaten. Despite their savage reputation, however, these master hunters have a hard time getting peace and quiet during the day.

Great horned owls search long and hard for a secluded treetop to roost in. They keep their ears erect and their feathers compressed, creating a slim, vertical shape that hides them from most passers-by. Unfortunately, however, crows see through the guise. As soon as an American crow spots a dozing owl, it

Great horned owl.

begins a raucous cawing that draws neighboring crows from far and wide. The mob gathers in the surrounding branches and begins a relentless taunting, until the owl, unable to stand it, flies away. Undaunted, the black mob trails after the owl and lands in tree after tree. It may be a long time until the owl can shake its harassers.

The shoe is sometimes on the other foot, however, as owls have been known to break up a sleeping flock, and on occasion, to make a meal of crow. Though they are adept at hunting anything from songbirds to geese, great horned owls specialize in mid-sized prey such as hares and grouse.

Look for great horned owls: at dusk and at night flying through branches or over meadows, searching for movement beneath them. A tree-roosting owl (daytime) is often right in the middle of a flock of crows.

Look for nests: 30–70 feet up, in stick nests abandoned by herons, hawks, or crows. Owls occasionally lay their eggs on the bare surfaces of cliffs or caves, or in natural cavities.

Listen for: a prolonged, tremulous hooting: "hoo, hoo-hoo, HOO HOO" that sounds like a distant fog horn or dogs barking far away. They are noisiest in midwinter, when their breeding season opens with bouts of competitive hooting among males for territory. When alarmed, they bristle their feathers and snap their bills. To find sleeping owls during the day, listen for crows making a ruckus in the treetops.

GRAY WOLF

Loons may laugh, and northern lights may flicker, but those who have heard howling agree: nothing says "northwoods" more eloquently than a wolf pack. A chorus begins with a single howl lifting clear out of the darkness. One by one, other wolves raise their voices, each in a different pitch, yet in concert with the one that came before. Once you've heard it, a part of you listens for it always.

Wolves have long fascinated us. They've been the

objects of reverence, fear, slander, and study. They were, at one time, the most widely distributed mammal beside humans. Today, after centuries of settlement and hunting, the gray wolf occurs in only a few unspoiled areas. Minnesota's population is 1,200, and wolves have also been sighted in northern Wisconsin and Michigan.

Wolves are like primitive human hunters in that they live in close-knit groups, and cooperate in order to catch prey that are much larger than themselves. A typical wolf pack has 5 to 8 members, mostly descendants of the dominant pair. They live by a strict caste system that determines which animals will breed (usually only the dominant pair), how food will be divided, and so on. This form of social control works to keep the population in balance with the ability of the environment to support the pack.

A pack is able to patrol a large range (40–400 square miles depending on prey density), marking it with urine "fenceposts" and defending it against intruders by using sound rather than fury. If resident wolves hear an intruder howling, they have two choices. They can remain silent and retreat, thus avoiding possible attack, or they can howl back, as if to say "We're here, come no further." Research has shown that wolves are more willing to make a vocal stand if they are protecting pups or if they are feeding on a recently killed moose or white-tailed deer. Also, in breeding season, when hormonal flux makes them more aggressive by nature, a resident pack is more likely to respond to an intruder. This vocal exchange is usually enough to scare off the intruder. Thanks to this long-distance defense system, wolves need not risk their lives in physical fights each time a boundary is crossed.

Howling is also used to gather members of a pack at "rendezvous sites" before or after a hunt. Pups stay behind at these rendezvous sites until they are strong enough to hunt with the older members of the pack.

On a typical hunt, wolves may travel 10 or more miles, eyes alert and noses tuned to scent trails. After carefully stalking an animal, they'll surround it and charge, thus testing its fitness. A healthy, adult moose can usually hold a wolf pack at bay by whirling and slashing out with its sharp hooves. If, however, the animal flees, like most deer do, the wolves will chase it for 100 to 5,000 yards. If they can't close in quickly, they usually give up. Prey that are brought down by the pack are usually the old, very young, weak, diseased, or injured—those that cannot fight or run fast enough for safety. This selective hunting actually helps deer and moose by checking the spread of their diseases, removing inferior genetic traits from the pool, and, in some cases, preventing their populations from exploding and crowding their habitats.

Look for gray wolves: traveling at night or sometimes during the day along all the same routes a person might choose: roads, trails, lakeshores, or ridgetops. In the snow, they stick to windswept areas such as lakes or high ridgetops where the snow will be crusted and hard. Wolves are highly efficient trotters, traveling an average of 10 miles a day with the smooth, swinging motion that is possible because their long legs are astride a narrow torso.

Gray wolf.

Look for dens: dug into the ground, in hollow logs, under ledges, or beneath piles of debris. Dens are usually in well-drained areas with a commanding view and water nearby. Wolves often "borrow" and enlarge dens built by other animals. Look for a pile of fresh dirt at the entrance hole, littered with skin, hair, and bone fragments. Wolves use these dens for raising pups to 8 weeks of age.

Look for tracks: a symmetrical, four-toed, doglike track with claws, 5¼ by 4¼ inches, in mud near ponds, or the dust of roads and trails. When traveling overland, one wolf breaks trail and the rest follow, so that most of the pack can conserve their strength. This forms a deep snow trough.

Look for "no trespassing signs": urine stains on snowbanks along roads or lakeshores. Also look for scratches in dirt.

Look for scat: 3–5 inches long, 1 inch in diameter, made of hair and bone fragments of prey. (To avoid hazardous parasites, don't handle wolf scat.)

Look for tag-along animals: that feast on the "table scraps" left by wolf kills. These include common ravens, American crows, foxes, fishers, gray jays, bald eagles, and black-capped chickadees.

Listen for: howling choruses at rendezvous sites in July–September, and in January and February as mating approaches. A typical howling performance begins with the howl of the high-ranking male, soon joined by the yaps, whines, and howls of other members—never in unison and always in a different pitch. The eerie chorus may be heard up to 5 miles away, at any time of day or night. Also listen for the whining, barking, and growling of family members. Wolves howl frequently when defending a fresh kill. A single howl may be a lone wolf that has been separated from the pack, or one that has left to establish a new territory. These wolves are sometimes allowed to join established packs that have lost one of their dominant wolves. Or, they can form their own packs with another lone wolf.

BOBCAT

Bobcats, even where they are plentiful, can live near people for years without being seen. Their spotted coat is a masterpiece of camouflage, and their hearing and eyesight are so keen that they usually have plenty of time to vanish before you ever spot them. They use the same powers of stealth to sneak up on unsuspecting prey, placing hind feet where their forefeet have been for a more silent gait.

Bobcat.

While their 500 separate muscles allow for liquid movement on the prowl, bobcats would probably lag behind in a long-distance race. Their long legs are better suited for sprints of 25–30 mph and adrenalin-rich bounds of 6–8 feet. Rather than run on endlessly, a bobcat being chased (usually by dogs) will try to outwit its harassers by circling, and will finally resort to a treetop escape.

Part of the bobcat's success lies in its ability to exploit many kinds of habitats and prey species. When snowshoe hares are not available, bobcats switch to squirrels, mice, young and weak deer, muskrats, foxes, and even an occasional porcupine. With such a varied menu, they wind up traveling through many different habitats on their nightly hunting forays.

Look for bobcats: in any kind of dense cover. In wilder areas and during the winter, you may spot them during the day, but they normally work at night. Look for them on dirt mounds, inclined logs, rocks, or stumps—places where they watch for danger or prey. In the winter, they often move to the protective cover of swamp conifers and shrub swamps.

Look for dens: in rocky caves or fissures, hollow trees, logs, or abandoned earth burrows. Remember that bobcats are only 2 feet tall and can fit into very small spaces. Smell for urine that they spray regularly on the entrance.

Look for tracks: round, and about as large as a medium-sized dog's, 2 inches by 2 inches, zigzagging in the mud, sand, or shallow snow. There are no nail marks because of their retractable claws. You're most likely to find them on roads crisscrossing shrub swamps in the winter. Hair grows between the toes in winter, and tends to obscure the features of the tracks.

Look for piles of droppings and sprays of urine: on rocks, trees, stumps, and grass, used to proclaim their presence. Look for scratching in the dirt where they've covered their droppings.

Look for scratches: on tree trunks where they have sharpened their claws. Also look for fallen bark below these posts.

Listen for: mewing and caterwauling of toms during mating season. Territorial fights are common and although opponents don't die, they carry shredded ears that tell the tale.

MASKED SHREW

Masked shrews are about as small as an animal can be if it is to maintain a body temperature that is warmer than its environment. As it is, their skin area is vast compared to their volume, providing a lot of surface through which heat can escape. Masked shrews solve this temperature problem by keeping their internal engines well-stoked with energy-rich insect food. At a minimum, they must consume their entire weight in food every day.

Masked shrew.

For their size, masked shrews could be considered ferocious. Captive shrews have been known to attack their kin and go after mice that are much larger than they are. In the wild, they normally stick to insect prey that they can find in the leaf litter of various habitats. As long as a habitat is somewhat moist and has some ground cover, a masked shrew will take up residence.

The masked shrew's transit system includes meadow vole runways, runways it builds itself, underground mole tunnels, or tunnels in the snow. Shrews bounce highpitched noises off the walls of these tunnels, reading the echoes to find out about their environment. They also rely heavily on memorized routes, touch, and on their long whiskers, always atwitch to give them information about their surroundings.

Look for masked shrews: running in the grass or emerging from an underground tunnel in heavy leaf litter, moss, grassy cover, or along moist water borders. A voracious appetite keeps them afoot night and day, in all seasons, but they're most active in early morning and just after dark. The onset of rain also seems to stimulate activity.

Look for nests: a 3-inch-wide grass ball with a ½-inch-wide inside chamber placed in the grass, or under logs, rocks, or brush.

In the winter: look for shrews exiting or entering underground tunnels. They are busy finding food to keep them warm.

Listen for: the twitterings and highpitched squeaks of fighting shrews.

BLACK BEAR

The season's silence is broken only by the sound of your skis schussing through powdery drifts. Suddenly, from a bank of snow before you, you hear high-pitched squeals, like small puppies wriggling together. It's not your imagination; it's a bear den, and inside are some of the most extraordinary animals in all the northwoods.

As fall turns to winter, black bears stuff themselves into crevices, caves, and hollow trees, not so much to escape the cold, but to survive a season without plant food. Here they will stay for 7 months, metabolizing at half their normal rate, and just barely breathing. Females rouse themselves in January to give birth to two or three cubs, which they nurse, tend, and keep warm in between bouts of deep sleep. Even though they don't eat, drink, urinate, or defecate for all those months, 99 percent of all hibernating bears will survive, making winter the lowest risk period of the year!

Scientists are intrigued. The chloresterol level of a hibernating bear is twice its normal level, and yet they don't develop hardening of the arteries or gallstones. In fact, they produce a bile juice that seems to dissolve gallstones, even in the human patients it has been tested on! By the same token, the urea that would poison most mammals (including us) doesn't harm bears. They break it down and use it to build protein, an adaptation that helps them maintain organ and muscle tissue during the long sleep.

Bears do lose weight during the winter, however—up to 30 percent of their fall weight—and when they emerge in spring, grasses and succulent forbs are not rich enough in carbohydrates to help them gain it back. The hungry bears must supplement their spring diet with insects, and an occasional frog, nest of eggs, or animal that has died of starvation over the winter. Once summer berries, fruits, and nuts begin to ripen, however, the black bear begins to feast in earnest, eating 11 to 18 pounds of food a day, which will accumulate into a 100-pound layer of insulative fat for the winter.

It is remarkable that an animal as large as a bear can build up this kind of a fat layer on a diet of small fruits, nuts, and insects. Part of its success is due to feeding adaptations that allow the bear to fully exploit these foods when they are in season. The bear's strong legs and feet, for example, are perfect for climbing, bending down fruit-laden branches, and tearing up logs in search of insects. Their digestive systems are designed to make the most of these small packets of energy. If forests of oaks or hazelnuts are not within the bear's range, they will travel up to 20 miles to reach these feeding meccas. To help them find their way back year after year, bears are equipped with memory, navigational ability, and the capacity to learn.

The fortunes of bears rise and fall depending on the quality and availability of food in their habitat. The better the food crop, the better the female's chances of giving birth to healthy offspring. After a year or two of poor food crops, bears may experience reproductive failures, and any cubs that are born will have a harder time making it through their first year.

Look for black bears: in open wooded areas that receive enough sun to produce the dense undergrowth that bears need for food and cover. They follow regular trails, and will often visit thickets with fruits and berries when they are in season. Look for napping bears in mud wallows, along a limb, or in day beds (piles of grass and leaves in concealed areas). Along their travels, bears will stand up occasionally on their hind legs to get a better view (bears are thought to be nearsighted). Their most active periods are: twilight in spring, during the day in summer, and both day and night in fall. When trying to avoid humans (at dumps, campsites, etc.), bears will become active by night instead of by day.

Look for dens: in hollow trees, brush piles, rock crevices, caves, excavated holes in hillsides, or under upturned tree roots. They have been known to den on exposed sites such as muskrat lodges, letting the snow build up around them. Inside the den is a bedding of leaves, grass, bark, and branches. Newborn

Black bear.

cubs may be squalling inside the den in late winter, or year-old cubs may be sleeping in the den with their mother.

Look for tracks: that look like the wide footprints of a barefoot child (except for the bear claws). They may be along trails that lead to regular eating places, such as blueberry thickets, or near regularly used shallow pools called wallows.

Look for "bear trees": that have marks where a bear has reached up on hind legs and clawed the tree, chewed the bark, or rubbed it bare. Researchers suspect that bears may mark these trees to warn intruding bears of their presence. A freshly visited bear tree may smell lightly of bear and there may be hairs stuck in the sap and bark crevices.

Look for black claw marks: high up on smooth-barked aspen or beech trees. Black bears are proficient climbers, sinking their short curved claws into the bark and hitching their way up. Sometimes their claws slip before they take hold, leaving long marks that blacken and remain as scars on the bark.

Look for signs of feeding: overturned logs or rocks; torn-apart stumps; twisted and broken branches of cherry, beech, or oak trees; upturned rocks; dug-up yellow-jacket and ant nests; claw marks on logs. Bears like burned-over areas where the stumps have rotted with age and are full of wood-chewing insects.

EASTERN GARTER SNAKE

At one time, it was fashionable for the well-dressed man to wear garters to hold up his socks. It is from these sometimes gaudy items that the longitudinally striped garter snake got its name.

The garter snake is the first snake that most people see, perhaps because it is one of our most common. It is perfectly harmless, as long as you don't object to the foul-smelling liquid that it discharges when it is frightened. It will flatten out its body if you corner it, and may try to strike with its tiny, nonpoisonous teeth.

The garter snake's teeth point backwards to help

it hold frogs, toads, salamanders, small birds, and mammals, as well as its mainstay, earthworms. Like many snakes, it opens wide its jaws and devours its victims head-first so that their long limbs can be pressed backward as they are engulfed. In turn, these slender predators make meals for hawks, other birds, raccoons, skunks, and larger snakes.

Look for eastern garter snakes: along the ground in every conceivable habitat, including the water. They are active both day and night, but most active at dawn and dusk. A good time to look is when they are gathered right before hibernation, or after emerging, in spring, when sunning themselves on rocks. A good time to check rocks is on a bright, sunny day after a rainy spell.

Look for hibernating snakes: in rock fissures, rock piles, building foundations, deserted ant mounds, and channels in banks where roots have decayed. (Don't disturb!) They follow established routes when migrating to these places, and many are killed crossing highways.

Smell for: the foul liquid that snakes exude if you pick them up.

Eastern garter snake.

WILDLIFE WATCHING HOTSPOTS

Certain places in the Lake States seem to have more than their fair share of great opportunities to view wildlife. Wildlife enthusiasts from far and wide come to these hotspots to see rare species or to see large numbers of birds and animals in migration or in nesting colonies. Hawk Ridge in Duluth, Minnesota is an example. On a typical fall day, hundreds or even thousands of hawks may be seen flying overhead en route to their wintering grounds farther south.

Check the listing of hotspots for each state to find out which habitats and species they are best known for. The Wildlife Events Calendar that follows will help you time your trips so they coincide with times of greatest wildlife activity. The reward for being in the right place at the right time may be some exceptional glimpses of wildlife communities.

Minnesota Hotspots

AGASSIZ NATIONAL WILDLIFE REFUGE
(61,500 acres)

A flat landscape of marshes and bogs—watery remnant of Glacial Lake Agassiz

grebes—all five North American species breed here

snow goose—migrant flocks arrive in October

ducks—although the 16 species that breed here are outstanding, the 250,000 birds that stop over in mid-October are the real treat

Franklin's gull—spring breeding colony of thousands has been noted

black tern—nests on floating mats of dead and fallen marsh vegetation *snowy owl*—frequently seen perched on fenceposts in mid-winter

beaver—quiet observation near dawn and dusk pays off, especially in fall, when beavers are actively stockpiling food for the winter

bobcat—tracks most easily found in freshly-fallen snow

moose—find antlered bulls in lakes munching aquatic plants in mid-summer

Contact: Refuge Manager, Middle River, MN 56737 (218/449-4115)

BELTRAMI ISLAND STATE FOREST
(600,000 acres)

Lowland tamarack/black spruce bogs and forested sand ridges of jack pine and aspen

spruce grouse—along jeep trails through jack pine, especially in early morning, late evening; easiest to locate from July through October

Connecticut warbler—returns to its territory in mid-May, located by its un-warblerlike song

gray wolf—active here, but hard to spot—may respond to human howling

moose—best viewing in lowland shrub swamps during September and October rutting season

Contact: Red Lake Wildlife Management Headquarters, Roosevelt, MN 56673 (218/783-6861)

BELTRAMI/MARSHALL COUNTIES
(near Grygla)

Aspen forest, shrub-sapling openings, open grassland, and farm fields mix here with lowland shrub swamps and sedge meadows

elk (wapiti)—reintroduced here in 1935; best viewing opportunities are before spring green-up and after leaf-fall in late September

Contact: Minnesota Dept. of Natural Resources Regional Headquarters, 2115 Birchmont Beach Road, Bemidji, MN 56601

Minnesota Hotspot Map

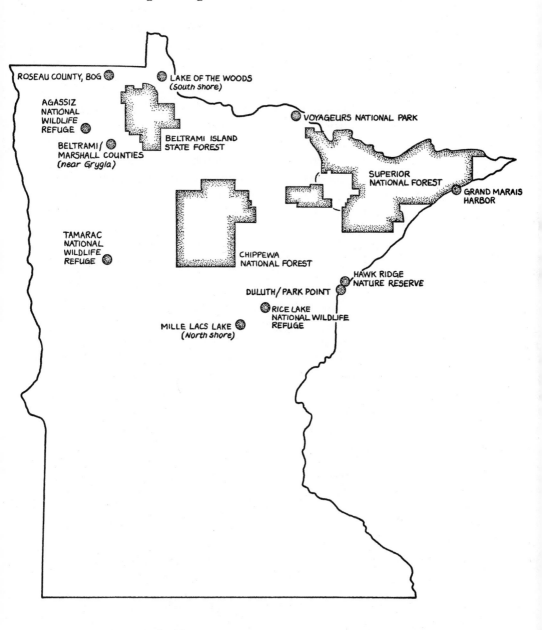

ROSEAU COUNTY, BOG

LAKE OF THE WOODS
(South shore)

AGASSIZ
NATIONAL
WILDLIFE
REFUGE

VOYAGEURS NATIONAL PARK

BELTRAMI/
MARSHALL COUNTIES
(near Grygla)

BELTRAMI ISLAND
STATE FOREST

SUPERIOR
NATIONAL FOREST

GRAND MARAIS
HARBOR

TAMARAC
NATIONAL
WILDLIFE
REFUGE

CHIPPEWA
NATIONAL FOREST

HAWK RIDGE
NATURE RESERVE

DULUTH/PARK POINT

RICE LAKE
NATIONAL WILDLIFE
REFUGE

MILLE LACS LAKE
(North shore)

CITY OF DULUTH, PORT TERMINAL

An odd habitat for most wildlife watchers; industrial harbor, grain elevators, and abandoned or neglected land and shoreline

sea ducks—many rarities on open waters of harbor each fall and winter

gyrfalcon—has been spotted hunting around grain elevators from December to February; look for panic-stricken pigeons pursued by large falcon

snowy owl—most likely around dawn and dusk from November through March

Contact: Duluth Audubon Society, c/o Biology Dept., University of Minnesota–Duluth, Duluth, MN 55812

CHIPPEWA NATIONAL FOREST
(661,500 acres)

A diverse mosaic of wetlands—streams, sloughs, shrub swamps, marshes, more than 1,300 lakes, and the meandering Upper Mississippi; upland forests of aspen, red pine, and jack pine

great blue heron—a dozen rookeries active each summer; look for feeding great blues along marshy shores and wooded banks

bald eagle—largest summer concentration in contiguous 48 states—more than 10 percent of nation's breeding bald eagles nest here; especially common near Lake Winnibigoshish

red-shouldered hawk—nests each spring in broadleaf trees in lowland forests, usually near open water

beaver—signs of activity are widespread—dams, cut trees, ponds, lodges

river otter—present throughout wetland areas; easiest to find in winter

Contact: Forest Supervisor, Cass Lake, MN 56633 (218/335-2226)

GRAND MARAIS HARBOR

Rugged rocky coastline, cobble beaches, grassy meadows; excellent spot for rare and odd bird sightings *sea ducks*—oldsquaw and other rare diving ducks seen in late fall and winter in sheltered bays, near mouths of north shore streams

scoters—all three species may occur in late October and November

Contact: Duluth Audubon Society, c/o Biology
Dept., University of Minnesota–Duluth,
Duluth, MN 55812

HAWK RIDGE NATURE RESERVE
(100 acres)

Lake Superior funnels migrating hawks along these high bluffs each fall; migration is best on days with strong breeze from west or northwest

northern goshawk—peak numbers occur in mid-October

broad-winged hawk—swirling clouds of thousands of birds rise on thermals in mid-September (31,891 broadwings counted on single day in 1978)

peregrine falcon—a few sightings expected mid-September through early October; best opportunity in northwoods area to see this endangered falcon

Contact: Duluth Audubon Society, c/o Biology
Dept., University of Minnesota–Duluth,
Duluth, MN 55812

LAKE OF THE WOODS
(south shore)

Huge open lake with wooded, brushy, and sandy shorelines, good vistas of water

American white pelican—one of only two spots in Minnesota to find breeding pelicans in the summer

piping plover—known to frequent isolated sand bars near Morris Point

gulls—Franklin's and Bonaparte's gulls are regular summer residents here

Caspian tern—can be seen flying low over shorelines throughout summer

Contact: Duluth Audubon Society, c/o Biology
Dept., University of Minnesota–Duluth,
Duluth, MN 55812

MILLE LACS LAKE
(north shore)

Open waters and wave-washed shorelines offer some good fall birding

common loon—congregate by the hundreds in October and November

scoters—these and other rare waterfowl seen rafted offshore each fall

Contact: Duluth Audubon Society, c/o Biology Dept., University of Minnesota–Duluth, Duluth, MN 55812

PARK POINT
(Minnesota Point)

A 6-mile-long sand spit separating Lake Superior from Duluth's harbor; brushy fields, needleleaf and broadleaf forests, as well as an extensive beachline

hawks—as merlin and American kestrel wing southward each fall, they pursue migrant warblers and woodpeckers

shorebirds—rare sightings such as dunlin, whimbrel, ruddy turnstone, and sanderling occur in spring

jaegers—a few seen mixed in with gull flocks from August through October

Caspian tern—may be seen flocking with gulls in May, along with other tern species

Contact: Duluth Audubon Society, c/o Biology Dept., University of Minnesota–Duluth, Duluth, MN 55812

RICE LAKE NATIONAL WILDLIFE REFUGE
(20,000 acres)

Bogs and shallow wild rice marshes separated by glacial moraines that are covered with forests and grassy openings

ring-necked duck—60,000 may gather here in mid-October

sandhill crane—breeds and nests here each spring and summer

352

sharp-tailed grouse—plentiful in large grassy fields from April to November

coyote—secretive, but highpitched howling may be heard at any season

black bear—prefers upland brush from May through September

white-tailed deer—abundant in brushy openings at dusk, especially during summer and fall

Contact: Refuge Manager, Rural Route 2,
      McGregor, MN 55760 (218/768-2402)

ROSEAU COUNTY, BOG

Wild, remote spruce bog and conifer forest north on route 130.

great gray owl—nests each spring in black spruce/ tamarack bogs near Canadian border

Contact: Duluth Audubon Society, c/o Biology
      Dept., University of Minnesota–Duluth,
      Duluth, MN 55812

SUPERIOR NATIONAL FOREST
(3,000,000 acres)

Complex mosaic of northern needleleafs and aspen/ birch forests clinging to ancient granite outcrops; land of hundreds of lakes and streams including the road-less, million-acre Boundary Waters Canoe Area

bald eagle—before snow and ice disappear in early spring, eagles flock to wolf-killed deer carcasses to feed

merlin—early spring nester in spruce or balsam fir crowns

spruce grouse—frequently seen along backroads through jack pine or spruce forests, especially from July until November

boreal owl—calling mid-April into early May from dusk until midnight

gray wolf—rarely seen, but there is a substantial breeding population here. Look for their trails in the snow or in muddy portions of back roads and trails.

black bear—active from May through September, commonly attracted to dumps

river otter—during spring thaw, look for them diving, fishing, and eating along holes in melting ice of rivers, lakes, and streams

moose—feeds on aquatic plants in slow-moving streams in June

mink frog—frequents mats of surface vegetation on slow-moving streams or in bogs, lakes, and ponds

Contact: Forest Supervisor, P.O. Box 338,
        Duluth, MN 55801 (218/720-5324)

TAMARAC NATIONAL WILDLIFE REFUGE
(44,000 acres)

An area of alternating ridges and wetlands; 21 shallow lakes and woodland potholes, shrub swamps, bogs, upland and lowland broadleaf and needleleaf forests and brush; Chippewa Indians still harvest wild rice by canoe here

scaups—flocks of 40,000 loaf until lakes freeze in late October, early November

bald eagle—common in spring and fall migration; you may see as many as 50 at once

bohemian waxwing—attracted to clusters of mountain-ash berries in winter

porcupine—"gnaws" at the bases of tamarack trees are signs of porkies

beaver—in fall, active ponds have freshly-packed mud on dams and fresh branches on lodges

mink—shores of wooded beaver ponds are good spots to check

river otter—social, often seen in pairs; watch for muddy "slides" on banks

gray treefrog—listen for trill call given from low shrubs near ponds in May and June

snapping turtle—active in mid-April through October in mud-bottomed ponds

Contact: Refuge Manager, Rural Route,
        Rochert, MN 56578 (218/847-2641)

VOYAGEURS NATIONAL PARK
(219,000 acres; 84,000 acres water area)

Ancient basalt knobs covered by spruce, fir, pines, aspen, and birch; lakes, vast and tiny, fill glacially-carved basins and surround isolated peninsulas

common loon—haunting territorial call echoes across lakes in May and June

double-crested cormorant—rookeries on islands in Rainy Lake

great blue heron—10 percent of Minnesota's great blues nest within the park

common tern—one of the few rookeries in the state is on an island in Kabetogama Lake

osprey—ideal habitat for this fish-eating raptor

bald eagle—congregate on Hoist Bay during September and October

snowshoe hare—seeks shelter from predators and weather in northern white-cedar swamps in winter

beavers—quiet observers will find evening entertainment at numerous ponds here

porcupine—easy to spot when feeding high in aspen trees in mid-winter

black bear—common in uplands, some 100–200 inhabit the park

mink—forages along shorelines and streambanks

river otter—common and curious, best viewed from a canoe as they frolic in water along banks

bobcat—tracks in snow are abundant, but cat is rarely seen

Contact: Superintendent, P.O. Box 50,
International Falls, MN 56649
(218/283-9821)

Wisconsin Hotspots

APOSTLE ISLANDS NATIONAL LAKESHORE
(66,500 acres)

Archipelago of nearly two dozen islands on Lake Superior; mostly upland forests of maple/birch with rocky shores and sand spits *double-crested cormorant*—rookeries on outer islands; often nests together with gulls

herring gull—much of western Lake Superior population breeds in area

hawks—stiff southerly breeze in April and May provides best hawk-watching as birds funnel up Bayfield Peninsula toward Lake Superior crossing

warblers—waves of spring migrants pass through these forested islands in early May

beaver—on islands with lowlands and streams; most visible in fall when refurbishing the lodge and stockpiling freshly cut branches in a winter food cache

black bear—can tolerate frigid waters; swims from island to island

mink frog—abundant along edge of sphagnum mats, where water flows slowly; can be heard calling in June

redbelly snake—diminutive, retiring snake of boreal forests often seen in and around moss-covered logs

Contact: Superintendent, Route 1, Box 4,
       Bayfield, WI 54814 (715/779-3397)

BRULE RIVER STATE FOREST
(38,500 acres)

Lowland stands of balsam fir, black spruce, and northern white-cedar border this narrow, fast-flowing stream as it rushes toward Lake Superior

osprey—frequently seen hovering above quiet stretches along the river

black-backed woodpecker—most often seen in winter; dead lowland stands of black spruce and northern white-cedar harbor this bark gleaner

warblers—many boreal nesters find suitable breeding habitat here

bobcat—better chance of finding bobcat here than anywhere else in Wisconsin; look for tracks in mud or snow

wood turtle—seen along forested banks of river; mainly terrestrial May through August, but never far from water

Wisconsin Hotspot Map

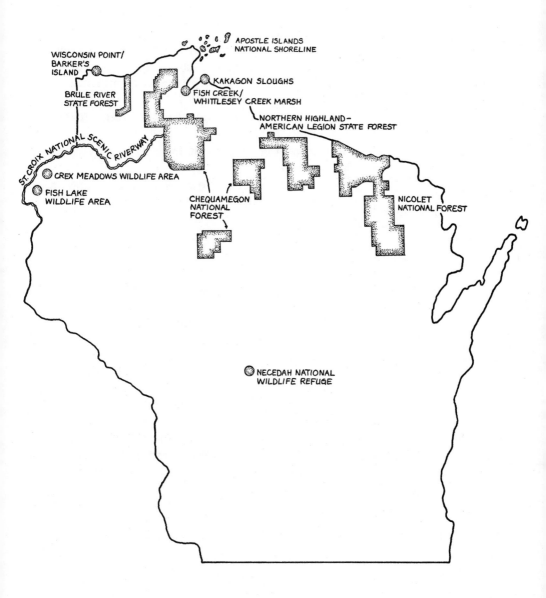

WISCONSIN POINT/
BARKER'S
ISLAND

BRULE RIVER
STATE FOREST

ST. CROIX NATIONAL SCENIC RIVERWAY

CREX MEADOWS WILDLIFE AREA

FISH LAKE
WILDLIFE AREA

APOSTLE ISLANDS
NATIONAL SHORELINE

KAKAGON SLOUGHS
FISH CREEK/
WHITTLESEY CREEK MARSH

NORTHERN HIGHLAND–
AMERICAN LEGION STATE FOREST

CHEQUAMEGON
NATIONAL
FOREST

NICOLET
NATIONAL FOREST

NECEDAH NATIONAL
WILDLIFE REFUGE

Contact: Forest Manager, Box 125, Brule, WI 54820
(715/372-4866)

CHEQUAMEGON NATIONAL FOREST
(848,500 acres)

A microcosm of entire northwoods; numerous lakes, lowland spruce/tamarack stands, open bogs, upland beech/maple forests, and groves of virgin white and red pine, and eastern hemlock

bald eagle—mated pairs return to breeding territories in late March

black bear—out and about from April to October; inactive over winter

fisher—this member of the weasel family recently re-introduced; porcupines are preferred prey

bobcat—quietly prowls remote uplands, lowland bogs, and needleleaf forests

redback salamander—moist hemlock logs often harbor several underneath

spotted salamander—breeds in woodland pools in early April

wood frog—abundant in temporary spring ponds, seeps; calls in early April

Contact: Forest Supervisor, 1170 4th Avenue S.,
Park Falls, WI 54552 (715/762-2461)

CREX MEADOWS WILDLIFE AREA
(30,000 acres)

Open sedge-cattail marsh, upland broadleaf forests, brushy fields, lakes; controlled burning and dikes are used to maintain northwoods/prairie border; 245 bird species recorded

grebes—look for migrants in April and May on lakes and ponds

great blue heron—rookeries are used year after year

sandhill crane—flocks commonly seen in mid- to late October

waterfowl—ducks and geese by the thousands stop over in October

osprey—successful nests built on artificial platforms; easily observed *greater prairie-chicken*—rare species, needs large grassy openings

sharp-tailed grouse—mating displays are best observed from blinds in April

short-eared owl—glides low over sedge meadows in search of meadow voles

yellow-headed blackbird—summer colonies of this primarily western species occur

prairie mammals—Franklin's ground squirrel and northern pocket gopher are prey for badger; all best observed in spring before vegetation grows too tall

Blanding's turtle—basks in spring sun on floating logs; forages both on land and in shallow waters of sloughs and marshes

eastern hognose snake—in dry bracken ferns; plays dead when threatened

Contact: Wisconsin Dept. of Natural Resources,
Box 367, Grantsburg, WI 54840
(715/463-2896)

FISH CREEK/WHITTLESEY CREEK MARSH

Extensive sedge marsh and shrub swamp complex located at head of Lake Superior's Chequamegon Bay

tundra swan—stops over in late March–May while awaiting ice-out further north

mute swan—adults and cygnets (young) are frequently seen in June

shorebirds—large numbers pass through in May; godwits, knots, sandpipers, and dowitchers among 25 species sighted

terns—Caspian and common terns arrive in April

black tern—nests above water in marsh vegetation

western chorus frog—the first frog voice of spring, males call from rafts of floating vegetation beginning in early April

wood turtle—semi-terrestrial; found along fast-flowing portions of creeks

Contact: Wisconsin Society for Ornithology,
W. 330 N. 8275 West Shore Drive,
Hartland, WI 53029

FISH LAKE WILDLIFE AREA
(13,000 acres)

Mixed oak, pine, and aspen uplands mixed with prairie-like fields and marshes

double-crested cormorant—shares rookery with herons

great blue heron—during early summer, adults make countless round trips from marsh to nest to provide food for nestbound young

great egret—among the most northerly nesting sites in state

black-crowned night-heron—unusual in northwoods, but can be seen here

shorebirds—probe exposed mudflats during periods of low water in fall

Contact: Wisconsin Dept. of Natural Resources,
Box 367, Grantsburg, WI 54840
(715/463-2896)

KAKAGON SLOUGHS

Sandy shores, shrub swamps, and marshes at remote spot near mouth of Chequamegon Bay, accessible only by boat or canoe

shorebirds—spring migrants gather at isolated beaches and backwaters

bald eagle—concentrate here each spring before crossing Lake Superior

Contact: Wisconsin Society for Ornithology,
W. 330 N. 8275 West Shore Drive,
Hartland, WI 53029

NECEDAH NATIONAL WILDLIFE REFUGE
(40,000 acres)

A patchwork of lakes, marshes, oak woodlands, and restored prairie

Canada goose—as many as 30,000 recorded late September through October

360

ducks—as many as 55,000 from late September through early November

bald eagle—gather here in October on journey southward

wild turkey—concentrate in brushy oak uplands each fall to feed on acorns

sandhill crane—boisterous courtship displays by hundreds of birds in April

whip-poor-will—call heard frequently on most summer evenings

badger—earth mounds in large grassy fields mark den sites

Contact: Refuge Manager, Box 386, Star Route West, Necedah, WI 54646 (608/565-2551)

NICOLET NATIONAL FOREST
(657,000 acres)

Upland forests of maple/birch, virgin groves of towering white pine and ancient hemlock; lowland forests, bogs, and numerous lakes provide headwaters for many rivers located in the region

bald eagle—watch for this broad-winged raptor soaring on summer thermals

spruce grouse—frequents dense needleleaf forest, easy to approach closely

black bear—omnivorous—feeds seasonally on blueberries in old burns, on acorns and beechnuts in mature forests, and on invertebrates in lakes and streams

marten—preys heavily on red squirrels in mature needleleaf forests

bobcat—a nocturnal hunter of grouse and snowshoe hare

salamanders—best viewing on warm spring nights; moist forest leaf litter shelters unusual species

Contact: Forest Supervisor, Federal Building, 68 S. Stevens, Rhinelander, WI 54501 (715/362-3415)

NORTHERN HIGHLAND–AMERICAN LEGION STATE FOREST
(218,000 acres)

A landscape heavily forested with aspen/oak/pine with numerous kettle-hole lakes, bogs, and slow-flowing streams scattered throughout

osprey—frequents the major lakes and streams

sandhill cranes—summer residents in a few of the large open bogs

beaver—numerous active colonies because of ample wetlands and aspen

porcupine—eats buds, twigs, inner bark; evidence of presence most obvious in winter

black bear—favors remote areas where mosaic of oak uplands and bogs occur

fisher—quick and cat-like in pursuit of red squirrel or porcupine meals

frogs—forested wetlands harbor a symphony of frog sounds in April and May

Contact: Forest Manager, Box 440, Woodruff, WI 54568 (715/356-5211)

ST. CROIX NATIONAL SCENIC RIVERWAY
(54,500 acres—northern unit)

Encompasses both Namekagon and upper St. Croix drainages; quiet pools, rapids, swamps, lakes, and second-growth needleleaf and broadleaf forests

great blue heron—rookeries located in lowland forests near river

bald eagle—common spring migrant and often a summer resident

bullfrog—baritone croaking heard in backwaters and ponds on summer evenings

turtles—river environments are excellent for locating hard-to-find or rare species like Blanding's turtle, wood turtle, and eastern spiny softshell

five-lined skink—rare in the northwoods; look around stumps and rotting logs in areas of oak and pine barrens for this nimble lizard

Contact: Superintendent, P.O. Box 708,
St. Croix Falls, WI 54024 (715/483-3284)

WISCONSIN POINT/BARKER'S ISLAND

A sandy barrier beach shields marshes, brushy grass-lands, and needleleaf and broadleaf forests from wave energy of open Lake Superior

waterfowl—scoters, loons, unusual sea ducks observed in late fall and winter in open waters

gulls—rare Iceland, Thayer's, and glaucous gulls sometimes occur from December through April

hawks—merlin, American kestrel, and other small hawks frequent area in fall migration

shorebirds—ruddy turnstone, dunlin, sanderling, and other rarities in excellent concentrations during late April and May

Contact: Wisconsin Society for Ornithology, W. 330
N. West Shore Drive, Hartland, WI 53029

Michigan Hotspots

BROCKWAY MOUNTAIN/KEWEENAW POINT

A windswept rock outcropping overlooking Lake Superior; an important spring migration route for raptors

hawks—peak flights between late April and late May, when hundreds may be seen on days with stiff south or southwesterly breezes

Contact: Michigan Audubon Society, 409 West "E"
Avenue, Kalamazoo, MI 49007
(616/344-8648)

HIAWATHA NATIONAL FOREST
(880,000 acres)

Shorelines on Lake Superior, Michigan, and Huron; upland sand plains of jack pine, bracken fern, and blueberry; lowland stands of mature balsam fir and northern white-cedar

osprey—as soon as shore ice breaks up in spring, watch for this whitish-looking hawk hovering over bays and shoreline shallows

porcupine—frequents the bare crowns of broadleaf trees in winter

black bear—rugged areas of densely-forested sandstone canyons and caves are preferred summer habitat

turtles—banks of winding Au Train River are good places to watch for turtles in summer

Contact: Forest Supervisor, 2727 North Lincoln
       Road, Escanaba, MI 49829 (906/786-4062)

HURON NATIONAL FOREST
(428,000 acres)

The wild and scenic Au Sable River's fast-flowing waters pass through 23 miles of mixed upland forests, including extensive stands of jack pine

Kirtland's warbler—4,000 acres of young jack pine provide nesting habitat for this endangered species. Fewer than 300 breeding pairs remain. Birds here may be viewed strictly by scheduled guided tour, offered by District Ranger Station in Mio, from mid-May through early July 1.

upland sandpiper—watch for them along roadsides in dry, grassy meadows

spruce grouse—feeds heavily on tough jack pine needles through the winter

wild turkey—flocks gather in brushy jack pine/oak stands in winter

eastern bluebird—commonly nests in old burns with plenty of dead trees that have cavities

coyote—forages in fields and forests for meadow voles, grasshoppers, beetles

smooth green snake—often seen as it ventures across backroads or sandy paths where its green camouflage is useless

Contact: Forest Supervisor, 421 S. Mitchell St.,
       Cadillac, MI 49601 (616/775-2421)

Michigan Hotspots Maps

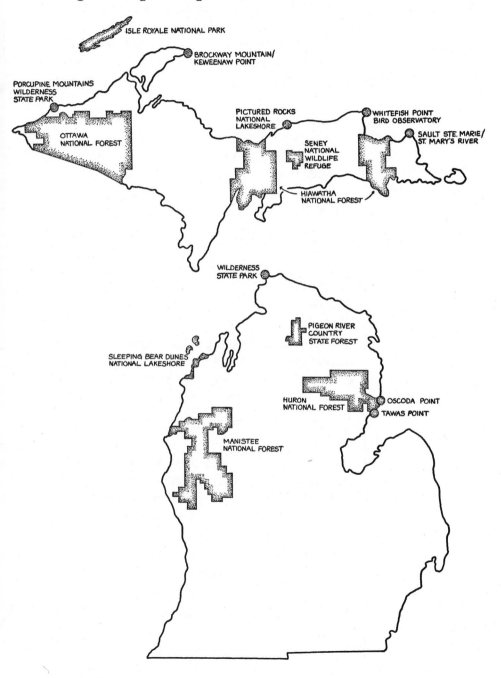

ISLE ROYALE NATIONAL PARK

BROCKWAY MOUNTAIN/
KEWEENAW POINT

PORCUPINE MOUNTAINS
WILDERNESS
STATE PARK

OTTAWA
NATIONAL FOREST

PICTURED ROCKS
NATIONAL
LAKESHORE

WHITEFISH POINT
BIRD OBSERVATORY

SAULT STE. MARIE/
ST. MARY'S RIVER

SENEY
NATIONAL
WILDLIFE
REFUGE

HIAWATHA
NATIONAL FOREST

WILDERNESS
STATE PARK

PIGEON RIVER
COUNTRY
STATE FOREST

SLEEPING BEAR DUNES
NATIONAL LAKESHORE

HURON
NATIONAL FOREST

OSCODA POINT

TAWAS POINT

MANISTEE
NATIONAL FOREST

ISLE ROYALE NATIONAL PARK
(572,000 acres; water areas comprise ¾ of park)

Isolated from the mainland since glacial retreat some 10,000 years ago; spruce/fir and maple/birch forests; inland lakes, fjord-like harbors, and 200 smaller islets

common loon—more than 10 percent of Michigan's breeding loons nest here in June

merlin—this hard-to-find falcon common here; nests in spruce crowns

warblers—26 different spring migrant or nesting species recorded

snowshoe hare—abundant some years, scarce others; often found in dense needleleaf cover

beaver—linear aspen-forested valleys are ideal sites for beaver activity

gray wolf—highest density of this canine known anywhere in the world

red fox—a bold scavenger that patrols hiking trails throughout the park

moose—roughly 1,000 present; especially active and vocal during September rutting season

Contact: Superintendent, 87 N. Ripley St., Houghton, MI 49931 (906/482-3310)

MANISTEE NATIONAL FOREST
(522,500 acres)

Pere Marquette River glides through a mixture of needleleaf and broadleaf forests; vast sandy dunes and extensive beaches stretch along Lake Michigan

waterfowl—summer breeders especially abundant in ponds and larger sloughs

beaver—likely to see adults and young together as fall progresses and winter draws near

mink—patrols roots and rocks along rivers and streams

river otter—a strong and graceful swimmer; fond of flowing waters

Contact: Forest Supervisor, 421 S. Mitchell St., Cadillac, MI 49601 (616/775-2421)

OTTAWA NATIONAL FOREST
(928,500 acres)

Ancient basalt rock exposures, breathtaking waterfalls, virgin hemlock/maple/birch forest filled with wildflowers and dotted with clear kettle-hole lakes

common loon—nests in isolated lakes with small islands in June and July

porcupine—often seen ambling along gravel roadsides at dawn or dusk

fisher—best seen in winter when fresh tracks and dark fur stand out; alarmed "churr" of red squirrels may direct you to a sighting

river otter—look for adults and young frolicking in fast-moving streams

Contact: Forest Supervisor, U.S. Hwy. 2 East,
        Ironwood, MI 49938 (906/932-1330)

PICTURED ROCKS NATIONAL LAKESHORE
(70,000 acres)

Multicolored sandstone cliffs rising abruptly from Lake Superior, inland lakes surrounded by young forests of maple/birch/beech, unbroken stretches of white sand and pebble beach, and the vast Au Sable Dunes

upland sandpiper—favors sandy soils and large grassy fields for nesting

ruffed grouse—especially abundant in brushy upland stands here

warblers—nearly two dozen migrants or summer residents present in May

Contact: Superintendent, P.O. Box 40,
        Munising, MI 49862 (906/387-2607)

PIGEON RIVER COUNTRY STATE FOREST
(93,000 acres)

Primarily forested uplands of aspen, birch, maple, and oak bisected by rivers and streams

elk (wapiti)—local population numbers near 1,000; active in morning and evening, seen feeding on new grass in fields after snowmelt in spring; watch for bull with harem during breeding season in mid-September

Contact: Forest Manager, Michigan Dept. of Natural Resources, Gaylord District, P.O. Box 667, 1732 W. Hwy. M-32, Gaylord, MI 49735 (517/732-3541)

PORCUPINE MOUNTAINS WILDERNESS STATE PARK
(58,000 acres)

Rugged basalt outcrops, virgin hemlock/maple/birch forests, and miles of rugged Lake Superior shoreline

osprey—dives from mid-air into water to grasp a sur-facing fish

bald eagle—scavenges along Lake Superior shore-lines and inland lakes

northern goshawk—remote, mature forests favored by this large bird of prey

pileated woodpecker—must have mature trees to nest successfully

black bear—seen frequently by visitors throughout the park

Contact: Park Manager, Star Route, Box 314, Ontonagon, MI 49953 (906/885-5275)

SAULT STE. MARIE/ST. MARY'S RIVER

Renowned for excellent winter birding when severe weather drives boreal species further south to open water; warm outflow from electric generating plant seems especially attractive

sea ducks—look for them in permanently open patches of water from January through April

gulls—rare northern or marine species known to oc-cur throughout winter

bald eagle—roosts in winter in large trees near open water along river

gyrfalcon—rare arctic falcon may pursue gulls and sea ducks when abundant

three-toed woodpecker—favors dead snags in semi-open swamps and bogs

bohemian waxwing—flocks irrupt southwards some winters, feed on berries available above the snow in early to mid-winter

northern shrike—returns to fields and marshes in late fall

Contact: Michigan Audubon Society, 409 West "E" Avenue, Kalamazoo, MI 49007 (616/344-8648)

SENEY NATIONAL WILDLIFE REFUGE
(95,000 acres; 7,000 acres open water)

Sedge marsh, sandy knolls with red and jack pine, and logged or burned-over lands

Canada goose—nesting and cruising around everywhere in June and July

sharp-tailed grouse—early morning mating displays occur in April and May

yellow rail—shy and retiring; distinctive call sounds like two stones tapped together

sandhill crane—observed in flocks of 300 in September and October

LeConte's sparrow—often difficult to spot; nests in sedges in early summer

black bear—feeds heavily on blueberries and other fall fruits

river otter—watch for them sliding down snowbanks in winter

bobcat—these cats are doing well in this land of bog and brush

Contact: Refuge Manager, Seney, MI 49883 (906/586-9851)

SLEEPING BEAR DUNES NATIONAL LAKESHORE
(72,000 acres)

Area named for massive coastal sand dunes and beaches on Lake Michigan; inland lakes, marshes, meadows, and rolling hills forested with beech and maple

piping plover—may still breed here on isolated strips of beach sand

herring gull—large breeding colony located on South Manitou Island

northern harrier—hunts by drifting just above marsh or meadow vegetation

beaver—inland lakes and streams have substantial beaver populations

Contact: Superintendent, 400½ Main St., Frankfort, MI 49635 (616/352-9611)

TAWAS POINT/OSCODA POINT

Pine/oak forests loom behind open sand beaches, sedge meadows, marshes, and mud flats

shorebirds—a collecting point for migrants each spring and fall; unusual species include piping plover, black-bellied plover, sanderling, ruddy turnstone, whimbrel, and dowitcher

Contact: Michigan Audubon Society, 409 West "E" Avenue, Kalamazoo, MI 49007 (616/344-8648)

WHITEFISH POINT BIRD OBSERVATORY

This broad peninsula extends into Lake Superior toward Canada 18 miles away; a natural concentration area for birds moving north in early April to mid-June; bird-banding station open March through end of June; (230 species recorded)

common loon—3,000–5,000 birds swim together along shores in April and May

shorebirds—sandy beaches and surf attract migrant sandpipers and plovers

raptors—15,000–25,000 seen each spring; 10,000 sharp-shinned hawks counted in May of one recent year, as well as northern goshawk, merlin, and peregrine falcon sightings

owls—great gray, boreal, northern hawk, saw-whet, and long-eared owls all observed in general vicinity of lighthouse and dunes

Contact: Michigan Audubon Society, 409 West "E" Avenue, Kalamazoo, MI 49007 (616/344-8648)

WILDERNESS STATE PARK
(8,000 acres)

Miles of Lake Michigan shoreline, including Waugoshance Point, a peninsula that juts three miles into Lake Michigan; beach habitat with stands of needleleafs

piping plover—rare but may still nest here on isolated sand shores

shorebirds—large concentrations of migrants appear in September

Contact: Park Manager, Carp River, MI 49718
(616/436-5381)

Cattails.

WILDLIFE EVENTS CALENDAR

"Phenology" is the study of seasonal timing in nature. When the first warblers arrive, when the trilliums bloom, when the hibernators curl up for winter: these are all examples of natural events that occur at certain times and in certain sequences relative to each other. Some of the events in nature's timetable are recorded in the monthly phenology calendar that follows.

Remember that the seasons change gradually, and spring comes earlier to the southern part of the northwoods than to the northern reaches. Lands that border the Great Lakes bask in a buffer zone of sorts, and receive unique lakeside weather patterns. To "synchronize" your seasonal watch with the rest of the region, look at weather information for various northwoods locations at the beginning of each month. You can estimate your own conditions depending on your distance north or south of these locations.

Seasonal Activities

Here in the snowbelt, winter is the best time for tracking, just as spring is the best time to search for bird nests or ponder the plight of returning migrants. Each month offers its own food for thought for the curious naturalist. In the margins of the Wildlife Watcher's Almanac, you'll find some hands-on activities to help you learn what's afoot in the natural world each month. Keep these in mind as you wander, observing and deciphering the rhythms and patterns that make up a wildlife year.

JANUARY

	Snowpack	Temperature	
	Inches	Ave. High	Ave. Low
Itasca, MN	12	18	−7
Grand Marais, MN	18	23	1
Spooner, WI	12	22	−2
Sturgeon Bay, WI	16	25	9
Houghton, MI	16	24	6
Seney NWR, MI	20	25	3

TAKING FIELD NOTES
Writing down what you see in the outdoors will improve your observation skills and allow you to compare the phenology of different years. Your records might also become a valuable resource for biologists and naturalists.

In January, when short, dark days keep you cabin-bound, consider organizing a notebook of your observations. You might want two sections. One with dates, places, and sightings would let you keep track of your travels, the general phenology, and other impressions. The second part could hold more detailed accounts of social behavior, food habits, etc. for species you observe repeatedly or have continued on next page

Short, cold days and deep, starry nights. At best, only 10 hours of daylight. Mammals are now most active towards midday, unlike in the summer, when dusk and dawn are peak times. The "lake effect" (the Great Lakes are now warmer than the air) warms the land near the lakeshores. Everywhere else is deepest cold. Make sure hands, face, and feet are well-insulated. Take back-country roads and trails only if well-prepared.

BIRDS

Pileated Woodpeckers Drum. Drumming proclaims the pair's territory; each pair may require a square mile or more of mature woodland.

Northern Finches Crave Salt. Pine and evening grosbeaks and red crossbills may be found feeding on salty (calcium chloride) grit along roads, presumably to satisfy their need for calcium.

Chickadees Sing. Despite the cold, black-capped chickadees are first heard singing their spring songs in response to lengthening days.

Ruffed Grouse Congregate. With deepening cold, ruffed grouse begin to roost together in dense needleleaf trees. When lacking cover in bitter weather, they roost in snow tunnels, leaving characteristic pellets of plant fibers. Occasionally this strategy backfires when freezing rain forms an impenetrable crust that blocks the bird's escape.

Crossbills May Nest. Red crossbills may begin nesting in January if the pine and spruce cone crop is good; they may be the first birds to nest in the new year. If not, these irregular breeders can nest any month of the year.

Chickadees Are Nucleus for Other Birds. If you find a flock of chickadees, look for associating nuthatches and woodpeckers. Such flocks increase vigilance for predators because there are more eyes on the lookout.

Cedar Waxwings Flock. Restless flocks of waxwings congregate to feed on the fruits of highbush cranberry, mountain-ash, and pin cherry, even when the fruits are frozen.

Northern Owls Invade. During invasion years, tame, day-active great gray owls and the more nocturnal boreal owls may be seen perched near swamps or openings in needleleaf forests.

Great Horned Owls Proclaim Territories. The heaviest of northwoods owls begins its characteristic, soft six-hooting to advertise its territory before nesting. Listen at twilight and early evening for the "whowhowhowhowho-who" calls.

MAMMALS

Lynx Hunt Snowshoe Hares. Lynx prey heavily on snowshoe hares in winter. If hare numbers are high enough, lynx won't bother to stalk. Instead, they will save energy and ambush their prey from a waiting place underneath snow-covered boughs.

Red Foxes Pair Up. After living alone most of the year, red foxes are seen together and may mate as early as January.

Bear Cubs Born. In dens beneath logs or in hillsides, sleeping bears wake to give birth to cubs the size of red squirrels.

White-tailed Deer Yard Up. Deer often "yard up"

a special interest in. If you are a student, these notes might become the basis of an independent study project. If you become a serious note-taker, consider getting a supply of permanent, 100 percent cotton paper (known as "rag") so your records won't yellow after 10 years. Also, share your notes with other wildlife watchers and encourage them to do the same. For more information, read Van Remsen's article on field notes in Vol. 31(5), pp. 946–953 in "American Birds" (1977).

(gather in groups) when deep snow limits their ranging. Yards are in or near food sources such as northern white-cedar swamps. Look here for shed antlers that bucks began dropping in late November.

Moose Browse Upland. Three-foot-tall legs allow moose to move through heavy snow to reach preferred browse plants: willows, birch, aspen, and mountain-ash.

Porcupines Are Aloft. Porcupines are often seen high in trees, feeding on bark despite rigorous wind chills. Like deer, they seem to be quite lethargic in extreme cold, perhaps to conserve energy and heat.

Red Squirrels Visit Food Caches. Red squirrels rely on their vigorously defended caches of spruce cones to survive the winter. They can be seen around midday in still, bright weather climbing trees or tunneling under the snow to visit their larder.

Wolf Sign on Ski Trails. Look for wolf tracks, scat, and urine used to mark the boundaries of the pack's territory. Some of the best places to see wolf sign are along state park ski trails on Minnesota's North Shore of Lake Superior. Wolves travel on these trails so they don't have to waste energy fighting thick woods or deep snow.

Muskrats Feed Below the Freeze Line. Muskrats are active throughout the winter, feeding on rootstocks below the freeze line. Unusually deep freezes may seal off these underwater foods. They huddle together inside lodges for warmth and sometimes eat the cattails from the walls.

REPTILES AND AMPHIBIANS

All Reptiles Are Inactive. With their body temperature close to freezing, reptiles are essentially paralyzed in ant mounds, lake bottoms, hollow logs, and other overwintering sites.

Some Frogs Are Partially Frozen. Frogs hibernating in soil encounter temperatures well below freezing. In some, the fluid between the cells, but not within the cells, will freeze. In the spring, they thaw out and resume activity.

FEBRUARY

	Snowpack	Temperature	
	Inches	Ave. High	Ave. Low
Itasca, MN	12	28	5
Grand Marais, MN	17	27	13
Spooner, WI	14	30	9
Sturgeon Bay, WI	17	30	16
Houghton, MI	17	31	11
Seney NWR, MI	23	31	9

Days continue to lengthen, deep cold moderates slightly, and the snow pack accumulates. February is the month of maximum snow depth in the northwoods. "Lake effect" snows are caused when moisture-laden air over the warmer Great Lakes hits the cooler land and snow precipitates out. Needleleaf trees at the northern extent of their range may show longitudinal freeze cracks. The cracks look like lightening scars but do not heal as quickly; wide-open wounds take on a "wing" or "buttress" shape. Look for them on hemlock, beech, and oak.

BIRDS

Ravens Perform Aerial Acrobatics. Ravens continue aerobatic flights, diving and tumbling in the presence of other ravens near cliff faces, open-pit mines, and wherever there are strong updrafts. They are best seen during clear, windy weather. These displays are important in courtship and territory defense. Listen for low "krruut-krruut-krruut" calls along lakeshores and other openings.

Barred Owls Are Sociable. Barred owls are vocal now, giving their eight-hoot calls along with other, stranger calls. Try imitating their call to lure them in; sometimes three or four are attracted and have a hooting conversation among themselves.

TRACKING
Like Robinson Crusoe discovering Friday's footprints, tracking reminds us that we are not alone. Whenever there is fresh snow, all walking creatures leave behind evidence of their passing. With a good field guide, you can identify most track-makers. Following their prints can be great fun. You may meet up with the animal if you front-track quickly enough, or you may discover its den location by back-tracking. Along its trail, look for remains of the animal's prey or food plants that it may have browsed. By picking apart droppings, you might be able to tell what the animal has been eating.
continued on next page

377

Many mammals have regular daily rhythms and may walk predictable "beats." The best times to stake out these heavily used trails are dusk and dawn, when "rush hour traffic" is at its peak. If you regularly visit an area, smooth the snow with a branch so that a fresh record of tracks can be left. Expert trackers take years to acquire their skills, but with experience they can read tracks and signs as easily as we read a book.

After the thaw, look along muddy lake shores and riverbanks for the tracks of semi-aquatic mammals and shorebirds. The fine detail in these tracks makes them easy to identify with the help of a good field guide. You can preserve tracks with sketches, photographs, or plaster casts. For further information, read Murie's "A Field Guide to Animal Tracks" in the Peterson series.

Watch For Winter Ducks on Open Water. Along the protected bays of the Great Lakes or other open water, look for the winter-resident ducks: common goldeneye, bufflehead, oldsquaw, and, with good fortune, white-winged scoter.

Pileated Woodpeckers Feed on Carpenter Ants. These crow-sized woodpeckers excavate large, rectangular holes in living and dead trees to reach sluggish carpenter ant colonies. Look for wood chips on the snow and listen for sounds of excavation ringing through the still air.

MAMMALS

Bats Hibernate in Caves and Mines. Big brown, little brown, and Keen's bats hibernate belowground at a constant 50 degrees F. No northwoods bats hibernate in trees—they would freeze in the sub-zero temperatures.

Deer May Face Starvation. In years when white-tailed deer numbers are high, snow is deep, and browse is scarce, smaller and younger deer may die. Because of the increase in logging and subsequent grassy openings, deer are 5 to 10 times more abundant than they were before Europeans arrived.

Ermines Active. The white-coated ermine must eat more during periods of cold. They tunnel through snow to find mice and voles, but will also feed on carrion. Look for them near road kills and deer carcasses.

Fisher Tracks Prominent in Remote Mature Woodland. In northern Wisconsin and the western section of Michigan's Upper Peninsula, the fisher is making a comeback after trapping greatly reduced its numbers. This population is now stable, thanks to reduced trapping and a good supply of the fisher's important prey—red squirrels and porcupines.

Southern Red-backed Voles Warm and Active Under Snow Cover. Beneath the insulating snow the temperature is usually close to freezing, although it may be −20 to −40 degrees F just above the snow.

378

Voles and mice sometimes build shafts to the surface, exposing them to waiting predators.

Badger Embryos Implant. After mating in the fall, the embryo's development is arrested until late winter, when it implants and matures. In a month, young badgers are born.

REPTILES AND AMPHIBIANS

Newts and Mudpuppies Active. Of all reptiles and amphibians, only newts and mudpuppies are active. Both are aquatic and have external gills to help them absorb dissolved oxygen from surrounding water. Look for swimming forms beneath clear ice in shallow water.

Hatchling Painted Turtles May Overwinter in Nest. If painted turtle eggs hatch late in the summer, the hatchlings may stay in the nest and wait until the following spring to emerge. Further south, the young always emerge and feed before winter, apparently because food is available later in the fall.

MARCH

	Snowpack	Temperature	
	Inches	Ave. High	Ave. Low
Itasca, MN	11	37	12
Grand Marais, MN	15	33	18
Spooner, WI	8	39	17
Sturgeon Bay, WI	8	37	22
Houghton, MI	19	36	14

Warmer temperatures allow more moisture to be held in the air, therefore snowfalls are often heavy. In late March, the freeze-thaw cycle triggers maple syrup flow. The crimson of red-osier dogwood stems deepens.

WHO'S DOING THE BROWSING?
By late winter, much of the previous year's woody growth near the ground has been heavily browsed. The browse line in northern white-cedar swamps is caused by large numbers of white-tailed deer feeding on the twigs and bark. Whenever they can find it, deer also nibble on Canada yew (a shrubby needle-leaf), thus limiting its distribution in the northwoods. Other preferred plants are eastern hemlock, sumacs, shrubby dogwood, and Usnea *lichen. On Isle Royale, moose browse American mountain-ash so heavily that the only mature mountain-ash survivors are those that grow close to the trunk of a spruce. Even though the umbrella-like boughs of the spruce shade the mountain-ash, they also protect it from hungry moose. During population peaks, the snowshoe hare may run out of tender shoots*
continued on next page

and begin to eat the bark of young willow, aspen, birch, pine, and spruce. In some areas, snowshoe hare browsing is so intense that the plants respond by synthesizing noxious chemicals that discourage return customers.

March is a good time to search for chewed bark and snipped shoots. To identify browsers, remember their trademarks: only porcupines eat bark high up on the trunk; hares gnaw circular areas on the stems of young saplings; mice leave minute teeth marks on young plants a few inches from the ground; and deer and moose snip twigs from above, but rarely debark trees unless they are starving. What plants seem to be most heavily browsed? Do some plants escape browsing even though their shoots or branches are available? For more information, read "American Wildlife and Plants: A Guide to Wildlife Food Habits" by Martin, Zim, and Nelson, and Murie's "A Field Guide to Animal Tracks."

Pussy Willows Bloom. This traditional sign of spring is also appropriate for the northwoods.

Buds of aspen and maple swell in anticipation. Skunk cabbage melts through lingering ice in southeastern parts of the northwoods.

BIRDS

Crows and Red-tailed Hawks Return. The birds that migrated the shortest distances to overwinter generally are the first migrants to return.

Gray Jays Nest. Gray jays are the first perching birds, except for the erratically breeding crossbills, to nest in the northwoods. Watch for them carrying lichens or bark to the nest.

Bald Eagles Return. Sometimes they are seen feeding on winter-killed deer and other carrion before spring food becomes available. One observer placed a deer carcass on a frozen lake and an eagle discovered it an hour later. The next day eight eagles were present. Did the eagle somehow communicate this information at its roost or did the eagles independently discover the food?

Male Red-winged Blackbirds Migrate Before Females. By late March, many male red-winged blackbirds have returned to the northern cattail marshes. Because females do not need to establish territories and do not start building nests until April, they stay south for 2 weeks longer than the males. In most migratory songbird species, the males precede the females for the same reasons.

MAMMALS

Red Squirrels Empty the Larder, Begin Courtship Chases. Red squirrels are still feeding on depleted fall stores—white spruce cones and acorns. Amorous males chase females over the fluffy snow, chattering noisily.

Young Otters Born. River otters give birth in dens near lakes or streams. In 2 months, the young will leave the den to forage with their mother.

380

Arctic Shrews Begin to Nest. You are most likely to find these active animals in northern white-cedar, tamarack, and black spruce swamps. Like other shrews, they are out day and night rooting in the leaf litter for insects and mice.

Snowshoe Hares Start Reverting to Brown. They continue to lose the white in their coats through March as the snowpack melts. By mid-April, when brown is peeking through the snow, all their white camouflage will be gone.

Chipmunks Emerge From Hibernation. In spring, chipmunks switch from eating only cached seeds to eating almost anything. Their new diet includes young birds, eggs, mice, insects, and even small snakes.

Meadow Vole Runways Become Visible. Runways that voles have used throughout the winter, under the cover of snow, are now visible in the matted grass. Examine closely for droppings, sleeping beds, and common areas.

APRIL

	Snowpack	Temperature	
	Inches	Ave. High	Ave. Low
Itasca, MN	3	56	28
Grand Marais, MN	5	47	31
Spooner, WI	3	56	31
Sturgeon Bay, WI	1	51	34
Houghton, MI	2	52	30
Seney NWR, MI	6	51	26

The snowmelt continues in earnest, although frost is possible until late-May in most areas. Ice-out is complete for most lakes by the end of the month, when aspen trees start shedding pollen. Notice in the table of temperatures that Grand Marais along chilly Lake

continued on next page

COLONIAL NESTING

Several types of birds nest together in colonies during the spring. Most conspicuous are the colonies of great blue herons, herring and ring-billed gulls, Caspian and common terns, and bank and cliff swallows. Many colonies are mixed; gulls and terns, herons and cormorants, or several different species of herons will nest together. Great blue herons choose tall trees isolated from human disturbance. From here, they may travel as far as 5 or 10 miles to find food for their young. They nest here year after year, until the constant "whitewash" of wastes poisons many of the trees, forcing the colony to relocate.

Nesting socially has its pros and cons. Some ornithologists believe group nesting allows birds to figure out where better foraging opportunities are by observing the foraging success of returning birds and following them back to the source. Large

Superior doesn't warm up as much during the day as inland sites. This "lake effect" delays the arrival of spring.

Aspen and alder catkins are prominent.

Late in month, bloodroots bloom in broadleaf forests.

Sedges and grasses green up soon after snowmelt.

BIRDS

Sharp-tailed Grouse Display on Their Leks. In extensive northern grasslands, male grouse now set up small territories (leks) to attract visiting females. Males inflate brightly colored air pouches on their necks which they use to make bizarre cooing noises while they "dance."

Saw-whet Owls Call. This little-seen but fairly common owl may be heard calling after 10 p.m. Visit dense needleleaf swamps and listen for the rhythmic "beeping" call that sounds like a spaceship has landed in the swamp.

Song Sparrows Establish Territories. This common bird nests on the ground in moist, shrubby habitat. It was the focus of a pioneering and classic study by an amateur ornithologist, Margaret Morse Nice.

Mergansers and Black Ducks Seen on Open Water. Fast-moving streams are the first to lose their lid of ice. Look for early spring waterfowl where these streams empty into lakes.

Horned Larks Flock in Open Areas. Look for them in bare fields once the snow cover is nearly gone.

Spruce Grouse "Flutter". In needleleaf forests with jack pine, spruce, and fir, look for a displaying male with black plumage and contrasting white dots. If it is quiet, you may hear the soft "flutter flight" display designed to impress female grouse.

Ospreys, Eagles, and Turkey Vultures Return. Most eagles have returned; pairs are performing courtship flights near their nests. Ospreys remain near open rivers until ice-out of lakes.

Brown Creepers and Winter Wrens Arrive. These birds return to the northwoods earlier than other insect eaters. Listen for their long, ringing songs in mature lowland forests. Within a month, both will be nesting. Creepers prefer to nest behind lose slabs of bark on a dead tree. Winter wrens make several covered nests, although the pair will only use one.

Ruffed Grouse Drum. Males advertise their territory from atop logs by beating the air with their wings. Sometimes the low frequency sound (a series of "shumps," starting slow and speeding up) is difficult to hear unless it is quiet. Listen for it at dawn and dusk.

First Sapsuckers Establish Their Territory. They choose the loudest and most resonant surfaces on which to drum: street signs, gutter down spouts, metal flashing, tin chimneys, and hard, hollow tree stubs.

First Flickers Return. Flickers feed largely on ants, which become active on warm April days. Flickers often break into ant nests with their bills if they can't find enough ants on the ground.

Great Blue Herons Start Returning to Nesting Colonies. Nest sites are defended vigorously. When building material is in short supply, watch as herons steal sticks from undefended nests.

Kingfishers Arrive. Listen for their "rattling" as they fly back and forth along an open stream. Soon they will excavate nestholes in sandy banks that are for human traffic.

Common Ravens Build Nests. April is the peak month for raven nest building. Look for adult ravens carrying *Usnea* lichen (old man's beard) and balsam fir branches which they will use to line the nest. Because young are messy, this fresh lining is applied periodically throughout the nesting period. Some raven nests are visible from canoe routes in the BWCA in Minnesota, and they may allow you to approach to within 130 feet.

Common Ravens Feed on Smelt. When the smelt run is strong, look for ravens feeding in the shallow

groups may also satiate the local predators, reducing the chance that any one nest will be destroyed. On the negative side, those birds nesting on the edges bear the bulk of the predation from owls, raccoons, and even snakes. Large colonies also tend to attract more parasitic flies and lice.

To avoid disturbing the bird colony, watch from a distance with a tripod-mounted spotting scope. Look for courtship displays, competition for nest sites, and sibling rivalry between heron nest-mates. Notice how noisy and aggressive terns are when their colony is threatened; this may be why the retiring piping plover often nests within the protective sphere of these well-guarded colonies.

eddies of rivers emptying into the Great Lakes. Ravens are cautious and won't be found near human smelt fisherman.

Black Phoebe Is First Migrating Flycatcher. During early springs, black phoebes may arrive in the northwoods in late April. Like bluebirds and swallows, they could starve if a late cold snap deprived them of their main food—flying insects. Look for nests under the eaves of little-used buildings.

Palm Warblers and Hermit Thrushes Return to Bogs. Territorial male palm warblers and hermit thrushes are the first migrants to begin singing in spruce bogs.

Tree Swallows Cluster to Avoid Cold. These early migrants congregate inside cavities or nest boxes during cold snaps to conserve energy. They fly with jerky wingbeats, hesitating outside the holes. It may not pay to be the first swallow to enter; the birds on the bottom are sometimes smothered.

Brown Thrashers Are Accomplished Mimics. In late April, listen in logged forest openings for the loud sounds of territorial thrashers. The song consists of phrases taken freely from the other birds and repeated frequently. Also listen carefully for warbling and melodious "whisper" songs.

MAMMALS

Black Bears Leave Dens. Fortified only by their mother's milk, cubs have grown to the size of housecats. They now leave with their mother to feed on a wide variety of plants and small animals.

Least Chipmunks Emerge from Hibernation. Chipmunks must guard themselves from a mob of predators including: fisher, marten, coyote, fox, bobcat, and weasel; northern goshawk, cooper's, sharpshinned, and broad-winged hawks; great horned, longeared, and barred owls.

Porcupine Pups Born. Inside rocky dens, or occasionally in large tree holes, single porcupines are born. Soft quills harden shortly after birth.

384

Rodents Gnaw Antlers. White-tailed deer and moose shed their antlers in the heart of winter, and voles, mice, and other mammals quickly chew them up. This helps wear down their growing teeth while providing needed calcium.

REPTILES AND AMPHIBIANS

Spring Peepers Begin to Call. Listen for their high, ascending trills in marshy areas, roadside ditches, and open or wooded areas. They produce a tremendous decibel level despite their small (1-inch-long) size. Eggs are attached singly or in small clusters attached to emergent stalks of water plants.

Wood Frogs Begin to Breed. The first true frog to call. Their highly explosive breeding season lasts only 2 weeks. To locate them, investigate duck-like, quacking calls coming from woodland pools.

Chorus Frogs Chorus. Towards the end of April, listen near woodland ponds and marshes for 1-second-long calls—a rapid series of "it" sounds that increase in tempo and rise in pitch. (Imagine the sound of a finger run along the teeth of an amplified comb.) Females, attracted to this din, begin to mate; in 2–3 months, metamorphosed froglets will leave the pond.

Painted Turtles Bask. Late in the month, this beautiful red and black turtle is the first to be seen basking in the spring sun. Like other reptiles, turtles cannot regulate their own thermostats; radiant heat from the sun allows them to warm up. When warm, a turtle can swim faster and chase prey more effectively.

Garter Snakes Exploit Breeding Frogs. When spring-breeding frogs congregate in local ponds, eastern garter snakes are often attracted by the concentration of prey. Snakes will remain in breeding ponds for several days to feast.

MAY

	Temperature	
	Ave. High	Ave. Low
Itasca, MN	68	39
Grand Marais, MN	54	38
Spooner, WI	70	42
Sturgeon Bay, WI	64	42
Houghton, MI	66	40
Seney NWR, MI	66	39

IDENTIFYING BIRDS BY SOUND

Beginning bird watchers usually identify common birds by sight with the help of binoculars. Most birds, however, are masterfully elusive, especially once trees leaf out in spring and summer. In the leafy seasons, bird watching can become mostly bird listening. During this time, most birds sing or give call notes that are unique to the species. By learning these vocalizations, you'll be able to identify birds at any season. To start, listen for songs, call notes, young birds begging, or woodpeckers tapping, then follow the sounds until you find the source. Or, after identifying a new bird by sight, continue watching until it vocalizes. You can also listen to recordings of bird songs to pin down that "voice in the woods" that escaped your gaze.

Keep notes to aid your memory. Or invent a mnemonic device to help you *continued on next page*

General warmth greens up grasses and many trees. Aspens, balsam poplar, and willows leaf out around mid-month. The chilling effect of the Great Lakes further delays spring along its shores. Most perching birds return during May. After a night of southerly winds, the trees may be filled with flight-weary male birds, greeting the day with ardent singing. During early or warm springs, the trees may leaf-out well before most of the migrants have arrived, a condition that frustrates birders.

Lavender and violet hepatica blooms in early May.

Fern fiddleheads push up through the leaf litter.

Eastern white pines may start to shed pollen late in the month; farther north, pollen may not fly until early July.

Aspen and birch buds burst; oaks and ashes follow 2–3 weeks later.

Wild asparagus is tall enough to harvest, as the deer and rabbits well know.

Morel mushrooms appear late in the month; look for the smaller species in the northwoods.

Canada mayflower blooms are set off by two or three lily-like leaves.

Wild strawberry and red-berried elder flower.

Marsh marigolds bloom in low, open swamps.

BIRDS

Yellow-rumped Warblers Are the First Warblers to Return. In early years, they may arrive in early April, before all the snow patches have melted. This flexible forager can survive late cold spells by feeding on a variety of insects and fruits. A few may winter just south of the northwoods, which is far north for a warbler.

Kirtland's Warblers Arrive. About mid-May, male Kirtland's warblers arrive in their territories. This extreme habitat specialist nests only in several Michigan counties. Habitat management and cowbird control have stabilized this endangered species at a population of less than 500. To avoid disturbing its nesting, take the organized tour to view the species.

Broad-winged Hawks Nest Near Woodland Pools. This tame broadleaf forest hawk prefers to nest in mature trees near a shallow pond and forest opening. A classic "sit and wait" predator, it perches silently until a moving frog, toad, rodent, or large insect betrays its location. Listen for a plaintive whistle like that of the eastern wood-pewee.

American Redstarts Are Vivid Migrants and Residents. The most animated May warbler is the American redstart which flits like a butterfly when catching insects. It fans its tail and droops its wings when singing and foraging, and in the process exposes bright orange and red flashes against a field of black feathers.

Common Snipes Begin "Winnowing" Territorial Flights. In wet sedge meadows and grassy spring seeps, listen during dawn or twilight for a bleating sound created by the wind vibrating the tail feathers of the male snipe as it plummets earthward.

Cooper's and Sharp-shinned Hawks Nest. Look for fast-flying birds darting through thick woods. Scan tall stumps or along elevated logs for plucked feathers or fur left at the kill site. Look for the remains of woodpeckers, northern flickers, red squirrels, and blue jays.

remember, e.g., "hic, three beers" for the song of the olive-sided flycatcher. Some field guides include sonograms, which are a visual display of the frequencies and duration of the bird's song that you can "read" to help identify the songster. The trickiest birds to identify are those that have a large repertoire of calls, some of which are given only at certain times of the year. These species will fool you for years until you learn all the songs they sing.

In May and June, birds are usually singing to attract females or proclaim territory. Peak song occurs between dawn and 8 a.m. By singing early in the day, songsters take advantage of the still air that lets their calls be heard from a greater distance. When songs and displays are not enough to settle disputes, rival males may chase each other in flight, often singing loudly. Their singing style varies by species. The persistent red-eyed vireo sings all day long,

continued on next page

387

while the cedar waxwing doesn't have a song to speak of. Some migrants will sing while in transit to more northern nesting territories, even though they are not seeking mates or advertising territory.
To increase your listening pleasure, keep conversation to a minimum, tread lightly, and pause frequently to listen. For more information, listen to Peterson's "Field Guide to Eastern Bird Songs."

Connecticut Warblers and Yellow-bellied Flycatchers Return to Bogs. These two species are the "rear guard" of the spring bird migration to the bogs.

Hairy Woodpecker Eggs Hatch. These year-round residents get a jump on the breeding season. Their young may fledge as early as late May. Listen for the loud call of nestlings from high nestholes.

Female Cowbirds Search for Nests to Parasitize. Brown-headed cowbirds lay their eggs in the nests of red-winged blackbirds, yellow warblers, scarlet tanagers, and other birds. Look for a drab, gray bird acting very secretive. A laying female cowbird is often followed by a small flock of displaying males eager to mate with her. These females do have territories; they defend nests of other species from parasitism by other cowbirds.

Wood Ducks Incubate. Eggs must be incubated during cool spring weather. Thanks to a thick insulating layer of feathers in the nest, the egg temperature drops only a few degrees during the 1 or 2 hours when the female must leave the nest to feed. To find the nest, look for large knot holes in mature trees (or artificial nest boxes) facing a body of water. Don't disturb!

Northern Harriers Nest in Sedge Meadows. A tussocky, treeless meadow is essential hunting and nesting habitat. Pesticides and loss of marshland have reduced the number of harriers.

MAMMALS

Young Woodchucks Leave Den. Young woodchucks begin to venture forth to feed on clover, grasses, and other herbaceous plants. Look for their dens on the edges of mixed woodland and grassy openings.

Cow Moose with Calves. You have a good chance of seeing moose along the Finland-Ely section of Highway #1 in Minnesota, in the Isle Royale National Park, and in the Upper Peninsula of Michigan. Cow moose are protective of their calves; be sure to keep your distance.

First Eastern Cottontails Out of Nest. Many young rabbits fall prey to hawks, weasels, and coyotes.

Beavers Fell Trees Near Water. Look for freshly cut trees, the sign of beavers setting up a new territory. They rarely cut farther than 100 feet from the water because they would be too vulnerable to wolves.

REPTILES AND AMPHIBIANS

Northern Leopard Frogs Breed. In open areas with quiet water, northern leopard frogs attach their eggs to submerged vegetation.

American Toads Trill. When marsh marigolds begin to bloom, listen for trilling at the edges of any body of water: ditches, vernal ponds, or bays of lakes. Look for distinctive long strings of eggs. Later, in June and July, look for schooling black tadpoles.

Redback Salamanders Active. This species may be found where eastern white pine, eastern hemlock, or mature broadleaf forests reign. Look for it under logs and stones in damp woodlands.

JUNE

	Temperature	
	Ave. High	Ave. Low
Itasca, MN	74	49
Grand Marais, MN	62	43
Spooner, WI	76	51
Sturgeon Bay, WI	74	51
Houghton, MI	74	48
Seney NWR, MI	74	47

June is the month of longest daylight (up to 16 hours), but the thermometer will not catch up with the day length until July or August. Most birds are incubating eggs or feeding young. A flush of caterpillars and plenty of daylight for foraging ease the burden of providing for young nestlings. Most orchids bloom during this month.

Yellow bladderwort flowers are abundant in northern white-cedar swamps and bogs.

White Canadian starflowers now reach peak bloom; both the petals and leaves are star-like.

Nodding bells of the pink twinflower appear in needleleaf forests and openings.

Bunchberry and bog-dwelling labrador tea are blooming.

Peak month for wild strawberries. Luna moths and other giant silkworm moths are flying.

Pin cherries and serviceberries continue to flower. Large-flowered trillium and bellworts begin their peak bloom.

Columbine is blooming in sunny openings.

American elm seeds fall.

Wood ticks are at their peak in grassy areas.

Yellow and showy lady's-slippers are in peak bloom.

BIRDS

Golden-winged Warblers Nest. With the loss of their preferred habitat (shrub-sapling openings) and aggressive hybridization from blue-winged warblers during the last 100 years, this species is becoming rarer. Look at individual birds carefully; most are partial hybrids and have some plumage characteristics of blue-winged warblers.

Female Baltimore Orioles Nest. It takes the female about a week to build the nest—a woven gray "sock"—where she incubates 4–6 eggs. Listen for the ascending calls of the hungry young in overhanging branches of American elms and other trees with drooping branches.

Wood Duck Broods Fledge. Late May and early June

is the peak period for wood duck fledging. In a per-
ilous trip, young wood ducklings jump from their
nest holes and follow their mother en masse to reach
the nearest lake or pond.

Alder Flycatchers Nest. In alder or willow thickets,
listen for the "peep" call or "fee-bee-o" song of this
secretive flycatcher. It cannot be distinguished vis-
ually from its southern cousin, the willow flycatcher,
which sings a sharp "fitz-bew" song.

Juneberries Begin Fruiting. Cedar waxwing flocks
visit juneberry stands with ripe berries. Notice the
fruits change color from green to red to blue as they
ripen. This tells the color-sensitive birds which fruits
have the highest sugar content and are therefore ready
to be eaten. Seeds pass unharmed through the bird's
digestive tract and are conveniently planted away from
the shade of the parent tree.

Common Nighthawks Nest. Look for the female
sitting on the ground incubating her eggs. There is
no nesting material! If you approach closely, you may
be surprised by her distraction display—a hissing
mouth gapes wide and wings flay out.

Eastern Kingbirds Are Good Neighbors. If you find
an eastern kingbird nest, look for other birds' nests
nearby. Sometimes orioles and American robins will
nest close to kingbirds, possibly to benefit from the
"sphere of protection" provided by the aggressive
kingbirds.

Northern Goshawks Defend Nests. When young
goshawks hatch, the parents are vigorous in their nest
defense, swooping dramatically towards any threat,
including hikers. Look for nests in remote, heavily
wooded forests.

*Male Hummingbirds Fly Courtship Loops, Defend
Sapwells.* Before nesting, ruby-throated hummingbirds drink from sapwells—holes made in birch trees
by yellow-bellied sapsuckers. Intruding hummingbirds are not welcome, and are driven away.

Chestnut-sided Warblers Nest. In young broadleaf
second growth, listen for the ringing song of the male.

FINDING BIRD NESTS

Few outdoor plea-
sures match the
thrill of discovering
a bird nest. It is
like looking through
a previously veiled
window and dis-
covering one of the
countless details of
nature that thank-
fully persist despite
our oblivion. June
is the best month to
look for nests in the
northwoods because
most species will be
either constructing
their nests, incubat-
ing eggs, or feeding
young. If you're
thorough, you can
discover nests of all
sizes—from the
lichen and spider-
web jewel made by
the ruby-throated
hummingbird to the
remote and fiercely
defended liar of the
northern goshawk.
Many nests are
camouflaged or
well-hidden for
good reason. In
some species at
least half of the eggs
and nestlings are
eaten by sharp-eyed
predators.

To find the nest of
a particular spe-
cies, read about its
preferred nesting
sites and nesting
phenology in ad-
vance. For exam-
ple, northern oriole
nests are most often
continued on next page

This bird was rare in Audubon's time—he saw only one—but extensive deforestation and regrowth have augmented its preferred habitat.

Ruffed Grouse Hatch. Shortly after hatching, 6–10 young grouse follow their mother looking for insects and seeds. The females are quick to defend the brood, sometimes faking injury in an attempt to distract the observer.

Wood Ducks Caravan with Young. Female wood ducks are often seen with their young, which cannot fly yet, but swim vigorously after their mother.

Barn Swallows Feed First Brood. The flush of insects has sustained the parent swallows, so they can now feed their young.

Sedge Wrens Build "Dummy" Nests. This secretive wren of grassy marshes is most easily detected by its unmistakable song, which sounds like the first start-up of an old sewing machine. Its wings vibrate stiffly as it appears to hover over the ground. The extra "dummy" nests may serve to confuse predators.

Common Loon Eggs Hatch. Young chicks are sometimes seen riding on their parent's back. Parents feed them a diet of small fish and aquatic insects.

Courtship Feeding in Cedar Waxwings. Waxwings may breed through August, but courtship feeding is most likely in June and July. Males and females pass a piece of food, usually a berry, back and forth repeatedly. When you see this behavior, look for a nest nearby (see Finding Bird Nests, page 390).

Ovenbird Nests a Challenge to Find. This common warbler nests on the ground but often sings its "teacher, teacher, TEACHER" song from an elevated perch. The bird's name comes from the dutch-oven shape of its nest. It is well-camouflaged with leaves and blends into the forest floor.

Yellow Warblers Sometimes Evade Cowbird Parasitism. Yellow warblers are frequent victims of brown-headed cowbird invasion. Some yellow warblers build new nests above the parasitized nest, lay a second clutch, and avoid raising an interloper.

found in the drooping branches of a large eastern cottonwood or American elm near open areas, and red-winged blackbird nests are concealed in cattails or low shrubs in or near a marsh. Scan likely locations. Sit quietly and wait in a concealed spot. Most females are very cagey near nests and won't return until they believe the danger has passed. Don't be fooled by distraction displays such as the broken wing act, or a noisy flight from the nest. Look for the nest or young in the direction opposite that taken by the distracting female. If you see birds courting or mating, you are probably near a nest site. Look for birds carrying nesting material or food, and then follow them discreetly toward the nest. Take care when approaching ground nests; humans leave a scent that is obvious to mammals that raid nests. These predators may follow your

continued on next page

Solitary Vireos Remarkably Tame on Nest. The first vireo to return to the north is a solitary denizen of deep woods. When discovered on the nest, it has allowed itself to be touched without flying away.

Nuthatches Prefer Different Habitats, Nest in Similar Cavities. Red-breasted nuthatches prefer mature needleleaf forests in the northern part of the northwoods, while white-breasted nuthatches predominate in broadleaf forests farther south. Both nest in cavities in dead limbs protruding from live trees, in knotholes, or in abandoned woodpecker holes.

MAMMALS

Moose Feed on Aquatic Plants. Throughout the summer moose wade into water 3 or 4 feet deep to feed on aquatic plants such as water lilies. These plants are full of sodium, which moose require a lot of. Moose are strong swimmers and may swim across a lake instead of taking the long way around by land.

Saplings Grow Rapidly. Most tree species are growing fastest now, and are browsed (in addition to aquatics and grasses) by moose and deer.

Red Foxes Are with Kits. Vixen may be seen away from the den with 3-month-old, playful kits.

Red Squirrel Pups Leave Nest. At first, the former nestmates are harmonious and even affectionate. But fighting and chasing increases as the pups grow and the food supply diminishes.

Black Bears Mate. Mating early in the summer allows bears to give their undivided energy to foraging when fruits ripen up in July and August.

REPTILES AND AMPHIBIANS

Green Frogs Breed. One of the last frogs to breed, green frogs need permanent water so their late-maturing tadpoles have enough water to swim in. Look for a thin film of eggs, 1 inch across, floating on the water. To witness mating and territorial skirmishes between males, view with flashlights or headlamps from late evening to early morning.

odor trail and wipe out all of the nests you have just visited! For more information, read Harrison's "Field Guide to Bird's Nests" in the Peterson series and Terres' excellent "Encyclopedia of North American Birds."

Mink Frogs Call in Bogs. At the edge of sphagnum mats, listen for the "knock-knock-knock" calls of mink frogs. The tadpole stage may take 1 or 2 years in the nutrient-poor bog waters. Look for them where water flows from bogs into lakes.

Redback Salamanders Guard Eggs. After laying about ten eggs under a log or on moss, the female guards them until they hatch 2 months later. She will drive off potential predators and apply an anti-fungal secretion to the eggs.

Ringneck Snakes Lay Eggs. This secretive, nocturnal snake hides under rocks, logs, and other debris. If you find a female at this time of year, she may be tending a clutch of eggs.

Snapping and Painted Turtles Dig Nest Holes and Lay Eggs. Both species lay eggs on open, slightly hilly areas. Look for painted turtles laying near sunset. Snapping turtles, which lay in early morning or early evening, go into a "trance" when laying and can be approached closely. Both species use water carried in their bladders from lakes or rivers to loosen soil while digging.

JULY

	Temperature	
	Ave. High	Ave. Low
Itasca, MN	82	55
Grand Marais, MN	72	56
Spooner, WI	82	58
Sturgeon Bay, WI	80	58
Houghton, MI	81	53
Seney NWR, MI	83	54

Many fruits, nuts, and seeds ripen in July. It's the sunniest month; and is clear nearly 75 percent of the

OBSERVING BIRD FORAGING BEHAVIOR

Although nesting activity slows down during July, you'll be able to watch the fledged young and adults busily feeding to gain fat for migration. On warm days, birds feed most often during the cool morning and late afternoon. Most birds cannot feed and be vigilant at the same time, so if they sense danger, they will flee. Therefore, keep yourself well-camouflaged, and don't approach too closely, even if your target bird goes out of view temporarily.

continued on next page

time. Heat waves are often followed by cooling thunderstorms. Lake Superior, the largest and northernmost of the Great Lakes, acts like a refrigerator throughout the summer. Temperatures are lower near the shores of the Great Lakes, and plant development may be 2 weeks slower than it is inland.

American basswood trees are fragrant; their flowers attract honeybees and bumblebees.

Bright red berries of wintergreen first appear in needleleaf forests.

Meadowsweet is blooming in alder thickets.

American mountain-ash is flowering.

Pin cherries are ripe.

Milkweeds bloom in fields and grassy forest openings.

The "doll's eyes" of white baneberry fruit first appear.

BIRDS

Peak Berry Month, Birds are Feasting. Blueberries, huckleberries, and juneberries ripen. Many birds feed on fruit: cedar waxwings, American robins, northern flickers, and wood thrushes, to name a few.

Ravens Switch to Fruit. With carrion and other food in low supply, ravens feast on raspberries, juneberries, and blueberries. Pellet analysis reveals fruit may comprise almost 100 percent of their summer diet. Look for pellets under nest trees and communal roosts.

Short-eared Owlets Growing Rapidly. At dawn and dusk, look for parent owls coursing over sedge meadows and marshes to feed their hungry young. When they spot a mouse or other rodent, they may drop straight down with their wings held up.

MAMMALS

Otters Fish, Float, and Feed. In deeper water, a river otter will catch fish underwater, return to the surface, then eat the catch while floating on its back,

The edges of habitats are good places to watch for birds. The fast-growing plants that thrive here offer fruits and insects that birds relish.

A bird's bill shape may be a good clue to its prevalent feeding method—whether it is a bark prober, foliage gleaner, ground feeder, or aerial feeder, for instance. The chisel beaks of woodpeckers are strong enough to hack out cavities in tree trunks. Compare the beaks of the hairy woodpecker and the yellow-bellied sapsucker. Which do you think does the most excavation? Short and pointed bills of warblers and vireos are efficient "tweezers" for gleaning insects. Flycatchers require a large trap area to help them capture flying insects during open-air "hawking." Their bill is widened at the base and equipped with bristles. Compare the flattened, spoon-shaped bill of the shoveler (which strains small food particles from the mud) with that of other ducks.

*Wildlife biologists study foraging be-**continued on next page*

havior to determine
the diet and habitat
needs of various
species. As you
watch, try record-
ing the types of for-
aging moves you
see (e.g., hover,
hawk, glean, probe,
excavate, steal,
etc.). Are some spe-
cies adept at sev-
eral behaviors?
Note the kind of
tree they are in,
where in the tree
they work, and
which food items
they eat. Are some
species specialists?
Note if the bird is
solitary or feeding
in a flock. Are there
interactions among
flock members?
What causes the in-
teractions? To make
your notes com-
plete, record tree
height, bird place-
ment, branch
diameter, etc. for
each foraging
move. These count-
ing and measuring
methods are easily
learned by an in-
terested amateur.
Chickadees are a
great species to
study because of
their abundance,
tameness, flock dy-
namics, and curios-
ity about many
kinds of food. For
more information,
read Stokes' "Guide
to Bird Behavior,"
Berger's "Bird
Study," and Van
Remsen's article on
taking field notes in
"American Birds,"
Vol 31 (5), (1977).

using its stomach as a table. Sea otters do the same with abalone and sea urchins.

Mink Pups Travel with Mother. After leaving the den, young mink follow their mother along lake shores, riverbanks, and woodlands not far from streams. Look for tracks in soft mud.

Mammals Relish Berries. Chipmunks, red squir-rels, raccoons, and black bears eat berries. Pin cher-ries ripen towards the end of the month.

Snowshoe Hares Breed Again. After the first litter of young are weaned, male hares chase females to initiate the second litter of the season.

REPTILES AND AMPHIBIANS

Green Frogs Still Breeding. Because this late-breeding frog lays its eggs in permanent ponds, there is less urgency than for those species using temporary ponds. Males call throughout the day, but females arrive and lay eggs only at night. Look for thin sheets of eggs floating on the water.

Young Toads Emerge. Toadlets feed upland and are easy prey for garter snakes and water snakes. Only adult toads are poisonous; when touched, large glands behind their eyes secrete bitter and toxic alkaloids.

Wood Turtles Forage in Uplands. All summer, wood turtles forage in open meadows or woodlands near fast-moving streams. They are found primarily in Wisconsin and Michigan, and are endangered in Minnesota.

Northern Water Snakes Feed on Frogs and Fish. This shy and harmless snake is usually seen only briefly as it rapidly swims away from humans. Its jaws and head are connected with elastic ligaments that allow it to swallow prey up to 5 inches long.

AUGUST

	Temperature	
	Ave. High	Ave. Low
Itasca, MN	80	54
Grand Marais, MN	72	56
Spooner, WI	80	57
Sturgeon Bay, WI	78	58
Houghton, MI	79	52
Seney NWR, MI	79	54

Temperatures finally catch up with shortening days; the latter half of August is noticeably cooler than July. Many warblers gain weight to prepare for migration. Violent thunderstorms are most likely in July and August. Destructive straight-line winds generated by strong downdrafts may knock over many square miles of forest. A July 4th, 1977 storm in Wisconsin damaged more than 2,500 square miles of forest.

Goldenrod blooming peaks in meadows.

Large leaf aster blooms in many types of forests.

Distinctive berries of the corn lily, or Clintonia, appear in pine and spruce-fir forests.

In open areas, fireweed is in bloom and American mountain-ash fruit is still green.

Highbush cranberries, red raspberries, and rose hips ripen.

Hazelnuts are ripe.

Sulphur shelf and other fungi appear after wet spells.

Late in the month, monarch butterflies begin to migrate south.

The first fall colors are solitary flames of red maple, sumac, and Virginia creeper.

BIRDS

Swallows Are the Earliest Conspicuous Migrants. In mid-to-late August, swallows gather for flights southward. They must migrate before other birds because their food supply (flying insects) may be sharply reduced by an early cold snap.

Red-Eyed Vireos Sing Persistently. Unlike most other birds, male red-eyed vireos still sing in early August, often throughout the day. The purpose of this late summer song is not known.

Common Nighthawks Migrate. Some years they move south in huge concentrations, often following shorelines. Look for flocks of thousands of birds late in August between 5 and 10 p.m. They follow the Mississippi Valley on their way to their wintering grounds in South America.

American Goldfinches Nest. When down is seen on thistle heads, look for goldfinch nests, which are lined with this material. Goldfinch are one of the last birds to nest.

Many Ducks Secretive During Molt. During molt or "eclipse" plumage, ducks fly poorly—if at all. They seek cover in remote marshes during this vulnerable period.

MAMMALS

Red Squirrels Show Increased Aggression. Fall territoriality begins and young squirrels disperse from their mother's territory, sometimes after being chased out by the female.

River Otter Fish in Beaver Ponds. Otters have found that beaver ponds are good places to fish. Look for otter tracks and scat on beaver dams.

Gray Wolves Howl. Wolf packs howl cooperatively to advertise their territories year round.

Chipmunks Clean Out Pin Cherries. This favorite food is harvested rapidly after the fruit is ripe. Many cherries are cached underground for winter food.

MIXED SPECIES FLOCKING

Many birds feed and migrate in interspecific (mixed species) flocks. Starting as early as mid-July, look for young warblers associating with flocks of chickadees. The warblers congregate in flocks near plentiful food sources, often following the cue of the presumably knowledgeable resident chickadees. For some reason, woodpeckers, nuthatches, and goldfinches associate with these flocks, even though they do not eat the same food. Perhaps predators are more quickly detected by *continued on next page*

Rodents, Deer, and Bears Feed on Fungi. If July has been wet, mushrooms are abundant, providing a favorite food for white-tailed deer and black bears. Red squirrels place them on tree limbs to dry, and chipmunks and mice nibble the caps. Look for telltale wedges cut out of the tops of mushrooms.

Red Squirrels Harvest Spruce Cones. Before white spruce cones mature and lose their seeds, red squirrels snip them from the tree. Listen for a rain of falling cones and territorial chatters. They don't linger on the ground long; squirrels quickly whisk them to underground caches for winter food.

Thirteen-lined Ground Squirrels Fatten. Within a month this lover of open fields and lawns will enter a 7–8-month hibernation. It feasts on green plants, flowers, seeds, grubs, ants, and even young mice and birds.

Striped Skunks Disperse. In late summer and fall, the young of the year disperse to find their own territories. Skunks are nocturnal, feeding on earthworms, ants, and other insects.

Raccoon Families Leave Dens. Mother and kits may range widely from the den site. They will remain as a family group well into the fall.

REPTILES AND AMPHIBIANS

Smooth Green Snakes Active. This day-active snake breeds in August, and becomes more active on wet summer nights or wet, overcast days.

American Toads Feed on Ants. Toads eat many kinds of insects, but in some areas they dine almost exclusively on ants. A researcher suggested that one way to survey ants might be to examine the stomach contents of toads. How they find so many ants is still a mystery.

Green Frog Tadpoles Still Transforming. This late-breeding frog is one of the last to have its tadpoles transform to froglets. Only 1½ months remain for them to feed and grow before hibernating for the winter.

these large groups. Watch what the other birds do in response to a chickadee's alarm call. Notice the similarity in call notes when chickadees, brown creepers, and kinglets are foraging together.

In late summer, shorebirds also begin "staging," or gathering, for their leap-frog migration farther south. In shallow lakes, look for competition within and between species for food items. Do the shorebirds segregate according to the depth of water in which they wade? Which individuals, if any, are dominant?

Four-toed Salamanders Live Under Stones and Logs. In Wisconsin and Michigan, look for this salamander in broadleaf forests bordering bogs. When a predator grabs the four-toed's tail, it breaks off easily and twitches, distracting the enemy. A new tail regenerates quickly.

SEPTEMBER

	Temperature	
	Ave. High	Ave. Low
Itasca, MN	66	44
Grand Marais, MN	61	47
Spooner, WI	69	46
Sturgeon Bay, WI	68	50
Houghton, MI	48	43
Seney NWR, MI	67	41

THE MIGRATION OF PERCHING BIRDS

During September, most migratory perching birds pass through the northwoods. Migration allows these birds to take advantage of the abundant insect supply in the North during the spring and summer, and then move to the South, where food is still available during the winter. Most songbird migrants fly south at night when favorable northern winds are blowing. Little southward progress is made during the day, because birds *continued on next page*

A definite chill returns to the northwoods, and a first frost is likely. In northern locations, fall colors peak during the latter half of the month, but are delayed by warm temperatures near the shores of the Great Lakes. Quaking aspens are brilliant yellow. Sugar maples start to change; they may turn yellow, orange, red, or russet brown. Dry, warm weather seems to intensify fall colors. Cold fronts bring in some of the clearest weather in months.

Older eastern white pine needles fall; needles younger than 3 years remain on the tree.

Orange jewelweed (spotted touch-me-not) blooms in moist, fertile soils. Its ripe pods explode when touched lightly.

Shaggy mane and puffball mushrooms appear soon after rains.

400

BIRDS

Ducks Begin to Harvest Wild Rice. Both humans and ducks relish the carbohydrate-rich grains. Look for ducks feeding in rice beds along the shores of shallow lakes.

Canada Geese Move South. Especially after a cold front, look for the characteristic "V" of a flying flock and listen for honking—the trumpet that heralds fall. The "V" shape helps reduce drag and increases flying efficiency.

Gray Jays Take Interest in Humans. Secretive other times of the year, gray jays now approach people. Are they looking for food? September and October are their peak months for visiting feeders and caching food.

Robins and Flickers Stage for Migration. Early in the month, flocks of American robins and northern flickers are seen on the sides of roads and edges of woods. Both feed on fruit and ground-dwelling insects before migration.

Flickers and Sapsuckers Are Only Woodpeckers that Migrate. These two birds have tastes that differ from other woodpeckers. The ants that northern flickers crave and the sap and free-crawling insects which yellow-bellied sapsuckers eat are only available in spring and summer in the north. These are the only woodpeckers, therefore, that migrate south in the fall.

Warbler Flocks Migrate. Look for large numbers of warblers associating with chickadees. Most are in confusing fall plumage; using a good field guide, test your identification skills. The males' bright plumage, which is used to attract females and advertise territory, won't be needed until next spring.

Listen for Early Evening Migrants. During clear weather with northerly winds, you can hear the chip notes of migrant warblers passing overhead in open fields. There is something poignant about these flocks of unseen, mysterious travelers advancing in front of autumn.

are busy fattening themselves (a phenomenon called "hyperphagia") for their long-distance flights. Their pre-migratory restlessness is called "zugunruhe" and results from hormonal changes triggered by the shortening day length.

Only recently have some of the mysteries of migration been unraveled. Researchers have found that birds use several directional cues in migration, including stars, the sun, polarized light, landmarks, magnetic fields, and possibly infrasound. Planetarium experiments have shown that the apparent rotation of the stars, but not the details of particular constellations, provides direction for some species such as the indigo bunting. On most nights there is enough light to see landscape features which may also serve as signposts for the migrant birds. Recent research suggests that American robins and bobolinks use the earth's magnetic field to aid in navigation. Perhaps the tiny iron needles found in the brains of bobo- continued on next page

401

links act as a compass during migration. The crashing of waves, thunderstorms, and winds produce ultra-low frequency sounds that we cannot detect, but that some birds, such as homing pigeons, may use as navigational cues.

Migration is risky for many species. Lights on tall television and microwave towers attract or confuse many birds, and thousands die each year in collisions. Radars have tracked the fate of migrating flocks on the East Coast. At least one flock lost its course and appeared to perish far out at sea. When radio transmitters are further miniaturized and the details of satellite tracking improved, much more will be learned about bird migration.

Harris' and White-crowned Sparrows Migrate. Look for these flocks frequenting weedy patches in forest openings.

Watch for Migrants Against the Full Moon. Using a telescope or strong binoculars, watch the face of the full moon between 10 p.m. and midnight late in the month and into October. You may see the silhouettes of herons, geese, and shorebirds flying in tight formation with the wind.

MAMMALS

Fawns Have Lost Spots, Adult Deer Grow Winter Coat. Now that fawns are moving about with their mother, the dappling that once provided camouflage on the forest floor would now make them conspicuous to sharp-eyed wolves. Thus, the change to a solid color is a survival adaptation. The adults' coat changes from a reddish-brown to a grayish-brown for the winter. It thickens with the growth of long hollow hairs.

Bur and Red Oak Acorns Mature. Red and gray squirrels feed on ripening acorns, even before they fall to the ground. During good mast years, red squirrels cache hundreds, defending the cache through winter. Gray squirrels bury acorns singly or in small groups, relying on a good memory to find dozens of small caches months later.

Beavers Refurbish Lodges. Beavers add sticks and mud to their lodge to thicken the walls that have deteriorated in rain, snow, and wind. The thickness of the lodge walls in part determines how warm the lodge will be in winter, and how much energy the beavers will need to keep warm.

Flying Squirrels Visit Oaks. As acorns mature, northern flying squirrels visit oaks to feast. During the day, look for partly chewed acorns under oak trees. To see squirrels, watch at a woodland edge after dark. First listen for them landing on and running up tree trunks, then use a powerful flashlight (with a red gel over the beam) to spot them.

Highbush Cranberries Are Bright Red. Upper branches bend over from the burden of heavy clusters of fruit. Chipmunks, squirrels, and waxwings relish the fruit.

Muskrats Build Winter Shelters. Muskrats use cattails, bulrushes, and mud to build these domed shelters that may reach 8 feet wide and 4 feet high.

Red Squirrel Siblings Become More Aggressive. With decreased food supply, red squirrels contest territories more fiercely. Those that don't have territories of their own must disperse to find them. Only about 30 percent of young red squirrels survive the winter.

Woodland Jumping Mice Enter Hibernation. This is the last month to be awakened in the middle of the night by these mice hopping across your sleeping bag. After fattening on seeds, fruit, fungi, and insects, these mice enter a 7–8-month hibernation.

REPTILES AND AMPHIBIANS

Redbelly Snakes In Motion. Overland and sometimes over-highway, redbellies migrate to ant mounds in early fall, where they will hibernate together with other snakes, as well as some frogs and toads.

Eastern Garter Snakes Catch Their Last Rays. On warm days, just before overwintering in rock piles, garter snakes may be seen sunning near foundations, and in deserted ant mounds.

Snapping Turtle Eggs Hatch. If the eggs have not been dug up by a striped skunk or raccoon, tiny hatchling turtles scuttle directly downslope to the nearby safety of rivers and lakes. Some of the late hatchers may overwinter underground and emerge the next spring.

Turtle Sex Determined by Temperature. Experiments show that in some species the sex of the hatchling turtle is determined by how hot or cold the eggs are when incubated. Low temperatures produced mainly males and high temperatures produced mainly females.

If you can find them, pellets and scats can provide even more information than tracks. Pellets are small balls made up of the parts of prey species that predators like owls, hawks, and gulls can't digest. They regurgitate these packets of bones, fur, or fish scales after they eat. Look for them beneath roosts or nest sites. Owls often roost and nest in dense stands of conifers. Hawks often have favorite perches in tall dead trees below which pellets accumulate. If a roost or nest site is used continuously, you can collect pellets over several seasons to determine how the bird's diet changes and how the prey food base changes over several years. With a reliable source of pellets, you could publish this information and make a valuable contribution to the scientific literature.

Although animal droppings may be less pleasant to examine, they are easy to find and can help improve

continued on next page

Tiger Salamanders Migrate to Wintering Sites. These salamanders, found only on the southern edge of the northwoods, migrate to wintering sites in building foundations, pocket gopher mounds, and under logs.

OCTOBER

	Temperature	
	Ave. High	Ave. Low
Itasca, MN	54	34
Grand Marais, MN	51	38
Spooner, WI	57	36
Sturgeon Bay, WI	56	40
Houghton, MI	55	36
Seney NWR, MI	59	29

Shorter days and more cloud cover herald the end of summer. Nearly all broadleaf trees are leafless by late October. Hard frosts have withered the ground cover. Some mammals begin hibernating and most insect-eating birds have migrated south within the last month. If it is a flight year, winter finches start to move in from the North.

Tamarack reaches peak golden color in swamps and along bog margins.

Cattail heads start to puff and release thousands of tiny seeds.

Club mosses produce clouds of microscopic spores with the slightest wind.

Eastern hemlock seeds fall from cones, but won't germinate until spring.

BIRDS

Snow Geese Moving South. Snow geese migrate later than Canada geese and often at a higher altitude.

Snow Buntings Pass Through. When nighttime temperatures routinely drop below freezing, look for flocks of snow buntings moving southward.

Diving Ducks Flock on Larger Lakes. Scaups, ring-necked ducks, buffleheads, and goldeneyes rest on local lakes en route to the southeastern U.S. and the Atlantic Coast.

Late Migrant Birds at Risk. If cold, windy weather prevents migration, sparrows, thrushes, and robins are forced to the ground to conserve energy. They sometimes cluster near roads, where they are at risk from cars. A naturalist's journal records an early snowstorm that grounded a flock of lesser golden plover on tennis courts.

Half-hearty Stragglers. Sometimes a few individuals of species that normally migrate will stay behind. They often rely on human-provided foods, such as suet and sunflower seeds. Look for yellow-rumped warblers, hermit thrushes, and American robins attempting to overwinter by feeding on leftover berries, fruits, and bird-feeder fare.

Common Raven Young Achieve Independence. Sibling groups of young ravens join larger flocks sometimes in spectacular pre-roost gatherings at sunset. Later in the fall, young ravens may fly 100 miles or more for a short visit to their parents' territory.

Blue Jays and Golden-crowned Kinglets Move South. Listen for the kinglets' thin, highpitched "seet-seet-seet" calls from the treetops. They are similar to call notes of a brown creeper. Both are short-distance migrants, wintering just south of the northwoods. A few may overwinter in warmer parts of the northwoods.

Spruce Grouse Specialize on Conifer Needles. Needles of jack pine, white spruce, and tamarack are their major food in fall and winter. A grouse's silhouette is almost indistinct against the dark branches;

your wildlife I.Q. Almost all mammals leave scats or droppings. Their size, shape, and contents are usually characteristic enough to identify their maker. They are often found along game trails, territory boundaries, sandy lake shores, and slightly elevated areas such as rocks or logs. Scats of mammalian predators are relatively "clean" and interesting to examine. (Warning: scats may contain pathogens; always wear gloves for your own safety!) The fur, hair, and bone fragments that they contain can help you identify the species that the predator has been eating. Pull "voucher" hairs from road-killed animals to provide a comparison with the ones you find in scats. Striped skunk scats are strange; they are often dry aggregations of insect parts. One scat contained more than 200 ants of four different species, many of which were queen carpenter ants! Droppings of browsing ungulates such as white-tailed deer become fibrous *continued on next page*

and dry when the
deer switch from
herbaceous to
woody forage.
Other information
on wildlife's food
habits comes from
examining caches,
food remains near
dens, midden
heaps, and kill
sites.

Mammals also
use scat and urine
to mark their terri-
tory. Unlike birds,
mammals are more
oriented to smell
than to sight and
sound, and they
usually have a
larger territory to
defend. For these
reasons, mammals
usually advertise
with scent, using
marks from special
glands, urine, or
scats. Human noses
are much less sensi-
tive to these odors,
so mammalian ter-
ritoriality is less
obvious to us. One
can expect territori-
ality in species that
have small hunting
ranges and re-
sources, such as
food and nests, that
are easily defended.
Red squirrels will
fiercely defend their
concentrated food
caches and a hand-
ful of productive
needleleaf trees.
Gray squirrels are
not territorial, how-
ever, because their
food sources are too
widely distributed.

continued on next page

carefully look for them sitting quietly in their preferred food trees.

Ruffed Grouse Eat a Vegetable Diet. Their diet
consists of paper birch leaves and buds of various
species, particularly aspen.

***Sandhill Cranes Flock in Sedge Meadows and
Marshes.*** Adults and young of the year congregate in
open sedge meadows, which are often dry at this time
of year. Cranes from western Minnesota winter in
Texas, while those from farther east migrate to Florida. The rust color of some adults is a feather stain
acquired while feeding in iron-rich soil.

MAMMALS

Felled Aspen Snag Tells Stories. An early October
entry from the field notes of one Minnesota wildlife
watcher: "Bats flew from a roosting site in an old
woodpecker hole as the tree fell. They could be a
migratory species or an overwintering species that
has not yet flown into caves or mine shafts to hibernate. This cavity also contained the cache of a flying
squirrel or red squirrel—several quarts of pea vine
seeds. To make it complete, a late gray treefrog was
20 feet up the trunk searching for insects."

Snowshoe Hares and Ermines Turn White. Early
in the month only the hares' ears and feet are white;
by the end of the month some snowshoe hares are
almost completely white.

Red Squirrels Cutting Spruce Tips. These tips are
not always cached like pine and spruce cones, but
are often eaten on the spot.

Mountain-Ash Berries Still On the Trees. Although
berries have been ripe for a month or so, they are
low in lipids (fats), and thus less likely to rot. Berries
and leaves are the preferred food of cedar waxwings,
evening grosbeaks, American robins, thrushes,
finches, black bears, moose, and snowshoe hares.
Bears make mini-migrations to feast on berries before
hibernation.

Beavers Add to Food Caches. Beavers cut and store woody branches (aspen is a favorite) in partly submerged piles near their lodges. When ponds freeze over, they swim underwater to reach the cache.

Black Bears Begin Hibernation. When tamaracks start to drop their yellow needles, bears retreat to dens ranging from well-protected earthen caves to open-air sites in clusters of large logs. If startled when starting sleep, they will look groggily at the intruder, then lapse back into unconsciousness. If acorns and other foods are available, some bears will stay aboveground until November, especially in Michigan and Wisconsin.

Raccoons Return to Their Winter Sleeping Quarters. Raccoons are not true hibernators but are largely inactive during the coldest winter months. They den in large hollow trees, culverts, and often beneath buildings.

Male White-tailed Deer in Rut. In November and December bucks often fight for possession of does, using both hooves and antler racks in the contest. The sound of two antlers rattling together may attract other deer.

Cattail Tubers Help Muskrats Fatten. Cattail tubers are rich in starch and are the preferred food of muskrats. Rich marshes support large muskrat populations that often peak and crash.

Moose in Rut. Like deer, male moose fight for access to females. Sometimes males will escort one another if females are nearby.

For the same reason, browsers and grazers such as deer and moose are rarely territorial. Defending their large feeding ranges would take too much energy. Besides, one or two more deer in the area would probably not deplete the food supply.

When watching mammals, look to see if they rub their rear end or snout on exposed branches. Such behavior often deposits a territorial scent. For more information, read Murie's "A Field Guide to Animal Tracks" in the Peterson Series and the Stokes' book on tracking.

NOVEMBER

	Snowpack	Temperature	
	Inches	Ave. High	Ave. Low
Itasca, MN	1	38	21
Grand Marais, MN	1	39	27
Spooner, WI	3	41	24
Sturgeon Bay, WI	2	44	30
Houghton, MI	1	43	25
Seney NWR, MI	2	43	27

IRRUPTIVE MIGRATIONS
Birds from Canada sometimes visit the northwoods when conditions in their own range are poor. Large numbers of their own species and failure of their food supply (scarce spruce and pine cones or low prey population) conspire to induce these "irruptive" flights. For example, lemming populations, on which snowy owls specialize, crash approximately every 4 to 10 years, and snowy owls must move south to the Lake States on a somewhat similar schedule. Pine grosbeaks, hoary redpolls, three-toed woodpeckers, and boreal, great gray, and hawk owls are most common during winter irruptive flights. Flocks of cedar waxwings and pine grosbeaks tend to move south with deepening cold, depleting the crop of mountain-ash berries as they go. Pine siskins, and red and white-winged crossbills are so erratic that their movement continued on next page

November is a "settling in" period. The northwoods is much quieter without its summer residents. Wildlife watchers need to know the food plants, habitat preferences, and activity patterns of their quarry if they wish to find them during this month of relative inactivity. Heavy snows are possible later in the month.

BIRDS

Boreal Chickadee Flocks Move South. Listen for the highpitched, buzzy calls of these brown-capped chickadees. Only occasionally do they form mixed flocks with black-capped chickadees.

Black-backed Woodpeckers More Visible. This rare northwoods specialist has unique habitat needs. They are most often seen feeding on dying and recently dead jack pine and other conifers. Listen for their unique chipmunk-like calls and the sound of bark being flaked off. They are fairly tame; approach them slowly for a close-up view.

Peak Migration for Scoters and Oldsquaws. These oceanic ducks are best seen on large inland lakes and on the Great Lakes. Unlike other ducks, they are usually well offshore. A few may persist during the winter if the water remains warm.

408

Downy Woodpeckers Wary at Roost Holes. All resident northwoods woodpeckers sleep in roost cavities. They make a beeline for them at dusk and enter without pausing. In the morning, they look out of the hole, retreat from view for a minute or two, then fly directly to a nearby tree. Ambushing owls and hawks are known to "stake out" woodpecker holes, which might explain this caution.

Search for Nests in Bare Woodlands. Take advantage of a leafless woodland to search for bird nests. Try to identify each nest's builders, and see if certain nests are found more often in particular habitats.

MAMMALS

Red Squirrels Are Quick Learners. A naturalist's notebook reads: "While feeding on and caching spruce branch tips, I notice that a red squirrel, to save "commuting" time, learns it is safe to jump down 12 feet onto 15 inches of snow. I never observed it jumping to bare ground from this height before the snowfall, so he or she must be pretty inventive."

Gray Squirrels Fatten. Gray squirrels fatten themselves on boxelder seeds and acorns, anticipating the lean days of winter. A forlorn sight is a gray squirrel feeding in a tree, exposed to the teeth of a November snowstorm.

Gray squirrel.

defies definition. These species seem to be true vagabonds that settle to breed only where food is plentiful.

To find these irruptive species, look in appropriate habitats during irruption years. Snowy owls perch on fence posts or low hills in open areas. Gyrfalcons, one of the rarest winter visitors, frequent cliffs near open water with ducks, or grain elevators with good populations of pigeons. Pine grosbeaks may be found feeding on American mountain-ash fruit. Keep your ears open for highpitched call notes overhead from arriving flocks of crossbills, grosbeaks, and pine siskins. Finding these irruptive migrants takes diligent work. For more background on how best to predict their arrival, read accounts in the state bird journals "The Loon," "The Passenger Pigeon," and "The Jack Pine Warbler," for Minnesota, Wisconsin, and Michigan, respectively.

DECEMBER

	Snowpack	Temperature	
	Inches	Ave. High	Ave. Low
Itasca, MN	7	19	1
Grand Marais, MN	5	26	10
Spooner, WI	9	25	6
Sturgeon Bay, WI	7	31	19
Houghton, MI	10	30	16
Seney NWR, MI	12	30	14

COVER AND WILDLIFE
In addition to providing food, plants shield wildlife from the eyes of predators and the vagaries of weather. In bitter cold, the ability to conserve energy is as important as the ability to find food. White-tailed deer tend to suffer without cover because their winter diet of low quality woody browse generates little heat. The densely packed northern white-cedars cut the wind, reduce radiant heat loss (much like cloud cover makes for a warmer night), and keep movement to a minimum so yarded deer can get the most out of their meager diet. Owls also tend to roost in dense
continued on next page

In most years, the northwoods takes on its "winter wonderland" aspect in December. Cross-country skiing is one of the best ways to see winter wildlife and their signs. Keep alert for tracks, scat, and browse marks along the trial. Pause often to listen for calls and scan for movement, and also to let the wildlife forget your presence.

BIRDS

Wild Food and Irruptive Finches. If food supplies farther north fail, pine grosbeaks, redpolls, pine siskins, and crossbills move south in search of food. They look for areas that have American mountain-ash berries, cones of white spruce, pine, and northern white-cedar, and seeds of ashes and birches.

Redpolls and Siskins Feast on Birch Seeds. Unlike larger finches and grosbeaks, these species feed on small food items, such as birch and weed seeds. Look for them in the crowns of birch trees.

Emaciated Northern Goshawk Found Dead in Tree. When the goshawk was found, the population of normal prey—snowshoe hare and ruffed grouse—was low. Usually, raptors will fly south until they find sufficient prey, then remain there for the winter. For instance, when prey populations are low in Canada, goshawk sightings are common in the northwoods and even farther south.

MAMMALS

Usnea *Lichen Important Deer Food.* With deepening snow, deer are limited to wood browse and *Usnea* lichen (old man's beard). Lichen grows profusely on the dead branches of budworm-damaged balsam fir; such stands attract many deer during hard winters.

Snowshoe Hares "Yard" in Conifer Swamps. In dense, lowland thickets of northern white-cedar and black spruce, hares find browse and shelter from predators. Look for tracks, droppings, and signs of browse. Follow the tracks to learn more about their natural history.

Voles and Mice Feed on Grasses and Cached Seeds. Snow cover does not stop hungry mice and voles. Voles make tunnels along the base of the snowpack to reach feeding areas.

Beaver Restricted to Lodge and Food Cache. By December most lakes have frozen over, restricting beaver families to their lodge and underwater exits.

Star-nosed Moles Still Active. This underground insectivore continues to find grubs, worms, and other arthropods in unfrozen soil. Snow cover insulates the ground and allows moles to tunnel closer to the surface.

stands of windshielding conifers, where they are hidden from the eyes of crows that would otherwise harass them. Ruffed grouse, when common, will group together at the base of conifers on cold days. Or, they may plunge headfirst into deep snow where they will roost and wait out bitter weather. Hares frequent needleleaf thickets where bobcat and lynx have a more difficult time catching them. Try cross-country skiing or snowshoeing into a needleleaf swamp this winter to catch some of these hardy species in action.

HOW TO GO BEYOND THIS BOOK

Volunteer and Educational Opportunities

The field of natural history owes a great debt of gratitude to amateur naturalists like you. Much of what we know about the more than 400 birds, mammals, reptiles, and amphibians in the northwoods comes from the meticulous notes of wildlife watchers from all walks of life. Margaret Nice, for instance, a homemaker from Iowa, conducted the definitive study of song sparrows from her kitchen window.

Today, researchers continue to be indebted to wildlife enthusiasts who volunteer their eyes and ears to enlarge the base of wildlife knowledge. Numerous organized censuses (studies that estimate numbers and locations of wildlife) are in the works, and they need your help. See the list that follows to find groups and agencies that are active in counting and monitoring efforts.

Besides census projects, there are other ways you can get involved in wildlife habitat management. You can teach a class, become politically active, or donate money to set aside acres of prime habitat. One of the best ways to make a lifelong contribution to the field is to first become better educated in the ways of wildlife yourself.

Educational opportunities run the gamut from home study (correspondence courses) to formal classroom or field study classes. You can learn by taking weekend jaunts with your local Audubon Society chapter, or by spending a summer as a member of a research team. Back home, you can apply what you learn about habitat management to your own land, whether it be a community garden plot or a back forty.

Further Reading

Next to hands-on experience, publications and periodicals are the mainstay of lifelong learning. Books such as this one owe their existence to the thousands of books, magazine articles, and research papers that came before. Some of the especially interesting sources used to compile this book are listed at the end of this section. If you want to build or add to your wildlife library, these selections may be a good starting point.

A curious raccoon.

Volunteer and Educational Opportunities

The following organizations offer a variety of volunteer and educational opportunities. We've included only the addresses of the headquarters. Once you reach the main office, explain the type of activity or service which interests you, and the operator will direct your call to the right person. If one organization can't help you, they can often refer you to a cooperating one.

Federal Agencies

USDA FOREST SERVICE
National Forests

Minnesota

Supervisor
Chippewa National Forest
Cass Lake, MN 56633   (218) 335-2226

Supervisor
Superior National Forest
Box 338
Duluth, MN 55801   (218) 720-5324

Wisconsin

Supervisor
Chequamegon National Forest
1170 4th Avenue S.
Park Falls, WI 54552   (715) 762-2461

Supervisor
Nicolet National Forest
Federal Bldg.
68 S. Stevens
Rhinelander, WI 54501   (715) 362-3415

Michigan

Supervisor
Hiawatha National Forest
2727 N. Lincoln Road
Escanaba, MI 49829   (906) 786-4062

Supervisor
Huron-Manistee National Forest
421 S. Mitchell Street
Cadillac, MI 49601   (616) 775-2421

Supervisor
Ottawa National Forest
East U.S. 2
Ironwood, MI 49938   (906) 932-1330

USDA SCIENCE AND EDUCATION
Extension Service

Leader
Wildlife and Fisheries Program
Extension Service
USDA
Washington, DC 20250   (202) 447-5468

Leader
Forest Resource Management Program
Extension Service
USDA
Washington, DC 20250   (202) 447-5119

USDI FISH & WILDLIFE SERVICE
National Wildlife Refuges

Minnesota

Manager
Agassiz National Wildlife Refuge
Middle River, MN 56737 (218) 449-4115

Manager
Minnesota Valley National Wildlife
  Refuge
4101 E. 80th Street
Bloomington, MN 55420 (612) 854-5900

Manager
Rice Lake National Wildlife Refuge
Route 2
McGregor, MN 55760   (218) 768-2402

Manager
Sherburne National Wildlife Refuge
Route 2
Zimmerman, MN 55398 (612) 389-3323

Manager
Tamarac National Wildlife Refuge
RR
Rochert, MN 56578   (218) 847-2641

Wisconsin

Manager
Necedah National Wildlife Refuge
Star Route West
Box 386
Necedah, WI 54646   (608) 565-2551

Michigan

Manager
Seney National Wildlife Refuge
Seney, MI 49883   (906) 586-9851

USDI NATIONAL PARK SERVICE
National Parks

Minnesota

Superintendent
Voyageurs National Park
P.O. Box 50
International Falls, MN 56649
(218) 283-9821

Wisconsin

Superintendent
Apostle Islands National Lakeshore
Route 1, Box 4
Bayfield, WI 54814   (715) 779-3397

Superintendent
St. Croix National Scenic Riverway
P.O. Box 708
St. Croix Falls, WI 54024
(715) 483-3284

Michigan

Superintendent
Isle Royale National Park
87 North Ripley Street
Houghton, MI 49931   (906) 482-3310

Superintendent
Pictured Rocks National Lakeshore
P.O. Box 40
Munising, MI 49862   (906) 387-2607

Superintendent
Sleeping Bear Dunes National
  Lakeshore
400½ Main Street
Frankfort, MI 49635   (616) 352-9611

Education & Advocacy Groups for
Federal Agencies

National Park Foundation
P.O. Box 57473
Washington, DC 20037   (202) 785-4500

National Parks and Conservation
  Association
1015 31st Street, NW
Washington, DC 20007   (202) 265-2717

National Wildlife Refuge Association
P.O. Box 124
Winona, MN 55987   (507) 454-5940

State Agencies

When contacting a State Department, please indicate which division or program you wish to contact (e.g., Wildlife, Environmental Education, Volunteer Program, Project Wild). We have listed the address and phone number of the headquarters of each department. The operator will direct your call.

DEPARTMENT OF NATURAL RESOURCES

Minnesota

Department of Natural Resources
500 Lafayette Road
St. Paul, MN 55155   (612) 296-6157

Wisconsin

Department of Natural Resources
Box 7921
Madison, WI 53707   (608) 266-2621

Michigan

Department of Natural Resources
Box 30028
Lansing, MI 48909   (517) 373-1220

DEPARTMENT OF EDUCATION

Minnesota
State Of Minnesota
  (Project Learning Tree)
Department of Education
644 Capitol Square Building
550 Cedar Street
St. Paul, MN 55101   (612) 296-4069

Wisconsin
Environmental Education
Wisconsin Department of Public
  Instruction
P.O. Box 7841
Madison, WI 53707   (608) 267-9266

Michigan
Science Specialist
Michigan Department of Education
P.O. Box 30008
Lansing, MI 48909   (517) 373-4223

Universities
Extension and Classroom Education

Minnesota
Director
Agricultural Extension Program
University of Minnesota
240 Coffey Hall
St. Paul, MN 55108   (612) 625-1915

Chairperson
Wildlife Department
232 Hodson Hall
University of Minnesota
St. Paul, MN 55108   (612) 624-3600

Wisconsin
Director
Cooperative Extension Programs
University of Wisconsin
432 N. Lake Street
Madison, WI 53706   (608) 263-2775

Chairperson
Wildlife Ecology Department
University of Wisconsin
226 Russell Laboratories
Madison, WI 53706   (608) 263-6882

Michigan

Director
Extension Service
Michigan State University
East Lansing, MI 48824 (517) 355-2308

Chairperson
Wildlife Education Department
8 Natural Resources Bldg.
Michigan State University
East Lansing, MI 48824 (517) 355-7493

Seminars in Ornithology:
  A Home Study Course in Bird
  Biology
Laboratory in Ornithology
Cornell University
159 Sapsucker Woods Road
Ithaca, NY 14850   (607) 254-2444

For more information about other ornithology courses, research programs welcoming amateurs, or where to find audio-visual and written information about conservation, try the *Conservation Directory*, available through the National Wildlife Federation and many libraries.

━━━━━ Citizen Organizations ━━━━━

━━━WILDLIFE OR HABITAT PRESERVATION GROUPS━━━

National Audubon Society
  (National Office)
950 Third Avenue
New York, NY 10022   (212) 832-3200

National Audubon Society
Great Lakes Region
7 N. Meridian
Suite 400
Indianapolis, IN 46204   (317) 631-2676

National Audubon Society
Minnesota Office
Suite 330, City Place
730 Hennepin Avenue
Minneapolis, MN 55403 (612) 375-9140

Sierra Club (National Office)
730 Polk St.
San Francisco, CA 94109(415) 776-2211

Sierra Club (MN, WI, MI)
Midwest Office
214 N. Henry Street
Suite 203
Madison, WI 53703   (608) 257-4994

The Izaak Walton League of America,
  Inc.
1701 N. Fort Myer Drive
Suite 1100
Arlington, VA 22209   (703) 528-1818

The Izaak Walton League of America,
  Inc.
Upper Mississippi Regional Office
6601 Auto Club Road
Minneapolis, MN 55438 (612) 941-6654

The Nature Conservancy
Suite 800
1800 N. Kent Street
Arlington, VA 22209   (703) 841-5300

The Nature Conservancy
Minnesota Field Office
328 E. Hennepin Avenue
Minneapolis, MN 55414 (612) 379-2134

The Nature Conservancy
Wisconsin Field Office
1045 E. Dayton Street
Room 209
Madison, WI 53703   (608) 251-8140

The Nature Conservancy
Michigan Field Office
531 N. Clipper Street
Lansing, MI 48912   (517) 332-1741

World Wildlife Fund—U.S.
1250 24th Street, NW
Washington, DC 20037 (202) 293-4800

─────────STATE ORNITHOLOGICAL UNIONS─────────

Minnesota

Minnesota Ornithologists' Union
James Ford Bell Museum of Natural
  History
10 Church Street SE
University of Minnesota
Minneapolis, MN 55455 (612) 546-4220

Minnesota Rare Bird Alert
(612) 544-5016

Wisconsin

The Wisconsin Society for Ornithology,
  Inc.
3352 Knollwood
West Bend, WI 53095   (414) 675-2443

Wisconsin Birder Hotline
(414) 352-3857

Michigan

Michigan Audubon Society
409 West E. Avenue
Kalamazoo, MI 49007   (616) 344-8648

Michigan Rare Bird Alert
(616) 471-2953 (daytime & evenings)
(616) 344-8648 (daytime)
(616) 345-7593 (evenings)

───────ENVIRONMENTAL EDUCATION ORGANIZATIONS───────

National Wildlife Federation
  (MI, MN, WI)
Region 7
735 E. Crystal Lake Road
Burnsville, MN 55337   (612) 774-6600

National Wildlife Federation
  (National Office)
1412 16th Street NW
Washington, DC 20036-2266
(202) 797-6800

The National Wildlife Federation publishes the *Conservation Directory*—a list of organizations, agencies, and people concerned with natural resource use and management. You can locate one at your local library or purchase one by writing to the national office listed directly above.

Environmental Education Seminars/
════════Nature Centers════════

────────────REGION-WIDE────────────

Many of the government agencies listed within this guide have visitor centers and/or naturalists who conduct seminars for the public. These include National Wildlife Refuges, National Parks, State Parks, County and City Parks, etc. Several citizen's organizations also offer such services. Refer to the sources below for an extensive list and description of centers and naturalists in your area.

National Association of Interpretation
6700 Needwood Road
Derwood, MD 20855   (301) 948-8844

The Naturalists' Directory and Almanac
(International) 43rd Edition (1979–
1980) compiled and Edited by:
Ross H. Arnett, Jr.
World Natural History Publications
1330 Dillon Heights Avenue
Baltimore, MD 21228

Minnesota

Naturalist
Environmental Learning Center
61 Mitawan Lake Road
Isabella, MN 55607   (218) 323-7733

Deep Portage Conservation Reserve
Route 1, Box 129
Hackensack, MN 56452 (218) 682-2355

Long Lake Conservation Center
Palisade, MN 56469   (218) 768-4653

Northwoods Audubon Center
Route 1
Sandstone, MN 55072   (612) 245-2648

For more information about
Minnesota's nature centers contact:
Minnesota Naturalists' Association
Westwood Hills Environmental
   Education Center
8300 West Franklin Avenue
St. Louis Park, MN 55426

Wisconsin

Central Wisconsin Environmental
   Station
7290 County MM
Amherst Junction, WI 54407
(715) 824-2428   (715) 346-2028

Sigurd Olson Environmental Institute
Northland College
Ashland, WI 54806
(715) 682-4531 ext. 223

Pigeon Lake Field Station
25 E. North Hall
UW–River Falls
River Falls, WI 54022   (715) 425-3256

Trees for Tomorrow Resources
   Education Center
611 Sheridan Street
Box 609
Eagle River, WI 54521   (715) 479-6456
                         (715) 479-6457

For more information about
Wisconsin's nature centers contact:
Department of Natural Resources
Education and Youth Programs
P.O. Box 7921
Madison, WI 53707   (608) 267-7529

Michigan

Isle Royale National Park Field
   Seminars
Isle Royale Natural History Association
87 N. Ripley
Houghton, MI 49931

Grand Traverse Natural Resources
   Education
1125 West Civic Center Drive
Traverse City, MI 49684

Sault Naturalists' Club
651 Dillon
Sault St. Marie, MI 49738

For more information about Michigan's
nature centers contact:
Chief
Information and Education Division
Department of Natural Resources
Box 30028
Lansing, MI 48909   (517) 373-3336

━━━━━━Volunteer Placement Services ━━━━━

Student Conservation Association, Inc.
Box 550
Charlestown, NH 03603 (603) 826-5206
(You don't have to be a student to be a
volunteer.)

In Michigan only:
Retired Senior Volunteers Program
   (RSVP)
507 1st Avenue N.
Escanaba, MI 49829

Recommended Reading

Watching Wildlife

Heintzelman, D. S. 1979. *A Manual for Bird Watching in the Americas.* New York: Universe Books. 255 p.

Kress, S. W. 1981. *The Audubon Society Handbook for Birders.* New York: Charles Scribner's Sons. 322 p.

McElroy, T. P. Jr. 1974. *The Habitat Guide to Birding.* New York: Alfred A. Knopf. 257 p.

Murie, O. 1975. *A Field Guide to Animal Tracks.* 2nd Edition. Boston: Houghton Mifflin. 367 p.

Pettingill, O. S. 1977. *A Guide to Bird Finding East of the Mississippi.* 2nd Edition. New York: Oxford University Press. 689 p.

Riley, W. 1979. *Guide to the National Wildlife Refuges.* Garden City, NY: Anchor Press. 653 p.

Roth, C. E. 1982. *The Wildlife Observer's Guidebook.* Englewood Cliffs, NJ: Prentice-Hall. 239 p.

Stokes, D. W. and L. Q. Stokes. 1986. *A Guide to Animal Tracking and Behavior.* Boston: Little, Brown and Company. 418 p.

About The Northwoods

Daniel, G. and J. Sullivan. 1981. *A Sierra Club Naturalist's Guide to the North Woods of Michigan, Wisconsin, Minnesota and Southern Ontario.* San Francisco: Sierra Club Books. 408 p.

Fladler, S. 1983. *The Great Lakes Forest.* Minneapolis: University of Minnesota Press. 336 p.

Leopold, A. 1966. *A Sand County Almanac.* New York: Oxford University Press. 269 p.

Regional Wildlife Guides

DeGraff, R. M. and D. D. Rudis. 1986. *New England Wildlife, Habitat, Natural History, and Distribution.* Gen. Tech. Rep. NE-108. Broomall, PA: U.S. Department of Agriculture, Forest Service, Northeastern Forest Experiment Station. 491 p.

MAMMALS

Baker, R. 1983. *Michigan Mammals.* Detroit: Michigan State University Press. 642 p.

Hazard, E. B. 1982. *Mammals of Minnesota.* Minneapolis: University of Minnesota Press. 280 p.

Jackson, H. H. T. 1961. *Mammals of Wisconsin.* Madison: University of Wisconsin Press. 504 p.

Savage, A. and C. Savage. 1981. *Wild Mammals of Northwest America.* Baltimore: Johns Hopkins University Press. 209 p.

BIRDS

Eckert, K. R. 1983. *A Birder's Guide to Minnesota.* Cloquet, MN: The Pine Knot, Cloquet Newspapers, Inc.

Godfrey, W. E. 1986. *The Birds of Canada.* Ottawa: National Museums of Canada. 595 p.

Green, J. C. and R. B. Janssen. 1975. *Minnesota Birds.* Minneapolis: University of Minnesota Press. 217 p.

Gromme, O. J. 1963. *Birds of Wisconsin.* Madison: University of Wisconsin Press. 219 p.

Roberts, T. S. 1936. *The Birds of Minnesota.* 2nd Revised Edition. 2 Volumes. Minneapolis: University of Minnesota Press. 459, 738 p.

Savage, C. 1985. *Wings of the North.* Minneapolis: University of Minnesota Press. 211 p.

Tessen, D. D. 1976. *Wisconsin's Favorite Bird Haunts.* Green Bay: The Wisconsin Society for Ornithology. 334 p.

AMPHIBIANS AND REPTILES

Breckenridge, W. J. 1944. *Reptiles and Amphibians of Minnesota.* Minneapolis: University of Minnesota Press. 202 p.

Vogt, R. C. 1981. *Natural History of Amphibians and Reptiles in Wisconsin.* Milwaukee: Milwaukee Public Museum. 205 p.

Regional Flora Guides

Barnes, B. V. 1981. *Michigan Trees: A Guide to the Trees of Michigan and the Great Lakes Region.* Ann Arbor: University of Michigan Press. 383 p.

Braun, E. L. 1950. *Deciduous Forests of Eastern North America.* Philadelphia: Blakiston. 556 p.

Curtis, J. T. 1971. *The Vegetation of Wisconsin.* Madison: University of Wisconsin Press. 657 p.

Lakela, O. 1965. *A Flora of Northeastern Minnesota.* Minneapolis: University of Minnesota Press. 541 p.

Rosendahl, C. O. 1955. *Trees and Shrubs of the Upper Midwest.* 2nd Edition. Minneapolis: University of Minnesota Press. 314 p.

Stokes, D. W. 1981. *The Natural History of Wild Shrubs and Vines of Eastern and Central North America.* New York: Harper and Row. 246 p.

Voss, E. G. 1972. *Michigan Flora.* 2 Volumes. Bloomfield Hills, MI: Cranbrook Institute of Science.

For The Amateur Naturalist

Brown, V. 1972. *Reading the Outdoors at Night.* Harrisburg, PA: Stackpole Books. 191 p.

Brown, V. 1969. *Reading the Woods.* Harrisburg, PA: Stackpole Books. 160 p.

Dillard, A. 1974. *Pilgrim at Tinker Creek.* New York: Bantam Books. 279 p.

Durrell, G. M. with L. Durrell. 1983. *The Amateur Naturalist.* New York: Alfred A. Knopf. 320 p.

Ehrlich, P. R. and A. Ehrlich. 1981. *Extinction.* New York: Random House. 305 p.

Martin, A. C., S. Zim and L. Nelson. 1961. *American Wildlife and Plants: A Guide to Wildlife Food Habits.* Reprint of 1951 Edition. New York: Dover Publications. 500 p.

Platt, R. 1965. *The Great American Forest.* Englewood Cliffs, NJ: Prentice-Hall. 271 p.

Stokes, D. W. 1983. *A Guide to Bird Behavior.* 2 Volumes. Boston: Little, Brown and Company. 336 p. each.

Stokes, D. W. 1976. *A Guide to Nature in Winter, Northeast and Northcentral North America.* Boston: Little, Brown and Company. 374 p.

Sutton, A. and M. Sutton. 1985. *Eastern Forests. (The Audubon Society Nature Guide Series.)* New York: Alfred A. Knopf. 638 p.

Tributsch, H. 1982. *How Life Learned to Live: Adaptation in Nature.* Cambridge, MA: MIT Press. 218 p.

Walker, L. C. 1984. *Trees: An Introduction to Trees and Forest Ecology for the Amateur Naturalist.* Englewood Cliffs, NJ: Prentice-Hall. 306 p.

Welty, J. C. 1975. *The Life of Birds.* 2nd Edition. Philadelphia: Saunders. 623 p.

Whitney, S. 1985. *Eastern Forests. (The Audubon Society Nature Guide Series.)* New York: Alfred A. Knopf. 671 p.

On The Reference Shelf

Bent, A. C. *et al.* 1919–1968. *Life Histories of North American Birds.* 23 Volumes. New York: Peter Smith and Dover.

Ernst, C. H. and R. W. Barbour. 1972. *Turtles of the United States.* Lexington: University of Kentucky Press. 347 p.

Grzimek, B. 1972. *Animal Life Encyclopedia.* 13 Volumes. New York: Van Nostrand Reinhold.

Hall, E. R. 1981. *The Mammals of North America.* 2nd Edition. 2 Volumes. New York: Wiley and Sons. 1181 p.

MacDonald, D. 1984. *The Encyclopedia of Mammals.* New York: Facts on File Publications. 895 p.

Nowak, R. M. and J. L. Paradise. 1983. *Walkers' Mammals of the World.* 4th Edition. 2 Volumes. Baltimore, MD: The Johns Hopkins University Press. 1362 p.

Oliver, J. A. 1955. *The Natural History of North American Amphibians and Reptiles.* Princeton, NJ: D. Van Nostrand. 359 p.

Palmer, R. S. 1962. *Handbook of North American Birds.* 3 Volumes. New Haven, CT: Yale University Press. 567, 521, 560 p.

Terres, J. K. 1980. *The Audubon Society Encyclopedia of North American Birds.* New York: Alfred A. Knopf. 1109 p.

Walker, E. P. 1983. *Mammals of the World.* 4th Edition. 2 Volumes. Baltimore: The Johns Hopkins University Press. 1500 p.

Periodicals

American Birds
Audubon
Defenders of Wildlife
National Wildlife
Natural History
Sierra
The Jack Pine Warbler
The Loon
The Passenger Pigeon
Wilderness

COMMON AND SCIENTIFIC NAMES

Plants classified according to:

Gleason, H.A. 1963. *The New Britton and Brown Illustrated Flora of the Northeastern United States and Adjacent Canada.* 3 Volumes. New York and London: Hafner Publishing Co., Inc.

Plant Names

TREES

American basswood	*Tilia americana*
American beech	*Fagus grandifolia*
American elm	*Ulmus americana*
American mountain-ash	*Sorbus americana*
balsam fir	*Abies balsamea*
balsam poplar	*Populus balsamifera*
bigtooth aspen	*Populus grandidentata*
black ash	*Fraxinus nigra*
black spruce	*Picea mariana*
eastern hemlock	*Tsuga canadensis*
eastern hophornbeam	*Ostrya virginiana*
eastern white pine	*Pinus strobus*
hawthorns	*Crataegus;* several species
northern white-cedar	*Thuja occidentalis*
paper birch	*Betula papyrifera*
pin cherry	*Prunus pensylvanica*
quaking aspen	*Populus tremuloides*
red maple	*Acer rubrum*
red pine	*Pinus resinosa*
striped maple; moosewood	*Acer pensylvanicum*
sugar maple	*Acer saccharum*
tamarack	*Larix laricina*
white spruce	*Picea glauca*
yellow birch	*Betula alleghaniensis*

TALL SHRUBS

alternate-leaf dogwood	*Cornus alternifolia*
American fly-honeysuckle	*Lonicera canadensis*
American green alder	*Alnus crispa*
beaked hazel	*Corylus cornuta*
Bebb willow	*Salix bebbiana*

bog birch	*Betula glandulosa*
bush-honeysuckle	*Diervilla lonicera*
chokecherry	*Prunus virginiana*
mountain maple	*Acer spicatum*
pussy willow	*Salix discolor*
red-berried elder; elderberry	*Sambucus pubens*
red-osier dogwood	*Cornus stolonifera*
sandbar willow	*Salix exigua*
serviceberry	*Amelanchier*; several species
smooth sumac	*Rhus glabra*
speckled alder	*Alnus rugosa*
swamp willow	*Salix pedicellaris*

LOW SHRUBS

bog laurel	*Kalmia polifolia*
bog rosemary	*Andromeda glaucophylla*
Canada yew	*Taxus canadensis*
creeping snowberry	*Gaultheria hispidula*
dwarf raspberry	*Rubus flagellaris*
highbush cranberry	*Viburnum trilobum*
labrador tea	*Ledum groenlandicum*
large cranberry	*Vaccinium macrocarpon*
leatherleaf	*Chamaedaphne calyculata*
low sweet blueberry	*Vaccinium angustifolium*
red currant	*Ribes triste*
red raspberry	*Rubus idaeus*
shrubby cinquefoil	*Potentilla fruticosa*
small cranberry	*Vaccinium oxycoccus*
smooth gooseberry	*Ribes hirtellum*
swamp birch	*Betula pumila*
sweet-fern	*Myrica aspleniifolia*
sweet gale	*Myrica gale*
velvetleaf blueberry	*Vaccinium myrtilloides*

HERBACEOUS PLANTS
(includes grasses and forbs)

alfalfa	*Medicago sativa*
arrow-leaved tearthumb	*Polygonum sagittatum*
arrowheads	*Sagittaria*; several species
asters	*Aster*; several species
bachelor's button; cornflower	*Centaurea cyanus*
beak rushes	*Rhynchospora*; several species
bellworts	*Uvularia*; several species
black-eyed susan	*Rudbeckia hirta*
bladderworts	*Utricularia*; several species
bloodroot	*Sanguinaria canadensis*
blue flag	*Iris versicolor*

bluegrasses	*Poa*; several species
bluejoint reedgrass	*Calamagrostis canadensis*
bracken fern	*Pteridium aquilinum*
buckbean	*Menyanthes trifoliata*
bulrushes	*Scirpus;* several species
bunchberry	*Cornus canadensis*
bur-reeds	*Sparganium;* several species
butterflyweed	*Asclepias tuberosa*
calopogon	*Calopogon pulchellus*
Canada mayflower	*Maianthemum canadense*
cattails	*Typha;* several species
cinnamon fern	*Osmunda cinnamomea*
clovers	*Trifolium;* several species
columbine	*Aquilegia canadensis*
common dandelion	*Taraxacum officinale*
common evening-primrose	*Oenothera biennis*
common mullein	*Verbascum thapsus*
corn-lily; clintonia	*Clintonia borealis*
cottongrasses	*Eriophorum;* several species
downy Solomon's seal	*Polygonatum pubescens*
duckweeds	*Lemna* and *Wolffia;* several species
false Solomon's seal	*Smilacina racemosa*
fireweed	*Epilobium angustifolium*
goldenrods	*Solidago;* several species
goldthread	*Coptis trifolia*
hedge bindweed	*Convolvulus sepium*
hepatica	*Hepatica americana*
hop clover	*Trifolium agrarium*
hornwort	*Ceratophyllum demersum*
horsetails	*Equisetum;* several species
jewelweed; spotted touch-me-not	*Impatiens capensis*
large-flowered trillium	*Trillium grandiflorum*
largeleaf aster	*Aster macrophyllus*
marsh fern	*Thelypteris palustris*
marsh marigold	*Caltha palustris*
meadowsweet	*Spiraea;* several species
milkweed	*Asclepias syriaca*
naked miterwort	*Mitella nuda*
multiflora rose	*Rosa multiflora*
narrowleaf meadowsweet	*Spiraea alba*
one-sided pyrola	*Pyrola secunda*
orange hawkweed	*Hieracium aurantiacum*
oxeye daisy	*Chrysanthemum leucanthemum*
panic grasses	*Panicum;* several species
panicled aster	*Aster simplex*
pearly everlasting	*Anaphalis margaritacea*
pickerelweed	*Pontederia cordata*
pipewort	*Eriocaulon septangulare*

pitcher plant	*Sarracenia purpurea*
pondweeds	*Potamogeton;* several species
poverty grass	*Danthonia spicata*
quack grass	*Agropyron repens*
quillworts	*Isoetes;* several species
red baneberry	*Actaea rubra*
rice grass	*Oryzopsis asperifolia*
rose pogonia	*Pogonia ophioglossoide*
rose twisted-stalk	*Streptopus roseus*
rough bedstraw	*Galium asprellum*
round-leaved sundew	*Drosera rotundifolia*
royal fern	*Osmunda regalis*
rushes	*Juncus;* several species
salvia; scarlet sage	*Salvia coccinea*
sedges	*Carex;* several species
sensitive fern	*Onoclea sensibilis*
shinleaf	*Pyrola elliptica*
showy lady's-slipper	*Cypripedium reginae*
silverweed	*Potentilla anserina*
skunk cabbage	*Symplocarpus foetidus*
spike rushes	*Eleocharis;* several species
spotted joe-pye-weed	*Eupatorium maculatum*
spotted wintergreen; spotted pipissewa	*Chimaphila maculata*
starflower	*Trientalis borealis*
swamp loosestrife; water-willow	*Decodon verticillatus*
sweet-scented bedstraw	*Galium triflorum*
tape grass	*Vallisneria americana*
three-way sedge	*Dulichium arundinaceum*
trailing arbutus	*Epigaea repens*
true watercress	*Nasturtium officinale*
turtlehead	*Chelone glabra*
twinflower	*Linnaea borealis*
water horehound	*Lycopus americanus*
water milfoils	*Myriophyllum;* several species
water smartweed	*Polygonum amphibium*
water shield	*Brassenia schreberi*
white baneberry	*Actaea alba*
white water lilies	*Nymphaea;* several species
wild celery	*Valisneria americana*
wild rice	*Zizania aquatica*
wild sarsaparilla	*Aralia nudicaulis*
wild strawberry	*Fragaria virginiana*
wintergreen; teaberry	*Gaultheria procumbens*
yarrow	*Achillea millefolium*
yellow lady's-slipper	*Cypripedium calceolus*
yellow pond lily	*Nuphar variegatum*

OTHER

club mosses	*Lycopodium;* several species
dwarf mistletoe (epiphyte)	*Arceuthobium pusillum*
feather mosses	*Pleurozium;* several species
filamentous algae	*Cladophora;* several species, and other algae
hairy-cap mosses	*Dicranium;* several species
old man's beard lichens	*Usnea;* several species
reindeer lichens	*Cladonia;* several species
sphagnum mosses	*Sphagnum;* several species
stoneworts (algae)	*Chara;* several species
trumpet creeper	*Campsis radicans*
Virginia creeper	*Parthenocissus quinquefolia*
virgin's bower (vine)	*Clematis virginiana*
wild grapes	*Vitis;* several species

DEFINITIONS

TREE—woody erect perennial, frequently more than 16 feet tall

TALL SHRUB—upright woody perennial, up to 16 feet tall

LOW SHRUB—creeping woody perennial, rarely more than 3 feet tall

HERB—non-woody annual, biennial, or perennial

OTHER—includes algae, lichens, mosses, and atypical vascular plants such as trailing or climbing vines and epiphytes

Animal Names

BIRDS

Alder Flycatcher	*Empidonax alnorum*
American Bittern	*Botaurus lentiginosus*
American Goldfinch	*Carduelis tristis*
American Kestrel	*Falco sparverius*
American Redstart	*Setophaga ruticilla*
American Woodcock	*Scolopax minor*
Bald Eagle	*Haliaeetus leucocephalus*
Bank Swallow	*Riparia riparia*
Barred Owl	*Strix varia*
Belted Kingfisher	*Ceryle alcyon*
Black-backed Woodpecker	*Picoides arcticus*
Black-throated Green Warbler	*Dendroica virens*
Boreal Chickadee	*Parus hudsonicus*
Broad-winged Hawk	*Buteo platypterus*
Brown Creeper	*Certhia americana*
Brown Thrasher	*Toxostoma rufum*
Chestnut-sided Warbler	*Dendroica pensylvanica*
Common Loon	*Gavia immer*
Common Snipe	*Gallinago gallinago*
Common Yellowthroat	*Geothlypis trichas*

Connecticut Warbler	*Oporornis agilis*
Eastern Bluebird	*Sialia sialis*
Eastern Phoebe	*Sayornis phoebe*
Evening Grosbeak	*Coccothraustes vespertinus*
Golden-crowned Kinglet	*Regulus satrapa*
Gray Catbird	*Dumetella carolinensis*
Gray Jay	*Perisoreus canadensis*
Great Blue Heron	*Ardea herodias*
Great Gray Owl	*Strix nebulosa*
Great Horned Owl	*Bubo virginianus*
Indigo Bunting	*Passerina cyanea*
Kirtland's Warbler	*Dendroica kirtlandii*
Le Conte's Sparrow	*Ammodramus leconteii*
Least Flycatcher	*Empidonax minimus*
Magnolia Warbler	*Dendroica magnolia*
Mallard	*Anas platyrhynchos*
Nashville Warbler	*Vermivora ruficapilla*
Northern Flicker	*Colaptes auratus*
Northern Goshawk	*Accipiter gentilis*
Northern Harrier	*Circus cyaneus*
Northern Parula	*Parula americana*
Olive-sided Flycatcher	*Contopus borealis*
Osprey	*Pandion haliaetus*
Ovenbird	*Seiurus aurocapillus*
Palm Warbler	*Dendroica palmarum*
Pied-billed Grebe	*Podilymbus podiceps*
Pileated Woodpecker	*Dryocopus pileatus*
Red-breasted Nuthatch	*Sitta canadensis*
Red-eyed Vireo	*Vireo olivaceus*
Red-shouldered Hawk	*Buteo lineatus*
Red-tailed Hawk	*Buteo jamaicensis*
Red-winged Blackbird	*Agelaius phoeniceus*
Rose-breasted Grosbeak	*Pheucticus ludovicianus*
Ruby-throated Hummingbird	*Archilochus colubris*
Ruffed Grouse	*Bonasa umbellus*
Rufous-sided Towhee	*Pipilo erythrophthalmus*
Sandhill Crane	*Grus canadensis*
Scarlet Tanager	*Piranga olivacea*
Sedge Wren	*Cistothorus platensis*
Short-eared Owl	*Asio flammeus*
Solitary Vireo	*Vireo solitarius*
Song Sparrow	*Melospiza melodia*
Spruce Grouse	*Dendragapus canadensis*
Tennessee Warbler	*Vermivora peregrina*
Veery	*Catharus fuscescens*
White-throated Sparrow	*Zonotrichia albicollis*
Wood Duck	*Aix sponsa*
Yellow Warbler	*Dendroica petechia*

AMPHIBIANS & REPTILES
Central Newt	*Notophthalmus viridescens*
Eastern Garter Snake	*Thamnophis sirtalis*
Four-toed Salamander	*Hemidactylium scutatum*
Mudpuppy	*Necturus maculosus*
Northern Leopard Frog	*Rana pipiens*
Northern Spring Peeper	*Hyla crucifer*
Northern Water Snake	*Nerodia sipedon*
Redback Salamander	*Plethodon cinereus*
Redbelly Snake	*Storeria occipitomaculata*
Ringneck Snake	*Diadophis punctatus*
Smooth Green Snake	*Opheodrys vernalis*
Snapping Turtle	*Chelydra serpentina*
Wood Frog	*Rana sylvatica*
Wood Turtle	*Clemmys insculpta*

MAMMALS
Arctic Shrew	*Sorex arcticus*
Badger	*Taxidea taxus*
Beaver	*Castor canadensis*
Black Bear	*Ursus americanus*
Bobcat	*Felis rufus*
Ermine	*Mustela erminea*
Fisher	*Martes pennanti*
Gray Fox	*Urocyon cinereoargenteus*
Gray Wolf	*Canis lupus*
Lynx	*Felis lynx*
Masked Shrew	*Sorex cinereus*
Meadow Vole	*Microtus pennsylvanicus*
Mink	*Mustela vison*
Moose	*Alces alces*
Muskrat	*Ondatra zibethicus*
Northern Flying Squirrel	*Glaucomys sabrinus*
Porcupine	*Erethizon dorsatum*
Raccoon	*Procyon lotor*
Red Bat	*Lasiurus borealis*
Red Fox	*Vulpes vulpes*
Red Squirrel	*Tamiasciurus hudsonicus*
River Otter	*Lutra canadensis*
Silver-Haired Bat	*Lasionycteris noctivagans*
Snowshoe Hare	*Lepus americanus*
Southern Bog Lemming	*Synaptomys cooperi*
Star-nosed Mole	*Condylura cristata*
13-lined Ground Squirrel	*Spermophilus tridecemlineatus*
Water Shrew	*Sorex palustris*
White-tailed Deer	*Odocoileus virginianus*
Woodchuck	*Marmota monax*
Woodland Jumping Mouse	*Napaeozapus insignis*

Index

Page numbers in italics refer to illustrations.

A

Acid precipitation, 60, 91–92
Acorn, 402
Agassiz National Wildlife Refuge (Minnesota), 347–48
Alder, 15, *110–12*, 147, 285, 382
American green, 7
speckled, *54–56, 72–74, 88–90, 110–12, 142–44,* 144–46, 211, *290–92*, 294
Algae, 58, 92–93, 113, 131
American Legion State Forest (Wisconsin), 362
Amphibians. *See also* specific species
seasonal activities, 35–38
Ant
carpenter, 246, 378, 405
Anthill, *170–72*, 172, 177, 198, 272–73, 403
Antler, *34,* 154
chewed, 384
rattling, 43, 215
shed, 34, 217–18
Api, 12–13
Apostle Islands National Lakeshore (Wisconsin), 355–56
April, 380–85
Arborvitae. *See* White-cedar, northern
Arbutus, trailing, *158–60, 250–52*
Area-sensitive species, 24
Arethusa, *302–4*
Arrowhead, *72–74,* 74, 77, *88–90, 110–12*
Ash, 268, 386
black, 145, *290–92,* 292–93, *321–22,* 323, 326
Asparagus, wild, 386
Aspen, 9–11, 15, *54–56, 72–74, 110–12, 184–86,* 380, 382, 386, 406
aspen-birch forest, 234–38, *239–40*
bigtooth, 7, 204, 222, 236, 277
mature upland mixed forest, 278, 285
mature upland needleleaf forest, 261
quaking, 5, 7, 155, 174, *200–2,* 204, *220–22,* 222, 236, *239–40,* 277

shrub-sapling opening, 202, 205
young upland broadleaf forest, 222–25
Aster, 144, *170–72, 184–86,* 187–88
largeleaf, *170–72, 200–2,* 203, *220–22, 239–40,* 397
panicled, *126–28*
red-stemmed, 130
August, 397–400
Auxin, 237

B

Bachelor's-button, 208
Backwaters, 94
Badger
characteristics and habitats, *184–86,* 188, 193–94, *193,* 196
hotspots, 359, 361
seasonal activities, 379
Baneberry
red, *258–60*
white, *232–34,* 395
Barberry, 211–12
Bark chips, 330
Barker's Island (Wisconsin), 363
Bark rub, 218
Basswood, American, 5, 223, 236–37, 277, 395
Bat, 78, 90
big brown, seasonal activities, 378
Keen's, seasonal activities, 378
little brown, seasonal activities, 378
red, characteristics and habitats, *170–72,* 174, 180–82, *181*
silver-haired, characteristics and habitats, *89–90,* 94, 101–2, *101*
Bat box, 102
Bay, 59
Beach, 59
Bear, black
characteristics and habitats, 94, 147, 166, *169,* 205–6, 254, 264, *290–92,* 294, 323–24, 330, 342–44, *343*
hotspots, 353, 355–56, 358, 361–62, 364, 368–69
observation of, 48
safety concerns, 48
seasonal activities, 35–36, 375, 384, 393, 396, 399, 407

Beaver
characteristics and habitats, *72–74,* 75, 77–78, 81–84, *83,* 90, 94, 224, 389
hotspots, 348, 350, 354–56, 362, 366, 370
seasonal activities, 35, 37, 402, 407, 411
Bedding site
red fox, 180
white-tailed deer, 217
Bedstraw
rough, 145
sweet-scented, *220–22, 239–40*
Beech
American, 5, 8, 223, 236, *274–76,* 277
maple-beech-birch forest, *232–34,* 237, 240
Beetle
bark, 205
diving, 139
elm bark, 293
whirlygig, 58
Behavior watching, 45–46
Bellwort, 390
large-flowered, *274–76*
Belly slide, river otter, 104
Beltrami/Marshall Counties (Minnesota), 348
Beltrami Island State Forest (Minnesota), 348
Berry, 202, 279
dried, *36*
mountain-ash, 406
rejected skins and pulp, 268
Bindweed
field, *184–86*
hedge, *200–2*
Binoculars, 39. *39*
Birch, *54–56, 110–12,* 223, 261, 276, 380, 386
aspen-birch forest, 234–38, *239–40*
bog, *302–4,* 306
paper, 7, 9, 11, 155, *200–2,* 202, *220–22,* 222, 224, *239–40, 258–60, 265–66,* 277
swamp, *126–28,* 130
yellow, 5, *274–76,* 277–78, *290–92,* 293
maple-beech-birch forest, *232–34,* 237, 240
Bird call, imitating, 43, *43,* 47–48
Bird feeder, 268, 405
Birds. *See also* specific species

behavior when disturbed, 47

he'per, 191

migration. *See* Migration

mixed species flocks, 398–99

seasonal activities, 35–37

in spring, 35

Bird song, identifying, 386–88

Bird watching, 386–88

Bittern, 78, 116

American, characteristics and habitats, *110–12*, 112, 117–19, *118*, 128

Blackberry, *157*, 206

Blackbird, 116

red-winged

characteristics and habitats, 22, *72–74*, *110–12*, 112, 119–20, *120*, *125*

seasonal activities, 380, 392

yellow-headed

characteristics and habitats, 22, *110–12*, 115

hotspots, 359

Black-eyed susan, *184–86*

Black light, 39

Bladderwort, 131

yellow, 390

Blinds, 42

Blister rust, 9, 262

Bloodroot, 382

Blueberry, 206, 260, 264, *265–66*, 395

low sweet, *250–52*, *302–4*

velvetleaf, 307

Bluebird, eastern

characteristics and habitats, *184–86*, 190–91, *190*

hotspots, 364

Blue flag, *72–74*

Bluegrass, 173, 175, *184–86*

Boat, 48

Bobcat

characteristics and habitats, 238, 307, 331, 339–40, *339*

hotspots, 348, 355–56, 358, 361, 369

observation of, 43

Bobolink, seasonal activities, 401

Body size, 19

Body waste, 45

Bog, *158–60*

black spruce, 319

definition, 160

formation, 7, 160–62

muskeg. *See* Needleleaf forest, semi-open lowland

perched, 162

temperature, 162

value to wildlife, 165–66

wildlife, 166–69

wildlife action, 166

Bog light, 165

Bones, 45

Borer, flat-headed, 311

Boundary Waters Canoe Area (Minnesota), 353–54

Boxelder, 268

Brambles, 205–6

Bridges, eastern phoebe nests on, 98–99

Bright object, waving, 43

Broadleaf forest

adaptations to winter, 14–15

mature lowland, *290–92*

definition, 292

formation, 292–93

value to wildlife, 293–94

wildlife, 294–300

wildlife action, 294

mature upland, *232–33*, *239–40*

definition, 234

formation, 235–37

value to wildlife, 238

wildlife, 240–49

wildlife action, 238–40

young upland, *220–22*

definition, 222

formation, 223–24

value to wildlife, 224

wildlife, 224–31

wildlife action, 224

Brockway Mountain/ Keweenaw Point (Michigan), 363

Browse line, 333, 379–80

Brule River State Forest (Wisconsin), 356–58

Bud, broadleaf tree, 235

Budworm, spruce, 266, 268

Bufflehead

characteristics and habitats, 60

seasonal activities, 378, 405

Bullfrog, hotspots, 362

Bulrush, *54–56*, 59, 74, 112–13, 128

Bunchberry, 7, *220–22*, *239–40*, 320, 390

Bunting

indigo

characteristics and habitats, 174, *200–2*, 212–13, *212*

seasonal activities, 401

snow, seasonal activities, 405

Burl, 293

Burning. *See* Fire

Bur-reed, *54–56*, *110–12*

Burrow

badger, 193–94

ermine, 214

13-lined ground squirrel, 196–97

mink, 122

muskrat, 124–25

red squirrel, 270

woodchuck, 182

woodland jumping mouse, 299

Bush-honeysuckle, *200–1*, 203, *250–52*, *265–66*

Butterfly, monarch, 397

Butterflyweed, *184–86*

C

Caddisfly, 92

Cairn, lynx, 334

Calling device, 43

Calopogon, *158–60*

Camera. *See* Photography

Camouflage of observer, 41

Camp robber. *See* Jay, gray

Canada bird. *See* Sparrow, white-throated

Canopy, 21, 23, 236

Carcass, 55

Castoffs, 45

Catbird, gray, characteristics and habitats, *200–2*, 209–10, *209*

Cattail, *54–56*, *72–74*, *88–90*, *110–12*, 112–15, *371*, 404, 407

cut, 124

Celery, wild, 76

Census projects, 413

Chequamegon National Forest (Wisconsin), 358

Cherry

fire. *See* Cherry, pin

pin, *200–2*, 202, 206, 222, 224, 390, 395–96, 398

Chickadee, 12, 147, 280, 304, 307, 324, 330, 374–75, 396, 398–99, 401

black-capped, characteristics and habitats, 339

boreal

characteristics and habitats, *302–4*, 309–10, *310*

seasonal activities, 408

Chipmunk

characteristics and habitats, 205, 240

eastern, *170–72*, *232–34*

seasonal activities, 380, 384, 396, 398–99

Chippewa National Forest (Minnesota), 65, 350
Chokecherry, *170–72*, 174, *184–86*, *200–2*, 206
common, *220–22*
Circadian rhythms, 81
Citizen organizations, 419–20
Clam, 59
Classroom education, 418–19
Clearcutting, 29
Clearing. *See* Woodland opening/edge
Climbing adaptations
brown creeper, 266
fisher, 283
gray fox, 246–47
northern flying squirrel, 285
northern spring peeper, 86
red squirrel, 269
Clintonia, *200–2*, *258–60*
Clover, hop, 173, 175
Cobble, 59
Coloration, 19
Columbine, *170–72*, 390
Cone. *See* Pine cone
Conifer. *See* Needleleaf forest
Coot, American,
characteristics and habitats, 74, *110–12*, 112, 116
Copepod, 58
Cormorant, 59, 382
double-crested, hotspots, 355–56, 360
Corn-lily. *See* Clintonia
Cottongrass, *158–60*
Cottonwood, eastern, 392
Courting grounds, spruce grouse, 328
Courtship behavior. *See* Display, courtship
Cove, 59
Cover for wildlife, 410–11
Cowbird, brown-headed
characteristics and habitats, 151, 174, 255–56, 281
seasonal activities, 388, 392
Coyote
characteristics and habitats, 194
hotspots, 353, 364
observation of, 43
Cranberry, 304
highbush, 397, 403
small, *302–4*, 307
Crane, sandhill
characteristics and habitats, *126–28*, 132–33, *132*, 165
hotspots, 352, 358, 361–62, 369
seasonal activities, 406
Creeper (bird), brown

characteristics and habitats, *258–60*, 265–67, 266–67, *316–18*, 330, 399
seasonal activities, 383
Creeper (plant)
trumpet, 176
Virginia, 397
Crex Meadows Wildlife Area (Wisconsin), 358–59
Crossbill, 12, 280, 410
red
characteristics and habitat, 19, 264
observation of, 35
seasonal activities, 374–75, 408
white-winged
characteristics and habitats, 19, 264
seasonal activities, 408
Crow, American
characteristics and habitats, 335–36, 339
seasonal activities, 380
Cryoprotectant, 299
Cud, 216
Currant, red, *321–22*
Current, water, 91–92

D

Daisy, oxeye, 173
Dam, beaver, 45, 81–84
Dandelion, 208
Dawn, at lake, 60
Daytime, animals active during, 38
DDT, 65, 190
December, 410–11
Deer, white-tailed
characteristics and habitats, 13, *49*, 56, 60, 77, 94, 147, 155, 174–75, 188, *200–2*, 202, 205–6, 215–18, *218*, *220–22*, 224, 255, 264, 294, 307, *321–22*, 323, 337–38, 405
hotspots, 353
observation of, 33, 43
seasonal activities, 35–37, 375–80, 393, 399, 402, 407, 410–11
Defense adaptations
American bittern, 117–18
northern water snake, 106
porcupine, 271
ruffed grouse, 226
Den. *See also* Nest
badger, 193–94
black bear, 343–44
bobcat, 340
ermine, 214
fisher, 284
gray fox, 247

gray wolf, 338
identification, 44–45
13-lined ground squirrel, 197
lynx, 334
mink, 121–22
porcupine, 271
raccoon, 100, 399
red fox, 179–80
river otter, 104
Diatom, 58
Digging adaptations
badger, 193
belted kingfisher, 95
pileated woodpecker, 245
woodchuck, 182
Disease
of American elm, 293
of eastern white pine, 9, 262
Display
camouflage, American bittern, 117–18
courtship
American goldfinch, 207
American redstart, 229
American woodcock, 148–49
bald eagle, 65
birds, 35, 387–88
cedar waxwing, 392
common snipe, 137
common yellowthroat, 150–51
eastern phoebe, 99
evening grosbeak, 269
gray catbird, 209
great gray owl, 325
least flycatcher, 228
magnolia warbler, 257
moose, 156, 407
mudpuppy, 69
northern flicker, 177
northern goshawk, 280–81
northern harrier, 136
osprey, 66
porcupine, 272
raven, 377
red fox, 179
red-shouldered hawk, 297
red-tailed hawk, 189
ruby-throated hummingbird, 176, 391
rufous-sided towhee, 209
sandhill crane, 132–33
scarlet tanager, 244
sharp-tailed grouse, 382
short-eared owl, 138
snowshoe hare, 332
solitary vireo, 281
song sparrow, 210–11
spruce grouse, 327–28, 382

white-tailed deer, 407
wood turtle, 107
distraction, 392
   common nighthawk, 391
   common snipe, 137
   Nashville warbler, 314
   olive-sided flycatcher, 312
   ovenbird, 240
   redbelly snake, 272
   ruffed grouse, 392
   rufous-sided towhee, 208
   short-eared owl, 139
   drumming
      pileated woodpecker, 246
      ruffed grouse, 226–28,
         383
      spruce grouse, 327
Distraction display. See
   Display, distraction
Disturbance range, 46–47
Diving adaptations, 19
   beaver, 82
   common loon, 62–63
   pied-billed grebe, 116
   river otter, 103
Dogwood, 205
   red-osier, 145, *142–44*, 155,
      203, *290–92*, 294, 379
   shrubby, 379
Dowitcher, hotspots, 359,
   370
Down, bits around nest, 297
Drag mark, northern flying
   squirrel, 286
Dragon-fly, 139–40
Drilling dust, 44
Droppings, 45
   arctic shrew, 168
   bobcat, 340
   identification, 405–6
   lynx, 334
   mink, 122
   porcupine, 271
   southern bog lemming,
      169
   star-nosed mole, 154
   white-tailed deer, 405
Drumming. See Display,
   drumming
Drumming log, ruffed
   grouse, 227
Duck, 347, 358, 361, 398,
   401
   black
      characteristics and
         habitats, 78
      seasonal activities, 382
   diving, characteristics and
      habitats, 78
   ring-necked
      hotspots, 352
      seasonal activities, 405
   sea, hotspots, 350–51, 363,
      368

wood
   characteristics and
      habitats, *72–74*, 77–80,
      79, *87*, 116, 238, 294
   seasonal activities, 388,
      390–92
Duck box, 286
Duck potato. See Arrowhead
Duckweed, 74, 76–77
Duluth port terminal
   (Minnesota), 350
Dunlin, hotspots, 352, 363
Dusk. See Twilight
Dust bath, 45
Dusting site, ruffed grouse,
   227
Dutch elm disease, 293

E

Eagle, 60, 282
   bald
      characteristics and
         habitats, *5*, *54–56*, 64–
         65, *64*, 339
      hotspots, 350, 353–55,
         358, 360–62, 368
Earthworm, 148
Echolocation, 101
Ecotone, 173–74
Edge, 23–24. See also
   Woodland opening/edge
Education, Department of,
   418
Educational opportunities,
   413
Eft, central newt, 85–86
Eggs
   central newt, 85
   four-toed salamander, 249
   frog, 93
   great gray owl, 325
   great horned owl, 336
   green frog, 393, 396
   northern leopard frog, 140,
      389
   northern spring peeper, 87
   painted turtle, 394
   redback salamander, 287,
      394
   ringneck snake, 288, 394
   snapping turtle, 394, 403
   turtle, 101
   wood frog, 299–300
Egret, 59, 78
   great
      characteristics and
         habitats, 62
      hotspots, 360
Elder, red-berried, *232–34*,
   386
Elk, hotspots, 348, 367–68
Elm, American, 208, 292–93,
   390, 392

Endangered species,
   Kirtland's warbler, 255–56
Energy budget, habitat, 46
Environmental education
   organizations, 420
Environmental education
   seminars, 421–22
Ermine
   characteristics and habitats,
      13, 166, *200–2*, 206, 213–
      15, *213*, *214*, *239–40*
   seasonal activities, 378, 406
Erratic, 6
Etiquette for wildlife
   watchers, 46–49
Evening-primrose, common,
   208
Evergreen. See Needleleaf
   forest
Everlasting, pearly, *184–86*
Evolution, 19
Extension Service, 415
Extinction, 26–28
   human vs. natural causes,
      27
Eyeshine
   lynx, 334
   raccoon, 101

F

Falcon, peregrine, hotspots,
   351, 370
Fall. See also specific months
   amphibians in, 37
   birds in, 36
   in broadleaf forest, 235
   lake overturn, 57–58
   mammals in, 36–37
   reptiles in, 37
Farming
   effect on gray fox, 247
   effect on Tennessee
      warbler, 313
   in field formation, 187
   in upland broadleaf forest
      formation, 230
   in woodland opening/edge
      formation, 173
February, 377–79
Federal agencies, 28, 415–17
Feeding signs, 44
Feeding adaptations
   American bittern, 118
   American kestrel, 192
   American woodcock, 148
   bald eagle, 64
   beak design and, 19
   belted kingfisher, 95
   black-backed woodpecker,
      329
   black bear, 343
   boreal chickadee, 309
   broad-winged hawk, 242

carnivorous plants, 131, 164–65
chickadee, 396
common snipe, 137
eastern garter snake, 344–45
ermine, 213–14
evening grosbeak, 268
fisher, 283
flycatcher, 395
gray jay, 308
gray wolf, 337–38
great gray owl, 325
hairy woodpecker, 395
northern flicker, 177
northern flying squirrel, 285
northern goshawk, 280
northern harrier, 135–36
osprey, 65–66
pied-billed grebe, 117
pileated woodpecker, 245–46
raccoon, 99–100
red-breasted nuthatch, 267
red-shouldered hawk, 296
red-tailed hawk, 189–90
red-winged blackbird, 119
rose-breasted grosbeak, 230
ruby-throated hummingbird, 175–76
ruffed grouse, 225
shoveler, 395
snapping turtle, 67
star-nosed mole, 153
Tennessee warbler, 313
vireo, 395
warbler, 395
white-tailed deer, 215–16
yellow-bellied sapsucker, 395
Feeding debris, muskrat, 124
Feeding hole, American woodcock, 149
Feeding house, muskrat, 124
Fern, 144, 187, 292, 294, 386
bracken, 170–72, 172–73, 187, 200–2, 203, 220–22, 260, 311
cinnamon, 142–44, 290–92, 321–22
marsh, 142–44
sensitive, 142–44
Field, 184–86
definition, 186
formation, 186–88
value to wildlife, 188
wildlife, 188–98
wildlife action, 188–89
Field notes, 374–75
Finch, 404
northern, seasonal activities, 374
Fir, balsam, 5, 7, 11

closed canopy lowland needleleaf forest, 318–19, 321–22, 323
mature lowland broadleaf forest, 293
mature upland broadleaf forest, 236, 239–40
mature upland mixed forest, 277–78
mature upland needleleaf forest, 258–60, 260–61, 265–66
white spruce-balsam fir forest, 261–62
young upland needleleaf forest, 252–53
Fire
adaptations to
aspen, 10–11
eastern white pine, 10
jack pine, 11
needleleaf trees, 263–64
paper birch, 11
red pine, 10
trees, 10–11
in broadleaf forest formation, 223, 236
controlled burning, 11
in field formation, 187
human control of, 253–54
in needleleaf forest formation, 253–55, 262, 319–22
in shrub-sapling opening formation, 203
succession after, 203–5
in woodland opening/edge formation, 173
Firebird. See Tanager, scarlet
Fireweed, 184–86, 203, 397
Fish, half-eaten, 122
Fish and Wildlife Service (USDI), 416
Fish Creek/Whittlesey Creek Marsh (Wisconsin), 359–60
Fisher
characteristics and habitats, 271, 274–76, 283–84, 283, 339
hotspots, 358, 362, 367
seasonal activities, 378
Fish Lake Wildlife Area (Wisconsin), 360
Flag, blue, 158–60
Flea, water, 58
Flicker, northern
characteristics and habitats, 170–72, 172, 176, 177–78, 206
seasonal activities, 383, 395, 401
Flock, interspecific, 398–99
Flooding
adaptations to

black spruce, 306
sedges, 130
animal behavior during, 38
Flora guides, 424
Fluorescent powder, 39
Flushing, ruffed grouse, 227
Fly, black, 92
Flycatcher, 238, 294, 307, 395
alder
characteristics and habitats, 142–44, 147, 149–50, 150
seasonal activities, 391
least, characteristics and habitats, 220–22, 228, 228, 239–40
olive-sided, characteristics and habitats, 302–4, 311–12, 311, 387
willow, characteristics and habitats, 391
yellow-bellied, seasonal activities, 388
Flying adaptations
broad-winged hawk, 242
northern flying squirrel, 284–85
Fly-honeysuckle, American, 258–60
Food store, 44
beaver, 407
boreal chickadee, 310
chipmunk, 398
gray jay, 308–9
gray squirrel, 402
northern flying squirrel, 285
red squirrel, 269–70, 376, 399, 402
Fool hen. See Grouse, spruce
Foraging behavior, birds, 394–96
Forbs, 187–88
Forest. See also Broadleaf forest; Mixed forest; Needleleaf forest
basement, 21
bog. See Needleleaf forest, closed-canopy lowland
canopy, 21, 23
climax, 261
floor, 21–22
land management, 29–30
shrub layer, 21
top story, 21
transition, 5
Forest Service (USDA), 415
Forms (frog resting spot), 140
Fox, 43, 77, 166, 206, 238, 240, 264, 339–40
gray, characteristics and

habitats, *199*, *232–34*,
246–48, *247*
red
  characteristics and
    habitats, 60, *170–72*,
    172, 178–81, *178*
  hotspots, 366
  seasonal activities, 375,
    393
Frog, 35, 37–38, 59, 74, 78,
93, 116, 362, 376
  discarded skins, 297
  green, seasonal activities,
    393, 396, 399
  mink
    characteristics and
      habitats, *158–60*, 166
    hotspots, 354, 356
    seasonal activities, 394
  northern leopard
    characteristics and
      habitats, *126–28*, 128,
      131–32, 139–41, *141*
    seasonal activities, 389
  western chorus
    hotspots, 359
    seasonal activities, 384
  wood
    characteristics and
      habitats, *290–92*, 299–
      300, *299*
    hotspots, 358
    seasonal activities, 384
Frost pocket, 173
Fruit, 394
Fungi
  brooming and, 324
  root, 285
  shelf, *170–72*
  soil, 263
  sulphur shelf, 397

G

Gale, sweet, *54–56*, *126–28*,
130, 164
Gaping, 119
Generalist, 20
Glacier
  action of, 6–8
  in bog formation, 161
  in broadleaf forest
    formation, 235
  in lake formation, 57
  legacies of, 6–7
  melting of, 6
  in needleleaf forest
    formation, 261
  in pond formation, 75
Glucose, as cryoprotectant,
299
Godwit, hotspots, 359
Goldeneye, 405
  common

characteristics and
    habitats, 60
  seasonal activities, 378
Goldenrod, 187–88, *142–44*,
184–86, 397
Goldfinch, American
  characteristics and habitats,
    200–2, 207–8, *207*, 398
  seasonal activities, 398
Goldthread, 320, *321–22*
Goose, 78, 358, 402
  Canada
    characteristics and
      habitats, 83, *109*
    hotspots, 360, 369
    seasonal activities, 401
  snow
    hotspots, 347
    seasonal activities, 405
Gooseberry, 212
  smooth, *142–44*
Gopher, northern pocket,
  hotspots, 359
Goshawk, northern
  characteristics and habitats,
    274–76, 280–81, *280*
  hotspots, 351, 368, 370
  seasonal activities, 391,
    410–11
Grand Marais Harbor
  (Minnesota), 350–51
Grape, wild, 205, 210
Grass, 129–30, 188, 294, 382
  balls of dried, 195
  blue joint, *72–74*
  cool-season, 187
  cut stems, 169
  exotic, 173
  meadow, 75
  poverty, *184–86*
  quack, *184–86*
  rice, *184–86*
Gravel, 59
Grebe, 60, 78, 347, 358
  pied-billed, characteristics
    and habitats, *110–12*,
    112, 116–17, *117*
Greenbrier, 212
Grosbeak
  evening
    characteristics and
      habitats, *258–60*, 265–
      66, 268–69, *268*, *316–18*
    seasonal activities, 374
  pine, seasonal activities,
    374, 408–10
  rose-breasted,
    characteristics and
      habitats, *220–22*, 229–30,
      230
Groundhog. *See* Woodchuck
Grouse, 238
  ruffed
    characteristics and

habitats, 147, 205–6,
  220–22, 222, 224–28,
  227, *239–40*, 280, *289*
  hotspots, 367
  seasonal activities, 374–
    75, 383, 392, 406, 411
sharp-tailed
  characteristics and
    habitats, 188
  hotspots, 353, 359, 369
  seasonal activities, 382
spruce
  characteristics and
    habitats, 252, 255, *316–
    18*, 323, 327–28, *327*
  hotspots, 348, 353, 361,
    364
  seasonal activities, 382,
    405–6
Gull, 59, 368
  Bonaparte's, hotspots, 351
  Franklin's, hotspots, 347,
    351
  glaucous, hotspots, 363
  herring
    characteristics and
      habitats, 382
    hotspots, 356, 370
  Iceland, hotspots, 363
  ring-billed, characteristics
    and habitats, 382
  Thayer's, hotspots, 363
Gyrfalcon
  hotspots, 350, 368
  seasonal activities, 409

H

Habitat
  aquatic. *See* Lake; Pond;
    River; Stream
  carrying capacity, 25
  complexity, 23
  definition, 17–18
  energy budget, 46
  forest. *See* Broadleaf forest;
    Mixed forest; Needleleaf
    forest
  horizontal zones, 21–23
  human's influences, 25–28
  interactions of organisms
    within, 24–25
  junctions between, 23–24
  maintenance, 28–30
  management, 25–28
  opening. *See* Field; Shrub-
    sapling opening;
    Woodland opening/edge
  patchiness, 23
  preferred, 18–20, 34
  selection of, 20–25
  size, 24
  special features, 24
  structure, 20–21

vertical layers, 21
wetland. *See* Bog; Marsh;
  Sedge meadow; Shrub
  swamp
Habitat preservation groups,
  419
Hare, snowshoe
  characteristics and habitats,
    5, 12, 146–47, 166, 205–6,
    224, *239–40*, 255, 283,
    308, *316–18*, 318, 323–24,
    331–34, *332*, 339
  hotspots, 355, 366
  seasonal activities, 35, 375,
    379–80, 396, 406, 411
Harrier, northern
  characteristics and habitats,
    83, *126–28*, 128, 131–32,
    135–36, *136*, 197
  hotspots, 370
  seasonal activities, 388
Hawk, 38, 43, 188, 202, 238,
    240, 264, 280, 307, 356,
    363, 404
  broad-winged
    characteristics and
      habitats, *170–72*, 206,
      232–34, 241–43, *242*
    hotspots, 351
    seasonal activities, 387
  Cooper's, seasonal
    activities, 387
  marsh. *See* Harrier,
    northern
  red-shouldered
    characteristics and
      habitats, 190, *290–92*,
      295–97, *296*
    hotspots, 350
  red-tailed
    characteristics and
      habitats, *184–86*, 186,
      189–90, *189*, 196, 296
    seasonal activities, 380
  sharp-shinned
    hotspots, 370
    seasonal activities, 387
  singing. *See* Hawk, red-
    shouldered
  sparrow. *See* Kestrel
Hawk Ridge Nature Reserve
  (Minnesota), 65, 241–42,
  351
Hawkweed, 187–88
  orange, *170–72*
Hawthorn, 205, 210, 212
Hazel, beaked, 155, *170–72*,
  200–2, 220–22, 203–5,
  265–66
Hazelnut, 264, 343, 397
Head-on stare, 39
Hearing, 19
  barred owl, 295
  great gray owl, 325

northern harrier, 135
short-eared owl, 135
silver-haired bat, 101
Heath plants, 164, 304–7,
  319, 323
Heavy metals, 26
Helper birds, 191
Hemlock, eastern, 5, 8, 25,
  237, 253, *274–76*, 277, 282,
  379, 404
Herbicide, 26
Heron, 59, 77–78, 402
  great blue
    characteristics and
      habitats, *54–56*, 56, 60–
      62, *61*, 94, 382
    hotspots, 350, 355, 358,
      360, 362
    observation of, 35
    seasonal activities, 383
  green-backed,
    characteristics and
      habitats, 116
Hiawatha National Forest
  (Michigan), 363–64
Hibernacula, 272
Hibernation, 36
  bat, 378
  black bear, 342, 407
  central newt, 85
  chipmunk, 380, 384
  eastern garter snake, 345
  emergence from, 36
  four-toed salamander, 249
  frog, 376
  13-lined ground squirrel,
    196
  northern leopard frog, 140
  northern spring peeper, 86
  northern water snake, 106
  redback salamander, 287
  redbelly snake, 272, 403
  ringneck snake, 288
  salamander, 77
  smooth green snake, 198
  snapping turtle, 68
  water snake, 77
  woodchuck, 182
  wood frog, 300
  woodland jumping mouse,
    298, 403
  wood turtle, 108
Homing ability, silver-haired
  bat, 102
Honeybee, 146
Honeysuckle. *See* Bush-; Fly-
Hophornbeam, Eastern,
  232–34
Hornwort, 76
Horsetail, *54–56*
Hotspots
  Michigan, 363–71
  Minnesota, 347–55
  Wisconsin, 355–63

Huckleberry, 395
Human's influence. *See also*
  Farming; Hunting; Logging;
  Trapping
  bird feeders, 268, 405
  clearing in forest, 173
  on extinction of species,
    27
  fire control, 253–55
  on habitat size, 24
Hummingbird, ruby-throated
  characteristics and habitats,
    170–72, 175–77, *175*
  seasonal activities, 391
Hummock, 300, 304, 306,
  308, 311, 313–14
Humus, 203, 278
Hunting, 8
  of duck, 80
  of gray wolf, 337
  of red fox, 178
  of spruce grouse, 327
Huron-Manistee National
  Forest (Michigan), 256
Huron National Forest
  (Michigan), 364
Hyperphagia, 401
Hypnum, water, 93

I

Ice Age, 6–8
Inlet, 59
Insecticide, 26, 198
Irruptive species, 326, 408–9
Island, 59
Isle Royale National Park
  (Michigan), 366, 388

J

Jacobson's organs, 272
Jaeger, hotspots, 352
January, 374–76
Jay, 307
  blue, seasonal activities,
    405
  gray
    characteristics and
      habitats, 260, *302–4*,
      304, 306, 308–9, 339
    seasonal activities, 380,
      401
Jewelweed, 176
Joe-pye-weed, spotted, *126–
  28*, 130
July, 394–96
Jumping adaptations,
  woodland jumping mouse,
  298
June, 389–94
Juneberry, 391, 395

K

Kakagon Sloughs
(Wisconsin), 360
Kestrel, American
characteristics and habitats,
184–86, 192–93, *192*
hotspots, 352, 363
Kettle (hawk), 242
Kettle hole, 7, 161
Kingbird, eastern, seasonal
activities, 391
Kingfisher, belted
characteristics and habitats,
88–90, 90, 94–96, *95*
seasonal activities, 383
Kinglet, 42, 324, 399
golden-crowned
characteristics and
habitats, *321–22*, 330–
31, *330*
seasonal activities, 405
ruby-crowned,
characteristics and
habitats, 276
Knot (shorebird), hotspots,
359
Knotweed, 311

L

Lady's-slipper, *316–18*, 320
showy, *321–22*, 390
yellow, *302–4*, 390
Lake, *54–56*
definition, 56–57
fall and spring overturn,
57–58
formation, 7, 57
layers within, 58–59
value to wildlife, 59–60
wildlife, 60–70
wildlife action, 60
in winter, 12
Lake effect, 377, 382
Lake of the Woods
(Minnesota), 351
Land management, 28–30
Land-use planning, 9
Lark, horned, seasonal
activities, 382
Larvae, insect, 59
Laurel, bog, *158–60*, 307
Lavender, 386
Layering (plant
reproduction), 205, 306
Leaf
dropping of, 235
position in canopy, 236
rummaging in litter, 208–9,
211–12
types, 236
Leatherleaf, *54–56*, *158–60*,
164, *302–4*, 307, *316–18*
Lek, sharp-tailed grouse, 382

Lemming, southern bog,
characteristics and habitats,
158–60, 165, 168–69, *168*,
264, *321–22*, 324, 408
Lichen, 7, 264
old man's beard, 319, 328–
29, 379, 411
Lily
corn, 397
pond, *72–74*
water, 59, 74, 76–77, *110–
12*, 112, 116, 393
Lily pad, 74
Liverwort, 93
Locust, honey, 212
Lodge
beaver, 81–84
muskrat, 116, 123–24
Log, 236
looking under, 48
Logging, 8–9, 29
black spruce, 320
in broadleaf forest
formation, 223, 236
effect on moose and deer,
155
effect on Tennessee
warbler, 313
in field formation, 186–87
in needleleaf forest
formation, 253, 262
northern white-cedar, 323
in shrub-sapling opening
formation, 212
in woodland opening/edge
formation, 173
Loon, 59–60, 363
common
characteristics and
habitats, 19, *54–56*, 62–
64, *63*, *71*
hotspots, 352, 355, 366–
67, 370
observation of, 35
seasonal activities, 392
Loosestrife
swamp, *72–74*, 75
Lower layer, lake, 59
Lumberman's chewing gum,
308
Lynx
characteristics and habitats,
26, 166, 307, *316–18*, 318,
331–35, *334*
seasonal activities, 37, 375

M

Mallard, characteristics and
habitats, *72–74*, 74, 78, 80–
81, *80*, 116, 132
Mammals. *See also* specific
species

behavior when disturbed,
46–47
seasonal activities, 35–37
Manistee National Forest
(Michigan), 366
Maple, 380
mountain, *258–60*, *274–76*
red, 145, *220–22*, *290–92*,
292–94, 397
striped, *232–34*
sugar, 5, 8–9, 11, *20*, 25,
170–72, *200–2*
maple-beech-birch forest,
232–34, 237, 240
mature upland broadleaf
forest, 234, 236, 238
mature upland mixed
forest, *274–76*, 277–78,
286
shrub swamp, 155
young upland broadleaf
forest, 223
Maple fruit, empty, 269
Maple key, 241
Maple seedling, 241
Maple syrup, 379
March, 379–81
Marigold, marsh, *290–92*,
292, 386
Markings, 45
Marsh, *110–12*
definition, 112
formation, 7, 113
value to wildlife, 115
wildlife, 116–25
wildlife action, 116
Marten (animal)
characteristics and habitats,
315
hotspots, 361
seasonal activities, 37
Martin (bird), observation
of, 38
May, 386–89
Mayflower, Canada, *220–22*,
265–66, *274–76*, 386
Mayfly, 90, 93
Meadow, sedge. *See* Sedge
meadow
Meadowlark, eastern, *47*
Meadowsweet, 395
narrowleaf, *142–44*
Merganser
characteristics and habitats,
59–60, 74
seasonal activities, 382
Merlin, hotspots, 352–53,
363, 366, 370
Methane gas, 165
Michigan hotspots, 363–71
Midden, 270
Migration
American crow, 380
American robin, 401

442

bank swallow, 97
birds, 35–36
black phoebe, 384
black-throated green
 warbler, 282
blue jay, 405
bobolink, 401
broad-winged hawk, 241,
 243
Canada goose, 401
common loon, 64
common nighthawk, 398
direction cues in, 401
golden-crowned kinglet,
 405
great gray owl, 326
Harris' sparrow, 402
indigo bunting, 401
irruptive, 408–9
magnolia warbler, 257
mallard, 80
Nashville warbler, 314
northern flicker, 401
northern leopard frog, 140
northern spring peeper, 86
oldsquaw, 408
palm warbler, 166
perching birds, 400–2
red bat, 181
redbelly snake, 272
red-shouldered hawk, 296
red-tailed hawk, 190, 380
red-winged blackbird, 380
risks involved, 405
ruby-throated
 hummingbird, 176
sandhill crane, 133, 406
scarlet tanager, 245
scoter, 408
silver-haired bat, 102
snow goose, 405
solitary vireo, 281
songbird, 400
stragglers, 405
swallow, 398
Tennessee warbler, 313
tiger salamander, 404
warbler, 401
white-crowned sparrow,
 402
yellow-bellied sapsucker,
 401
Milfoil, water, 72–74
Milkweed, 184–86, 395
Mille Lacs Lake (Minnesota),
 352
Mink
 characteristics and habitats,
  54–56, 60, 77, 94, 110–
  12, 116, 120–22, 121, 166
 hotspots, 354–55, 366
 seasonal activities, 37, 396
Minnesota hotspots, 347–55
Mississippi Flyway, 80

Mistletoe, dwarf, 306, 324
Miterwort, naked, 321–22
Mixed forest, upland, 274–
 76
 definition, 276
 formation, 276–78
 value to wildlife, 279
 wildlife, 280–88
 wildlife action, 279–80
Moccasin, water, 106
Moisture loss, adaptations to
 bog plants, 162–63
 needleleaf tree, 263
 redback salamander, 286–
  87
Mole, star-nosed
 characteristics and habitats,
  142–44, 78, 147, 152–54,
  154
 seasonal activities, 411
Molehill, 152–54
Molting, 45, 45
 duck, 398
 mallard, 81
 red-winged blackbird, 120
 scarlet tanager, 244
 smooth green snake, 198
Moose
 characteristics and habitats,
  13, 77, 94, 144, 146, 148,
  154–56, 156, 174, 202,
  205, 224, 255, 264, 307,
  323, 337–38
 cow and calf, 142–44
 hotspots, 348, 354, 366
 safety concerns, 48
 seasonal activities, 35–36,
  376, 379–80, 388, 393,
  407
Moraine, 6
Morel, 386
Moss, 7, 264, 304–5
 club, 274–76, 404
 cushion, 93
 feather, 306, 319
 fountain, 93
 sphagnum, 158–60, 160–
  63, 249, 304, 306, 316–
  18, 318–19, 323
Moth, 390
Motorboat, 48
Mountain-ash, American,
 155, 258–60, 379, 395, 397,
 406, 409
Mouse, 37, 194, 202, 264,
 380, 384, 399, 411
 deer, characteristics and
  habitats, 205, 234–36
 woodland jumping
  characteristics and
  habitats, 290–92, 298–
  99, 298
 seasonal activities, 403
Muck, 59, 129, 145, 152, 292

Mud
 holes in, 44
 lake bottom, 58–59
 river, 93–94
 tracks in, 378
Mud pie, 83–84
Mudpuppy
 characteristics and habitats,
  56, 59, 69–70, 70, 95
 seasonal activities, 379
Mullein, 188
 common, 184–86
Mushroom, 264, 269–70, 285,
 386, 399
Muskeg. See Needleleaf
 forest, semi-open lowland
Musk gland, 178
Muskrat
 characteristics and habitats,
  77, 82, 110–12, 113–16,
  122–25, 124, 340
 seasonal activities, 37, 376,
  403, 407
Mussel, 93
Mussel shells, 124

N

National Forests, 415
National Parks, 416–17
National Park Service
 (USDI), 416–17
National Wildlife Refuges,
 416
Natural Resources,
 Department of, 417
Natural selection, 19–20
Nature centers, 421–22
Necedah National Wildlife
 Refuge (Wisconsin), 360–
 61
Nectar, 176
Needle (tree), 74
 tamarack, 307
Needleleaf forest
 adaptations to winter, 14
 closed-canopy lowland,
  316–18, 321–22
 definition, 318–19
 formation, 319–23
 value to wildlife, 323
 wildlife, 324–34
 wildlife action, 324
 mature upland, 258–60,
  265–66
 definition, 260–61
 formation, 261–62
 value to wildlife, 264
 wildlife, 266–73
 wildlife action, 266
 semi-open lowland, 302–4
 definition, 304
 formation, 304–7
 value to wildlife, 307–8

wildlife, 308–14
  wildlife action, 308
young upland, *250–52*
  definition, 252
  formation, 253–54
  value to wildlife, 254
  wildlife, 255–57
  wildlife action, 254–55
Needleleaf tree, adaptations of, 262–64
Nest. *See also* Den
  alder flycatcher, 150, 391
  American bittern, 118
  American goldfinch, 207–8, 398
  American kestrel, 192
  American redstart, 229
  American woodcock, 149
  arctic shrew, 168
  bald eagle, *54–56*, 65
  Baltimore oriole, 390
  bank swallow, 97–98, 382
  in bare woodland, 409
  barred owl, 295
  belted kingfisher, 95–96
  black-backed woodpecker, 329–30
  boreal chickadee, 310
  broad-winged hawk, 242, 387
  brown creeper, 267, 383
  brown-headed cowbird, 255–56, 388, 392
  brown thrasher, 212
  Canada goose, 83
  Caspian tern, 382
  chestnut-sided warbler, 230
  cliff swallow, 382
  colonial, 382–83
  common loon, 63
  common nighthawk, 391
  common raven, 383
  common snipe, 138
  common tern, 382
  common yellowthroat, 151
  Connecticut warbler, 313
  Cooper's hawk, 387
  cormorant, 382
  dummy, 134, 392
  eastern bluebird, 190–91
  eastern kingbird, 391
  eastern phoebe, 98–99
  evening grosbeak, 268
  finding, 391–93
  four-toed salamander, 249
  golden-crowned kinglet, 331
  golden-winged warbler, 390
  gray catbird, 209
  gray jay, 309
  great blue heron, 61–62, 382–83
  great gray owl, 326

great horned owl, 336
  hawk, 280
  herring gull, 382
  identification, 44–45
  indigo bunting, 213
  Kirtland's warbler, 255–56
  least flycatcher, 228
  Le Conte's sparrow, 135
  magnolia warbler, 257
  mallard, 81
  masked shrew, 341
  meadow vole, 195
  mudpuppy, 69–70
  Nashville warbler, 314
  northern flicker, 178
  northern flying squirrel, 286
  northern goshawk, 281, 391
  northern harrier, 83, 136, 388
  northern oriole, 391–92
  northern parula, 328–29
  nuthatch, 280
  observation of, 39, 47
  olive-sided flycatcher, 312
  osprey, 66
  ovenbird, 240–41, 392
  owl, 280
  palm warbler, 166
  pied-billed grebe, 117
  pileated woodpecker, 246
  redback salamander, 287
  red-breasted nuthatch, 267–68, 393
  red crossbill, 375
  red-eyed vireo, 244
  red-shouldered hawk, 297
  red squirrel, 270
  red-tailed hawk, 190
  red-winged blackbird, 120, 392
  ring-billed gull, 382
  rose-breasted grosbeak, 230
  ruby-throated hummingbird, 177
  ruffed grouse, 227
  rufous-sided towhee, 209
  sandhill crane, 133
  scarlet tanager, 245
  sedge wren, 134, 392
  sharp-shinned hawk, 387
  short-eared owl, 139
  smooth green snake, 198
  snapping turtle, 68
  snowshoe hare, 332
  solitary vireo, 281–82, 393
  song sparrow, 211
  southern bog lemming, 169
  spruce grouse, 328
  squirrel, 280
  star-nosed mole, 153
  Tennessee warbler, 314
  tern, 383

tree swallow, 191
  veery, 298
  water shrew, 105
  white-breasted nuthatch, 393
  white-throated sparrow, 311
  winter wren, 383
  woodchuck, 183
  wood duck, 78–80, 388
  woodland jumping mouse, 299
  woodpecker, 280
  wood turtle, 107–8
  yellow warbler, 151–52
Nest box
  bat, 102
  eastern bluebird, 190–91
  wood duck, 80, 388
Newt, 379
  central, characteristics and habitats, 84–85, *84*
Niche, 21
Nicolet National Forest (Wisconsin), 361
Nighthawk, common, seasonal activities, 391, 398
Night-heron, black-crowned, hotspots, 360
Nightingale. *See* Sparrow, white-throated
Nighttime
  animals active during, 38
  migration of birds during, 402
  observing wildlife during, 39, *39*
  at pond, 82
Nitrogen source, 131, 145, 164–65
Northern Highland-American Legion State Forest (Wisconsin), 362
November, 408–9
Nut, 269–70, 394
  gnawed, 44, 286
Nuthatch, 238, 280, 330, 375, 398
  red-breasted
    characteristics and habitats, *258–60*, 267–68, *267*
    seasonal activities, 393
  white-breasted, *316–18*
    seasonal activities, 393
Nutrients, release by fire, 10

O

Oak, 7–8, 252, 277, 343, 386
  bur, 402
  northern pin, *250–52*
  red, 402
Oakfern, *258–60*

Observation tips
  behavior watching, 45–46
  etiquette, 46–49
  extending senses, 39
  hiding by observer, 41–42
  luring wildlife, 42–43
  reading signs, 44–45
  site selection, 34–35
  stalking, 40–41
  thinking like an animal,
    33–34
  time of day, 38
  time of year, 35–38
October, 404–7
Odor, 45
  eastern garter snake, 344–
    45
  ermine, 215
  mink, 122
  porcupine, 272
  red fox, 178, 180
  ringneck snake, 287–88
  skunk cabbage, 146
Oldsquaw, seasonal
    activities, 378, 408
Open bog. *See* Bog
Opening. *See* Field; Shrub-
  sapling opening; Woodland
  opening/edge
Orchid, 164, 319
  ram's head, *250–52*
Oriole
  Baltimore, seasonal
    activities, 390
  northern
    characteristics and
      habitats, 116
    seasonal activities, 391–
      92
Ornithological unions, state,
    420
Oscoda Point (Michigan),
    370
Osprey
  characteristics and habitats,
    25, 54–56, 56, 59–60, 65–
    66, *65*
  hotspots, 355–56, 358, 362,
    364, 368
  seasonal activities, 382
Ottawa National Forest
    (Michigan), 367
Otter, river
  characteristics and habitats,
    77, *88–90,* 90, 94, 102–4,
    103
  hotspots, 350, 354–55, 366–
    67, 369
  seasonal activities, 37, 380,
    395–96, 398
Ovenbird
  characteristics and habitats,
    24, *232–34,* 238, 240–41,
    241

seasonal activities, 392
Overstory, 236
Owl, 38, 43, 202, 240, 264,
    280, 307, 310, 404, 410–11
  barred
    characteristics and
      habitats, *290–92,* 294–
      96, *295*
    seasonal activities, 377
  boreal
    hotspots, 353, 370
    seasonal activities, 375,
      408
  great gray
    characteristics and
      habitats, 5, 13, 165, 308,
      316–18, 324–27, *325*
    hotspots, 353, 370
    seasonal activities, 375,
      408
  great horned
    characteristics and
      habitats, 196, *219,* 238,
      331, 335–36, *335*
    hotspots, 370
    seasonal activities, 375
  long-eared, hotspots, 370
  northern hawk
    characteristics and
      habitats, 308
    seasonal activities, 408
  saw-whet
    characteristics and
      habitats, 308, *321–22*
    hotspots, 370
    seasonal activities, 382
  short-eared
    characteristics and
      habitats, 25, *126–28,*
      131–32, 135, 138–39,
      138, 165
    hotspots, 359
    seasonal activities, 395
  snowy
    hotspots, 348, 350
    seasonal activities, 408–9

P

Parabolic reflector, 39
Park Point (Minnesota), 352
Parula, northern,
  characteristics and habitats,
    321–22, 324, 328–29, *328*
Peat. *See also* Bog; Broadleaf
  forest, mature lowland;
  Needleleaf forest, closed-
  canopy lowland;
  Needleleaf forest, semi-
  open lowland
  formation, 7
  patterned, 129
Pecking order, Tennessee
  warbler, 313

Peeper, northern spring
  characteristics and habitats,
    72–74, 86–87, *86*
  seasonal activities, 384
Pelican, American white,
  hotspots, 351
Pellets (regurgitated), 45
  barred owl, 295
  ermine, 215
  formation, 404
  hawk, 404
  owl, 404
  raven, 395
Perch tree, belted kingfisher,
    96
Periodicals, 426
Pesticide, 65–66, 149, 190
Pets, 48
Phoebe
  black, seasonal activities,
    384
  eastern, characteristics and
    habitats, *89–90,* 94, 98–
    99, *98*
Photography, 39, *41,* 47
Pickerelweed, *72–74, 110–
    12*
Pictured Rocks National
  Lakeshore (Michigan), 367
Pigeon, homing, 402
Pigeon River Country State
  Forest (Michigan), 367–68
Pine, 8, 261, 380
  eastern white, 5, *7–10, 8,*
    252–53, 262–63, *265–66,*
    277, 386
  forest, 262
  jack, 7, 9, 11, *11,* 204, *250–
    52,* 252–56, 261–62, 264,
    277
  red, *2,* 5, 7–8, 10, *27, 250–
    52,* 252–53, 255, 262–63,
    265–66, 277
Pine cone, 44, 269–70
  eastern white pine, *11*
  jack pine, 11, *11, 204*
  piles of scales from, 270
  red pine, *2*
Pipewort, *54–56*
Pishing, 42–43
Pitcher plant, *158–60,* 164–
    65, *302–4*
Plants
  accumulator, 164
  aquatic, 93
  carnivorous, 164–65
  colonizing, 203–4
  emergent, 113
  floating-leaved, 113
  free-floating, 113
  hummingbird-adapted, 176
  marsh, 113–14
  pond, 75–76

scientific and common
  names, 427–31
submergent, 113
suspended in water, 113
Plover
  black-bellied, hotspots, 370
  piping, hotspots, 351, 369–
    71
  upland, characteristics and
    habitats, 188
Plum, wild, 212
Plunge hole
  great gray owl, 326
  woodchuck, 183
Pogonia, rose, *158–60*
Pollinator, 176
Pollution, 26, 60, 65–66, 91
Pond, *72–74*
  definition, 74
  formation, 75
  plants in, 75–76
  value to wildlife, 77
  wildlife, 78–89
  wildlife action, 77–78
Pondweed, *54–56*, *88–90*
Poplar, balsam, 293, 386
Popple. *See* Aspen
Population cycle
  great gray owl, 325–26
  lemming, 408
  lynx, 333
  meadow vole, 195
  muskrat, 123
  red-breasted nuthatch,
    267–68
  ruffed grouse, 227
  snowshoe hare, 331–32
Porcupine
  characteristics and habitats,
    224, 238, 255, *258–60*,
    264, 270–72, *271*, *274–76*,
    283, *316–18*, 323, 340
  hotspots, 354–55, 362, 364,
    367
  seasonal activities, 376,
    380, 384
Porcupine Mountains
  Wilderness State Park
  (Michigan), 368
Prairie, 8, 188
Prairie-chicken, greater,
  hotspots, 359
Preacher bird. *See* Vireo,
  red-eyed
Preening, 326
Preservation groups, 419
Pussy willow, *72–74*, *110–
  12*, *142–44*, 146, 285, 294,
  380
Pyrola, one-sided, *258–60*

Q
Qali, 12
Quill, porcupine, 270–71

R
Rabbit, cottontail,
  characteristics and habitats,
    5, *170–72*, 389
Rabies, bat-transmitted, 102
Raccoon
  characteristics and habitats,
    60, 74, 77, *88–90*, 94, 99–
    101, *99*, 238, 294, *414*
  observation of, 43
  seasonal activities, 396,
    399, 407
Ragweed, 311
Rail, 116
  black, characteristics and
    habitats, 112
  Virginia, *72–74*, *110–12*
  yellow, hotspots, 369
Rain, animals active during,
  38
Raspberry, 395
  dwarf, *321–22*
  red, *200–2*, 205, 211, 397
Rat, black, characteristics
  and habitats, 335
Raven, common
  characteristics and habitats,
    339
  seasonal activities, 377,
    383–84, , 395, 405
Recommended reading, 423–
  26
Redcedar, eastern, 211
Redhead, characteristics and
  habitats, 60
Redpoll, 147, 410
  hoary, seasonal activities,
    408
Redstart, American
  characteristics and habitats,
    23, *220–22*, 229, *229*
  seasonal activities, 387
Reedgrass, bluejoint, 130
Regeneration
  central newt, 85
  salamander tail, 248–49,
    400
Rendezvous site, gray wolf,
  337, 339
Reptiles. *See also* specific
  species
  behavior when disturbed,
    47
  seasonal activities, 36–38
Resin, 308
Resource management, 9
Resting area, snowshoe hare,
  332–33
Rhizome, 114, 130

Rice, wild, *88–90*, 401
Rice Lake National Wildlife
  Refuge (Minnesota), 352–
  53
Ridge, star-nosed mole, 153–
  54
River, *88–90*
  definition, 90
  formation, 91
  seasonal changes, 91–92
  value to wildlife, 94
  wildlife, 95–108
  wildlife action, 94–95
Riverbank, 44, 94–97
River bottom, 93–94
River current, 91–92
Roadway, 198, 272, 345
Robin, American
  characteristics and habitats,
    20
  seasonal activities, 395,
    401, 405
Rocks
  lake, 59
  looking under, 48
  river, 92–93
Rodent, shovel-footed, 34–35
Rookery, great blue heron,
  61–62
Roosting area, red bat, 182
Root, pond plants, 75–77
Rose, multiflora, 210–11
Roseau County bog
  (Minnesota), 353
Rose hips, 397
Rosemary, bog, *158–60*, 307
Rotifer, 58
Running adaptations, bobcat,
  339
Runway, 45
  American bittern, 118
  arctic shrew, 167–68
  masked shrew, 341
  meadow vole, 195, 380
  muskrat, 124
  southern bog lemming,
    168–69
  star-nosed mole, 153
  woodchuck, 182–83
Rush, *110–12*, *126–28*
  beak, *54–56*
  scouring, *54–56*
  spike, *54–56*

S
Safety of wildlife watcher,
  48–49, 67–68
St. Croix National Scenic
  Riverway (Wisconsin),
  362–63
St. Mary's River (Michigan),
  368–69

446

Salamander, 35–38, 77–78, 94, 206, 254, 279, 361
blue-spotted, *200–2*, *239–40*
four-toed
characteristics and habitats, *158–60*, 166, *232–34*, 248–49, *249*, 294, 307–8
seasonal activities, 400
redback
characteristics and habitats, *274–76*, 286–87, *287*
hotspots, 358
seasonal activities, 389, 394
spotted
characteristics and habitats, *37*
hotspots, 358
tiger, seasonal activities, 404
Salt craving
northern finches, 374
porcupines, 271
Salvia, 176
Sand, 59
Sanderling, hotspots, 352, 363, 370
Sandpiper, 60, 77, 359, 370
spotted, characteristics and habitats, 94
upland, hotspots, 364, 367
Sand ridge, 98
Sap, 14–15, 44, 263, 267, 286
Sapsucker, yellow-bellied
characteristics and habitats, 176, *239–40*, 395
seasonal activities, 383, 401
Sarsaparilla, wild, *200–2*, 203, *239–40*, *274–76*
Sault St. Marie/St. Mary's River (Michigan), 368–69
Sawfly, 308
larch, 323–24
Scape (bare patch of ground), 218
Scat, 45
ermine, 215
gray fox, 247–48
gray wolf, 338
identification, 404–6
moose, 155
raccoon, 101
red fox, 180
striped skunk, 405
Scaup
hotspots, 354
seasonal activities, 405
Scent. See Odor
Scent markings
beaver, 83–84
gray fox, 247–48

porcupine, 272
river otter, 104
territorial, 406–7
Science and Education (USDA), 415
Scientific names
animals, 431–433
plants, 427–31
Scoter
hotspots, 351–52, 363
seasonal activities, 378, 408
SCUBA gear, 39
Sedge, *54–56*, *110–12*, 129–30, *142–44*, 144, 294, 382
three-way, *54–56*
Sedge meadow, *126–28*
definition, 128–29
formation, 129
value to wildlife, 131
wildlife, 132–41
wildlife action, 132
Seeds, 394
weed, 188
Seney National Wildlife Refuge (Michigan), 369
September, 400–4
Serviceberry, *170–72*, *200–2*, *274–76*, 390
Shallows, pond, 78
Shinleaf, *265–66*
Shorebirds. See also specific species
characteristics and habitats, 399
hotspots, 360, 371
Shoreline, 59, 77, 94
Shoveler, characteristics and habitats, 395
Shrike, northern, *184–86*
Shrew, 37, 147, 194, 205, 307–8
arctic
characteristics and habitats, 131, *158–60*, 165, 167–68, *167*
seasonal activities, 380
masked, characteristics and habitats, 340–41, *341*
water, characteristics and habitats, *88–90*, 90, 95, 104, *104*
Shrike, northern, hotspots, 369
Shrub, 204–5
Shrub-sapling opening, *200–2*
definition, 202
formation, 203–4
value to wildlife, 205–6
wildlife, 207–18
wildlife action, 206
Shrub swamp, *142–44*
definition, 144
formation, 145

value to wildlife, 147
wildlife, 148–56
wildlife action, 147–48
Sight. See Vision
Signs, reading, 44–45
Silverweed, *54–56*
Siskin, pine, seasonal activities, 408, 410
Sitzmark, northern flying squirrel, 286
Skin
rodent, 44
snake, 45
Skink, five-lined, hotspots, 362
Skull, meadow vole, 196
Skunk, striped
characteristics and habitats, 77, 405
seasonal activities, 399
Skunk cabbage, *142–44*, 145–47, *290–92*, 380
Skyscraper, 192
Sleeping Bear Dunes National Lakeshore (Michigan), 369–70
Smartweed, water, *54–56*
Smell, sense of, 19
snake, 272
Smelt run, 383–84
Snail, 59, 93
Snake, 36–37, 188, 206, 255, 279
eastern garter
characteristics and habitats, *18*, 166, *170–72*, 272, 307–8, 344–45, *345*
seasonal activities, 384, 403
eastern hognose, hotspots, 359
eastern ribbon, *158–60*
gopher, *184–86*
green, characteristics and habitats, 175, 188
northern water
characteristics and habitats, 74, 77–78, *88–90*, 106, *106*
seasonal activities, 396
redbelly
characteristics and habitats, *258–60*, 272–73, *273*
hotspots, 356
seasonal activities, 403
ringneck
characteristics and habitats, *274–76*, 287–88, *288*
seasonal activities, 394
smooth green
characteristics and

habitats, *184–86*, 198, *198*, 272
hotspots, 364
seasonal activities, 399
Snipe, common
  characteristics and habitats, *126–28*, 128, 132, 137–38, *137*
  seasonal activities, 387
Snorkeling, 39
Snow, 12–13. *See also* Winter
  blood in, 34
  melting, 13, 91–92, 195
  tracking in, 377–78
  tracks in, 37
  on trees, 14–15
Snowberry, creeping, 307
Sod, 173, 187
Soil
  buffering ability, 60
  formation, 6–7
  fungi in, 263
  woodland opening, 173
Soil stabilizer, 203–4
Solomon's seal, *170–72*
  downy, *232–34*, *274–76*
  false, *316–18*
  smooth, *200–2*
Sora, *110–12*, *126–28*
Sparrow, 240
  Harris', seasonal activities, 402
  Le Conte's
    characteristics and habitats, *126–28*, 131, 134–35, *135*
    hotspots, 369
  Lincoln's, *158–60*
  song
    characteristics and habitats, *200–2*, 210–11, *210*
    seasonal activities, 382
  swamp, characteristics and habitats, 116, 132
  white-crowned, seasonal activities, 402
  white-throated, characteristics and habitats, 25, *302–4*, 310–11, *311*
Spathe, skunk cabbage, 146
Spotting dog, 39
Spotting scope, 39
Spring. *See also* specific months
  amphibians in, 35–36
  birds in, 35
  lake overturn, 57–58
  mammals in, 35
  reptiles in, 36
Spring beauty, *232–34*
Spruce, 261, 276–77, 380
  black, 7, *158–60*, 160–61,

302–4, 304–6, 318, 323–26, 329
  black spruce bog, 319
  black spruce-tamarack forest (swamp), *316–18*, 319–20, 323–24
  white, 5, 11, 236, 252–53, 260, 399
  spruce-balsam fir forest, *258–60*, 261–62
Squeaking, 43
Squirrel, 19, 37, 205, 234, 240, 264, 280, 307
  flying
    characteristics and habitats, 19, 238
    observation of, 38
    seasonal activities, 402
  Franklin's ground, hotspots, 359
  gray
    characteristics and habitats, 406, *409*
    seasonal activities, 402, 409
  ground, observation of, 43
  13-lined ground
    characteristics and habitats, *184–86*, 188–89, 196–97, *197*
    seasonal activities, 399
  northern flying, characteristics and habitats, *274–76*, 284–86, *284*
  red
    characteristics and habitats, 12, *258–60*, 260, *265–66*, 269–70, *269*, 306, 308, *316–18*, 323–24, 406
    observation of, 38
    seasonal activities, 376, 380, 393, 396, 398–99, 402–3, 406, 409
  southern flying, characteristics and habitats, 5, 276
Stalking, 40–41
Starflower, *200–2*, *274–76*
  white Canadian, 390
Starling, characteristics and habitats, 178
State agencies, 417–18
Stick
  debarked, 77
  gnawed, 83
Stimulation broom, 324
Stonefly, 93
Strawberry, wild, *170–72*, 386, 390
Stream, 22, *88–90*
  current, 91–92
  definition, 90

formation, 91
  seasonal changes, 91–92
  value to wildlife, 94
  wildlife, 95–108
  wildlife action, 94–95
Streambank, 44, 94
Stream bottom, 93–94
Succession
  bog, 160–62
  field, 187–88
  after fire, 203–5
  lake, 57
  lowland broadleaf forest, 292–93
  lowland needleleaf forest, 304–7, 319–23
  marsh, 113
  pond, 75
  sedge meadow, 129
  shrub-sapling opening, 203–4
  shrub swamp, 145
  upland broadleaf forest, 223–24, 235–37
  upland mixed forest, 276–78
  upland needleleaf forest, 253–54, 261–62
  woodland opening/edge, 173
Suckering (plant reproduction), 204, 223
Sumac, 379, 397
  smooth, *170–72*
Summer. *See also* specific months
  amphibians in, 36
  birds in, 36
  mammals in, 36
  reptiles in, 36
Sundew, 164–65
  round-leaved, *158–60*
Superior National Forest (Minnesota), 353–54
Surface layer, lake, 58
"Survival of the fittest," 19–20
Swallow, 38, 78, 90, 398
  bank, characteristics and habitats, *88–90*, 94, 97–98, *97*, 382
  barn, seasonal activities, 392
  cliff, characteristics and habitats, 382
  tree
    characteristics and habitats, 191
    seasonal activities, 384
Swamp. *See also* Broadleaf forest, mature lowland
  black spruce-tamarack, 323–24

northern white-cedar, 319, 323–24
shrub. *See* Shrub swamp
Swan, 78
  mute, hotspots, 359
  tundra, hotspots, 359
Sweet-fern, 203, *239–40*
Swimming adaptations
  beaver, 82
  central newt, 84–85
  pied-billed grebe, 116
  river otter, 103
  water shrew, 105

T

Tadpole, 78, 86, 93, 95, 131, 139–40, 389, 399
Tamarack, 5, 7, *302–4, 307,* 404
  black spruce-tamarack forest (swamp), *316–18,* 319–20, 323–24
  bog, *158–60,* 160–61
  lowland needleleaf forest, 304–8, 318, 323, 326, 329
  mature upland mixed forest, 277
  mature upland needleleaf forest, 261
Tamarac National Wildlife Refuge (Minnesota), 354
Tanager, scarlet, characteristics and habitats, *232–34,* 244–45, *244*
Tannin, 164
Tape recordings, 39, 47–48
Tawas Point/Oscoda Point (Michigan), 370
Tea, labrador, *158–60, 302–4,* 304, 307, *316–18,* 390
Tearthumb, arrow-leaved, *142–44*
Teal, characteristics and habitats, 132
Tern, 59, 78, 383
  black
    characteristics and habitats, 60
    hotspots, 347, 359
  Caspian
    characteristics and habitats, 382
    hotspots, 351–52, 359
  common
    characteristics and habitats, 382
    hotspots, 355, 359
  Forster's, characteristics and habitats, 116
Territory, marking, 406
Thicket, 212
Thistle down, 207
Thrasher, brown

characteristics and habitats, *200–2,* 210–12, *211*
seasonal activities, 384
Thrush, 264
  hermit, seasonal activities, 384, 405
  willow. *See* Veery
  wood, seasonal activities, 395
Tick, wood, 390
Timber management, 29–30
Toad
  characteristics and habitats, 78, 188, 206, 254
  observation of, 38
  seasonal activities, 389, 396, 399
Tongue, snake, 272
Touch, sense of
  northern flying squirrel, 285
  raccoon, 99–100
Towhee, rufous-sided, characteristics and habitats, 25, *200–2,* 208–9, *208*
Tracking, 39–41, 377–78
Tracks, 45. *See also* Trail
  arctic shrew, 168
  badger, 194
  black bear, 344
  common snipe, 138
  dog, 180
  ermine, 214
  fisher, 284, 378
  gray fox, 247–48
  gray wolf, 338
  lynx, 334
  meadow vole, 195
  mink, 122
  moose, 155
  muskrat, 124
  northern flying squirrel, 286
  raccoon, 100
  red fox, 180
  river otter, 104
  ruffed grouse, 227
  in snow, 37
  snowshoe hare, 331–32
  white-tailed deer, 217
  woodchuck, 183
Trail, 45. *See also* Tracks
  American bittern, 118
  black bear, 343
  gray fox, 247
  gray wolf, 338
  river otter, 104
  ski, 376, 410
  snowshoe hare, 332
  white-tailed deer, 216–17
Trapping, 8
  of fisher, 283
  of mink, 120
  of muskrat, 123

of red fox, 178
Tree. *See also* specific species
  "bear", 344
  chewed, 156, 271–72, 379–80
  clawed, 45, 101, 340, 344
  deciduous, 235
  dominant, 277–78
  gnawed, 83, 196, 286
  holes in, 44
  snag, 294–95, 406
  white patches on trunk, 330
  wood chips at base, 178
Treefrog, 86, 165
  gray, hotspots, 354
Tree stump, 83
Trillium
  large-flowered, *170–72, 232–34, 274–76,* 390
Tubeworm, 59
Tundra, 6–7
Tunnel, 45
  bank swallow, 97–98
  belted kingfisher, 95–96
  masked shrew, 341
  red squirrel, 270
  southern bog lemming, 168
  star-nosed mole, 152–54
  water shrew, 105
Turkey, wild
  characteristics and habitats, *31*
  hotspots, 361, 364
Turnstone, ruddy, hotspots, 352, 363, 370
Turtle, 36–38, 59, 77–78, 94, 116, 364, 403
  Blanding's, hotspots, 359, 362
  eastern mud, *110–12*
  eastern spiny softshell, hotspots, 362
  painted
    characteristics and habitats, 95, 166
    seasonal activities, 379, 384, 394
  snapping
    characteristics and habitats, *54–56,* 56, 67–68, *68*
    hotspots, 354
    seasonal activities, 394, 403
  wood
    characteristics and habitats, *88–90,* 90, 107–8, *108*
    hotspots, 356, 359, 362
    seasonal activities, 396
Turtlehead, *142–44*

Tussock, *126–28*, 130
Twig, chewed, *34*, 44, 217, 271
Twilight
  animals active during, 38
  barred owl, 295
  at lake, 60
  northern flying squirrel, 284–86
  at pond, 78, 82
Twinflower, *258–60*
  pink, 390
Twisted-stalk, rose, *274–76*

U

Understory, 236
University extension, 418–19
Upper layer, lake, 58
Urine
  bobcat, 340
  red fox, 180

V

Veery, characteristics and habitats, *290–92*, 297–98, *297*
Velvet (antler), 45, 218
Violet, *170–72*, *232–34*
Violet hepatica, 386
Vireo, 42, 395
  red-eyed
    characteristics and habitats, *232–34*, 238, 243–44, *243*, 387
    seasonal activities, 398
  solitary
    characteristics and habitats, *274–76*, 281–82, *281*
    seasonal activities, 393
Virgin's bower, 145
Vision, 19
  barred owl, 295
  broad-winged hawk, 242
  lynx, 333
  northern flying squirrel, 284–85
  red squirrel, 269
  red-tailed hawk, 189
Vole, 202, 279, 308, 384, 411
  meadow
    characteristics and habitats, 25, *126–28*, 128, 131, 165, *184–86*, 188, 194–96, *194*, 264
    seasonal activities, 380
  southern red-backed
    characteristics and habitats, 205, 238
    seasonal activities, 378–79
Volunteer opportunities, 413

Volunteer placement services, 422
Voyageurs National Park (Minnesota), 355
Vulture, turkey, seasonal activities, 382

W

Walking adaptations, wood duck, 78–79
Wallow, moose, 156
Wapiti. *See* Elk
Warbler, 42, 147, 238, 307, 324, 356, 366–67, 395, 398, 401
  bay-breasted, observation of, 34
  blackburnian
    characteristics and habitats, 282
    observation of, 34
  black-throated green, characteristics and habitats, *274–76*, 282–83, *282*
  blue-winged, 390
  chestnut-sided
    characteristics and habitats, *220–22*, 230–31, *231*
    seasonal activities, 391–92
  Connecticut
    characteristics and habitats, *302–4*, 308, 312–13, *312*
    hotspots, 348
    seasonal activities, 388
  golden-winged, seasonal activities, 390
  hybrid, 390
  Kirtland's
    characteristics and habitats, *250–52*, 254–56, *255*
    hotspots, 364
    seasonal activities, 387
  magnolia
    characteristics and habitats, *250–52*, 254, 256–57, *257*, 282
    observation of, 34
  mourning, characteristics and habitats, 148
  Nashville, characteristics and habitats, *302–4*, 308, 314, *314*
  palm
    characteristics and habitats, 166–67, *166*
    seasonal activities, 384
  Tennessee, characteristics and habitats, 313–14, *313*

  wood, characteristics and habitats, 264
  yellow
    characteristics and habitats, *142–44*, 151–52, *152*
    seasonal activities, 392
  yellow-rumped, seasonal activities, 387, 405
Waterbug, 74
Watercress, true, 93
Waterfall, 93
Water jump, fox tracks at, 180
Water shield, *88–90*
Waterthrush, Northern, *88–90*
Water "walking," water shrew, 104–105
Waxwing
  bohemian, hotspots, 354, 369
  cedar
    characteristics and habitats, 388
    seasonal activities, 375, 391–92, 395, 408
Weasel, short-tailed. *See* Ermine
Weed, 188
Wetland. *See* Bog; Marsh; Sedge meadow; Shrub swamp; Swamp
Whimbrel, hotspots, 352, 370
Whip-poor-will, hotspots, 361
Whistle pig. *See* Woodchuck
White-cedar, northern, 216, 293, 319, *321–22*, 379, 410
  northern white-cedar forest (swamp), 319–24
Whitefish Bay Bird Observatory (Michigan), 370
Whitewash, 45, 382
  great gray owl, 326
Whittlesey Creek Marsh (Wisconsin), 359–60
Wide-ranging wildlife, 335–45
Wilderness State Park (Michigan), 371
Wildfire. *See* Fire
Wildflowers, 304–5
Wildlife guides, 423–24
Wildlife management, 29–31
Wildlife preservation groups, 419
Wildlife research, 30
Will-o'-the-wisp, 165
Willow, 145, 147, 155, 380, 386
  black, *290–92*
  sandbar, *88–90*

shrubby, 307–8
slender, *126–28*
swamp, *302–4*, 306
Windstorm, 25
Winter. *See also* specific
  months
adaptations to. *See also*
  Hibernation; Migration
  animals, 12–13
  arctic shrew, 167
  beaver, 81
  black bear, 342–43
  boreal chickadee, 309
  broadleaf trees, 14–15,
    235
  cattail, 114
  ermine, 214, *214*
  great gray owl, 326
  moose, 13, 155
  mudpuppy, 70
  muskrat, 123–24
  needleleaf trees, 14, 262–
    63
  northern leopard frog,
    140
  pond plants, 76–77
  porcupine, 272
  raccoon, 99–100
  ruffed grouse, 227
  short-eared owl, 139
  snowshoe hare, 12, 331
  spruce grouse, 328
  white-tailed deer, 13,
    216–17
  wood frog, 299–300
amphibians in, 37
birds in, 37
circadian rhythms during,
  81
mammals in, 37
reptiles in, 37–38
Wintergreen, 203, *250–52*,
  395

Wisconsin hotspots, 355–63
Wisconsin Point/Barker's
  Island (Wisconsin), 363
Witches' broom, 306, 324
Wolf, gray
  characteristics and habitats,
    301, 336–39, *338*
  hotspots, 348, 353, 366
  seasonal activities, 37, 376,
    398
Wolf pack, 337–39, 398
Woodchuck
  characteristics and habitats,
    170–72, 175, 182–83, *183*
  seasonal activities, 388
Woodcock, American,
  characteristics and habitats,
    142–44, 144, 147–49, *148*,
    206
Woodland opening/edge,
  170–72
  definition, 173
  formation, 173
  value to wildlife, 174–75
  wildlife, 175–83
  wildlife action, 175
Woodland pond. *See* Pond
Woodpecker, 19, 34, 38, 175,
  234, 238, 280, 330, 375,
  398
  black-backed
    characteristics and
      habitats, *158–60*, *321–
      22*, 329–30, *329*
    hotspots, 356
    seasonal activities, 408
  downy, *239–40*
    seasonal activities, 409
  hairy
    characteristics and
      habitats, 238, 395
    seasonal activities, 388
  pileated

characteristics and
  habitats, *17*, *232–34*,
  240, 245–46, *245*, 324
hotspots, 368
seasonal activities, 374,
  378
three-toed
  characteristics and
    habitats, 324
  hotspots, 368
  seasonal activities, 408
Wood-Pewee, eastern,
  characteristics and habitats,
  23
Worm, burrowing, 93
Wren, 307
  marsh, characteristics and
    habitats, *33*, 72–74, *110–
    12*, 115–16, 133
  sedge
    characteristics and
      habitats, *126–28*, 128,
      131–34, *134*
    seasonal activities, 392
    winter, seasonal activities,
      383

Y

Yarding up, white-tailed
  deer, 216–17, 375–76
Yarrow, common, 173
Yellowthroat, common,
  characteristics and habitats,
  116, 132, *142–44*, 150–51,
  151
Yew, Canada, 211, 379

Z

Zugunruhe, 401

Illustration Credits

Georgine Price

Illustrations by Georgine Price, reprinted courtesy of Wisconsin Department of Natural Resources, pages 1, 2, 5, 11, 18, 25, 26, 49, 87, 109, 169, 199, 219, 301, 315, 334, 409, 414.

Jim McEvoy

Illustrations by Jim McEvoy, reprinted courtesy of Wisconsin Department of Natural Resources, pages 7, 8, 14, 28, 31, 33, 71, 125, 157, 289, 371.

Karen Sullivan

Illustrations © Karen Sullivan, pages 12, 13, 17, 20, 22, 34, 35, 36, 37, 39, 40, 41, 43, 44, 45, 132, 135, 167, 193, 197, 204, 213, 225, 255, 273, 307, 312, 328, 338.

Vera Ming Wong

Illustrations © Vera Ming Wong, cover illustration, pages 54–55, 72–73, 88–89, 110–11, 126–27, 142–43, 158–59, 170–71, 184–85, 200–01, 220–21, 232–33, 239, 250–51, 258–59, 265, 274–75, 290–91, 302–03, 316–17, 321.

R.A. Alexander

Illustrations © R.A. Alexander, pages 83, 99, 101, 103, 104, 121, 124, 154, 156, 168, 178, 181, 183, 194, 214, 218, 247, 269, 271, 283, 284, 298, 332, 339, 341, 343.

Charles Joslin

Illustrations by Charles Joslin, Charlemont, MA, are reprinted from *New England Wildlife: Habitat, Natural History, and Distribution* by Richard M. DeGraaf and Deborah D. Rudis, USDA Forest Service, Northeastern Forest Experiment Station, pages 47, 61, 63, 64, 65, 79, 80, 95, 97, 98, 117, 118, 120, 134, 136, 137, 138, 149, 150, 151, 152, 166, 175, 177, 189, 190, 192, 207, 208, 209, 210, 211, 212, 227, 228, 229, 230, 231, 241, 242, 243, 244, 245, 257, 267, 268, 280, 281, 282, 295, 296, 297, 309, 310, 311, 313, 314, 325, 327, 329, 331, 336.

Abigail Rorer

Illustrations by Abigail Rorer are reprinted from *New England Wildlife: Habitat, Natural History, and Distribution* by Richard M. DeGraaf and Deborah D. Rudis, USDA Forest Service, Northeastern Forest Experiment Station, pages 68, 70, 84, 86, 106, 108, 141, 198, 249, 287, 288, 299, 345.

Lisbeth Quade

Habitat symbols designed by Lisbeth Quade.

The area covered by the 'Northwoods Wildlife Guide"

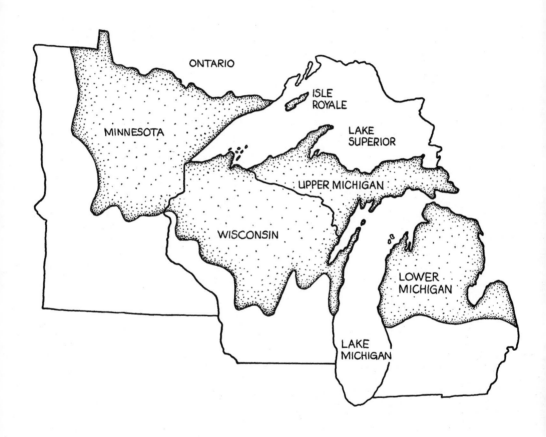